Children, Changing Families and Welfare States

Children, Changing Families and Welfare States

Edited by

Jane Lewis

Professor of Social Policy, London School of Economics, UK

Edward Elgar
Cheltenham, UK • Northampton, MA, USA

Published by
Edward Elgar Publishing Limited
The Lypiatts
15 Lansdown Road
Cheltenham
Glos GL50 2JA
UK

Edward Elgar Publishing, Inc.
William Pratt House
9 Dewey Court
Northampton
Massachusetts 01060
USA

Paperback edition 2008
Paperback edition reprinted 2013

A catalogue record for this book
is available from the British Library

Library of Congress Cataloguing in Publication Data
Children, changing families and welfare states / edited by Jane Lewis.
    p. cm.
  Includes bibliographical references and index.
  1. Children—Government policy. 2. Family policy. 3. Welfare state. I. Lewis, Jane (Jane E.).
  HQ789.C42753 2006
  362.7—dc22
                               2006041326

MIX
Paper from
responsible sources
FSC
www.fsc.org FSC® C021018

ISBN 978 1 84542 523 4 (cased)
     978 1 84720 987 0 (paperback)

Printed in Great Britain by Berforts Information Press Ltd

Contents

Figures

Tables

Contributors

Fran Bennett works half time as a senior research fellow at the Department of Social Policy and Social Work, University of Oxford, UK. In the other half of her time, she works in a self-employed capacity, often for non-governmental organisations. She is interested in poverty and income distribution, participatory research and ways of working, gender and social security issues. Her recent publications include *Gender and Benefits*, for the Equal Opportunities Commission (2005) and (with Moraene Roberts), *From Input to Influence: Participatory Approaches to Research and Inquiry into Poverty*, for the Joseph Rowntree Foundation (2004).

Ulla Björnberg is Professor of Sociology at the University of Göteborg, Sweden. She has a long record of research on forms of life in families, gender equality, lone mothers, and the reconciliation of employment and family life. She has been engaged in several international projects on family policy and family life in Eastern and Western Europe and is currently directing a research programme on 'Family Ties between Generations: Transfers of Material and Social Support among Individuals in Different Family Forms', and leading the development of an interdisciplinary and international research programme on asylum-seeking children in Europe. Her recent publications include: with Anna-Karin Kollind, *Individualism and Families* (Routledge, 2005); (as editor), *The Asylum-seeking Child in Europe* (Göteborg CERGU, 2005); and with Stefán Ólafsson and Guðný Björk Eydal, 'Education, Employment and Family Formation: Differing Patterns', in J. Bradshaw and A. Hatland (eds), *Social Policy, Employment and Family Change in Comparative Perspective* (Edward Elgar, forthcoming).

Jonathan Bradshaw is Professor of Social Policy and Head of the Department of Social Policy and Social Work at the University of York, UK. His research interests are in child poverty and well-being, family policy, and comparative social policy. He is currently working for UNICEF on an Innocenti Report Card on Child Well-being in the OECD.

Ann-Zofie Duvander has a PhD in sociology from Stockholm University, Sweden. She has worked at the National Social Insurance Board and is currently a researcher at Statistics Sweden, unit for Demographic Analysis and

Gender Equality. Her most recent article is Parents' Workplace Situation and Fathers' Parental Leave, together with Magnus Bygren, forthcoming in the *Journal of Marriage and the Family* (2006).

Karin Halldén is a doctoral student working on several projects on labour market careers at the Swedish Institute for Social Research (SOFI) at Stockholm University. Her most recent publication is: 'Globalisation, Work Intensity and Health Inequalities – a Cross National Comparison', forthcoming in I. Lundberg, C. Hogstedt and T. Hemmingson (eds), *Work and Social Inequalities in Health in Europe* (Peter Lang).

Barbara Hobson is a Professor of Sociology at Stockholm University, Sweden. She has published numerous articles on gender and welfare states, focusing on gender and citizenship, men and social politics, and social movements and gender diversity in welfare states. Her publications include the following books: (as editor,) *Recognition and Social Movements: Contested Identities, Agency and Power* (Cambridge University Press, 2003); *Making Men into Fathers: Men, Masculinities and the Social Politics of Fatherhood* (Cambridge University Press, 2002). She is founder and a current editor of the journal: *Social Politics: International Studies of Gender, State and Society*. She would like to acknowledge the support of the European Science Foundation grant: 'The changing relationship between work, welfare and gender equality in Europe'.

Jane Jenson was awarded the Canada Research Chair in Citizenship and Governance at the Université de Montréal in 2001, where she is Professor of Political Science. Between June 1999 and 2004, she was the Director of the Family Network of Canadian Policy Research Networks, Inc, a policy think tank located in Ottawa. She has published widely on family policy in Canada and Europe. See www.cccg.umontreal.ca.

Ute Klammer is Professor of Social Policy at the Niederrhein University of Applied Sciences, Mönchengladbach, Germany. Recent co-authored publications include *Working Time Options Over the Life Course: Changing Social Security Structures* (European Foundation for the Improvement of Living and Working Conditions, 2005); *WSI- FrauenDatenReport 2005* (Sigma, 2005). Research interests include family policy, pension systems, flexicurity, European and comparative social policy, labour market participation and social protection of women.

Marie-Thérèse Letablier is a sociologist, senior researcher in the Centre National de la Recherche Scientifique (CNRS/Centre d'Etudes de l'Emploi) in Paris, France. Her main research interests include work, family and gender issues from a European and comparative perspective. She has been participating in several European Research Networks, on family policies, women's employment and work–family balance issues. Her publications include (with Linda Hantrais) *Families and Family Policies in Europe* (Longman, 1996); (with Jeanne Fagnani) *Familles et travail: contraintes et arbitrages* (la Documentation Française, 2001); and (with J.C. Barbier), *Social Policies: Epistemological and Methodological Issues in Cross-national Comparison* (Peter Lang, 2005).

Jane Lewis is Professor of Social Policy at the London School of Economics, and a Fellow of the British Academy. She has written numerous articles on gender and welfare regimes, family policies and the history of social policies. Her most recent books are: *The End of Marriage? Intimacy and Relationship* (Edward Elgar, 2001); and *Should We Worry about Family Change?* (University of Toronto Press, 2003).

Ruth Lister is Professor of Social Policy at Loughborough University. She is author of *Citizenship: Feminist Perspectives* (2nd edn, Palgrave, 2003) and *Poverty* (Polity, 2004). Her research interests include citizenship, poverty, gender, welfare reform.

Rianne Mahon is Chancellor's Professor and Director of the Institute of Political Economy, Carleton University. Co-editor (with Sonya Michel) of *Child Care Policy at the Crossroads: Gender and Welfare State Restructuring* (Routledge, 2002). Recent articles include 'Rescaling Social Reproduction: Childcare in Toronto/Canada and Stockholm/Sweden', *International Journal of Urban and Regional Research*, 29 (2, 2005) and (with Robert Johnson), 'NAFTA, the Redesign and Rescaling of Canada's Welfare State', *Studies in Political Economy*, 76 (2005).

Peter Moss is Professor of Early Childhood Provision at the Thomas Coram Research Unit, Institute of Education, University of London, UK. His research interests include children's services and their workforce, and the relationship between employment and caring, in particular leave policies; much of his work is cross-national. Recent books include *Ethics and Politics in Early Childhood Education* (with Gunilla Dahlberg), *Care Work: Present and Future* (edited with Janet Boddy and Claire Cameron) and *From Children's Services to Children's Spaces* (with Pat Petrie) all published in London by Routledge.

Diane Perrons is the Director of the Gender Institute at the London School of Economics, UK. She recently published *Globalization and Social*

Change: People and Places in a Divided World (Routledge, 2004) and has just finished editing the anthology *Gender Divisions and Working Time in the New Economy: Changing Patterns of Work, Care and Public Policy in Europe and North America* (Edward Elgar, 2006) with Colette Fagan, Linda McDowell, Kathryn Ray and Kevin Ward. Diane's research focuses on the social and spatial implications of global economic restructuring, paying particular attention to the changing composition of employment, gender and regional inequalities and the social reproduction of daily life.

Birgit Pfau-Effinger is Professor of Sociology and Co-Director of the Globalisation and Governance Centre at the Department of Social Sciences, University of Hamburg, Germany. She has published widely in the fields of comparative welfare state analyses, labour market analyses, sociology of family, childcare and elderly care, gender relations, and sociology of transformation. Her recent books include *Culture, Welfare State and Women's Employment in Europe* (Ashgate, 2004) and (edited, with B. Geissler) *Care and Social Integration in European Societies* (Policy Press, 2005).

Acknowledgements

The contributors to this volume first presented their papers to a conference held under the auspices of the EC's 6th Framework Programme Coordinated Action project: 'The Well-being of Children: the impact of changing family forms, working conditions of parents, social policy and legislative measures', coordinated by Professor Lluis Flaquer and the Institut d'Infància I Mon Urbà, Barcelona. The project grant also supported Matthew Grant, who provided invaluable assistance in preparing the manuscript.

1. Introduction: children in the context of changing families and welfare states[1]

Jane Lewis

The nature of the relationship between children, parents and the state has been central to the growth of the modern welfare state and has long been a problem for western liberal democracies. Historically, children have been conceptualised as belonging to the private world of the family and thus to their parents, and policymakers have been preoccupied with the question: in what circumstances can, or should, the state intervene to protect children or to ensure that opportunities exist for their development? Many governments have been concerned that state intervention on behalf of children will serve to relieve parents of their responsibilities, and it has often proved difficult to establish a relationship that is not adversarial. As Hendrick (1990) has pointed out, such issues have played an important part in defining the very meaning of modern childhood. More recently, there has been increased emphasis on the idea that collective investment in children is crucial to the welfare of society, leaving open the extent to which the welfare of the child *qua* child is a central consideration. This has raised additional questions about how far children's views are taken into account at a time when academic commentators have been stressing the importance of listening to the voice of the child.

At the level of the individual household, the family has tended to be left alone except when a child has been abused or neglected, or when the child has been considered to constitute a (criminal) threat. In these instances the state has taken action to remove the child. But commentators have mounted a strong defence of 'family privacy' in liberal democracies (for example, Elshtain 1990; Mount 1983), although as Gordon (1988) showed in her historical study of social work/domestic violence in Boston, state intervention by embryonic social workers at the household level was often taken on behalf of the powerless – women and children – in the context of an essentially patriarchal family form.

1

But the nature of the relationship between child, parent and state has developed very differently in different nation states. English-speaking countries have had much more suspicion of state intervention in the family, and have tended historically to limit direct intervention not only at the household level but also in respect of the collective support of children via cash benefits and services, particularly childcare services. Only the USA failed to develop any system of universal 'family allowances' or child benefits, which provide (varying amounts) of recognition as to the cost of raising a child, but the care of children has been much more likely to be treated as a 'family' (usually women's) responsibility in large tracts of Europe as well as North America. In the UK, for example, the problem of childcare was not considered to be an issue for state policy until the late 1990s; men and women were free to enter the labour market, but were expected to make their own arrangements regarding care for their children. This sort of approach has contrasted markedly with that in other Northern and Western European countries, where it has been considered first, a duty on the part of the state to support children financially and in respect of their care; and second, where this duty is seen as one to be undertaken in partnership with parents, particularly in the Scandinavian countries.

Nevertheless children have come to the fore on policy agendas in recent years in most western states, with both the policy drivers and the policy responses taking many forms. In respect of the former, first there is what has been termed by most recent writers on welfare state change 'the demographic challenge' (for example, Pierson 2001). All western countries are ageing, birth rates are falling and the worsening dependency ratios mean that pensions and health and social care for older people are becoming harder to afford. Thus a major reason for putting children on the policy agenda is their absence. Most recently policies addressing childcare and support have been framed in terms of what might 'enable' parents to have the number of children they desire (for example CEC 2005).[2] Second, there has been a greater interest in the relationship between family change and welfare state change. Indeed, many analysts have begun to realise the extent to which household change in respect of both family form and the contributions that adult men and women make to families is driving policy (for example Esping-Andersen 1999), as well as being shaped by it. The first substantive section of this introduction explores these relationships as a means of providing the background for what is a fundamental shift in thinking about the orientation of welfare states that also has major implications for children.

Broadly speaking, states have pursued what has been termed a more 'active' approach to social entitlements for adults by drawing a tighter link between employment and social provision, and a stricter social investment approach to welfare spending in general. In this context, considerable attention has focused on children as future citizen workers, but responses have been varied and not necessarily of a piece. The tensions can be particularly stark in some countries at the household level. For example in the UK, as many commentators have pointed out, there have been moral panics about both the threat posed by a-social and criminal behaviour on the part of children, which has resulted in the effective lowering of the age of criminal responsibility to ten (the lowest in the EU), at the same time as there has been massive outcry about the failure to protect children abused by kin and carers (see James and James 2001 for a particularly critical review of UK government policy).

But the focus of this book is more on the implications of social policies to do with the arrangements for the care and support of children than on the nature of intervention at the level of the household,[3] and here too it is possible to identify very different approaches. One major strand in the early English-speaking commentary on changes in family form, and the increasingly high rates of lone parenthood resulting from high and stable divorce rates and high rates of cohabitation, has been the perceived collapse of family values and the lack of proper socialisation of children,[4] with the solution being sought in the traditional, married, two-parent family, and a rolling back of state support. This is a response that stands to have a detrimental impact on the welfare of children in poor families, certainly in the present generation, and that has proved more influential in the USA than in Europe, other than in the UK during the 1980s and early 1990s (Kiernan et al. 1998; Lewis 1997).

However, since the late 1990s, the demographic challenge has resulted in something of a premium being attached to children in EU member states, all of which have experienced a decline in their birth rates (the decline has been precipitous in Southern Europe; Douglass 2005). One of the most striking recent developments in European countries has been the emphasis on 'investing' in children as part of a social investment state (explored further in Part I of this book). A focus on children's welfare because of their future role as adult citizens is hardly new in and of itself: the whole apparatus of state education was designed to do just that in the service of both the child, and also, crucially, of economic growth and social harmony. However, the reorientation of the modern welfare state toward expenditure that can be represented in terms of investment, whether in the form of active labour market policies (rather than 'passive' welfare benefits for the unemployed), or family policies to support children as future investments is new. This stronger focus on children looks as though it should bring unadulterated benefits. But one of the major issues that arises from this new orientation is how far the policy responses are actually child-centred.

A major issue in the literature on the sociology of childhood is the extent to which children are viewed as agents, rather than acted on. This literature, which is explored in the second substantive section of this introduction, has particular policy relevance in regard to measures that impact directly on households – for example, in respect of post-divorce parenting – but is important for our purposes in this book for the way in which it alerts us to how far policy responses are actually driven by concerns about the welfare of children *per se*. We explore two areas of policy of fundamental importance to children: their financial support and care. One of the issues we explore is how far such policies may be described as 'instrumental', in other words, how far they are about issues other than the welfare of the child, such as encouraging fertility and women's employment, both of which are argued to be necessary to address the problem of the deteriorating dependency ratio, or encouraging economic growth, by investing in children's early learning. Such a policy may bring very real benefits for children but, as this introduction argues, it is nevertheless important to consider what more genuinely child-centred policymaking might look like, and to take into account children's own perspectives.

CONTEXT: FAMILY AND WELFARE STATE CHANGE

It is now widely recognised that family change, involving *both* demographic change and the changing nature of the contributions that adults make to families via paid and unpaid work, is of major importance to our understanding of the complex relationship between families, markets and states. Dramatic and interlinked changes in families and households, in labour markets, and in systems of social provision and regulation have been underway for some time now. Families and labour markets are moving towards increasing 'individualisation', with the erosion of traditional family bonds (manifested in low fertility, higher rates of divorce, extra-marital births, lone parenthood and increasing numbers of single-person households) and, with steadily rising rates of female participation in the workforce, more economic independence among women.

Traditional patterns of social provision in welfare states assumed the existence of a particular kind of family form, comprising a stable, two-parent, primary male earner and primary female carer model, and sought to provide protection against specified eventualities or risks – such as ill health and unemployment – within the confines of that family model. Core forms of social provision, for example in the form of social insurance benefits (and core approaches to family law, for example in respect of establishing fault and hence entitlement to alimony on divorce) rested on these basic assumptions as to what the family looked like and how it worked. It has recently been suggested that the erosion of the traditional family model has brought with it 'new social risks' (Bonoli 2005), which by definition cannot be addressed within the old frameworks. Thus, for example, the recent effort at EU level and by policymakers in most member states to further increase the level of female employment has also brought with it more attention to the provision of childcare, even in countries where this has been historically a low policy priority. This section attempts to summarise family and welfare state change, both of which have major implications for the support and care of children.

The Nature of Family Change

The settlement at the heart of modern welfare states was that between capital and labour. But it is increasingly recognised that there was a second key settlement between men and women at the household level. Partly as a result of feminist critique (for example, Lewis 1992; Orloff 1993), and partly because the nature and pace of change have made it much harder to ignore, recent comparative work on social provision has paid far greater attention to family arrangements and to gender relations (Crouch 1999; Esping-Andersen 1999; Huber and Stephens 2001; Korpi 2000). The old labour contract was designed first and foremost for the regularly employed male breadwinner and provision had to be made alongside it for women and children. The gendered nature of the settlement meant that those marginal to the labour market received cash cover via dependants' benefits paid to the male breadwinner. The male breadwinner family model was based on a set of assumptions about male and female contributions at the household level, with men being expected to take primary responsibility for earning, and women for household work and caring for the young and the old. Female dependence was inscribed in the model, and with it the dependence of children. In the inter-war period, the British feminist and campaigner for family allowances, Eleanor Rathbone (1924), raised the question that has remained crucial ever since: what is the wage for? Designed as a reward for individual effort in the labour market, it has always been difficult to see how a male wage can provide effectively for wives and differing numbers of children. In recognition of this, dependants' allowances were written into different kinds of cash benefits, and some effort was made in all western countries except the USA to provide a benefit in the form of a 'family allowance' in respect of all children, usually paid to the mother. However, this has remained a relatively small, albeit important, part of social security systems.

Crucially, the male breadwinner model built into the post-war settlement assumed regular and full male employment *and* stable families, in which women and children would be provided for largely via their husbands' earnings and their husbands' social contributions. High rates of family instability; much greater fluidity in intimate relationships (such that cohabitation may precede marriage and post-date divorce, and high rates of extra-marital childbearing in many western countries); together with rising rates of female labour market participation, especially among mothers of young children, made it impossible to sustain the traditional gender settlement that underpinned social provision and regulation in modern welfare states. Above all, the rising proportion of lone mother families have made considerable claims on social provision.

Thus the male breadwinner model family has substantially eroded in two key respects: the changing pattern of women's and to a much lesser extent men's contributions to the family in respect of cash (more than care), and the changing structure of the family itself. It seems that on both the work and the family front we are seeing more individualisation. Elizabeth Beck-Gernsheim (1999, p. 54) has described the effects of individualisation on the family in terms of 'a community of need' becoming 'an elective relationship'. Elias (1991, p. 204) expressed a similar idea in the following: 'The greater impermanence of we-relationships, which at earlier stages often had the lifelong inescapable character of an external constraint, puts all the more emphasis on the I, one's own person, as the only permanent factor, the only person with whom one must live one's whole life.' In this interpretation, the family used to be a community of need held together by the obligations of solidarity. But women's increased labour market participation, together with family instability and fluidity, has resulted in new divisions between biography and family.

Changes in family form and in patterns of both income and working time impact directly on the welfare of children, especially when policymakers begin to assume that adults can increasingly be treated as fully individualised, in the sense of being economically independent. In increasingly fluid families, children still tend to end up living with biological mothers (and often subsequently in families with men who are not their biological fathers), so arrangements that are made to support women as mothers become particularly important. Divorce is high and stable in northern Europe, with more moderate rates in continental Western Europe and low rates in the South, albeit with rising rates of separation. There have been extraordinary rises in the proportion of live births outside marriage in northern Europe, wide variations in the increase in the continental Western European countries (high in France, low in the former West Germany), and wide variations in Southern European countries (Portugal had a higher rate than many northern countries as early as 1960 and a higher rate than Germany in 1995; Lewis 2003a). Divorce and unmarried motherhood are routes to lone motherhood, with cohabitation driving much of the change, and the proportions of lone mother families have therefore increased. It remains the case that children's material welfare depends disproportionately on the welfare of women. Thus children have been adversely affected by the well-documented increase in the feminisation of poverty (for example, Sharma 2005).

Changes in the nature of the contributions men and women make to families also vary between countries, with particular implications for children. Nowhere is there a fully fledged adult worker model family. Indeed, while in Western Europe there is evidence of substantial movement away from the male breadwinner model towards a citizen worker model (Crompton 1999; Lewis 2001), it is most common to find some form of transitional dual breadwinner model than a full dual career model. Indeed, dual-earner families have become the norm in most western countries, although the number of hours women work outside the home varies hugely (Rubery et al. 1999). Labour participation rates are low in Southern Europe, but women tend to work full time, while in much of Western Europe more women work, but part time, in a one-and-a-half earner model, extending to a one-and-three-quarter model in the Scandinavian countries. In most Western European countries part-time work for women has been the main way of reconciling work and family responsibilities and hence providing for the care of children, especially in countries like the UK, the Netherlands and Germany where a large proportion of women work short part-time hours (under 15 hours a week). The vast majority of men have continued to work full time and in the English-speaking countries a significant proportion (just over 31 per cent of UK fathers with children under 16) work more than the 48 hours laid down by the European Commission's 1996 Working Time Directive (Gershuny 2000; Smith 2004).

It is often assumed that the increased employment of women has a beneficial effect on child poverty rates. This may be so, but in countries where formal childcare costs are high and the gender pay gap is wide, for example in the UK (see Manning and Petrongolo 2005), it is less likely to be the case. Changing patterns of time-use on the part of adults also affect children, indeed, Mutari and Figart (2001) have argued that gender differentiation in families is increasingly based on time. These different patterns of male and female employment at the household level are accompanied by very different ways of making provision for the care of children. But as the hours women work lengthen, so mothers and fathers in two-parent families must either engage in 'shift parenting' (very common in the UK and the USA), or seek help from kin, or a daycare place. Countries differ enormously in how much state help has been offered to parents by providing either childcare services, or cash benefits that enable parents (usually mothers) to stay at home or to buy childcare.

Adults increasingly undertake a series of transitions over the lifecourse, in and out of intimate relationships and in and out of paid and unpaid work. These must be negotiated. Considerable caution is nevertheless needed when assessing the extent of change. After all, a majority of children are still brought up in two-parent families in which women are far from economically independent. However, first, it is striking how processes of individualisation are often discussed without mention of the implications for children. Second, and more problematic from the point of view of everyday living, when policymakers begin to *assume* greater economic independence on the part of adults, this may have particularly grave consequences for children, who often end up living with their relatively poorer mothers. As those mothers are encouraged to increase their hours of paid work, children may also experience childcare that is not necessarily high quality.

'New Social Risks' and the Changing Assumptions Underpinning Policy

The structure of modern welfare systems has never provided well for those who were marginal in some way to the labour market. Thus we might expect part-time women workers and lone mothers to have been relatively poorly provided for. In the case of the latter – by definition women with children and without men – only widows have been able to rely on derived benefits, consisting of social insurance benefits paid for by their husbands' contributions. These are invariably higher than the means-tested social assistance benefits that the growing proportion of divorced and unmarried mothers end up depending on, supplemented by whatever money the state is able to extract from the 'absent' father. In most western countries these women and their children have remained disproportionately poor. In other words, changes in the labour market, particularly in respect of women's precarious place in it, and in family form have thrown up new groups facing the old risk of poverty.

The links between men, the labour market and the traditional family have been eroded by more fluid families, more female employment and more flexible employment. At the same time, the linkage between labour markets and welfare, broadly defined, has intensified over the past two decades, with new forms of conditionality being imposed via welfare-to-work schemes. Thus, alongside labour market and family change, welfare state restructuring has made the welfare of all adults, male and female, increasingly dependent on their success in the labour market at a time of increasing flexibilisation. As Yeandle (1999, p. 142) has observed, a complex relationship between individuals and labour markets is emerging

across the life course, which is 'fraught with risk' and 'requires skilful negotiation'. In addition, recent research has revealed the extent to which children are also involved in negotiations arising from family change, whether
at the household level, for example, following family breakdown (Smart
et al. 2001), or attendant on the changing pattern of women's employment
and its effects on children's household work and the organisation of their
time (for example Brannen et al. 2000).

Individualisation in the sense of increasing economic independence and
more autonomy to choose and to move between different kinds of intimate
relationships has increasingly been matched by new assumptions on the
part of policymakers regarding the part men and women play in families.
What is crucial from the perspective of children are the terms and conditions on which this shift in assumptions has been pursued. In practice, the
nature of the policy logics that underpin different adult worker models in
different countries varies enormously. Only in the USA and in some of the
Nordic countries have policies been based on the assumption that men and
women will be fully engaged in the labour market. However, these models
work in very different ways. In the US case, the obligation to enter the
labour market is embedded in a residual welfare system that often borders
on the punitive, whereas in Scandinavia it is supported by an extensive
range of care entitlements in respect of children in particular. In addition,
only in the Nordic countries has policy attempted to address the way in
which unpaid work is shared at the household level, by making it possible
for men to take paid 'daddy leave'. In the USA, an adult worker model
family has been promoted with no support for care work in the family.
Perhaps not surprisingly, studies of the 'time squeeze' and of family stress
have most commonly emanated from the USA (Schor 2001; Skocpol 2000;
Heymann 2000).

There also remains a substantial strand of opinion that promotes
more traditional family roles and relationships, particularly in the English-
speaking countries, but also in many continental European countries. In
Germany, for example, the Federal Government and Länder have long promoted the 'choice' for mothers of young children to stay at home or enter
employment, and mothers continue to express a preference for part-time
work (European Foundation 2000); and the tax system is still not individualised (Dingeldey 2001). Nevertheless, there is considerable convergence
between different countries in terms of governments' efforts to promote an
'adult worker model family' in the hope of doing many things: promote
economic growth, tackle poverty, further gender equality (in the labour
market), and combat the problem of deteriorating dependency ratios. All
of these rationales have been mentioned by different groups and political
parties in different countries at different moments. They are not equally

important policy drivers, and some, particularly gender equality, are largely rhetorical (Stratigaki 2004, 2005), but increasingly, as policy assumptions change, all adults will be at risk (particularly in respect of pension provision), if they are not in the labour market. Indeed the shift to an adult worker model family can be read as evidence of the privatisation of risk to the individual and/or the family (Brush 2002).

The policy drivers behind the new assumptions of an adult worker citizen signal the extent to which the shift in the policy assumptions has been instrumental: the welfare of women, whose behaviour is expected to change most, is not necessarily at the centre of policymaking (Lewis 2002). Nor are the policy implications in respect of children's welfare a central matter for consideration. 'Active' welfare provision, entailing tighter conditionality between social provision and the labour market has been extended to adult women as well as tightened for adult men, raising the question of how we make provision for the care of children. The new assumptions regarding the desirability of an adult worker model family are framed within the need to take a 'social investment' approach to welfare expenditure, justifying it on the basis of future returns, whether in relation to cash benefits designed to promote economic activity on the part of adults and hence economic growth, or expenditure on early years learning, designed in the main to produce more employable workers in the future. This new orientation to welfare has meant that more attention has been directed towards children, albeit more on the basis of their 'becoming' rather than their 'being'. Nevertheless, there have also been substantial benefits for children in the here and now, particularly in terms of the way in which child poverty has moved rapidly up the policy agenda.

The policy trends may be illustrated briefly by reference to developments at the EU level. Employment growth has been seen as a key social policy goal and as a means of promoting social inclusion, a position shared by European social democrats (for example Vandenbroucke 2001). However, the emphasis in respect of the promotion of women's employment, especially of lone mothers, has been somewhat different, having much to do with tackling poverty and limiting expenditure on welfare benefits (Rowlingson and Millar 2001). But, this may ignore the perceptions on the part of lone mothers that the risk their absence from home poses to their children may be greater than the absence of income, and their desire to put childrearing first (Duncan and Edwards 1999).

Over the last decade the European Commission has increasingly stressed the importance of the effective use of women's skills in a competitive, knowledge-based economy (CEC 2000), and has received academic backing for its position. Women have been seen as an untapped labour reserve. Reports to the Portuguese Presidency in 2000 (Ferrera et al. 2000) and to the Belgian Presidency in 2001 (by Esping-Andersen, 2001) favoured higher female labour market participation for instrumental reasons, as a means of increasing both competitiveness and the tax base of the continental European social insurance welfare states. The Lisbon Council set a target of 60 per cent for female labour market participation in member states by 2010 (Council of the European Union 2000), and the following year the Stockholm European Council set an interim target of 57 per cent by 2005 (Council of the European Union 2001). The Commission has called in addition for 'reforms of means-tested benefits so that each member of the household has an incentive to work' (CEC 2002). However, in most countries there has been insufficient attention to the terms and conditions under which the transition to an adult worker model family is undertaken, and in particular to the linked problems of how carework for children (and older people) is to be accomplished.

Increasing women's paid work is part of, but not the whole, solution to the problem of poverty, particularly child poverty, not least because of the gender pay gap, which has proved difficult to shrink (Rubery 2002), and because women continue to do a disproportionate amount of unpaid carework. The trend in welfare state restructuring towards an adult worker model family increasingly assumes that more care will become commodified and that women will become paid rather than unpaid carers (for example Esping-Andersen et al. 2002). Policymakers have increasingly promoted non-familial childcare in conjunction with the shift to an adult worker model family, as well as in order to promote 'early learning' and thus better opportunities in the labour market in the future (for the UK, see Lewis 2003b). In 2002 a benchmark for childcare was set by the Barcelona Council in 2003, whereby at least 33 per cent of children under three years of age and at least 90 per cent of children between three and the mandatory school age should have access to childcare by 2010, but again the rationale was phrased more in terms of the welfare of the child and of society in the future rather than in the present. There is in fact an increasingly complicated and mutually reinforcing set of drivers behind the promotion of formal childcare at EU and member state level. For example, in Germany during the 1990s, the desirability of childcare outside the family became increasingly accepted, fuelled by falling fertility rates (to 1.29 in 2001), Germany's poor showing in the OECD's PISA report on performance in schools (OECD 2001), and increased female labour market participation rates (Evers et al. 2006).[5]

Thus women's work has been broadly encouraged, and for a wide variety of reasons. The care of, and support for, children has also become more of a policy priority, in large part because of the changing contribution to family life made by their mothers, and also because of the increased attention given to the importance of investing in the next generation. Indeed, the benefits for the economy and society have tended to take precedence over those for individual women and children. In particular, increased female labour force participation has created a new imperative for childcare provision. Institutional provision has found new support in the research evidence, which has increasingly swung away from condemning the effects of maternal employment on young children and towards endorsing formal daycare, at least for children over three (Gregg and Washbrook 2003), with the proviso that it is high quality care. However, outside the Scandinavian countries – where daycare was developed much earlier and where arguments about the welfare of the child were much more central (see Borchorst 2000 on Denmark; see also Dahlberg et al. 1999) – the approach has also tended to be rather instrumental, with the desire to promote female employment, and, most recently, concerns to help women reconcile work and family as a means of increasing birth rates (CEC 2005) taking precedence over the needs of children.

CHILDREN AND THE NEED FOR A MORE CHILD-CENTRED APPROACH TO POLICYMAKING

Children have become increasingly 'precious' at both household and societal levels. Zelizer (1985) argued that as children lost their economic value to their parents and became a drain on their material resources, they also became emotionally 'priceless'. Beck and Beck-Gernsheim (1995; see also Beck-Gernsheim 2002) have argued that as adult relationships have become more individualised, so the emotional link with children has become more attractive. At the societal level, both the 'scarcity' of children due to the fall in the birth rate, and increased recognition of the need for a highly educated workforce in the 'knowledge economy' have moved children up the policy agenda, but in relation more to children's future role as citizen workers than to the welfare of the child *qua* child.

Despite the focus on children by the end of the twentieth century, evidence regarding their welfare was far from encouraging, particularly in terms of child poverty rates (Bradshaw 2000; Vleminckx and Smeeding 2001; Ritakallio and Bradshaw 2006). At the turn of the new century, the USA, the UK, Canada and Italy had child poverty rates well above their overall poverty rates, although between 1996 and 2001 child poverty fell in most EU countries, including the UK, Germany and the Netherlands. Considerable (and often polemical) fears have also been expressed over the effects on children of family breakdown and the freedom of adults to move from relationship to relationship.[6] Gillis (2003) has suggested that we are increasingly living through children, rather than reciprocally with them. While early twenty-first century children may have more symbolic power, they have lost actual power (Jensen 2003).

There has been relatively little analysis of the position of children in the context of changing families and welfare states. As adults become increasingly individualised in the sense of being economically independent, children remain economically dependent for longer on their families. And as adult women play a greater role in the public sphere, children are increasingly confined to the private world of the family, because of anxieties about their safety and because of the changes in leisure patterns wrought by new technology and media (Livingstone 2002).

Nor do children have much power of voice or exit over the changing ways in which family life is organised, particularly in respect of the politics of time, which has special significance for the lives of children (Jensen and McKee 2003). The idea of the 'hurried child' has been used to suggest both that childhood is more fleeting (Lynott and Logue 1993) and that in the new adult worker model family, children and adults may be on different time schedules (Gillis 2003). In the last chapter of her pathbreaking book, Zelizer (1985) suggested that the role of children may change in the future because of women's increasing labour market participation, in other words, children may again be expected to do more by way of domestic labour (see also Miller 2005). As Brannen et al. (2000) have pointed out, the processes of individualisation that have affected adult family members have implications for children, who must also re-negotiate their family practices in terms of both the contributions they make to housework and, indeed, to carework (for empirical evidence, see Solberg 1997; Becker et al. 1998; Olsen 2000) and how they fit their schedules to those of their parents. They may also often spend less time with their (working) parents.

In addition, more also tends to be expected of children at school. Governments have focused increasingly on the welfare of children, but their orientation in most western countries has been on the child as a future 'worker citizen'. Thus in the UK the announcement of more investment in childcare in 2004 was justified in terms of the national interest: helping parents to reconcile work and family life, and helping children to get a good start in life because they are 'the citizens, workers, parents and leaders of the future' (HM Treasury 2004, paras 2.8, 2.11). The publication of international league tables on children's performance in school (for example OECD 2001) has resulted more generally in the promotion of early learning, standardising curricula and more educational testing.

This may be represented as an extension of the traditional concern to meet the needs of children. Certainly, the well-established developmental view of children, which clearly demarcated the boundary between child and adulthood, has served to recognise children's needs, mainly in terms of health and education (Thomas 2005). But historically children have been 'acted upon'. Indeed, comparisons of the treatment of children can be made with that of women in the nineteenth century, who were considered by lawmakers to be 'childlike' in terms of their lack of competence and autonomy (Lewis 1984; Land 2003; Näsman 1994). The boundary drawn by developmental psychologists between child and adulthood in terms of 'natural growth and development', has in fact much to do with economic dependence and power relations (Gittins 1998). Nevertheless, children are increasingly expected to take more responsibility for themselves and their development. In addition, the boundary seems in any case to be increasingly unclear. Postman (1994) has – controversially – argued that childhood is disappearing beneath the weight of consumerism and a media-dominated culture. Less spectacularly, it is possible to point out the extent to which education, historically the prerogative of the child, is now conceptualised as 'life-long', or the way in which sexual maturity is reached earlier and earlier, while economic dependency is prolonged. In Southern European countries in particular, young adults are continuing to live at home with their parents throughout their twenties.

Children are being affected by family and welfare state change, which raises the question of how to make policy more genuinely focused on children, especially when government policy tends to take an instrumentalist approach towards children's 'becoming' rather than being. The view of more recent academic work, particularly on the sociology of childhood, and of many of those working in supra-national organisations to prioritise the welfare of children, has been that the way forward lies in recognising the importance of the agency of the child in shaping childhood, rather than assuming the overwhelming importance of structures, particularly the institutions of the family and the school (see Prout and James 1997 for a review). Thus, for example, as Brannen and O'Brien (1996) put it, the focus should be on 'children in families' rather than on 'families with children'. Seeing children as agents with rights to participate in decisions affecting them raises a question mark over the more traditional developmental approach to childhood, which has tended to result in children being excluded from having a voice in the way they are treated by parents and law-makers. Recent research, for example with children on their welfare in post-divorce families (Smart et al. 2001), has revealed the extent to which they cannot be considered immature, irrational and incompetent social actors, in contra-distinction to mature, rational and competent adults.

However, the logical end of solutions stressing agency and extending children's right to participation has limits that are not always acknowledged by some proponents (James and James 2004). If children's agency is over-emphasised to the exclusion of the need for protection, it is difficult to avoid making them at least in part responsible for securing their own welfare. As Minnow (1986) pointed out, confusion has arisen as a result of both advocates of greater protection for children – in the form of welfare rights – and the more extreme 'child liberationist' school, which would treat children as autonomous and equivalent to adults (for example Holt 1974) using the language of 'rights'. Any simple emphasis on rights threatens to play down the obligations that more powerful and better endowed adults have towards individual children and children as a group. After all, recent research on children's perspectives has shown the extent to which poverty limits children's capacity to make choices (Ridge 2002). Jones (2005) commented on the extent to which children in the UK feel more 'individualised' than do German children in terms of feeling more responsible for their success or failure, but are less able to capitalise on their choices because of structural disadvantage. Qvortrup (1995) argued strongly that children's lack of command over resources is unfair, given that their work at school, which is in the interests of society rather than the family, goes unrewarded until they reach adulthood. Adults 'choose' to have children, but children do not choose to be poor (see also Wintersberger 1994). The problem remains as to who is to speak for the child when it comes to resource allocation (O'Neill 1994), how far the child should also have a voice, and whether in any case this would be sufficient to guarantee his or her welfare.

What these academic debates and findings usefully do is alert us to the importance of the child's perspective in relation to social policymaking. Children have never been recognised as full citizens. T.H. Marshall (1950) gave them only limited rights, as 'citizens in the making'. If childhood and adulthood are firmly demarcated, then children will in all likelihood be 'acted-upon'. Family law has insisted that this be in their 'best interests', but, again, there remains a problem as to who will determine what these are. It is a major challenge to find the best way of conceptualising and representing children's interests. But the need to do so has become more pressing with rapid family and welfare state change. Much debate has focused on ways to move away from the traditional approach of simply protecting children, towards giving more recognition to some form of 'children's citizenship', and in particular to ways of allowing children to 'participate' and to have a say in their treatment (for example Stasiulis 2002). Ben-Arieh and Boyer (2005) have argued that children's participation is necessary if they are to be guaranteed their welfare entitlements. The most important formal document in this respect has been the 1989 UN Convention on the Rights of the Child, but there has also been more radical discussion, for example about the possibilities of extending the vote to children (for example, Ringen 1997; van Parijs 1999; see also Cutler and Frost 2001 who recommend lowering the voting age to 16 in the UK). However, some of these proposals are not necessarily child-centred, for example van Parijs's (1999) main preoccupation is to do something about the threat of gerontocracy in the face of population ageing.

To claim full citizenship for children of all ages is difficult. The UN Convention puts considerable emphasis on what might be considered the traditional 'welfare rights' of the child (to health and education), but also recognises the right of the child to 'voice' (Daniel and Ivatts 1998; James and Richards 1999). Neale (2002, p. 470) has advocated a 'social model of citizenship' that 'grounds the individualised rights of recognition, respect and participation within the relational ethics of care, responsibility and interdependence'. This also seeks to combine the more traditional concern about children's 'welfare rights'[7] with the new recognition of the importance of participation. Some form of partial citizenship (Roche 1999) or 'citizenship in context' (Smart et al. 2001), offering a flexible model of citizenship for children with different kinds of participation at different levels, which endeavours to incorporate the idea of children as agents without losing sight of the fact that they are often in need of protection, has become more evident in the recent literature. This is similar to Stasiulis's (2002) vision of children's citizenship as protection and participation. The UNICEF Innocenti Research Centre has gone one step further by making an explicit effort to link the UN Convention's stress on the importance of participation on the part of children (Article 12), with its statement (in Article 5) that those with responsibility for children must take into account the 'evolving capacities' of the child to do so, by suggesting ways of promoting and measuring 'evolving capacity' (Lansdown 2005).

Children's views do provide an interesting and important commentary on family change and have implications for policy debates. For example, recent research with children has shown the extent to which they value 'ordinary time', and how longer parental working hours are perceived to reduce this (Christensen 2002; see also Brannen et al. 2000; Klammer, Chapter 11 this volume). It may also be that not all children need or want to keep in contact with both parents after divorce (Smart 2002, also James and James 1999). Hearing the voice of the child makes it harder to generalise on what is in the best interests of (all) children.

However, rights-based, citizenship models necessarily focus on the individual child and his or her need and capacity for protection and participation. One of the main messages of the chapters in this book is that policies affecting children as a group need to be child-centred if children are to thrive. This is not necessarily to make an argument that children can or should be treated as an undifferentiated group, but rather to draw additional attention to the policy drivers. As Minnow (1986) remarked two decades ago, children are all too often not the real focus of legislation directed towards them, which is often guided by other adult social interests and goals. The contributors to this volume focus on the two dimensions of financial support of and care for children. Efforts on the part of governments to tackle child poverty would appear to be unambiguously beneficial for children. But those efforts have included promoting female labour market participation, and there has been considerable debate about the consequences of this and of doing relatively little to promote the greater involvement of fathers in unpaid carework (see Hobson et al., Chapter 13 this volume) for children. Nevertheless, it is possible to argue that if parental time becomes more rare in the lives of children, the concept of 'quality time' can make up the difference. In the UK, where men's working hours are the longest in the EU, government has insisted that flexibility rather than the absolute number of working hours is key to securing children's well-being. However, not only do the views of children about family time (cited above) bring these positions into question, but it is also necessary to consider the extent to which the shift to an adult worker citizen model for adults has taken priority over consideration of what is best for children. A similar point can be made using the example of childcare provision. If the increase in formal childcare places is driven mainly by the fact that more mothers are in the labour market, then the priority is likely to be maximising the number of childcare places available. A more child-centred childcare policy will push the issue of quality, rather than quantity, up the policy agenda. As Lister (2005) has argued, it is necessary to look 'at children's well-being and citizenship together'; it is this that constitutes a child-centred approach to policymaking. Many of the contributions in this book look at the outcomes for children; where policy has been more child-centred, the outcomes are generally better.

The reorientation of welfare systems towards making a more 'active' link between the individual and the labour market, together with the new challenge being posed by population ageing, has resulted in more attention being paid to children. In large measure, this has resulted in a 'futurist' approach to children, which has to a great extent always characterised social policy. Children are protected, educated and valued for what they will become: future citizens. This 'social investment' approach, which has characterised the recent approach to social expenditure more generally, is explored by Jenson (Chapter 2) and Lister (Chapter 3) in Part I of the book. The approach has brought substantial benefits to children; the idea that future citizens cannot develop well in poverty has driven measures to reduce child poverty rates in those EU member states where the record was poorest, as Part II shows. Bradshaw (Chapter 4) provides an update of the amount of cash available for children in the tax and social security systems in

15 countries, while both Björnberg (Chapter 5) and Bennett (Chapter 6) review the cross-national policy trends. While these are far from simple or convergent, many policy issues are common to a number of member states; for example, how far cash transfers in respect of children are made to depend on parents' performance as workers or as parents, and what kind of claim fathers, as opposed to mothers, are able to make on behalf of children.

The focus on the duty of adults to be in the labour market has made the issue of childcare more pressing. Part III of the book focuses on the care of children, with Pfau-Effinger (Chapter 7) showing both the extent to which the boundaries between formal and informal carework have become blurred, and the way in which parents have made a double claim to time to care on the one hand, and to childcare services on the other. Moss (Chapter 8) takes up the issue of childcare services and examines the limited meaning that is all too often given by providers to the idea of childcare, while Mahon (Chapter 9) explores the very different views of childcare that can be found in two recent and influential OECD reports on the subject. Finally, Part IV explores the tension between longer and/or more flexible hours in the labour market, which may lift more children out of poverty, but may also deprive children of ordinary family time. Letablier (Chapter 10) examines the complex interplay between greater flexibility at work, legislation limiting working hours, and the highly developed childcare system in France. Klammer (Chapter 11) and Perrons (Chapter 12) focus more on the problems and possibilities of flexibility in Germany and the UK, while Hobson et al. (Chapter 13) address the issue of fathers' working hours in particular, and the issues they raise for both children's welfare and mothers' choices about how to combine paid and unpaid work.

As Part IV shows, negotiating the shift to the adult worker model family is difficult, the interests of mothers, fathers and children at the household level may not be the same, and there may also be conflict between mothers, fathers, children and the state. Social policies may often prove to be rather a blunt instrument, but it is nevertheless possible to promote the same policy, for example, early years learning, with a more or less child-centred focus, and this matters for the welfare of children. Focusing on 'being' rather than 'becoming' requires a more child-centred approach.

NOTES

1. I am grateful to Ruth Lister for helping me think about the issues raised in this introduction. I have profited particularly from her recent writings on the subject (Lister 2005).
2. There is evidence to suggest that there is a gap between ideal and actual family size in Western European states (European Foundation for the Improvement of Living and Working Conditions 2005).

3. We would also wish to acknowledge the wide range of policy issues that are crucial to children's welfare beyond financial support and care. The role of new media and the increased danger of public spaces in increasing the isolation of children are key.
4. The classic statement is that of Charles Murray (1984), but see also the idea of a 'parenting deficit' developed in the literature on social capital and community (Coleman 1988; Etzioni 1994).
5. The participation rates of mothers with dependent children increased by 10 per cent in West Germany, albeit that 52 per cent of them worked for fewer than 20 hours, a picture not so dissimilar from that in the UK.
6. These are pressing issues, but Pryor and Rodgers (2001) have shown the difficulties in assessing their effects.
7. Well-being may be a more appropriate term (Lister 2005; Dean 2006). See Bradshaw (2005) for a range of indicators to measure material well-being.

REFERENCES

Beck-Gernsheim, E. (1999), 'On the way to a post familial family: from a community of need to elective affinities', *Theory, Culture and Society*, **15**(34), 53–70.

Beck-Gernsheim, E. (2002), *Reinventing the Family: In Search of New Lifestyles*, Cambridge: Polity Press.

Beck, U. and E. Beck-Gernsheim (1995), *The Normal Chaos of Love*, Oxford: Polity Press.

Becker, S., J. Aldridge and C. Dearden (1998), *Young Carers and their Families*, Oxford: Blackwell.

Ben-Arieh, A. and Y. Boyer (2005), 'Citizenship and childhood', *Childhood*, **12**(1), 33–53.

Bonoli, G. (2005), 'The politics of the new social policies: providing coverage against new social risks in mature welfare states', *Policy and Politics*, **33**(3), 431–49.

Borchorst, A. (2000), 'Danish childcare policy: continuity or restructuring', paper given to the GEP Conference, Vilvorde KursusCenter, Denmark, 18–20 August.

Bradshaw, J. (2000), 'Child poverty in comparative perspective', in D. Gordon and P. Townsend (eds), *Breadline Europe*, Bristol: Policy Press.

Bradshaw, J. (2005), *The Well-being of Children in the UK*, London: Save the Children.

Brannen, J., E. Heptinstall and K. Bhopal (2000), *Connecting Children. Care and Family Life in Later Childhood*, London: Routledge Falmer.

Brannen, J. and M. O'Brien (eds) (1996), *Children in Families: Research and Policy*, Brighton: Falmer Press.

Brush, L.D. (2002), 'Changing the subject: gender and welfare regime studies', *Social Politics*, **9**(2), 161–86.

Christensen, P.H. (2002), 'Why more "quality time" is not on the top of children's lists: the "qualities of time" for children', *Children and Society*, **16**, 77–88.

Coleman, J.S. (1988), 'Social capital in the creation of human capital', *American Journal of Sociology*, **94**(supplement), S95–S120.

Commission of the European Communities (CEC) (2000), *Towards a Community Framework Strategy on Gender Equality (2001–2005)*, COM (2000) 335 final, 7 June, Brussels.

Commission of the European Communities (CEC) (2002), *Increasing Labour Force Participation and Promoting Active Ageing*, COM (2002) 9 final, Brussels.

Commission of the European Communities (CEC) (2005), 'Confronting Demographic Change: A New Solidarity between the Generations', green paper COM (2005) 94 final, Brussels, 16 March.

Council of the European Union (2000), 'Conclusions of the Presidency', Lisbon European Council of 23–24 March.

Council of the European Union (2001), 'Conclusions of the Presidency', Stockholm European Council of 23–24 March.

Crompton, R. (ed.) (1999), *Restructuring Gender Relations and Employment: The Decline of the Male Breadwinner*, Oxford: Oxford University Press.

Crouch, C. (1999), *Social Change in Western Europe*, Oxford: Oxford University Press.

Cutler, D. and R. Frost (2001), *Taking the Initiative: Promoting Young People's Involvement in Public Decision-making in the UK*, London: Carnegie UK Trust.

Dahlberg, G., P. Moss and A. Pence (1999), Beyond Quality in Early Childhood Education and Care: Postmodern Perspectives, London: Routledge.

Daniel, P. and J. Ivatts (1998), *Children and Social Policy*, Basingstoke: Macmillan.

Dean, H. (2006), *Social Policy*, Cambridge: Polity Press.

Dingeldey, I. (2001), 'European tax systems and their impact on family employment patterns', *Journal of Social Policy*, **30**(4), 653–72.

Douglass, C.B. (ed.) (2005), *Barren States. The Population 'Implosion' in Europe*, Oxford: Berg.

Duncan, S. and R. Edwards (1999), *Lone Mothers, Paid Work and Gendered Moral Rationalities*, Basingstoke: Macmillan.

Elias, N. (1991), *The Society of Individuals*, Oxford: Blackwell.

Elshtain, J.-B. (1990), 'The family and civil life', in D. Blankenhorn, S. Bayme and J.-B. Elshtain (eds), *Rebuilding the Nest: A New Commitment to the American Family*, Milwaukee; WI: Family Service America.

Esping-Andersen, G. (1999), *Social Foundations of Post-industrial Economies*, Oxford: Oxford University Press.

Esping-Andersen, G. (2001), 'A new welfare architecture for Europe?', final version of a report submitted to the Belgian Presidency of the European Union.

Esping-Andersen, G., D. Gallie, A. Hemerijcke and J. Myles (2002), *Why We Need a New Welfare State*, Oxford: Oxford University Press.

Etzioni, A. (1994), *The Spirit of Community: The Reinvention of American Society*, New York: Touchstone Books.

European Foundation for the Improvement of Living and Working Conditions (2000), *Employment and Working Time in Europe*, Dublin: European Foundation.

European Foundation for the Improvement of Living and Working Conditions (2005), *Fertility and Family Issues in an Enlarged Europe*, Dublin: European Foundation.

Evers, A., J. Lewis and B. Reidel (forthcoming 2006), 'Developing Childcare Provision in England and Germany: Dilemmas of Governance', *Journal of European Social Policy*, **15**(3).

Ferrera, M., A. Hemerijck and M. Rhodes (2000), *The future of social Europe recasting work and welfare in the New Economy*, report for the Portuguese Presidency of the European Union.

Gershuny, J. (2000), *Changing Times*, Oxford: Oxford University Press.

Gillis, J. (2003), 'Childhood and family time: a changing historical relationship', in A.-M. Jensen and L. McKee (eds), *Children and the Changing Family: Between Transformation and Negotiation*, London: Routledge Falmer.

Gittins, D. (1998), *The Child in Question*, Basingstoke: Macmillan.

Gordon, L. (ed.) (1988), *Heroes of Their Own Lives: The Politics and History of Family Violence, Boston 1880–1960*, New York: Viking.

Gregg, P. and E. Washbrook (2003), 'The effects of early maternal employment on child development in the UK', CMPO working paper.

Hendrick, H. (1990), 'Constructions and reconstructions of British childhood: an interpretative survey, 1800 to the present', in A. James and A. Prout (eds), *Constructing and Reconstructing Childhood: Contemporary Issues in the Sociological Study of Childhood*, London: Routledge.

Heymann, J. (2000), *The Widening Gap. Why America's Working Families are in Jeopardy and What Can be Done about it*, New York: Basic Books.

H.M. Treasury (2004), *Choice for Parents, the Best Start for Children: A Ten Year Strategy for Childcare*, London: H.M. Treasury.

Holt, J. (1974), *Escape from Childhood: The Needs and Rights of Children*, Harmondsworth: Penguin.

Huber, E. and J. Stephens (2001), *Development and Crisis of the Welfare State. Parties and Policies in Global Markets*, Chicago: University of Chicago Press.

James, A.L. and A. James (1999), 'Pump up the volume: listening to children in separation and divorce', *Childhood*, **6**(2), 189–206.

James, A.L. and A. James (2001), 'Tightening the net: children, community and control,' *British Journal of Sociology*, **52**(2), 211–28.

James, A. and A.L. James (2004), *Constructing Childhood. Theory, Policy and Social Practice*, Basingstoke: Macmillan.

James, A.L. and M.P.M. Richards (1999), 'Sociological perspectives, family policy, family law and children: adult thinking and sociological tinkering', *The Journal of Social Welfare and Family Law*, **21**(1), 23–40.

Jensen, A.-M. (2003), 'For the children's sake. Symbolic power lost?', in A.-M. Jensen and L. McKee (eds), *Children and the Changing Family: Between Transformation and Negotiation*, London: Routledge Falmer.

Jensen, A.-M. and L. McKee (2003), 'Introduction: theorizing childhood and family change', in A.-M. Jensen and L. McKee (eds), *Children and the Changing Family: Between Transformation and Negotiation*, London: Routledge Falmer.

Jones, G. (2005), *Young Adults and the Extension of Economic Dependence*, London: National Family and Parenting Institute.

Kiernan, K., H. Land and J. Lewis (1998), *Lone Motherhood in Twentieth-century Britain*, Oxford: Oxford University Press.

Korpi, W. (2000), 'Faces of inequality: gender, class, and patterns of inequalities in different types of welfare states', *Social Politics*, **7**(2), 127–91.

Land, H. (2003), 'Children, families, states, and changing citizenship', in J. Scot, J. Treas and M.P.M. Richards (eds), *The Blackwell Companion to the Sociology of Families*, Oxford: Blackwell.

Lansdown, G. (2005), *The Evolving Capacities of the Child*, Florence: UNICEF Innocenti Research Centre and Save the Children.

Lewis, J. (1984), *Women in England, 1870–1950*, Brighton: Harvester/Wheatsheaf.

Lewis, J. (1992), 'Gender and the development of welfare regimes', *Journal of European Social Policy*, **3**, 159–73.

Lewis, J. (ed.) (1997), *Lone Mothers in European Welfare Regimes*, London: Jessica Kingsley.

Lewis, J. (2001), 'The decline of the male breadwinner model: the implications for work and care', *Social Politics*, **8**(2), 152–70.

Lewis, J. (2002), 'Gender and welfare state change', *European Societies*, 4(4), 331–57.

Lewis, J. (2003a), *Should We Worry About Family Change?*, Toronto: University of Toronto Press.

Lewis, J. (2003b), 'Developing Early Years Childcare in England, 1997–2002: The Choices for (Working) Mothers', *Social Policy and Administration*, 37(3), 219–38.

Lister, R. (2005), 'Children, well-being and citizenship', paper presented to the Social Policy Association Annual Conference, University of Bath, 27–29 June.

Livingstone, S. (2002), *Young People and New Media*, London: Sage.

Lynott, P.P. and B.J. Logue (1993), 'The "Hurried Child": The Myth of Lost Childhood in Contemporary American Society', *Sociological Forum*, 8(3), 471–89.

Manning, A. and B. Petrongolo (2005), *The Part-time Pay Penalty*, London: DTI.

Marshall, T.H. (1950), *Citizenship and Class and other Essays*, Cambridge: Cambridge University Press.

Miller, P. (2005), 'Useful and priceless children in contemporary welfare states', *Social Politics*, 12(1), 3–41.

Minnow, M. (1986), 'Rights for the next generation: a feminist approach to children's rights', *Harvard Women's Law Journal*, 9(1), 1–24.

Mount, F. (1983), The Subversive Family: An Alternative History of Love and Marriage, London: Allen and Unwin.

Murray, C. (1984), *Losing Ground: American Social Policy 1950–1980*, New York: Basic Books.

Mutari, E. and D. Figart (2001), 'Europe at a crossroads: harmonization, liberalization, and the gender of work time', *Social Politics*, 8, 36–64.

Näsman, E. (1994), 'Individualization and institutionalization of childhood in today's Europe', in J. Qvortrup, M. Bardy, G. Sigritta and H. Wintersberger (eds), *Childhood Matters. Social Theory, Practice and Politics*, Aldershot: Avebury.

Neale, B. (2002), 'Dialogues with children. Children, divorce and citizenship', *Childhood*, 9(4), 455–75.

Organisation for Economic Co-operation and Development (OECD) (2001), *Knowledge and Skills for Life: First Results from PISA 2000*, Paris: OECD.

Olsen, R. (2000), 'Families under the microscope: parallels between the young carers debate of the 1990s and the transformation of childhood in the late nineteenth century', *Children and Society*, 14, 384–94.

O'Neill, J. (1994), *The Missing Child in Liberal Theory*, Toronto: University of Toronto Press.

Orloff, A. (1993), 'Gender and the social rights of citizenship. State policies and gender relations in comparative research', *American Sociological Review*, 58(3), 303–28.

Parijs, P. van (1999), 'The disfranchisement of the elderly, and other attempts to secure intergenerational justice', *Philosophy and Public Affairs*, 27, 292–333.

Pierson, P. (ed.) (2001), *The New Politics of the Welfare State*, Oxford: Oxford University Press.

Postman, M. (1994), *The Disappearance of Childhood*, New York: Vintage Books.

Prout, A. and A. James (1997), 'A new paradigm for the sociology of childhood? Provenance, promise and problems', in A. James and A. Prout (eds), *Constructing and Reconstructing Childhood. Contemporary Issues in the Sociological Study of Childhood*, London: Routledge Falmer.

Pryor, J. and B. Rodgers (2001), *Children in Changing Families. Life after Parental Separation*. Oxford: Blackwell.

Qvortrup, J. (1995), 'From useful to useful: the historical continuity of children's constructive participation', *Sociological Studies of Children*, 7, 49–76.

Rathbone, E. (1924), *The Disinherited Family*, London: Edward Arnold.

Ridge, T. (2002), *Childhood Poverty and Social Exclusion: From a Child's Perspective*, Bristol: Policy Press.

Ringen, S. (1997), *Citizens, Families, and Reform*, Oxford: Clarendon Press.

Ritakallio, V.-M. and Bradshaw (2006), 'Family poverty in the European Union', in J. Bradshaw and A. Hatland (eds), *Social Policy, Employment and Family Change in Comparative Perspective*, Cheltenham; UK and Northampton, MA, USA: Edward Elgar (in press).

Roche, J. (1999), 'Children: rights, participation and citizenship', *Childhood*, **6**(4), 475–93.

Rowlingson, K. and J. Millar (eds) (2001), *Lone Parents, Employment and Social Policy: Cross-national Comparisons*, Bristol: Policy Press.

Rubery, J. (2002), 'Gender mainstreaming and gender equality in the EU employment strategy', *Industrial Relations Journal*, **33**(5), 30–56.

Rubery, J., M. Smith and C. Fagan (1999), *Women's Employment in Europe*, London: Routledge.

Schor, J. (2001), *The Overworked American*, New York: Basic Books.

Sharma, V. (2005), *Women's and Children's Poverty: Making the Links*, London: Women's Budget Group.

Skocpol, T. (2000), *The Missing Middle: Working Families and the Future of American Social Policy*, New York: W.W. Norton & Company.

Smart, C. (2002), 'From children's shoes to children's voices', paper presented to the seminar on 'The Children of Divorce: Parentage and Citizenship', Institute d'Infancia i Món Urbà, Barcelona, 19–20 September.

Smart, C., B. Neale and A. Wade (2001), *The Changing Experience of Childhood, Families and Divorce*, Oxford: Polity Press.

Smith, A. (2004), 'Who cares? Fathers and the time they spend looking after children', paper presented to the International Conference on Work and Family, CRFR, University of Edinburgh, 30 June–2 July.

Solberg, A. (1997), 'Negotiating childhood: changing constructions of age for Norwegian children', in A. James and A. Prout (eds), *Constructing and Reconstructing Childhood: Contemporary Issues in the Sociological Study of Childhood*, London: Falmer Press.

Stasiulis, D. (2002), 'The active child citizen: lessons from Canadian policy and the children's movement', *Citizenship Studies*, **6**(4), 507–36.

Stratigaki, M. (2004), 'The co-optation of gender concepts in EU policies: the case of "reconciliation of work and family"', *Social Politics*, **11**(1), 30–56.

Stratigaki, M. (2005), 'Gender mainstreaming vs positive action. An ongoing conflict in EU gender equality policy', *European Journal of Women's Studies*, **12**(2), 165–86.

Thomas, N. (2005), 'Interpreting children's needs: contested assumptions in the provision of welfare', in J. Goddard, S. McNamee, A. James and Allison James (eds), *The Politics of Childhood. International Perspectives, Contemporary Developments*, Basingstoke: Palgrave Macmillan.

Vandenbroucke, F. (2001), 'European social democracy and the third way: convergence, divisions, and shared questions', in S. White (ed.), *New Labour: The Progressive Future?*, Basingstoke: Palgrave.

Vleminckx, V. and T.M. Smeeding (eds) (2001), *Child Well-being, Child Poverty and Child Policy in Modern Nations*, Bristol: Policy Press.

Wintersberger, H. (1994), 'Costs and benefits – the economics of childhood', in J. Qvortrup, M. Bardy, G. Sigritta and H. Wintersberger (eds), *Childhood Matters. Social Theory, Practice and Politics*, Aldershot: Avebury.

Yeandle, S. (1999), 'Gender contracts, welfare systems and non-standard working: diversity and change in Denmark, France, Germany, Italy and the UK', in A. Felstead and N. Jewson (eds), *Global Trends in Flexible Labour*, Basingstoke: Macmillan.

Zselizer, V. (1985), *Pricing the Priceless Child: The Changing Social Value of Children*, New York: Basic Books.

PART I

Children as a social investment

2. The LEGO™ paradigm and new social risks: consequences for children

Jane Jenson

Effective economic policies are complementary to effective social policies in extending opportunities and mobilising more assets than are currently available. Equally, effective social policies are necessary to generate economic dynamism and contribute to flexible labour markets; to ensure that childhood experiences do not lead to disadvantage in adulthood; to prevent exclusion from the labour market and society; and to ensure a sustainable system of support for the elderly. Social policies must be pro-active, stressing investment in people's capabilities and the realisation of their potential, not merely insuring against misfortune. (Final communiqué, 2005 Meeting of OECD Social Affairs Ministers,[1] OECD 2005a)

INTRODUCTION

Social policy thinking has been profoundly altered in recent years, as the policy pronouncement of Organisation for Economic Co-operation and Development (OECD) social policy ministers about future social architecture reveals. Now policy communities assert that economic dynamism depends on effective social policies, that social policies must involve investment (not 'merely insuring against misfortune'), and that one of the goals of a new social architecture is to prevent intergenerational transfer of disadvantage. Social protection constituted the basic notion of post-1945 welfare regimes but pooling resources to protect against consequences of ageing, ill-health, or job loss is no longer considered sufficiently cutting edge, at least according to these representatives of the 30 members of the OECD. Now the goal is to be proactive rather than compensatory. One result of this shift in ideas is that the best policy mix envisioned often targets children.

This reworking of policy analysis is not due to chance. There are sociological, political and ideational reasons for it. Rising life expectancy rates and falling fertility rates as well as increases in women's labour force participation and in female-headed lone-parent families have all undermined assumptions about the best mix of public and private responsibility for care in the work–family balance. The lingering influence of neo-liberalism and the commitment to 'activation' as the way to ensure a modernised social model has brought a redefinition of 'full employment' from its Keynesian meaning of the male half the population to employment of virtually everyone. Left and centre-left formations have come to understand that protection of hard-won social rights will depend on solving several deep conundrums about financing social programmes in the present and in the future.

In previous policy paradigms, children were not targeted specifically; families and adults were. Now, as in the quotation at the head of the chapter, childhood experiences of disadvantage are understood to have long-term effects, and preparing for the future proactively, including by spending on children and their human capital, is sometimes considered more important than protecting adults against the misfortunes of the present. This chapter maps some of the policy ideas that have made such statements self-evident policy dogma and that shape policy interventions in many places. I argue that such widespread thinking follows from the identification of and a convergent set of responses to new social risks. In effect policy prescriptions for a social architecture now resemble what we characterise as the LEGO™ paradigm (Jenson and Saint-Martin forthcoming).[2] In this paradigm, which is meant to address in particular the new social risks, the main features are an emphasis on social policy as a productive factor; on investments for the future more than on social protection; and on re-mixing responsibility for employment and family responsibilities. Not all versions of the paradigm, however, target children; LEGO™ for adults does exist. Indeed, the degree to which children are the focus marks a significant difference between a social investment version of the LEGO™ paradigm and other versions.

In this chapter I set out the dimensions of the LEGO™ paradigm, locating it in relation to the analysis of new social risks. I then compare, within the general LEGO™ paradigm, the social investment perspectives adopted in Great Britain and Canada. Finally, I sketch an alternative expression of the same paradigm, deployed in the discourse of the European Union. The social investment version of the paradigm has brought significant attention to the circumstances of childhood and of children. Comparison reveals, however, that while many institutions share an adherence to the LEGO™ paradigm, they maintain a clear focus on the needs of adults, especially women, and on workers and their families. A brief examination of European Union policies documents this variation and the consequences for policy choices about how to confront new social risks.

NEW SOCIAL RISKS AND THE LEGO™ PARADIGM

Many of the principles of policy redesign are similar across countries. Social policy communities claim that social policy is a necessary support for economic well-being (for example, European Commission 2005, plus the OECD ministers cited above). They identify new social risks and argue that these risks call for spending on human capital, lifelong learning and training, so that virtually all adults will seek and retain employment. The notion of new social risks (Pearson and Scherer 1997, p. 6; Esping-Andersen et al. 2002, pp. 30ff; Bonoli 2005; Jenson 2004a; Taylor-Gooby 2004) provides a framework for understanding innovations in social policy design and spending, even as the programmes established in the so-called golden age of the welfare state (such as pensions, post-secondary education, and health care, for example) are mired in controversy and threatened with cutbacks.[3]

The new social risks result from income and service gaps in post-industrial labour markets. Compared to the labour market of the industrial era, there has been a loss of well-paid and traditionally male jobs in production and an increase in low-paid and often precarious service jobs that make many people the 'working poor'. There has also been an increase in the female employment rate. Socially, family transformations mean smaller families and a significant increase in lone-parent families. Demographically, there has been a decline in the fertility rate and an increase in life expectancy. Such restructuring of labour markets and transformations of family and demography create challenges to social care arrangements as well as income security. For example, women's labour force participation means reduced availability for full-time caring while lone-parent families can not count on a relatively well-paid male breadwinner. More generally, the polarisation of the post-industrial income structure in many countries has generated an increase in low-income rates among young families, whether lone-parent or couples, and therefore the appearance of what has been termed 'child poverty' in many policy circles (for example, UNICEF 2000, 2005; European Commission 2005, p. 10). These patterns are often also concentrated among minority ethnic groups and in cities.

Gradually a set of shared responses has emerged to the new social risks and they have significant consequences for the situation of children and families. Attention has shifted from supposedly passive spending on social protection against risk to 'investments' that will generate an active society and an active citizenship and proactively insure against the new social risks. Thus one widely shared policy response has been to try to increase the employment rate. Termed *activation* in the language of the European

Union, and therefore many European countries, the objective is to raise the proportion of the population involved in the paid labour force.[4] One goal of activation policies is to ensure the future of expensive social programmes protecting against 'old' social risks, such as pensions and healthcare, by increasing the contributions to or tax base of such programmes as well as by reducing the number of claimants among the working age population. But additionally, it is to ensure that in the post-industrial labour market, families will combat the effects of low wages and instability of employment by moving all adults into employment, thereby maintaining their market income.

Activation policies clearly have knock-on effects for social policy and services. Gaps in caring regimes are obvious, as women are moved into employment. Training, even in basic skills, is required as efforts are made to move everyone into the labour force. Indeed, in this policy paradigm, the two domains are frequently linked. Early childhood education and care are often promoted as both a way to care for children while their parents – that is mothers – work, and as an investment in prevention, to reduce the chance of school failure and therefore the need for basic skills training later in life as well as the likelihood of encounters with the criminal justice system. The title of the 2004 pre-budget document, with which the British Labour government went into the 2005 election, says it all: *Choice for Parents, the Best Start for Children: A Ten Year Strategy for Childcare* (HM Treasury et al. 2004).

Therefore, an active society requires some new public spending. Between 1980 and 1999 spending levels on services for the elderly and disabled and services for families as well as for active labour market support increased in all welfare regime types (Taylor-Gooby 2004, Table 1.1, p. 16). Nonetheless, and despite the common pattern, the specifics of activation and support for activation have varied. In continental Europe, for example, some countries have initiated policies and programmes that limit support for those providing full-time care of children by requiring lone parents to seek employment and by removing incentives for women in couple families not to participate in the labour market (Lewis 2001). At the same time they have improved services, including childcare, and developed mechanisms, such as care allowances, that maintain or even create a link to the labour force (by accumulation of pension rights, for example) for the many women caring for family members with disabilities or the vulnerable elderly (Jenson and Jacobzone 2000). Another mechanism that has found favour addresses income insecurity from low-paid work by providing income supplements 'to make work pay'. Sometimes termed 'in-work benefits', they are instruments for supplementing low earnings and ensuring activation. Attention to skills acquisition, and other forms of investment in human capital, especially for the groups considered most vulnerable, such as children, women heading lone-parent families, young workers, and the long-term unemployed also fall under the rubric of 'making work pay'.

In many cases these interventions have involved re-mixing public and private provision. The market and family sectors are assigned greater responsibility for programmes designed to address 'old' social risks, such as pensions, health care, post-secondary education and the other classic service areas of the welfare state. At the same time, the family sector is relieved of some responsibility for caring, as public support for early childhood education and care (ECEC) increases and new benefits to pay for care of elderly and disabled persons are added to the social policy mix. In addition, wage supplements make the state and the market sectors jointly responsible for the earnings package of a significant proportion of the employed, a role that the state rarely assumed in the 'golden age' of the welfare state.

Explicit attention to poverty, to children, families and work–family balance, and to pre-school education as well as elder care are all central to the discussion of new social risks. Poor children are by no means the only focus, nor are lone-parent families. Also targeted are parents increasingly preoccupied by labour market participation, struggling to earn enough in service jobs that may be poorly paid, and challenged by the stress of balancing work and family, whether the family is composed of one or two adults.

Our proposition in this chapter is that such responses to new social risks have prompted a future-oriented policy strategy that often evokes intergenerational solidarity more than the needs of male breadwinners and their families, as was the case in the 'golden age'. In some liberal welfare regimes, the promise is to 'invest in children' to ensure a future of well-trained, flexible and productive workers (Saint-Martin 2000; Jenson 2001; Lister 2003). Several international organisations also share this focus on investing in children, whether the organisation is traditionally concerned with childhood or not (UNICEF 2000, 2005; OECD 2001, 2005b).[5] Elsewhere, investment in adults human capital, particularly women and youths, is the expression of concern about new social risks.

Such signs of convergence around ideas for a social architecture of activation and investment to reduce the effects of new social risks, prompt us to identify a common shift towards a LEGO™ paradigm, one that shapes thinking about the new social risks, while providing policy prescriptions for limiting the effects of the social changes that produce these risks. The principles of this paradigm are captured well by this quote from the website of the toy company:

> Children are our role models. Children are curious, creative and imaginative. . . .
> Lifelong creativity, imagination and learning are stimulated by playful activities
> that encourage 'hands-on and minds-on' creation, fun, togetherness and the
> sharing of ideas. People who are curious, creative and imaginative, i.e. people
> who have a childlike urge to explore and learn, are best equipped to thrive in a
> challenging world and be the builders of our common future.[6]

This quotation from the corporate website describing the company's philosophy illustrates at least three key features of what we term the LEGO™ paradigm. First, while LEGO is a toy, involving play, it is also about a life-long commitment to learning in order to work. Indeed, play *is* work because work is – supposedly – creative and playful. Second, this philosophy is future-oriented. Children now are already creating the future.[7] Ensuring intergenerational solidarity will depend on what happens to them. Finally, for LEGO, successful play in childhood benefits more than individual children; it enriches our common future. Activity in the present is beneficial for the community as a whole.

This discourse of constant learning, knowledge acquisition, involvement and engagement captures a good deal of thinking about the knowledge-based economy of the present as well as the need to invest now to ensure collective advantage in the future. Therefore, the LEGO™ name serves our purposes in two ways. It is a metaphor, describing convergence around some basic building blocks of a possible emerging social architecture. It is also an ideal-type, capturing the key features of the future-oriented, investment-centred activation strategy currently advocated as a blueprint for welfare state redesign.

The LEGO™ paradigm is a general one, just as Keynesianism served as a general paradigm in the decades after 1945. However, just like the earlier one, it is translated into policy in various ways in different jurisdictions.[8] We can observe at least two variations in the way that the LEGO™ paradigm is used. One variation is in the extent to which a social investment perspective is explicitly adopted. A second variation is in the extent to which a focus on children displaces attention to families and adults.

THE SOCIAL INVESTMENT PERSPECTIVE: ONE VERSION OF THE LEGO™ PARADIGM

In the mid-1990s both international organisations and some centre-left political parties developed a new response to the straightforward neo-liberalism of the right that had arrived at an ideational and political impasse. As early as 1994, OECD documents were identifying a continuing need to spend in the social realm rather than simply cut back (Deacon 2001, p. 74). By 1997,

OECD reports were saying, 'by shifting from a social expenditure to a social investment perspective, it is expected that considerable progress can be made in transforming the welfare state and ensuring social cohesion' (OECD 1997, p. 14). Social policy experts were also moving towards a treatment of 'welfare as social investment' (Esping-Andersen et al. 2002, p. 9).

The social investment perspective that emerged has been dominant since the mid-1990s in both Canada and Britain, the cases examined here. As a response to new social risks, this policy perspective casts government spending differently from that in the post-1945 years. Income transfers and credits designed to end child poverty and the intergenerational cycle of poverty as well as to 'make work pay' justify spending on child benefits and income supplements as an 'investment', while simultaneously reducing spending on protection against loss of income due to unemployment (Powell 1999, p. 21; Boychuk 2004, pp. 15–18). Beyond putting children at the centre of much social policy (Jenson 2001; Myles and Quadagno 2000), there is a clear emphasis on ensuring greater levels of activation by investing in learning and in the future, because it will supposedly pay off for everyone.

The social investment perspective is an elaborated version of the three principles of the LEGO™ paradigm: an emphasis on work and life-long learning, orientation towards the future, and the belief that there is a general benefit from everyone being actively engaged. It provides a set of ideas for politicians and policymakers and has generated tangible effects: it has justified some new spending; it makes sense of the growing, albeit still inadequate, commitment to publicly funded childcare in both Canada and Britain; and it underpins the enthusiasm for distributing assets and encouraging savings.

A Focus on Work: Child Poverty and Parental Employment

Reducing child poverty has been one of the big policy ideas of the Labour government since 1999 when Tony Blair pledged to halve child poverty by 2010 and eliminate it by 2020. Gordon Brown, Chancellor of the Exchequer, then set out to 'tackle child poverty'. Income transfers and credits were no gift, however. As Brown bluntly put it: 'The Government will do all it can to support parents, but in turn it is right that parents fulfil their responsibilities too' (HM Treasury 2001, pp. iii–iv), and this included doing their part to end the scourge of Britain's high rate of 'worklessness'.[9]

Promoting parental employment was also the major idea behind the 1999 overhaul of Canadian social policy and intergovernmental relations, via the National Child Benefit (NCB).[10] Under the heading 'Ending Child Poverty', the federal, provincial and territorial social service ministers said: 'The National Child Benefit aims to help prevent and reduce the depth of child poverty, and help parents find and keep jobs by providing benefits and services that better support low-income families and their children.'[11]

The focus on employment to reduce child poverty rates had concrete policy consequences, of course. One was a set of measures to cajole and compel parents into employment. The NCB was supposed 'to ensure that low-income families are better off in jobs' than they would be on social assistance. Neo-liberalism had insisted, and continued to insist in some Canadian provinces, that 'any job is a good job'. The social investment perspective, in contrast, tempered its enthusiasm for employment with a human capital dimension as well as recognition that if responsible parents were to leave social assistance for a low paying job without private social benefits, they would need new services and supports (Finn, 2003; Mendelson 2005).

In the 1998 Green Paper, 'The learning age: a renaissance for a new Britain', individuals were encouraged to invest in their own training and learning throughout the life course, with some financial support from the state (Dobrowolsky and Jenson 2005, pp. 210–11). This emphasis on learning throughout the life course is a central element of the LEGO™ paradigm. Skilling and re-skilling can benefit any kind of worker, but there are two versions of the diagnostic that target particular categories of potential workers. It is here that lone mothers and women in general come into the picture, being one of the groups identified as in need of skill upgrading because they have been too long out of the labour force or because they missed out on basic skills in the first place. In Britain, the emphasis on basic skills training and upgrading predominates in programmes such as Sure Start as well as Excellence Action Zones and Excellence in Cities which target adult learners. Initially, New Labour talked more about training than acting, but the second term (2001–2005) brought increased attention to building skills and sustaining people in work (Dobrowolsky and Jenson 2005, p. 213). Canada went in the opposite direction. In the early 1990s Canada had been, in international terms, one of the biggest spenders on training, but as intergovernmental responsibility for social policy was reworked in parallel with the NCB, labour market measures were devolved to the provinces and spending fell off (Lazar 2002, p. ix).

Supportive services are also seen as a measure that could both limit child poverty and increase parental employment. In Canada, the NCB provided for provincial 'reinvestments' to access publicly financed supplementary health benefits (for example, dental care and prescription drugs) in order to 'lower the welfare wall'. For a transitional period, as parents moved from social assistance to a low-wage job, they would retain these benefits, thereby making it more likely they would see an advantage to taking a low-paying job without private insurance for supplementary health care (for details see Canada 2005, Appendix 2).

In both Britain and Canada, however, the major incentive for parents to move into employment came from the income supplements put into place from the late 1990s onward. Reliance on tax credits, both refundable and non-refundable, had emerged during the 1980s as a preferred social policy instrument – less intrusive than means testing; less dependent on costly state employees, because handled by computers dealing with tax returns; less transparent because changes were part of complicated tax codes, and therefore useful for doing 'social policy by stealth'.[12] In Britain a series of 'child-tested' credits[13] were designed and redesigned. Spending rapidly increased after 1999, and its targets changed from the universal child benefit to in-work benefits and from being weighted towards lone-parent families towards including couple families, especially low-income ones (Joseph Rowntree Foundation 2004; OECD 2005b). Treasury documents and speeches by Tony Blair and Gordon Brown regularly summarised the number of children 'lifted out' of poverty by these measures. In Canada, the child-tested tax credits in the NCB also are designed to supplement income. Although paid to families whether they have income from employment or not, they have been implemented in a way that any increase in income was initially seen only by families whose income came from sources other than social assistance.[14]

Both countries have experienced a reduction in child poverty since the mid-1990s, some of which must be attributed to these policies, although a good deal is also due to changes in labour market conditions. In 2005 UNICEF predicted the UK would meet 'the interim target of a 25 per cent reduction in the number of children living in households below 60 per cent of median income by 2004/2005' (UNICEF 2005, p. 15). In Canada the story is bleaker. There has been an almost 75 per cent increase in the amount of benefit between the pre-NCB level (1997) and the announced levels for 2007, and a much higher proportion of low-income families' revenue comes from such income supplements (Mendelson 2005, pp. 2–3). Nonetheless, Campaign 2000 reported in 2004: 'not only is Canada's record on child poverty actually worse than it was in 1989, Canada's rate of poverty jumped for the first time in 2002, following five straight years of decline'. The child poverty watchdog group called on the government to live up to its promises, saying 'too many children in poverty for too long. Canada needs a social investment plan for children and families' (Campaign 2000, 2004, p. 1).[15]

Thus child poverty remains widespread, despite the increase in the employment rate due, in part, to the labour force participation of lone mothers. In Canada between 1996 (that is before the NCB reforms) and 2003, the employment rate of women heading lone-parent families with children under age 3 rose 14 percentage points, while that of all women heading lone-parent families with children under 16 rose 15 percentage points, to 46.9 per cent and 64.9 per cent respectively. This meant a substantial reduction in the gap between the employment rates of women in couple families (who were much more likely to be employed) and in lone-parent families. In 1996, the gap for women with children under three was 28.1 percentage points and in 2003 it was fully 10 points less, while that for women with children under 16 fell from a 14-point difference to one of only 4 points (Statistics Canada 2004, p. 15). Thus the activation strategy was showing larger amounts of change than the anti-poverty strategy in Canada's social investment perspective.[16]

In Britain, in contrast, the reduction of child poverty occurred despite a very small reduction in workless households and only a slight increase in employment rates of women heading lone-parent families with children under 16. Between 2000 and 2005 their employment rate rose from 51.0 per cent to 56.2 per cent, while that of married or cohabiting mothers with children under 16 was basically stable (going from 70.7 per cent to 71.9 per cent) (UK National Statistics 2005, p. 5).[17] This relatively low employment rate for women heading lone-parent families can in part be accounted for by the unwillingness of the Labour government to impose work requirements on them (Dobrowolsky and Jenson 2005, p. 224). The New Deal for Lone Parents, for example, seeks to foster labour force participation, but only requires lone parents with children of school age to attend an interview with a personal adviser to talk about employment and training options.

The 'Children's Agenda' – Fixed on the Future

The child poverty focus also resonates within the LEGO[TM] paradigm because it can be framed in terms of the future, providing the rationale for using the label *child* poverty rather than simply poverty and thereby avoiding 'merely insuring against misfortune', as the OECD social ministers put it. Child poverty is time-sensitive because childhood lasts for very few years and what happens in those years will have long-term consequences. Such ideas have appeared in numerous academic studies and policy papers reporting on the long-term negative effects of a childhood spent in poverty.[18] They are also promoted by advocacy groups in civil society, which adopted the child poverty frame for social justice claims well before the policy initiatives of 1999.[19]

Terms such as 'sure start', 'best start' and 'good start in life' abound in the social investment perspective and they go well beyond a poverty focus.[20] Publicly supported early childhood education and care, both non-parental and parental, are oft-chosen instruments to concretise this future focus. They supposedly do triple duty: fighting the long-term effects of childhood poverty; helping parents balance work and family; and preparing all children for the labour market of the future. All three arguments are used where childcare is discussed as a social investment.

At first, in its 1998 Green Paper 'Meeting the childcare challenge', the Labour government maintained an employability lens for childcare, as well as a focus on the particular needs of low-income children (Randall 2002). Special attention was paid to lone parents, who were described as both facing high costs for non-parental care and forming a potential pool of paid childcare workers. In the second Labour government, however, ECEC became an investment target because it would benefit everyone. This quotation from the 2003 Treasury paper, *Balancing Work and Family Life: Enhancing Choice and Support for Parents*, is one example among many (quoted in Dobrowolsky and Jenson 2005, p. 219):

> Enabling parents to balance work and family responsibilities can make the difference between their participation in the labour market, or their exclusion. For the employer, it can make the difference between being able to retain a valued member of staff or incurring the costs of recruitment and further training. And for children, it gives them the best possible start in life.

The government of the province of Ontario elected in 2003, after years of resistance to new spending on childcare by its neo-liberal predecessor, has placed its Best Start programme within a classic social investment frame. As the Minister of Children and Youth Services said when presenting the programme: 'This is an investment that keeps growing as our children grow. How we choose to support them now will determine the quality of their lives and the lives of all Ontarians in the future.'[21]

The Collective Good – Activity and Engagement

As this last quote makes clear, the social investment perspective, in true LEGO™ fashion, is oriented towards the future of the whole society. Canada's social ministers justified the increased dollars going into NCB benefits and investments this way: 'Helping children get off to a good start in life is crucial, and governments have recognized that child poverty has long-term consequences for children and society' (Canada 2005, p. i).[22] But how is society affected? Policy communities identify three long-term general benefits from a social investment policy stance.

One benefit is that their own and their parents' experience with social engagement will generate social inclusion and limit their involvement in anti-social behaviour. The OECD was quick to make the link between social cohesion and a social investment welfare state (OECD 1997). Both

Britain and Canada have developed social development strategies around services for children intended to increase parents' engagement in their community and 'good citizenship' more generally. Sure Start is one example, as are many of the youth-focused programmes that seek to combat the risks of social exclusion (Kidger 2004). Canadian examples are Aboriginal Head Start and the Community Action Program for Children. A key goal of the head start programme, for example, is to help children learn about and retain Aboriginal culture, a perspective that is set firmly within the social investment frame. The mission and mandate states: 'First Nations people, Métis and Inuit recognize children as their nations' most valuable resource.'[23]

The notion behind such programmes is not only to provide support in the here and now but also to lower the risk of anti-social behaviour and poor citizenship in the future. The British discourse and actions are much more central to public policy interventions than is the Canadian approach on this matter. Tony Blair's campaign against anti-social behaviour, wrapped in the language of the rights and responsibilities of citizenship, and the Anti-Social Behaviour Orders in place since 2004 have no equivalent in Canadian political discourse. The community focus of Blair's initiatives is clear, as is the relationship to negative school experiences; the PM singled out 'abuse from truanting school age children' as one of the leading forms of behaviour to be combated. He also framed the development of anti-social behaviours using the key actions of the social investment perspective (Blair 2003):

> To those who say the answer is tackling the causes as well as the symptoms of Anti-Social Behaviour I don't disagree. We are investing heavily in the biggest anti-poverty programme for over half a century. Record investment in education, the New Deal, the Working Families Tax Credit, record increases in child benefit and income support, and Sure Start. Our commitment to equalising opportunity has meant sustained support for families under pressure. The life-chances of children are hugely influenced by their earliest experiences, which is why access to post-natal support, parenting classes and early years provision is so important.

A second claim is that collective well-being is advanced by employment, and not only because it contributes to a healthy economy. Adults are considered to be behaving as responsible citizens and building healthy community when they respect the social contract or covenant implied by taking social benefits and using social services; in exchange they should engage in employment and in 'responsible parenting'.[24] In the same way, investing in children's ECEC as well as schooling will benefit us all by making them both well-prepared workers and responsible citizens (Lister 2003).

A third way that engagement is good for 'us all' is that it teaches responsible middle-class behaviours such as saving and investing. Both Britain and Canada have programmes explicitly designed to encourage low- and middle-income families to aspire to accumulating assets. Canadian programmes are, for the moment, limited to savings for post-secondary education. The Canada Savings Education Grant and the Learning Bond augment the savings of low- and middle-income families who have established tax-sheltered registered education savings plan (RESP). The British government describes saving and asset ownership as a complement to the work and skills, income, and public services pillars of the welfare strategy. Encouraging the accumulation of assets has been one of the big ideas since the earliest days of New Labour. For example, the Chief Secretary to the Treasury, Alistair Darling, said in 1998: 'We want to build the savings culture. That is good for individuals. It is good for businesses and is therefore good for the country as a whole' (quoted in Dobrowolsky and Jenson 2005, p. 220). Programmes such as the Child Trust Fund and the Savings Gateway were advocated as the best way to realise the social investment agenda. As Gordon Brown said when introducing the plans for the programme: 'Child poverty is a scar on the soul of Britain and it is because our five year olds are our future doctors, nurses, teachers, engineers and workforce that, for reasons not just of social justice but also of economic efficiency, we should invest in not just – as in the past – some of the potential of some of our children but invest, as we propose today, in all of the potential of all of our children' (Brown 2001).

THE LEGO™ PARADIGM: SOME VARIATIONS COMPARED

Paradigms are implemented differently in various jurisdictions. While commitment to underlying principles is shared widely, expression in policy varies. We saw this with the implementation of Keynesian thinking from the 1940s through the 1960s and we can observe it too with the LEGO™ paradigm (Hall 1989; Jenson and Saint-Martin forthcoming). The previous section noted some differences in implementation in Britain and Canada, despite a shared enthusiasm for the social investment perspective. In this section, I will account for some of these differences and also briefly document the variation visible when the social investment perspective, with its focus on children, is not the predominant response to new social risks within the LEGO™ paradigm. To understand these differences it is helpful to observe the interacting effects, within the political institutions of each country, of political ideologies deployed by parties and governments as well as their choices; in particular the decision to reject or continue the trajectory set out by previous governments. In each case, because of the constraints of space, particular attention will be paid to one policy domain – childcare, which is central to any discussion of children's well-being.

Institutional Effects: Politics and Choices Compared

Canadian governments took much longer than Whitehall to engage significant action on Early Childhood Education and Care (ECEC). Indeed, Canada devotes only half the public spending to childcare that the UK now does (OECD 2005b, Table 1.1), and this despite the federal government dropping new money into the system. In contrast, the UK more than doubled spending on childcare between the late 1990s and 2003–04. Nonetheless, it continues to lag behind not only Sweden but even Quebec, which now devotes 0.8 per cent of its GDP to childcare (0.28 per cent to parental leave), while the corresponding UK figures are 0.4 per cent and 0.11 per cent (OECD 2005b, Table 1.1). Both the UK and Canada have chosen to devote substantially more to child allowances, in both cases intended to, among other things, 'make work pay'.[25]

In Canada, calls for significant reform of childcare policy have been heard for over two decades (for this history see Mahon and Phillips 2002). We can pick up the controversy in the late 1990s when social policy thinking at the federal level was converted to the social investment perspective (Saint-Martin 2000). Federal politicians and bureaucrats and their allies in civil society put forward a well-developed social investment reading of the need for investing in children; public support for childcare was identified, along with the in-work benefits of the NCB, as a central instrument for implementing this perspective (details are in Jenson 2004b). Childcare was designated one of the possible reinvestments provinces and territories might make within the NCB, and then an additional promise of new federal spending resulted in the federal government signing with provinces and territories the Early Childhood Development (ECD) initiatives in 2001.

Institutions and politics were clearly in play. Social policy (as opposed to direct income transfers to individuals) is a provincial competence in Canadian federalism. The central government can try to incite action but it can not legislate what provinces do. Moreover, the recent history of federalism since the mid-1990s has been one of provincial governments being increasingly recalcitrant to federal intrusion in their policy domains. Even when they share the social investment perspective and a clear commitment to spending on children, they resist direction from the centre. When they do not share the same policy perspective – for example, when they are firmly neo-liberal – then public funding of childcare is not a priority. This opposition is reinforced by the presence in federal as well as provincial politics of a strong neo-liberal populist party that both forms the official opposition and has, since the 1990s, constituted a convincing political threat to the Liberal Party in elections.

With the exception of Quebec,[26] then, Canada has taken much longer to move toward any real new spending on childcare, despite the presence of an 'investing in children' discourse. In Ontario, for example, between 1995 and 2003 the Conservatives led by Premier Mike Harris simply refused to increase spending on childcare services. Indeed, despite their neo-liberal commitment to activation (expressed among other places in their workfare programme, 'Ontario Works'), the government preferred to allow mothers heading lone-parent families to substitute parental childcare for employment until the youngest child reached school age, one of the highest ages of exemption of any province or territory. The significant amount of funds received from Ottawa under the ECDI agreement went to many other services, including a benefit (somewhat misleadingly labelled the 'Ontario Child Care Supplement for Working Families') that could be accessed by a stay-at-home parent providing a couple's own childcare. Advocates of early childhood education and care term this stance 'ABC' – anything but childcare (Jenson 2004b, p. 188). Similar resistance comes from the official opposition at the federal level, the Conservative Party. It advocates spending 'childcare' funds on allowances to families who use only parental care.

Provincial reluctance is visible even in the 2004–05 'great leap forward'. Four months after the first agreement in principle (that permits a province to access the new money) at the end of April 2005, only six of 13 provincial and territorial governments had signed the accord with the federal government that is the requirement for obtaining a share of the promised US$5 billion of federal funding. The slow movement can be attributed to a number of factors, the three main ones being chariness about recognising Ottawa's involvement in an area of provincial constitutional competence; lack of enthusiasm for public funding of early learning and continued interest in providing support for parental care; and disputes over the legitimacy of limiting public funding to non-profit care providers and excluding the commercial sector.

This brief overview shows that federal and electoral institutions have hindered the full-scale application of the social investment perspective in Canada, and therefore of the childcare policies so crucial to it. The British situation is different, for several reasons. First, opposition to the Labour government's social policy initiatives, even in 2005, have had little political resonance. The Conservatives have yet to find their feet in the post-Thatcher era. This political weakness has allowed the social investment perspective to garner a hegemonic position that it does not enjoy in

Canada. Second, while certain important policies, including childcare, have been devolved to Scotland, Wales and Northern Ireland, it is Westminster that acts for England. The Labour government does not have to deal with a strong sub-national government with responsibility in the area and its own ideology.

When we examine Labour's choices around childcare, we can observe an important and early political decision, one that nonetheless set limits to an effective translation of all the talk about investing children into a coherent system of childcare provision or even one that fully supports the activation agenda. Immediately after its first election, the Labour government decided to continue one key element of the Conservative government's Early Years policy. The fact that the Major government was already active in the policy realm meant that the Blair government had to decide quickly whether to reconfigure the whole domain – toward for example an ECEC model of full-time educational care – or to continue along the same road as the Conservatives.[27] Rather than waiting, the new government immediately reaffirmed 'the Conservative pledge, and indeed funding commitment, to provide nursery education for all four-year-olds' (Randall 2002, p. 234), a year later extending it to cover all children three and older. Then, 'when the new child care policy was launched in March 1998 it was in a sense grafted onto this Early Years policy' (Randall 2002, p. 235).

This decision to meet the social investment perspective's commitment to early learning and care with nursery schools had two consequences. Because nursery schools only provide half-day services, parents are still left searching for care for the rest of the day, as well as for younger and school-age children. The Labour government decided that these needs could be filled by tax credits or informal care. The legitimacy of informal care was thereby reinforced; this is a second consequence of the 1997 decision. The 10-year strategy for childcare set out in 2004 reinforces this legitimacy by including informal care on the tray of choices (HM Treasury et al. 2004).

Parents of pre-school children are compelled to cobble together part-time nursery school (the public component) with parental or non-parental care for the rest of the day. This key decision to maintain the emphasis on extending access to part-time nursery schools contributes to the UK's low labour force participation rate by mothers of young children, a high rate of part-time employment (and therefore low female earnings), expensive childcare and low rates of centre-based care (OECD 2005b, Table 4.3 and passim). The weak spots in this system have been identified and singled out by the Babies and Bosses team, which writes:

> families still find it hard to reconcile work and family life, and further efforts are needed if British parents are to have the same opportunities as those in the

best-performing countries . . . The offer of free early education . . . in nursery schools is aimed at strengthening child development and reducing the parental share of the cost of childcare. The government is promising to extend free early education to 15 hours/week for 38 weeks/year. This will still leave many parents resorting to private day care and taking time off to transport children from one care source to another – an organisational challenge which could force many more out of full-time employment. *Babies and Bosses* suggests that childcare support needs to be provided in a more coherent way. The quality, cost, and opening hours of childcare facilities in the UK are also thorny issues for parents.[28]

In other words, large gaps remain to be filled if the social investment version of the LEGO™ paradigm is to be fully instituted in these two countries. Such gaps can be attributed to institutional rigidities as well as governmental preferences and choices.

The LEGO™ Paradigm for Adults: As Seen by the European Union

The LEGO™ paradigm is composed of three elements: an emphasis on work and life-long learning, orientation towards the future, and the belief that there is a general benefit from everyone being actively engaged. One difference that emerges in any comparison beyond Britain and Canada is the extent to which children's needs are privileged over those of adults in discourse and action. Examination of the European Union's social policy perspectives helps to see how the LEGO™ paradigm can vary across jurisdictions.

The European Union has taken to the LEGO™ paradigm with enthusiasm. We owe the term 'activation' to Eurospeak. Raising employment rates in the face of ageing societies, declining birth rates, and costly pensions has become the way to 'save' social protection. At least since the 2000 European Council in Lisbon the institutions of the EU, through the European Employment Strategy and other social policy areas, have promoted an increase in the employment rate of both women and men. This is done, as the EU documents constantly reiterate, so that Europe can become 'the most competitive and dynamic knowledge-based economy in the world capable of sustainable economic growth with more and better jobs and greater social cohesion' (for example, European Commission 2000, p. 2). This is a future orientation that sees active engagement as the way to ensure individual well-being (better jobs) and the collective success of the European economy.

At the same time, European institutions are in the forefront of promoting the notion that economic well-being in the future as well as the present depends on a modernised social policy focused on human capital and

capable of facing all the new social risks. One example: 'While robust economic and employment growth is a vital precondition for the sustainability
of social protection systems, progress in achieving higher levels of social
cohesion is, together with effective education and training systems, a key
factor in promoting growth' (European Commission 2005, p. 7).

While clearly adhering to the three principles of the LEGO™ paradigm,
the EU's version targets children much less than the social investment perspective does. In the immediate post-Lisbon Social Agenda, children were
mentioned only twice, both times in reference to the International Labour
Organisation's convention on child labour. The poverty analysis focused on
unemployment as the major risk factor for poverty, leading to the objective
'to prevent and eradicate poverty and exclusion and promote the integration and participation of all into economic and social life' (European
Commission 2000, pp. 12, 20, 25). In the Social Agenda issued in 2005 for
the years 2006–10, children are not mentioned either. Intergenerational
transmission of poverty and social exclusion have emerged, however, as
significant concerns; indeed the Communication applies an intergenerational approach focused on young people (European Commission 2005).
Thus the future orientation of the LEGO™ paradigm is present at the
heart of the analysis, but without necessarily adopting the 'investing in children' discourse.

One place where European institutions have begun to target the child,
however, is in analyses of social exclusion. For a number of years, the *Joint
Reports on Social Inclusion* have identified eliminating child poverty as a
policy objective and in doing so have linked the problem to the new social
risks of low-income and lone-parent families (for example, European
Commission 2005, pp. 10–11). However, child poverty is only one category
and its elimination only the fourth of seventh objectives. Analysis remains
overwhelmingly focused on the poverty–employment link – that is the situation of adults facing new kinds of labour markets and low wage jobs – and
activation and training are the first two priorities for fixing it (European
Commission 2005, p. 10).

The focus on adults is also confirmed by the way that childcare is framed
in European Union discussions. It remains overwhelmingly within a
work–family frame. There is continuity here, despite the best efforts of
experts on early childhood to promote the idea that *all* children benefit
from high quality early childhood education and care. As Janneke
Plantenga and Melissa Siegel (2004) put it in their position paper for the
Dutch presidency's major conference on childcare:

> Confirming the goal of full employment, the Barcelona European council
> agreed that: 'Member States should remove disincentives to female labour force

participation and strive, taking into account the demand for childcare facilities and in line with national patterns of provision, to provide childcare by 2010 to at least 90 per cent of children between 3 years old and the mandatory school age and at least 33 per cent of children under 3 years of age'.

This is a reading of the need for childcare and parental leave framed by employment policy. It indicates that the EU maintains its focus on 'reconciling work and family' that depends on article 119 of the Treaty of Rome (Ross 2000). The consequence is that it targets only rates of coverage; the issue of quality is left aside. This position persists despite pressure to focus on the quality issue and the analyses of the advantages of good quality care that were presented in the mid-1990s by its own Childcare Network (Moss 2004, p. 4 and passim). Even the OECD's Babies and Bosses analysis, most concerned about parental employment, has recognised the need to incorporate a quality focus (as we saw in the quote in the previous section) and in doing so is more attentive to the early childhood education issue than are the institutions of the EU, for whom childcare remains a service for parents.

CONCLUSION

We see clearly, then, that adherence to the LEGO™ paradigm does not automatically lead to attention to children's well-being. The paradigm may focus on adults' needs more than children's, even while it gives rise to policies designed to increase human capital and social services. In the European Union this means that the new social risks are analysed from the perspective of workers and parents, from the perspective of intergenerational solidarity among the old as well as the young, and from the perspective of integrating employment and social policy. The social investment perspective of the British and Canadian versions of the paradigm is only one among several in use. It does open the policy door to notions of investing in children, but as we have also seen, the talk is not always translated into policy actions that increase their well-being.

By identifying this variation within the social perspective and across the paradigm, this chapter seeks to uncover both the structure of assumptions and diagnosis that are increasingly being applied to discussions of new social risks and social architectures to confront them. We are living in new times, ones that will structure the well-being of future generations, and it is therefore important to understand not only the presence of new social risks but also the consequences of parsing them in policy discourse one way or another.

NOTES

This chapter is part of the project 'Fostering Social Cohesion: A Comparison of New Policy Strategies', supported by the Social Sciences and Humanities Research Council of Canada (SSHRC).

1. Final communiqué, 1 April 2005. Available at: www.oecd.org/document/47/0,2340,en_21571361_34360727_34668207_1_1_1_1,00.html, consulted 28 August 2005.
2. The United States since the welfare reform of the mid-1990s is a notable exception to this generalisation. It cannot be considered to share the same commitment to social investment as other liberal welfare regimes, and is probably best described as 'conservative' or 'neo-conservative'. As a result, the US case is excluded from the analysis and the generalisations developed in this chapter.
3. There is no single list of *the* new social risks. For example, Taylor-Gooby (2004, pp. 4–5) and Bonoli (2005, p. 435) identify the effects of policy design (inadequate pension coverage for some groups, for example) or redesign (privatisation, for example) as a new social risk. I prefer to treat them as *policies*, and then assess the extent to which they respond well or poorly to the new patterns of risk that individuals and families encounter in the labour market or families.
4. The choice of the term 'activation', which involved creation of a concept, allows policy communities to make an explicit link to the 'active labour market policies' long favoured by countries such as Sweden and somewhat later by the OECD.
5. There are multiple sources of this emphasis on investments to combat new social risks, including the OECD, the European Union (especially the Portuguese presidency in 2000 and the Belgian presidency in 2001), individual countries (especially Britain under New Labour since 1997), and policy intellectuals. For some discussions of the origins see Saint-Martin (2000), Dobrowolsky and Jenson (2005, pp. 204–7), and some key policy documents (for example, OECD 1997; Giddens 1998; Esping-Andersen et al. 2002).
6. This quotation is from the web page entitled 'fundamental beliefs', consulted 26 July 2005, www.lego.com/eng/info/default.asp?page=beliefs.
7. This may seem little more than a banal statement, but controversy over addressing children 'in the here and now' or treating them as 'adults in becoming' is a lively one. See, for example, Lister (2003) and OECD (2001, p. 8).
8. Peter Hall's (1989) useful book describes the variety of ways that the general paradigm of Keynesianism was 'domesticated' differently in a wide range of countries.
9. In the neo-liberal years of Thatcherism there had been a significant rise in workless households, contributing to a child poverty rate after taxes and transfers of 20 per cent, a 'score' higher than all OECD countries but Italy and the United States (UNICEF 2000, pp. 13–14 and 15). While a correlation between worklessness and poverty might seem obvious, the underlying notion was that, without employment, social transfers of the residual sort Britain had always provided could not move people out of poverty. Thus the main idea about how to end child poverty was to combat 'worklessness' (HM Treasury 2001, Chapter 2) by moving at least one parent into employment.
10. Instituting the NCB involved a major reform in social assistance. It 'removed children from social assistance' by locating their support in other programmes (the quasi-universal Canada Child Tax Benefit and the NCB Supplement targeted to low-income families) and was paid directly by the federal government rather than by the provinces and territories, as the child portion of social assistance had been (Jenson 2004b, pp. 177–8).
11. A message from ministers responsible for social services at www.nationalchildbenefit.ca/ncb/ncb_e19.html#anchor5100397, consulted 29 July 2005.
12. Myles and Quadagno (2000, p. 159) have rightly insisted on the importance of such policy instruments. For a presentation of their advantages, from a policymaker's perspective, see Mendelson (2005, pp. 1–2).
13. These are benefits that are accessed by adults responsible for a dependent child, usually under 18 or still in school. They are sometimes called 'child contingent' benefits.

14. Initially, all but two provincial governments 'clawed back' (reduced) their social assist-
     ance benefits by the amount of the federal tax credits. However, as the amount of the
     benefits has risen since 1999, even some families on social assistance have seen an
     increase in income.
15. Campaign 2000 is the successor group to the Child Poverty Action Group created in
     1983. It takes its name from the House of Commons pledge, voted unanimously in 1989
     to honour the retirement of Ed Broadbent as leader of the New Democratic Party, 'to
     seek to achieve the goal of eliminating poverty among Canadian children by the year
     2000' (Jenson 2004b, pp. 185, 170).
16. In a 2005 simulation of what family incomes would have been without the NCB,
     Statistics Canada reported: 'The results show that because of the NCB, there was a
     reduction of 8.9 per cent in the number of low-income families, meaning that 94,800 chil-
     dren in 40,700 families were not living in low-income situations. For these families, the
     average disposable income was higher by an estimated 9.2 per cent (about $2200).' The
     analysis also found that the NCB had a positive impact on families with children who
     remained in low-income situations.
17. Comparing the UK and Canadian situations, we note that in both cases the increase over
     five years was 5 percentage points, but the UK has a much lower rate of labour force par-
     ticipation by women who are lone parents. The Canadian rate in 2003 was 68 per cent
     and the British rate in 2005 was 56 per cent.
18. For the British studies, many of which benefited from long-running longitudinal analy-
     ses, see Dobrowolsky and Jenson (2005, pp. 209, 224). In Canada, because the longitu-
     dinal studies are more recent, the focus has been more on school readiness. See the
     studies cited in Jenson (2004b, pp. 180, 187) for example.
19. In 1994, for example, Canada's Campaign 2000 pre-figured later state preoccupations in
     its *Report on Children and Nationhood*, the message being 'If we neglect the next gener-
     ation, we're jeopardizing the future of our country.' The *Globe and Mail*, Canada's main
     newspaper, headlined its article this way: 'Child poverty seen as a threat to Canada's
     future' (28 June 1994, A8).
20. *Sure Start* is the name of Britain's community-based programme. British government
     ministers and their documents constantly intone the need for programmes that will give
     children the 'best possible start in life'. Ontario now has a *Best Start Plan*, and the NCB
     promises to help children 'to get off to the best possible start in life'.
21. 'McGuinty Government Expands Best Start Plan for Children', press release, 28 July
     2005. Available at: www.ontarioliberal.ca/news_20050728.htm, consulted 1 August 2005.
22. The language of investment permeates the NCB documents, especially the provincial
     reports which use a template in which they distinguish 'investments' from other spend-
     ing (Canada 2005, Appendix B).
23. From www.phac-aspc.gc.ca/dca-dea/programs-mes/ahs_overview_e.html#mission, con-
     sulted 1 August 2005.
24 . A clear expression of this position is: 'But you can't build a community on opportunity
     or rights alone. They need to be matched by responsibility and duty. That is the bargain
     or covenant at the heart of modern civil society. Frankly, I don't think you can make the
     case for Government, for spending taxpayers money on public services or social exclu-
     sion in other words for acting as a community – without this covenant of opportunities
     and responsibilities together' (Blair 2000).
25. The UK rate of 0.90 per cent is virtually the same as Sweden's 0.93 per cent and Canada
     is at 0.63 per cent (OECD 2005b, Table 1.1).
26. In 1998 Quebec instituted an affordable, high quality, universal ECEC programme, thus
     far the only one in Canada (Jenson 2002). The fourth volume of the OECD's *Babies and
     Bosses* series (OECD 2005b) focuses on Quebec, holding it up as a model for the rest of
     Canada.
27. New Labour did, however, abandon the notion of providing vouchers to parents, choos-
     ing instead to mix tax credits and some spending on ensuring supply.
28. From the summary of the reports conclusion, available at www.oecd.org/document/
     39/0,2340,en_2649_33933_34916903_1_1_1_1,00.html, consulted 28 August 2005.

REFERENCES

Blair, T. (2000), 'Values and the power of community', Prime Minister's speech to the Global Ethics Foundation, Tübigen University, Germany, 30 June, accessed 1 August, 2005 at: www.number-10.gov.uk/output/Page1529.asp.

Blair, T. (2003), 'Prime Minister's speech on anti-social behaviour at the QEII Centre, London', 14 October, accessed 1 August, 2005 at: www.pmo.gov.uk/output/Page4644.asp.

Bonoli, G. (2005), 'The politics of the new social policies: providing coverage against new social risks in mature welfare states', *Policy and Politics*, **33**(3), 431–49.

Boychuk, Gerard (2004), 'The Canadian social model: the logics of policy development', CPRN report F36, Ottawa, accessed at www.cprn.org.

Brown, G. (2001), 'Statement by Chancellor Gordon Brown at the press launch of the Saving and Assets for All consultation', 26 April, accessed 1 August, 2005 at www.hm-treasury.gov.uk/Newsroom_and_Speeches/Press/2001/press_54_01.cfm.

Campaign 2000 (2004), 'One million too many. Implementing solutions to child poverty in Canada', 2004 report card on child poverty in Canada, Toronto: Campaign 2000, accessed at www.campaign2000.ca.

Canada (2005), 'The National Child Benefit. Progress report 2003', catalogue number: SP-119-03-05E, accessed at: http://www.nationalchildbenefit.ca.

Commission of the European Communities (2000), 'Social policy agenda', COM (2000) 379 final.

Commission of the European Communities (2005), 'Social Policy Agenda', COM (2005) 33 final.

Deacon, B. (2001), 'Les organisations internationales, l'Union Européenne et la politique sociale globalisée', *Lien Social et Politiques-RIAC*, **45**, 73–87.

Dobrowolsky, A. and J. Jenson (2005), 'Social investment perspectives and practices: a decade in British politics', in Martin Powell, Linda Bauld and Karen Clarke (eds), *Social Policy Review*, **17**, 203–30.

Esping-Andersen, G., D. Gallie, A. Hemerijcke and J. Myles (2002), *Why We Need a New Welfare State*, Oxford: Oxford University Press.

European Commission (2005), *Joint Report on Social Protection and Social Inclusion 2005*, Luxembourg: Office for Official Publications of the European Communities.

Finn, D. (2003), 'The "employment-first" welfare state: lessons from the New Deal for young people,' *Social Policy and Administration*, **37**(7), 709–24.

Giddens, Anthony (1998), *The Third Way: The Renewal of Social Democracy*, Cambridge: Polity Press.

Hall, P.A. (ed.) (1989), *The Political Power of Economic Ideas*, Princeton, NJ: Princeton University Press.

HM Treasury (2001), *Tackling Child Poverty: Giving Every Child the Best Possible Start in Life*, A Pre-Budget Document, London: HM Treasury, December, accessed at: www.hm-treasury.gov.uk.

HM Treasury, et al. (2004), *Choice for Parents, the Best Start for Children: A Ten Year Strategy for Childcare*, Norwich: HM Treasury, December, accessed at www.hm-treasury.gov.uk.

Jenson, J. (2001), 'Rethinking equality and equity: Canadian children and the social union', in E. Broadbent (ed.), *Democratic Equality. What Went Wrong?*, Toronto: University of Toronto Press.

Jenson, J. (2002), 'Against the current: child care and family policy in Quebec', in S. Michel and R. Mahon (eds), *Child Care Policy at the Crossroads. Gender and Welfare State Restructuring*, London: Routledge.

Jenson, J. (2004a), '*Canada's new social risks: directions for a new social architecture*', CPRN report F43, Ottawa, accessed at www.cprn.org.

Jenson, J. (2004b), 'Changing the paradigm. Family responsibility or investing in children', *Canadian Journal of Sociology*, **29**(2), 169–92.

Jenson, J. and S. Jacobzone (2000), '*Care allowances for the frail elderly and their impact on women care-givers*', OECD labour market and social policy occasional papers 41, Paris.

Jenson, J. and D. Saint Martin (forthcoming), 'Building blocks for a new social architecture: the LEGO™ paradigm of an active society', *Policy and Politics*.

Joseph Rowntree Foundation (2004), 'The financial costs and benefits of supporting children since 1975', *Findings*, January.

Kidger, J. (2004), 'Including young mothers: limitations to New Labour's strategy for supporting teenage parents', *Critical Social Policy*, **24**(3), 291–311.

Lazar, H. (2002), '*Shifting roles: active labour market policy in Canada under the labour market development agreements*', *CPRN conference report*, Ottawa, accessed at www.cprn.org.

Lewis, J. (2001), 'The decline of the male breadwinner model: implications for work and care', *Social Politics. International Studies in Gender, State and Society*, **8**, 152–69.

Lister, R. (2003), 'Investing in the citizen–workers of the future: transformations in citizenship and the state under New Labour', *Social Policy and Administration*, **37**(5), 427–43.

Mahon, R. and S. Phillips (2002), 'Dual-earner families caught in a liberal welfare regime? The politics of child care policy in Canada', in S. Michel and R. Mahon (eds), *Child Care Policy at the Crossroads. Gender and Welfare State Restructuring*, London: Routledge.

Mendelson, M. (2005), *Measuring Child Benefits: Measuring Child Poverty*, Ottawa: Caledon Institute of Social Policy, accessed at www.caledoninst.org.

Moss, P. (2004), 'Getting beyond childcare, quality . . . and the Barcelona targets', presentation to Child Care in a Changing World Conference, Groningen, the Netherlands, 21–23 October, accessed at www.childcareinachangingworld.nl.

Myles, J. and J. Quadagno (2000), 'Envisioning a third way: the welfare state in the twenty-first century', *Contemporary Sociology*, **29**(1), 156–67.

Organisation for Economic Co-operation and Development (OECD) (1997), *Societal Cohesion and the Globalising Economy. What Does the Future Hold?*, Paris: OECD.

OECD (2001), *Starting Strong: Early Childhood Education and Care*, Paris: OECD.

OECD (2005a), 'Extending opportunities. How active social policy can benefit us all', summary report prepared for the meeting of social ministers of the OECD, Paris, accessed at www.oecd.org/socialmin2005.

OECD (2005b), *Babies and Bosses. Reconciling Work and Family Life, Vol. 4, Canada, Finland, Sweden and the United Kingdom*, Paris: OECD.

Pearson M. and P. Scherer (1997), 'Balancing security', *OECD Observer*, **205**, April–May, 6–9.

Plantenga, J. and M. Siegel (2004), 'Position paper – child care in a changing world', prepared for *Child Care in a Changing World*, Groningen, the Netherlands, 21–23 October, accessed at www.childcareinachangingworld.nl.

Powell, M. (1999), 'Introduction', in M. Powell (ed.), *New Labour: New Welfare State?*, Bristol: The Policy Press.

Randall, V. (2002), 'Child care in Britain, or, how do you restructure nothing?', in S. Michel and R. Mahon (eds), *Child Care Policy at the Crossroads. Gender and Welfare State Restructuring*, London: Routledge.

Ross, G. (2000), 'Europe: an actor without a role', in J. Jenson and M. Sineau (eds), *Who Cares? Women's Work, Childcare, and Welfare State Redesign*, Toronto: University of Toronto Press.

Saint-Martin, D. (2000), 'De l'État-providence à l'État d'investissement social?', in L.A. Pal (ed.), *How Ottawa Spends 2000–2001: Past Imperfect, Future Tense*, Toronto: Oxford University Press.

Statistics Canada (2004), *Women in Work: Work Chapter Updates 2003*, catalogue no. 89F0133XIE, Ottawa: Statistics Canada.

Taylor-Gooby, P. (ed.) (2004), *New Risks, New Welfare*, Oxford: Oxford University Press.

UK National Statistics (2005), 'First release. Work and worklessness among households July 2005', London: National Statistics, accessed at www.statistics.gov.uk.

UNICEF (2005), '*Child poverty in rich countries 2005*', UNICEF Innocenti Research Centre report card no. 6, Florence, Italy, accessed at www.un-ngls.org/UNICEF-child-poverty-in-rich-countries-2005.pdf.

UNICEF (2000), '*A league table of child poverty in rich nations*', Innocenti Research Centre report card no. 1, Florence, Italy, accessed at http://www.unicef-icdc.org.

3. An agenda for children: investing in the future or promoting well-being in the present?[1]

Ruth Lister

INTRODUCTION

The purpose of the title of this chapter is not to pose a false dichotomy between a future-oriented 'investing in children' strategy and a strategy that promotes children's well-being in the present. The two are not mutually exclusive and part of the argument will be that an agenda for children should – and to a more limited extent does – embrace elements of both. Instead, this construction is used to provide a framework for an analysis of the current UK government's agenda for children in an emergent 'social investment state' in which children represent 'citizen–workers of the future' (Lister 2003, p. 433).

The chapter starts with a brief account of how children have been prioritised in the UK 'social investment state'. It then details the key policies that have been developed to promote investment in children alongside more regulatory policies designed to encourage and enforce responsibility among children and their parents. The second half of the chapter explains why, despite the unprecedented investment in children, there are criticisms of how children are being positioned in the UK 'social investment state'. The conclusion offers a more normative sketch of how the social investment approach might be modified in the interests of children's well-being and flourishing in the present.

Children: '100 per cent of our Future' in the Social Investment State

'Social investment' has emerged in recent years as an ideal, promoted by the OECD and the EU among others. The term 'social investment state' was coined by Anthony Giddens as an alternative to the traditional welfare state in order to promote 'investment in *human capital* wherever possible, rather than direct provision of economic maintenance' (Giddens 1998,

p. 117, emphasis in original). A number of welfare state analysts have used the notion to make sense of current developments in the liberal welfare states of Canada and the UK (Lister 2003; Dobrowolsky and Jenson 2005; see also Jenson, Chapter 2 in this volume).

Children, especially young children, represent the main 'human capital' to which Giddens refers. Investment in young children takes on key strategic significance for a state keen to equip its citizens to respond and adapt to global economic change so as to enhance competitiveness in the knowledge economy. A key *Strategic Audit*, drawn up by the UK government's Strategy Unit, emphasises the importance of 'ensuring people have the skills and qualities for future jobs, lives and citizenship' (Strategy Unit 2003, p. 37). In particular, it points to 'the very strong evidence on the cost-effectiveness of targeted investment in children' (Strategy Unit 2003, pp. 78–9). Social policy is thus accorded a central role but it is primarily an instrumental role. It is still, in Richard Titmuss's phrase, the 'handmaiden' of economic policy (Titmuss 1974, p. 31).

The *Strategic Audit* exemplifies the future-oriented nature of the 'social investment state' (Jenson 2004). This is illustrated also in the justification provided for investing in children in the government's childcare strategy document. This states that:

> it is in everyone's interests that children are given the opportunity to fulfil their potential. This is all the more important in the context of an ageing society, where current generations will depend more heavily on those who follow . . . Investment in children to ensure that they have opportunities and capabilities to contribute in positive ways throughout their lives is money well spent and it will reduce the costs of social failure. (HM Treasury 2004, p. 7)

This future orientation is also reflected in New Labour's preoccupation with equality of life-long opportunity rather than the more traditional social democratic concern with equality as such (Lister 2000a). It underpins its welfare philosophy, which holds up paid work as the route out of poverty.

Children emerged as key figures in New Labour's nascent 'social investment state' early in 1999 when, in his Beveridge Lecture, the Prime Minister pledged the government to eradicate child poverty in two decades. Echoing the Commission on Social Justice, he explained that children were the Government's 'top priority' because they are '100 per cent of our future' (Blair 1999, p. 16).[2]

Although the pledge to end child poverty was made by the Prime Minister, the real drive behind the child poverty strategy has come from the Chancellor of the Exchequer, who had taken up the cause of child poverty when a back-bench MP. In a series of reports, speeches and Budget statements, Gordon Brown has developed the theme of investing in Britain's children, and in particular children living in poverty, as investment in the country's future. Moreover, he has argued that 'tackling child poverty is the best anti-drugs, anti-crime, anti-deprivation policy for our country' (Brown 2000). The 2003 Budget Report went so far as to claim that 'support for today's disadvantaged children will therefore help to ensure a more flexible economy tomorrow' (2003, para 5.4).

As Harry Hendrick points out, from a historical perspective government investment in children for the greater good of the nation is nothing new. What is new is the way in which New Labour has 'put children at the *centre* of a social investment strategy' and of social policy making (Hendrick 2005, p. 8, emphasis in original).

Policies for Children: Investing and Regulating

Investment in children involves improvements to both cash support and services. At the same time, investment is matched with more regulatory policies. These are designed to ensure that the investment pays off in terms of promoting social cohesion and security and turning children and young people into responsible adult citizens. This particular inflection of the 'social investment state' in the UK reflects New Labour's third way philosophy that with opportunities come responsibilities (Lewis and Surender 2004). The dual approach to investment in children and young people is summed up by Tony Blair with reference to citizenship education which, he states:

> gives us our best chance to teach young people about responsibility . . . One thing that we know is that the more we invest in young people at the earliest possible age, the better chance we have of making sure that they become responsible adults – hence the importance of programmes such as Sure Start. That is why it is important that, as well as clamping down on antisocial behaviour, we should continue to invest in the education of our young people. That education, of which citizenship is a part, is the best way to ensure a more secure society in the future. (Blair 2004a)

Time and again it is made clear that policy will be used to encourage and if necessary enforce the responsibility of parents 'to bring up children as competent, responsible citizens' (Blair 1998, p. 12).

Cash Support

Apart from a one-off real increase in the universal child benefit (for the first child only), investment in cash support has been primarily through an evolving tax credit scheme, which has replaced a means-tested benefit paid to low-income working families with children. The scheme has been influenced by similar schemes in Canada, Australia and the USA. It represents what Sylvia Bashevkin has described as an increasingly 'fiscalized social policy' (Bashevkin 2002, p. 114) in liberal welfare states. It also represents a further shift in the balance of financial support to the income-related targeting, typical of liberal regimes. New Labour invokes the principle of 'progressive universalism' – that is, 'giving everyone a stake in the system while offering more help to those who need it most' (HM Treasury 2002, para 5.5).

Tax credits target resources on children in low to moderate income families through two schemes. One, the child tax credit, is designed as 'a single, seamless system of income-related support for families with children' paid direct to the caring parent with child benefit (HM Treasury 2002, para. 5.17). The other, the working tax credit, is designed 'to make work pay' and it incorporates a childcare element (payable to the caring parent).

The child tax credit is constructed to replace social assistance payments for children. These payments have already been increased significantly in real terms, particularly for children aged under 11, for whom the value of financial support has doubled. New Labour tends not to trumpet this progressive policy, for it does not fit the third way philosophy it articulated on coming to power: that social security payments for those not in paid work represent 'dependency'-inducing 'handouts'.

The two other main innovations on the cash support side are more in line with New Labour's philosophy. One is the introduction of statutory means-tested educational maintenance allowances to encourage young people from low-income families to stay on at school. The other is a universal 'child trust fund' under which every new-born child will be given a modest capital sum (with additional payments for children in low-income families) accessible only when they reach 18. This is a form of 'asset-based welfare', which has itself been characterised as a key building block of the 'social investment state' (Sherraden 2002).

Services

From the outset, New Labour has stressed that 'welfare is not just about benefits. Active welfare is about services too' (Blair 1999, p. 13). An early mantra was 'education, education, education', seen as the key to achieving economic success, tackling child poverty and promoting equality of opportunity and social mobility. Education's pivotal role is symbolised in the transfer of responsibility for policymaking for the care and protection of children to the Department for Education and Skills, in 2003, under a new Minister for Children and Young People.

Of particular consequence, has been the priority given early-years child development and education services and childcare. The Sure Start programme, established in over 500 deprived areas by 2005, has been at the forefront of the drive to invest in young children's development. The broader childcare strategy, for all its weaknesses, represents a breakthrough in British social policy in its recognition of public as well as private responsibility for the care of children. Blair has heralded 'a nationwide universal early years service for the under fives based on the personal needs of each child and their parents' as 'a new frontier for the welfare state' (2004b). This will be provided by a network of children's centres, which represent the transformation of Sure Start into a universal programme (see also below). In addition, New Labour is promising wrap-around care from 8 am to 6 pm for primary school children.

More generally, children's services are being redeveloped following a broad-ranging Green Paper in 2003, 'Every child matters'. Local health, education and social services for children will work in partnership through new children's trusts. A Children's Commissioner for England has been established, after considerable pressure, but with more limited powers than elsewhere including the devolved administrations of the UK, where Children's Commissioners were introduced at an earlier date (see also below).

Regulation and Responsibility

While the main emphasis in the 2003 Green Paper, 'Every child matters', is on the protection of children, children and their parents are also required to exercise responsibilities. A number of regulatory policies have been introduced to enforce these responsibilities. Fawcett et al. argue that 'many of the initiatives are predicated on parents changing their own behaviour' and that common to a number of policy areas is 'the increasing social control of childhood' and a marked authoritarianism (2004, pp. 43, 113). This is best exemplified by the Crime and Disorder Act 1998 and the subsequent Anti-Social Behaviour Act 2003. Among their provisions are compulsory parenting orders designed to ensure parents control their children's behaviour; child curfews; and anti-social behaviour orders (nearly half of which have been applied to children and young people). According to the civil liberties organisation Liberty, the rights of under-16 year olds 'on the streets have been gradually eroded' since 1997 (Gallagher 2005, p. 5). Tim Gill, outgoing director of the Children's Play Council observes that 'there is growing hostility to children in public space. Behaviour that would a few years ago have been "larking about" is now labelled antisocial' (Gill 2004).

Parents can be fined, or even jailed, in cases of persistent child truancy, although a proposal to dock their child benefit was abandoned in face of opposition (internal as well as external). In a letter to a government task group, Blair has also raised the possibility of pupils suspended from school because of bad behaviour being legally required to stay at home accompanied by a parent who would have to take time off from work if necessary. He wrote 'it is clearly essential that parents fully accept their responsibilities if we are to improve discipline and respect in schools' (quoted in the *Independent*, 2 July 2005).

Henricson and Bainham suggest that these measures to enforce children's and parents' responsibilities 'may have gone too far', simultaneously eroding both children's and parents' rights against the spirit of the UN Convention on the Rights of the Child and the Human Rights Act (Henricson and Bainham 2005, p. 86).

WHY ONLY TWO CHEERS?

Children have moved from the margins to the heart of social policy. Overall spending on both financial support and childcare/early-years services has increased significantly. This policy shift has occurred in a country described as 'a serious contender for the title of worst place in Europe to be a child' (Micklewright and Stewart 2000b, p. 23). This label reflects not only a dominant liberal social welfare philosophy, which severely limited state intervention to promote the interests of children, but also what the new Children's Commissioner for England has described as a 'deep ambivalence' towards children and childhood (cited in the *Guardian*, 2 March 2005; see also Lister 2000b). Children are simultaneously sentimentalised as little angels and feared as little devils, most notably in the growing use of the term 'feral children' by the media. In this context, a discourse of investment is being used to good effect to promote a children's agenda.

Given this transformation in state policy towards children, one has to ask why those who have been arguing for such an agenda for years are now able to muster only two cheers at best. Of course, governments can always be criticised for not doing enough. However, this is not just a question of not moving as fast as the children's lobby would like. There is also some disquiet among both analysts and activists about the way in which children are being positioned in this brave new world of social investment. This section outlines four main sources of disquiet.

'Beings' or 'Becomings'?

The first concern is rooted in what has been called a 'new paradigm of childhood', which values children as 'beings' in the present and not just as potential adults or 'becomings' (Fawcett et al. 2004, p. 17). The government explains that it is in 'the nation's social and economic interests' to ensure 'children get a good start in life' because 'children are the citizens, workers, parents and leaders of the future' (HM Treasury 2004, p. 7). As the Children's Forum declared in their official statement to the UN General Assembly 'you call us the future, but we are also the present' (cited in Stasiulis 2002, p. 508). Thus, paradoxically, the iconisation of the child in the 'social investment state' has involved the partial eclipse of *childhood* and the child *qua* child. Childcare and education policies are more oriented towards employment priorities – current and future – than towards children's well-being. The gap between this orientation and children's own priorities is underlined by research with children carried out by the children's charity, Barnardo's. In discussions around the Green Paper, 'Every child matters', the children emphasised their desire for better opportunities for play and fun. Instead, the main outcomes of the consultation process relate to 'achievement but not enjoyment; education and not play', which, Barnardo's argues, 'suggests a view of children as adults in waiting' whereas 'play and enjoyment are in their very essence about the quality of children and young people's lives' (Kelley 2004, pp. 34–5). According to Gill 'politicians and Whitehall mandarins insist on hard evidence of the benefits of outdoor play, the implied message to children being, "we'll only let you out if you prove to us it'll do you good"' (Gill 2004). Play is an aspect of children's lives that does not fit so well into the social investment template, and which is therefore accorded relatively low priority.[3]

Lisa Harker, chair of a leading childcare charity, has suggested that an important lesson for the development of childcare provision in the UK is the need 'better to reflect on the totality of a child's experience, and that the best early years services are . . . child-centred'. She holds up, as a model, the approach taken by the Italian city of Reggio Emilia, which is 'informed by an image of the child . . . as a being with extraordinary potential' (Harker 2004; see also Moss, Chapter 8 this volume). In contrast to such a model, Norman Glass, the godfather of Sure Start, has warned that the programme's initial child-centred focus is at risk because it is in danger of 'becoming a New Deal for toddlers', captured by the 'employability agenda' (Glass 2005, p. 2).[4]

For older children, education is reduced to a utilitarian achievement-oriented measurement culture of tests and exams, with insufficient attention paid to the actual educational experience. In the words of the children's author, Philip Pullman, the government wants 'to turn children into bright little units of production and consumption' rather than develop the whole child (quoted in the *Observer*, 19 October 2003). Likewise, the

New Economics Foundation suggests that 'our secondary education system is not supporting young people to naturally grow and flourish, which implies that they have lower wellbeing, both currently and across their lives, than they might have done if the education system' explicitly promoted 'individual and societal well-being' (Shah and Marks 2004, p. 12).

Citizens of the Present Or the Future?

It is as citizen–workers of the future that children figure as the prime assets of the 'social investment state'. Criticisms of this model centre both on its elevation of paid work as the primary obligation of citizenship, to the detriment of care and voluntary work, and on the limits of its acknowledgement of children as rights-bearing members of the citizenship community. The first element of the critique has been well rehearsed elsewhere (see, for instance, Levitas 1998; Lister 2002) and is not central to the argument developed here. We therefore focus on the second criticism.

A number of bodies, including the UN Committee on the Rights of the Child and the parliamentary Joint Committee on Human Rights, have criticised the government's piecemeal and partial approach to children's rights. The latter criticises it for its failure to build 'a culture of respect' for children's human rights (cited Williams 2004, p. 421). Pivotal documents such as 'Every child matters' make no reference to the UN Convention on the Rights of the Child to which the UK is signatory. The model adopted for England's children's commissioner has been widely criticised for its weakness with regard to championing children's rights.

In general the government has been more willing to countenance rights for children who do not live with their parents than to intervene in the private sphere of the family to uphold the rights of those who do. This is most notable in the refusal to ban smacking, for fear of being labelled 'the nanny state', with an incursion into the private sphere too far (Toynbee 2004). Henricson and Bainham comment that 'retention of the defence of reasonable chastisement to the assault of a child by a parent remains a baffling violation of children's rights in deference to parental autonomy' (Henricson and Bainham 2005, p. 106). Smacking has been strongly criticised by the UN Committee as constituting 'a serious violation of the dignity of the child' (Committee on the Rights of the Child 2002, para. 35).

The same imbalance applies to children's participatory rights, which, on the whole, have been better developed for looked after children than for others. The main exception has been the efforts made by the Children and Young Person's Unit to consult and involve children and young people in imaginative ways. However, it has been abolished as a free-standing unit and subsumed within the new Children and Families Directorate within the

Department for Education and Skills. There is also a considerable amount of consultation going on at local authority level, although the quality of listening and responding has been questioned (Neale 2004). Moreover, consultation falls short of genuine participation, a point underlined by the incoming Children's Commissioner, Al Aynsley-Green. In a radio interview to mark his first day in post, he twice argued that 'children are now citizens' to make his case for their participation in decision-making, which he explicitly distinguished from consultation.[5]

All Or Some Children?

One of the criticisms made by Fawcett et al. in their study of New Labour's policies for children is that not all children have the same strategic significance as future citizen–workers for the 'social investment state'. They point in particular to disabled children and young people who, they argue, have not been targeted 'for intervention to the same extent that other groups can be seen to have been targeted. One reason for this', they suggest, 'could be that disabled children do not fit into the social investment state as either "threats" to civil order or "opportunities" for promoting a more market-friendly society' (Fawcett et al. 2004, p. 123).

However, in response to criticism, the government has now committed itself to improving support for families with young disabled children through childcare and early education, and attention to their additional needs. All national evaluations of children's services will 'assess the impacts on families with disabled children, and recommend specific actions to address barriers to their inclusion' (Strategy Unit 2005, p. 11). This commitment has been well received although there are fears that it could be undermined by the government's reluctance to ringfence the necessary funding, so that it has 'left itself precious few levers to get local authorities and health services to deliver improvements on the ground' (Bates 2005).

Gypsy and traveller children have been identified as a group even more marginalised within the 'social investment state', an expression of the second-class citizenship status of their parents and of gypsy and traveller communities generally. Gypsy and traveller children and their families are largely invisible other than when they are deemed to constitute a public nuisance. They do not comprise a category in the statistics on child poverty or in policies to combat it. However, there is evidence to suggest they are a group at considerable risk of poverty (Cemlyn and Clark 2005). This poverty, it has been argued, 'reflects the group's wider relationship with the dominant settled society and the discrimination and denial of human rights across a range of aspects of day-to-day living' (Cemlyn and Clark 2005, p. 154).

The children of asylum-seekers are effectively excluded from the 'social investment state' altogether. In one of his first media interviews, the Children's Commissioner for England expressed concern about the treatment of 'the most vulnerable who come to our shores' (Revans 2005, p. 27). Pamela Fitzpatrick points to the conflict between asylum policy and 'policies on child welfare, social inclusion and anti-discrimination' (Fitzpatrick 2005, p. 92). It has been described as a strategy of 'selective inclusion', as asylum-seeking families have suffered a 'progressive reduction' in material support and 'marginalisation . . . from mainstream services and society' (Burchardt 2005, pp. 209, 224).

A series of reports published by Save the Children has documented the problems faced by the children of asylum-seekers and unaccompanied children. One of these looks at children who had been detained for purposes of immigration control. The study provides evidence of the damage done to the children's education and health, and in particular their mental health. The report's main recommendation is that 'if the Government is serious about protecting and safeguarding the interests of children in the UK, then asylum-seeking and other migrant children must be treated as children first and foremost' (Crawley and Lester 2005, p. ix). Another study by Save the Children talked to asylum-seeking children living in the community. The report 'highlights the fact that despite their obvious vulnerability, children seeking asylum face constant discrimination, and it illustrates (in children's own words) how their rights are violated and routinely infringed by a state that seems to have forgotten that they are children' (Hewett et al. 2005, p. 1). It underlines that these children 'are in need of care and protection; moreover, they are a potential asset to our society and not a burden' (Hewett et al. 2005). However, they are not seen as such. Instead, 'they are treated as a threat and, whilst their resilience is often noted, their skills and talents are not encouraged to flourish as they might' (Stanley 2005, p. 187; see also Malikzada and Qadri 2005). One might speculate that the government does not consider them to be a good investment in the 'social investment state', in part because it does not see them as long-term residents and future citizens and does not wish them to see themselves as such.

Children and Parents

While the prioritisation given to children has been welcome, it has, in some ways, been at the expense of their parents. Great emphasis is placed on parenting and the responsibilities of parents. Although this has been backed up with some support services, as observed above there is also a strong whiff of authoritarianism in the measures adopted to ensure that parents (in practice, typically mothers, see Scourfield and Drakeford 2002) turn their children into responsible citizens. Henricson and Bainham are critical of the implications for human rights and point out that 'the attribution of blame to parents for their children's behaviour up to the age of 16 underestimates children's independence and overestimates the ability of parents to control the behaviour of young people as they grow older' (Henricson and Bainham 2005, p. 103).

In some cases the responsibilities expected of parents come into conflict with each other, placing strains on lone mothers in particular. On the one hand they are increasingly being encouraged to participate in the labour market as responsible citizens while, on the other, they are exhorted to do more to control their children's behaviour and involve themselves in their education as responsible parents. Juggling the two sets of responsibilities, within very real time constraints, can create considerable strain (Standing 1999; Horgan 2005).

The fulfilment of parental responsibilities has to be understood in relation to parental capacity, which is affected by the financial and material circumstances within which parenting takes place. Henricson and Bainham have questioned the way in which child poverty is addressed separately from the family poverty of which it is a part (2005). The point has been made at greater length by the Women's Budget Group. It argues that 'the well-being of children cannot be divorced from that of their mothers' and that 'the stress of poverty can undermine parental/maternal capacity to perform effectively the parental role, which is identified by the Government as crucial to its child poverty strategy' (Women's Budget Group 2005, p. iii).

This has implications for the financial support provided for non-employed parents which, unlike support for children, has seen no real increase and which has thus fallen further and further behind average earnings. This is beginning to emerge as an issue, including for children's organisations such as the Child Poverty Action Group who argue that family income needs to be looked at in the round. Henricson and Bainham analyse these issues as part of a more general study of how policy addresses the respective interests of children and parents. They conclude that the two sets of interests would be better recognised and reconciled within a rights based framework. They argue that:

> rights provide a framework and point of reference for handling interests. They flush individual and collective entitlements out into the open. They create expectations of a balance of interests that cannot disappear so readily as it might under a discretionary welfare model of government investment. (Henricson and Bainham 2005, p.110)

CONCLUSION – BACK TO THE PRESENT: PROMOTING WELLBEING

This chapter has provided an overview of how children are positioned in the UK, which, together with Canada, represents the clearest example of a liberal 'social investment state'. It has demonstrated how children are now at the heart of social policy as the objects of both investment and regulatory policies. New Labour may assert that 'every child matters' but children appear to matter more for their potential and future productivity as citizen–workers than as children in the here and now. Moreover, some groups of children matter less than others.

While its critical analysis of New Labour's approach to child welfare should not be read as a statement that all of its policies for children are reducible to the social investment template, this template does, nevertheless, provide a dominant frame for its agenda for children. It is one that is not rooted in the values of organisations working in the field. A study of national voluntary organisations by Fiona Williams and Sasha Roseneil found that, while, on the one hand, many organisations adopt a social investment discourse strategically, on the other, they:

> largely share a discursive centering of the child, which stands at some critical distance from New Labour's social investment approach to children. Many, though not all, were advancing considerably more holistic frameworks for thinking about the care and well-being of children and more radical frameworks for promoting social justice and equality for children than the government and, most important, were operating with an idea of children as moral subjects, rather than merely as the objects of policy intervention. (Williams and Roseneil 2004, p. 208)

This suggests a degree of consensus around the need to temper the futuristic and instrumentalist social investment approach, in the interests of children's wellbeing in the present and recognition of their status as child–citizen members of our society (see also Prout 2000). It means, I have argued elsewhere, that 'the Government's emphasis on children as investments needs to be balanced by a more explicit appeal to principles of social justice and to the human rights of children *qua* children' (Lister 2004, p. 59). A report published by UNICEF offers some pointers. It concludes that 'in societies throughout the world, more could be done to create environments in which children achieve their optimum capacities and greater respect is given to children's potential for participation in and responsibility for decision-making in their own lives' (Lansdown 2005, p. xi). This will, the report argues, require a cultural change 'so that children are protected appropriately in accordance with their evolving capacities, and also respected as citizens, as people, and as rights bearers' (Lansdown 2005, p. xi).

The reference to children's continued need for protection also serves as a reminder that the current emphasis on children's life-chances needs to be rooted in an equal concern with children's well-being and flourishing *as children*, which does more than pay lip-service to such ideals. Micklewright and Stewart suggest 'four key functionings that . . . a child needs to lead a "good life" ', which reflect the concept of children's well-being and development in the UN Convention on the Rights of the Child: 'material well-being, health and survival, education and personal development, and social inclusion/participation' (Micklewright and Stewart 2000a, p. 7). The New Economics Foundation's *Well-being Manifesto for a Flourishing Society* ends with the declaration that 'all policy-makers should ask "What would policy look like if it were seeking to promote well-being?" This should be one of the defining questions of politics in developed countries' (Shah and Marks 2004, p. 17). It is a question that could do much to reshape the agenda for children across the whole range of policies affecting them.

NOTES

1. A different version of this chapter appears in *Critical Social Policy* 26(2) 2006 as 'Children (But Not Women) First: New Labour, Child Welfare and Gender'.
2. The Commission was appointed by the previous Leader of the Labour Party, the late John Smith, to advise the party on its strategy for economic and social reform.
3. This is not to say that it is ignored completely. The Big Lottery Fund announced, in 2005, a new £155 million funding programme for innovative play facilities in England, focused on areas where facilities are poorest. Around the same time the Secretary of State for Culture, Media and Sport acknowledged the importance of play in an article on the subject (Jowell 2005).
4. Norman Glass was a Treasury civil servant who led the interdepartmental review out of which Sure Start was developed. Since leaving the civil service he has been a vocal critic of the shifts in the programme's focus and its transmutation into a more universalistic network of children's centres with limited, non-ringfenced, resources and less parental led local autonomy. Some students of Sure Start have, however, counselled against 'knee jerk' pessimism in reaction to these shifts (Featherstone 2005).
5. The Radio 4 *Today* programme 1 July 2005. The nature of children's citizenship and its relationship to that of adults needs greater exploration (see Lister 2005).

REFERENCES

Bashevkin, S. (2002), 'Road-testing the third way: single mothers and welfare reform during the Clinton, Chrétien and Blair years', in S. Bashevkin (ed.), *Women's Work is Never Done. Comparative Studies in Care-giving, Employment and Social Policy Reform*, New York and London: Routledge.

Bates, F. (2005), 'Think tank', *Society Guardian*, 9 March.

Blair, T. (1998), *The Third Way: New Politics for the New Century*, London: Fabian Society.

Blair, T. (1999), Beveridge Lecture, Toynbee Hall, London, 18 March, reproduced in R. Walker (ed.), *Ending Child Poverty*, Bristol: Policy Press.

Blair, T. (2004a), oral answers, *House of Commons Hansard*, 11 February, col. 1410.

Blair, T. (2004b), speech to the National Association of Head Teachers, Cardiff, 3 May.

Brown, G. (2000), speech to the Children and Young Person's Unit conference, Islington, London, 15 November.

Burchardt, T. (2005), 'Selective inclusion: asylum seekers and other marginalised groups', in J. Hills and K. Stewart (eds), *A More Equal Society? New Labour, Poverty, Inequality and Exclusion*, Bristol: Policy Press.

Cemlyn, S. and C. Clark (2005), 'The social exclusion of gypsy and traveller children', in G. Preston (ed.), *At Greatest Risk. The Children Most Likely to be Poor*, London: Child Poverty Action Group.

Committee on the Rights of the Child (2002), *Concluding Observations of the Committee on the Rights of the Child: United Kingdom of Great Britain and Northern Ireland*, Geneva: Office of the High Commissioner for Human Rights, accessed at www.unhchr.ch.

Crawley, H. and T. Lester (2005), *No Place for a Child. Children in UK Immigration Detention: Impacts, Alternatives and Safeguards*, London: Save the Children.

Dobrowolsky, A. and J. Jenson (2005), 'Social investment perspectives and practices: a decade in British politics', in M. Powell, L. Bauld and K. Clarke (eds), *Social Policy Review, 17*, Bristol: Policy Press.

Fawcett, B., B. Featherstone and J. Goddard (2004), *Contemporary Child Care Policy and Practice*, London and New York: Palgrave.

Featherstone, B. (2005), 'From Sure Start to children's centres: charting the journey', paper presented to Social Policy Association Annual Conference, University of Bath, 27–29 June.

Fitzpatrick, P. (2005), 'Asylum seeker families', in G. Preston (ed.), *At Greatest Risk. The Children Most Likely to be Poor*, London: Child Poverty Action Group.

Gallagher, C. (2005), 'The unrepresented: under-18s and civil liberties', *Liberty*, (Summer), 4–5.

Giddens, A. (1998), *The Third Way. The Renewal of Social Democracy*, Cambridge: Polity Press.

Gill, T. (2004), 'Bred in captivity', *Guardian*, 20 September.

Glass, N. (2005), 'Surely some mistake?', *Society Guardian*, 5 January, 2–3.

Harker, L. (2004), 'Lessons from Reggio Emilia', *Guardian*, 11 November.

Hendrick, H. (2005), 'Child welfare: the historical background', in H. Hendrick (ed.), *Child Welfare and Social Policy. An Essential Reader*, Bristol: Policy Press.

Henricson, C. and A. Bainham (2005), *The Child and Family Policy Divide*, York: Joseph Rowntree Foundation.

Hewett, T., N. Smalley, D. Dunkerley and J. Scourfield (2005), *Uncertain Futures. Children Seeking Asylum in Wales*, Cardiff: Save the Children Wales.

HM Treasury (2002), *Budget Report 2002*, London: HM Treasury.

HM Treasury (2003), *Budget Report 2003*, London: HM Treasury.

HM Treasury (2004), *Choice for Parents, the Best Start for Children. A Ten Year Strategy for Child Care*, London: HM Treasury.

Horgan, G. (2005), 'Welfare-to-work policies and child poverty in Northern Ireland', *Social Policy and Administration*, **39**(1), 49–64.

Jenson, J. (2004), 'Changing the paradigm. Family responsibility or investing in children', *Canadian Journal of Sociology*, **29**(2), 169–94.

Jowell, T. (2005), 'Play-makers', *Community Care*, 21–27 April, 36–7.

Kelley, N. (2004), 'Child's play', *Community Care*, 1–7 July, 34–5.

Lansdown, G. (2005), *The Evolving Capacities of the Child*, Florence: UNICEF Innocenti Research Centre.

Levitas, R. (1998), *The Inclusive Society?*, Basingstoke: Macmillan.

Lewis, J. and R. Surender (eds) (2004), *Welfare State Change. Towards a Third Way?*, Oxford: Oxford University Press.

Lister, R. (2000a), 'To RIO via the third way: Labour's "welfare" reform agenda', *Renewal*, **8**(4), 9–20.

Lister, R. (2000b), 'The politics of child poverty in Britain from 1965 to 1990', *Revue Française de Civilisation Britannique*, **XI**(1), 67–80.

Lister, R. (2002), 'The dilemmas of pendulum politics: balancing paid work and citizenship', *Economy and Society*, **31**(4), 520–32.

Lister, R. (2003), 'Investing in the citizen–workers of the future: transformations in citizenship and the state under New Labour', *Social Policy and Administration*, **37**(5), 427–43.

Lister, R. (2004), 'Ending child poverty: a matter of human rights, citizenship and social justice', in P. Doran (ed.), *Ending Child Poverty in 2020. The First Five Years*, London: Child Poverty Action Group.

Lister, R. (2005), 'Children, well-being and citizenship', paper presented to Social Policy Association Annual Conference, University of Bath, 27–29 June.

Malikzada, K.M. and A. Qadri (2005), 'Postscript on asylum seekers and refugees', in M. Barry (ed.), *Youth Policy and Social Inclusion*, London and New York: Routledge.

Micklewright, J. and K. Stewart (2000a), *The Welfare of Europe's Children*, Bristol: Policy Press.

Micklewright, J. and K. Stewart (2000b), 'Child well-being and social cohesion', *New Economy*, **7**(1), 18–23.

Neale, B. (ed.) (2004), *Young Children's Citizenship*, York: Joseph Rowntree Foundation.

Prout, A. (2000), 'Children's participation: control and self-realisation in British late modernity', *Children and Society*, **14**, 304–15.

Revans, L. (2005), 'Take me as I am', *Community Care*, 26–7.

Scourfield, J. and M. Drakeford (2002), 'New Labour and the "problem of men"', *Critical Social Policy*, **22**(4), 619–40.

Shah, H. and N. Marks (2004), *A Well-being Manifesto for a Flourishing Society*, London: New Economics Foundation.

Sherraden, M. (2002), 'From a social welfare state to a social investment state', in C. Kober and W. Paxton (eds), *Asset-based Welfare and Poverty*, London: National Children's Bureau.

Standing, K. (1999), 'Lone mothers and "parental" employment: a contradiction in policy?', *Journal of Social Policy*, **28**(3), 479–95.

Stanley, K. (2005), 'Young asylum seekers and refugees in the UK', in M. Barry (ed.), *Youth Policy and Social Inclusion*, London and New York: Routledge.

Stasiulis, D. (2002), 'The active child citizen: lessons from Canadian policy and the children's movement', *Citizenship Studies*, **6**(4), 507–38.

Strategy Unit (2003), *Strategic Audit: Discussion Document*, London: Cabinet Office.

Strategy Unit (2005), *Improving the Life Chances of Disabled People*, London: Cabinet Office.

Titmuss, R.M. (1974), *Social Policy*, London: Allen & Unwin.

Toynbee, P. (2004), 'Nanny Blair would win it', *Guardian*, 2 July.

Williams, F. (2004), 'What matters is what works: why every child matters to New Labour', commentary on the DfES Green Paper 'Every child matters', *Critical Social Policy*, **24**(3), 406–27.

Williams, F. and S. Roseneil (2004), 'Public values of parenting and partnering: voluntary organizations and welfare politics in New Labour's Britain', *Social Politics*, **11**(2), 181–216.

Women's Budget Group (2005), *Women's and Children's Poverty: Making the Links*, London: Women's Budget Group.

PART II

Paying for children

4. Child benefit packages in 15 countries in 2004

Jonathan Bradshaw

BACKGROUND

All industrialised countries have a package of tax benefits, cash benefits, exemptions from charges, subsidies and services in kind, which assist parents with the costs of raising children. This package plays a part, along with labour market income, in tackling market-driven child poverty. Parts of the package assist parents in employment: by subsidising low earnings, subsidising childcare costs, creating or structuring financial incentives or disincentives to be in employment or to work part time or full time or, in couples, have one parent or two parents working. Other parts of the package assist parents to stay out of the labour market, enabling them to stay at home to care. The package may influence the number of children a women will have and the birth spacing. It may also have an impact on family form, making it more or less easy for a parent to separate or bring up a child alone.

The analysis in this chapter updates earlier work on the child benefit package undertaken in a series of studies (Bradshaw and Piachaud 1980; Bradshaw et al. 1993; Bradshaw et al. 1996; Ditch et al. 1995, 1996, 1998; Bradshaw and Finch 2002; Bradshaw and Mayhew 2006).

This chapter represents the situation of 15 countries as at January 2004. Eight of the countries (the Nordic countries, Germany, the Netherlands and the UK) were the subject of a comparative study (Bradshaw and Hatland 2006) funded by the Nordic Council of Ministers. The other countries were added as a result of national informants agreeing to provide their data to match that already collected for the Nordic project. The mix is therefore somewhat ad hoc.

THE MODEL FAMILIES MATRIX

The model family method is an attempt to compare social policies on a systematic basis. The procedure is to identify a specific range of model families and, with the help of national informants, to calculate what cash benefits, tax benefits and subsidies they would obtain given the rules in force at a particular time (in a particular place where necessary). In order to do this we select a number of model families:

- A childless married couple,
- A lone parent divorced with one child under 3 receiving full-time formal childcare,
- A lone parent with one child aged 7,
- A couple with one child aged 7,
- A couple with two children aged 7 and 14,
- A couple with three children aged 7, 14 and 17, all at school.

This choice enables us to compare childless couples and families with children; the treatment of childcare costs for a lone parent; and variations in the package for couples by the number of children.

For each family a variety of income cases have to be specified. In this project they were as follows:

- One earner on half average earnings or the minimum wage for a 35-hour week, whichever is the highest,
- One earner on average earnings,
- Two earners on average and half average earnings or the minimum wage for a 35-hour week, whichever is highest,
- Two earners, both on average earnings,
- On social assistance, no earnings.

These income cases were chosen to enable us to compare how the package varies with earnings and the number of workers, and how it compares with a base case not in employment.

The policies that are taken into account in the package are:

- Tax benefits,
- Income-related cash benefits,
- Non-income-related cash benefits,
- Social insurance contributions,
- Rent/housing benefits,
- Local taxes/benefits,
- Childcare costs/benefits,
- Social assistance,
- Guaranteed child support,
- Other.

In order to reduce the burden of work for national informants, we reduced the range of family types and income cases from those used in Bradshaw and Finch (2002). In that study we also included the costs and benefits of schooling and a standard package of health care. These were not found to be important elements of the package for most countries. However among our countries, health costs and educational costs (for secondary school pupils) had a negative impact on the package in the Netherlands, and educational benefits (free school meals) made a positive contribution to the package in Finland, Sweden and the UK (for the social assistance case).

Housing costs are particularly difficult to handle in this kind of comparative research and there is no good solution. We have opted to follow the OECD method of assuming that our families are tenants and that rent is 20 per cent of average earnings and does not vary with family size and type. There is further discussion of these problems in Kuivalainen (2002), Bradshaw and Finch (2002) and Bradshaw and Finch (2004).

There is of course scope for argument about these assumptions. For example in the context of a Nordic study there are probably too many one-earner family cases. The method is designed to ensure that like is being compared with like. The results are illustrative not representative. They present a formal picture of how policy *should* operate given the law and regulations, not necessarily how it *does* operate. In particular no allowance is made for non-take-up of income-tested cash benefits or tax benefits. Also after the impact of the package, families have to pay different prices for commodities, and in some countries they have to pay for services that are free or subsidised in other countries. We have taken some account of variation in the costs of living by expressing the value of the package in terms of the latest (2003) euro purchasing power parities (PPPs) available (OECD 2004).

The situation described is at January 2004.

RESULTS

In the rest of this chapter we will be examining the structure and value of the child benefit package by showing the difference between the net disposable income of a childless couple and that of a family with children on the same earnings – this represents the contribution of the state in respect of children (and being a lone parent). However this relative difference in net income may hide quite large differences in absolute net incomes. So in Figure 4.1 we first compare the net disposable incomes of a couple with two children where both parents are employed (one on national average and one on half national average earnings). It can be seen that the Netherlands has the highest earnings and New Zealand and Ireland the lowest. However

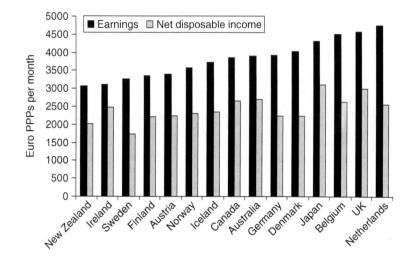

Figure 4.1   *Comparison of gross earnings and net disposable income per*
month after taxes, benefits and housing costs, couple plus
two children, two earners on average and half average earnings.
Euro purchasing power parities per month, January 2004

after the impact of taxes, benefits and housing costs Japan has the highest
net disposable resources and Sweden the lowest by some way.

We now begin to examine the structure of the child benefit package using
the illustrative cases. In Figure 4.2 we show how the package is made up for
a poor lone parent – a lone mother on half average earnings with a
preschool-age child requiring childcare. The money amount is the extra net
income per month that the family has over what a childless couple would
receive at these earnings – thus it is what the family receives in respect of
their children from the state. It can be seen that the UK has the highest child
benefit package for this family type, mainly delivered through Child Tax
Credit, with Child Benefit and Housing Benefit. However the UK also has
the highest net childcare costs and so the generosity of the package is
undermined. Contrast Austria, which has a Guaranteed Child Support
scheme, a non-income-related child benefit and very low childcare costs.
Among the Nordic countries Finland has the lowest package at this earnings level. What is significant to note in Figure 4.2 is the variety of different
elements that go to make up the way in which a low-paid lone parent with
a preschool-age child is supported.

Then in Figure 4.3 we present the structure for an 'average family' – a
couple with two children and one earner on national average earnings. For

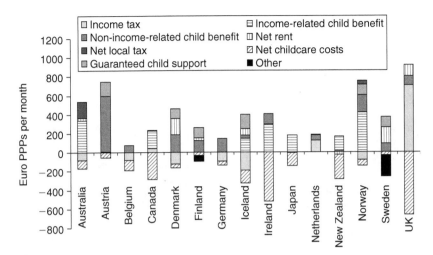

*Figure 4.2   Structure of the child benefit package, lone parent plus one
child under three, one earner on half average earnings. Euro
purchasing power parities per month, January 2004*

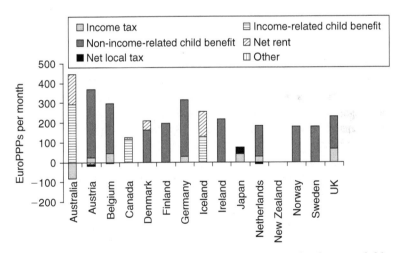

*Figure 4.3   Structure of the child benefit package, couple plus two children,
one earner on average earnings. Euro purchasing power parities
per month, January 2004*

this family the structure is much simpler with mainly non-income-related
child benefits and/or child tax benefits making up the packages. In
Australia, Canada and Iceland some income-related child benefits is still
payable and Australia, Denmark and Iceland have housing benefit.

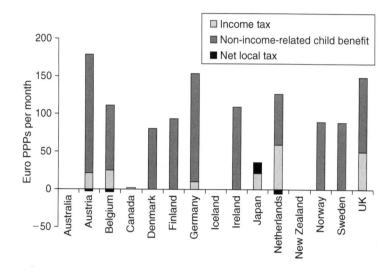

Figure 4.4   Structure of the child benefit package, couple plus one child,
two earners both on average earnings. Euro purchasing power
parities per month, January 2004

Figure 4.4 presents a picture of the structure of the child benefit package
for a small well-off family – a couple with one child, with two earners both
on average earnings. The main component of the package in most countries is now non-income-related child benefits. Belgium also has child tax
allowances that benefit families at this earnings level but not lower income
families However in Australia, Iceland and New Zealand there is no child
benefit paid at this income level and Canada's is very small. With the exception of Iceland the main component of the package at this level of earnings is non-income-related child benefit. Housing benefits are important in
Denmark and Iceland and tax benefits contribute in all the non-Nordic
countries.

So far we have been concerned with structure – how the child benefit
packages are made up. Now we turn to compare the level of the packages.
Figure 4.5 provides a picture of how the whole child benefit package varies
with earnings for the same family type (a couple with two school-age children). Australia, Iceland and New Zealand pay no child benefit package to
the best off family and Canada pays very little. However Australia, Ireland
and the UK are much more generous to the low earning family and
Denmark, Finland, Sweden and Norway pay social assistance and/or
housing benefit to supplement the income of very low earning families.
Austria, Belgium and Japan all have slightly regressive elements to their

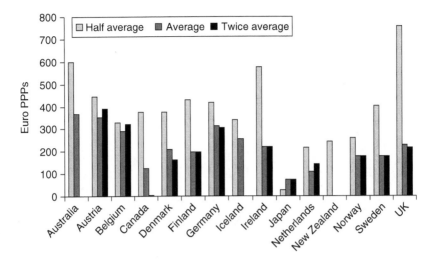

Figure 4.5 *Child benefit package by earnings (euro ppps per month) after taxes, benefits and housing costs, couple plus two children, January 2004*

packages, which increase with earnings. The Netherlands package also has an income-related element, and when earnings rise beyond that level the package is comparatively small.

This picture is complicated by the two other ways in which the child package varies. Figure 4.6 shows how it varies by the number of children in the family – for couples and keeping earnings constant. In New Zealand only the three child family receives any more than a childless couple. The other countries are making rather different judgements about the relative needs of families of different sizes. Austria is more generous for the third child and so are Belgium, the Netherlands and Sweden to a lesser extent. Australia is more generous to the second child and the UK is unusual in favouring the first child. In Finland the family gets no more benefit for the third child. In Iceland families receive less for the third child than the first and second. In the other countries each child receives equal amounts.

Figure 4.7 compares how the tax benefit package treats families of different types – lone parents and couples with the same earnings. Again New Zealand has no package at this earnings level. A lone parent with one school-age child in Belgium, Germany and Japan is treated less well in the tax benefit system than a childless couple or a couple with one child – hence the negative child benefit package. Iceland treats lone parents families less generously than couples with the same number of children. In contrast all

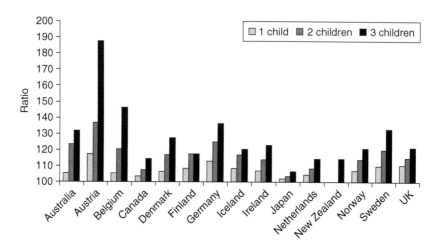

Figure 4.6   Child benefit package by number of children (childless couple = 100), after taxes, benefits and housing benefits

the other Nordic countries and the Netherlands are very much more generous to lone parents than to couples. In Australia, Canada, Ireland and the UK the package is neutral between couples and lone parents.

An important element of the overall package is the treatment of child-care costs. We asked national informants to assess what a lone parent with one preschool-age child would have to pay for full-time preschool childcare of the most prevalent type in their country. Figure 4.8 presents the results for lone parents at two earnings levels. Two countries, Austria and Norway, have positive childcare costs because they have benefits for a lone parent with a preschool child that more than offset the charges for childcare – in Austria it is *Kinderbetreuungsgeld* and Norway it is the Transitional Allowance. Ireland, New Zealand and the UK have by far the highest child-care costs – though in New Zealand and the UK these are reduced for the low earnings lone parents. All the other countries have childcare that is sub-sidised, and all of these except Iceland have reductions in charges which vary with earnings.

Marginal tax rates are a measure of the incentives in the tax benefit system for working more. They are normally presented as the marginal tax rate on each additional unit of income, but here we are observing the average marginal tax rate over a wider range of earnings. What we are esti-mating is how much of the extra earnings a family lose when they increase their earnings from half average to average – as a result of working longer hours, changing their jobs or working overtime. It can be seen in Figure 4.9

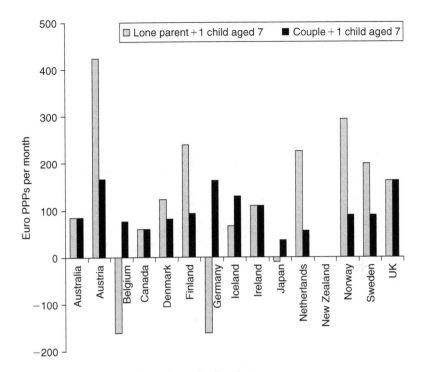

*Figure 4.7   Child benefit package by family type, one earner on average
earnings, after taxes, benefits and housing costs. Euro ppps per
month, January 2004*

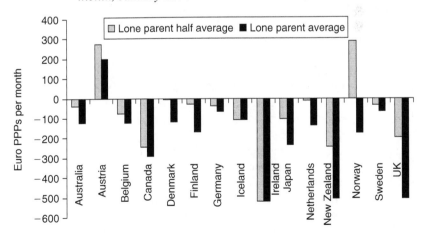

*Figure 4.8   Net costs of full-time childcare. Euro ppps per month, January
2004*

Paying for children

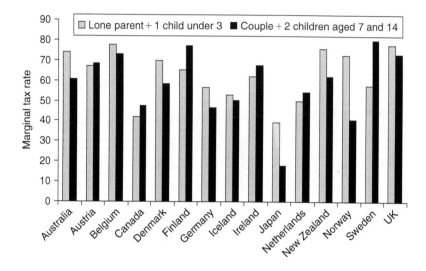

Figure 4.9   Marginal tax rates on moving from half average earnings to average earnings

that the marginal tax rates are highest for lone parents when childcare subsidies are income related, such as in New Zealand, Norway and the UK. For couples, Sweden and Finland have the highest marginal tax rates. Canada, Germany, Iceland, Japan and Norway have relatively low marginal tax rates for couples.

Figure 4.10 gives the marginal tax rate for couple families moving from having one earner on average earnings to two earners on average and half average earnings. It therefore shows the incentive effect on a second earner starting to work part time. Second earners in Iceland keep less than half of their earnings, and Denmark and Germany also have high marginal tax rates for second earners. Austria, Finland, Japan, New Zealand and the UK have considerably lower marginal tax rates and therefore stronger incentives for a second parent to be employed – though this analysis takes no account of childcare costs that might be involved.

So far we have been comparing how the tax benefit package impacts on the net income of families in employment. In Figure 4.11 we compare the levels of social assistance paid to families out of employment who have children, in euro purchasing power parities per month. Social assistance for a lone parent is relatively low in Austria, Canada and Germany and relatively high in Denmark, Iceland and Norway. For the large couple family social assistance is highest in Australia, Austria, Denmark, Japan and the UK and relatively low in Canada and New Zealand.

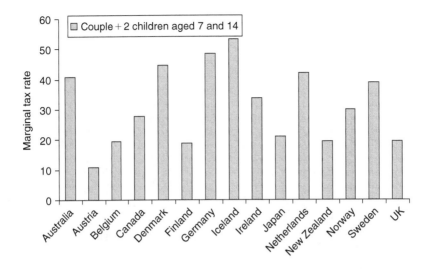

Figure 4.10   Marginal tax rates for couples, moving from one earner on
average earnings to two earners, one on average earnings
and one on half average

These data on social assistance payable to families, combined with the
in-work incomes enables us to estimate notional replacement rates. The
replacement rate is the proportion of net in-work income that would be
'replaced' by social assistance if the family were unemployed. It is commonly used as an indicator of the incentives facing people – in the UK it
is sometimes known as the unemployment trap. It is notional in this
instance because the numerator is the net income of the two family types
on social assistance, whereas in a number of countries it would not
be social assistance that they received if unemployed, but earnings-related
contributory unemployment benefit that would be almost certainly higher
than social assistance. So the replacement rate here is a notional minimum
rate. Further, we use as our denominators the net income of the two family
types earning half average earnings. The actual replacement rates would be
lower at higher earnings levels. Nevertheless we chose this level of earnings
on the grounds that it is the level where financial incentives are likely to be
most salient in influencing labour supply decisions.

Figure 4.12 shows that there are very substantial variations in the
replacement rates between countries, with Austria, the Nordic countries
(except Finland) and Japan having rates for couple families well in excess
of 100 per cent – these families would be better off not working. The
Anglophone countries and the Netherlands tend to have lower replacement rates for the couple families. Canada and the Netherlands have low

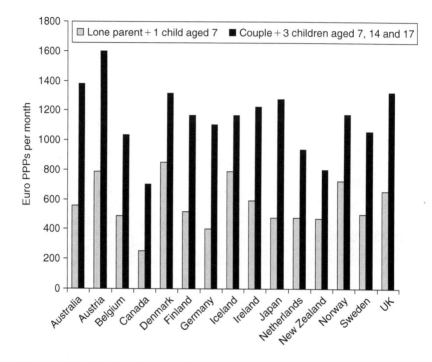

Figure 4.11   The level of out of work social assistance per month in ppps

replacement rates for lone parents, while for Denmark, New Zealand and
Norway they provide very little if any financial incentive to work.

   As we argued earlier, the model family method can only reliably illustrate differences in the child benefit package. However, as we have seen, the
package varies in level according to earnings, employment status, type of
family, number of children and according to whether the comparisons are
made before or after childcare. It is difficult to see the true values with all
this variation. So in order to summarise and compare the packages overall
we take an illustrative sample of family types and earnings levels, selected
from our model families with a crude weighting on the more common
types (see Appendix) and estimate an overall average child benefit package.
Figure 4.13 presents the summary 'league' table based on purchasing
power parities. Austria has the most generous child benefit package by
some margin. The UK has the next most generous package and is similar to a group that includes Norway, Australia, Denmark, Belgium,
Germany, Sweden, Finland and Ireland. Next comes a group of the
Netherlands, Iceland and Canada, and then the laggards are Japan and
New Zealand.

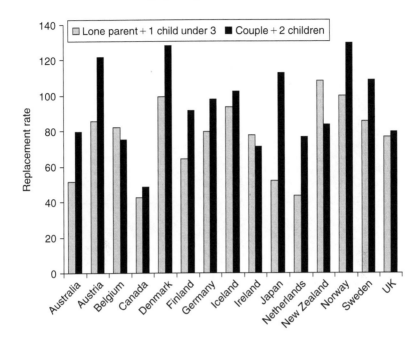

Figure 4.12   Replacement rates at half average earnings (NDI after all)

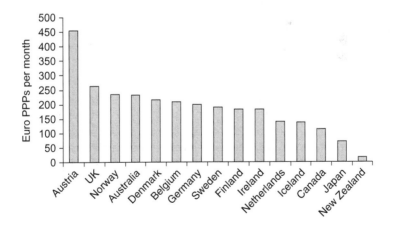

Figure 4.13   Overall 'average' child benefit package after taxes, benefits, childcare and housing costs (difference from childless couple). Euro ppps per month, January 2004

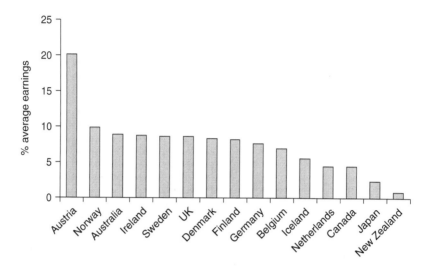

Figure 4.14   *Overall 'average' child benefit package after taxes, benefits,
childcare and housing costs (difference from childless couple).
% average earnings, January 2004*

This picture is complicated by the fact that a rather different league table
is produced if the value of the package is expressed as proportion of
average earnings instead of purchasing power parities. In Figure 4.14 the
UK moves down the league table and there are some other changes in
ranking, however the groupings remain broadly the same. There is no way
of reconciling these two measures – they each have their advantages and
disadvantages.

Tables 4.1a and 4.1b compare the rankings obtained in 2001 with those
obtained in this study at 2004. It would be wrong to make too much of these
comparisons. The assumptions about earnings were not entirely consistent
between 2001 and 2004 and there may have been other inconsistencies. In
Table 4.1a we compare the rankings after taking account of taxes and
benefits only. Austria is at the top of the league table for both years. In comparison with average earnings there is a mixed picture, with reductions in
Japan, New Zealand, the Netherlands and especially Belgium. In most
other countries the values of the package has improved, but most improvement has taken place in Austria which was already the best.

Table 4.1b makes the comparisons after taking into account housing
benefits. Japan and New Zealand become more clearly laggards. However
the overall league table has changed very little – Sweden and Denmark
move up and Belgium moves down the league table.

Table 4.1a *Comparisons of the ranking of child benefit packages in July 2001 and January 2004, after taxes and benefits only*

Ranking in 2001 as % average earnings		Ranking in 2004 as % average earnings	
Austria	16.3	Austria	20.1
Ireland	12.7	Ireland	11.8
Belgium	12.1	UK	10.3
UK	11.6	Norway	9.1
Norway	9.6	Belgium	8.8
Germany	9.0	Australia	8.2
Finland	8.7	Finland	8.1
Australia	7.6	Germany	7.5
Sweden	6.7	Sweden	6.3
Denmark	6.2	Canada	6.1
Netherlands	5.8	Denmark	6.1
Canada	5.8	Netherlands	5.1
New Zealand	5.2	Iceland	3.6
Japan	4.9	New Zealand	3.5
		Japan	2.6

Table 4.1b *Comparisons of the ranking of child benefit packages in July 2001 and January 2004, after taxes, benefits and housing costs*

Ranking in 2001 as % average earnings		Ranking in 2004 as % average earnings	
Austria	18.3	Austria	20.7
Belgium	12.1	Ireland	11.9
Ireland	12.0	UK	11.3
Norway	11.5	Norway	10.6
UK	10.9	Australia	9.6
Germany	9.8	Sweden	9.0
Finland	9.5	Finland	8.8
Sweden	9.2	Denmark	8.7
Australia	9.1	Germany	7.8
Denmark	8.7	Belgium	7.6
Netherlands	6.2	Canada	6.3
Canada	5.8	Iceland	6.3
Japan	5.7	Netherlands	4.9
New Zealand	4.5	Japan	3.2
		New Zealand	3.2

Note: for technical reasons this comparison does not take into account childcare costs.

DISCUSSION

One question that arises from this analysis is do these differences matter?
For example:

- Is there any association between the child support system and
  mothers' employment rates?
- Does the child benefit package have any relationship to fertility rates
  in these countries?
- Is the child poverty rate in any way a function of the level of the child
  benefit package?

Mothers' Employment

Figure 4.15 examines the relationship between the marginal tax rates on a
mother going to work part time for half national average earnings and the
mothers' employment rates derived from OECD data. There is a clear relationship between the two, but in the opposite direction to what economic

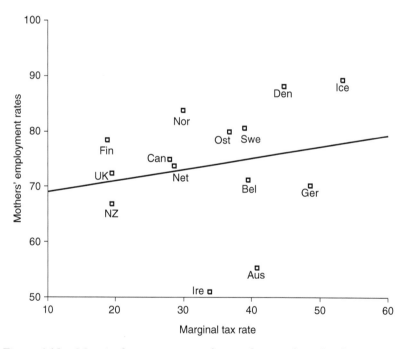

*Figure 4.15   Marginal tax rate on mother working and mothers'
employment rates*

theory would suggest. Higher marginal tax rates are associated with higher employment rates!

It would be interesting to examine the relationship between lone mothers' employment rates and the replacement rates they experience. Unfortunately we do not have up-to-date lone mothers' employment rates for all our countries. However Bradshaw et al. (2005) found no relationship between lone parent labour supply and replacement rates and they suggested that whether or not labour supply was regulated by a work test might have a stronger influence on labour supply.

Fertility

Figure 4.16 shows the relationship between the total fertility rate and the value of the child benefit package. There is a regression line drawn on the Figure indicating a negative relationship – the higher the child benefit package the lower the fertility rate – but the correlation is not statistically significant. There is no clear relationship between the generosity of the package in these countries and their fertility level. If the Southern European

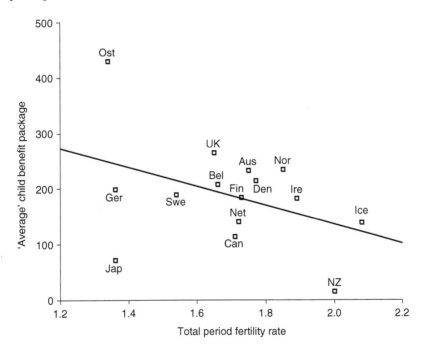

Figure 4.16   Total fertility rate and average value of the child benefit package

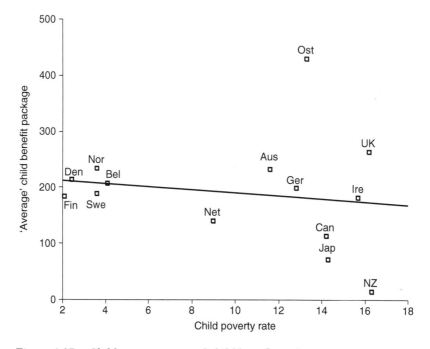

Figure 4.17   Child poverty rate and child benefit package

countries had been included in this analysis the relationship would have been a positive one, with higher fertility rates in the countries with more generous packages (see Bradshaw and Finch 2002).

Child Poverty

The problem with comparing the child poverty rates and the child benefit package is that the periods do not coincide. The latest child poverty rates available are for circa 2000 and the child benefit package is for January 2004. Figure 4.17 compares the child benefit package as a percentage of average earnings with the child poverty rates obtained by Forster and D'Ercole (2004). There is a weak relationship in the direction one would expect – those countries with the more generous child benefit packages have lower child poverty rates. However Austria ('Ost' in Figures 4.15 to 4.18) is a big outlier, and the UK has a child poverty rate higher than the child benefit package would suggest and the Netherlands has a lower rate. It may be that more recent child poverty data might improve the relationship.

It might be expected that there would be a closer relationship between the child poverty rate and the level of the package paid to families with low

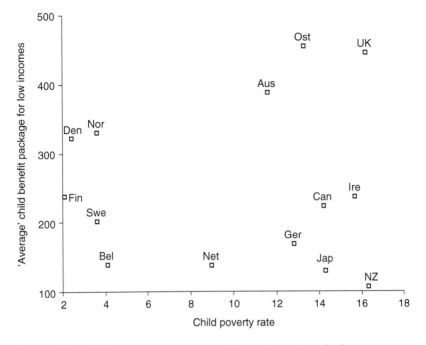

Figure 4.18 Child poverty rate and child benefit package for low-income families

incomes. This is explored in Figure 4.18, and there is really no evidence of any relationship. The Nordic countries and Belgium have low child poverty rates and varying child benefit packages. Austria, Australia and the UK have generous packages and high child poverty rates, and Ireland, Canada, Germany, Japan and New Zealand have the relationship one would expect to find – low child benefits and high child poverty.

CONCLUSION

In terms of the level of the child benefit package, Austria is a clear outlier. The Nordic welfare states may be surprised that they are not the leaders of the countries in this study. The structure (and objectives) of the package are still rather different. The Anglophone countries are much more generous at low incomes and the Nordic countries, except Iceland, more universal in their arrangements. The Nordic countries' packages are in general not much concerned (at least in their effect) with work incentives.

REFERENCES

Bradshaw, J., J. Ditch, H. Holmes and P. Whiteford (1993), 'Support for children: a comparison of arrangements in fifteen countries', Department of Social Security research report 21, London.

Bradshaw, J. and N. Finch (2002), 'A comparison of child benefit packages in 22 countries', Department for Work and Pensions research report 174, London, accessed at www.dwp.gov.uk/asd/asd5/rrep 174.asp.

Bradshaw, J. and N. Finch (2004), 'Housing benefits in 22 countries', *Benefits*, **12**(2), 87–94.

Bradshaw, J., N. Finch and E. Mayhew (2005), 'Financial incentives and mothers' employment: a comparative perspective', in P. Saunders (ed.), *Welfare to Work in Practice: Social Security and Participation in Economic and Social Life*, International Studies in Social Security, vol. 10, Aldershot: Ashgate.

Bradshaw J., and A. Hatland (eds) (2006), *Social Policy, Employment and Family Change in Comparative Perspective*, Cheltenham, UK and Northampton, MA, USA: Edward Elgar.

Bradshaw, J., S. Kennedy, M. Kilkey, S. Hutton, A. Corden, T. Eardley, H. Holmes and J. Neale (1996), *Policy and the Employment of Lone Parents in 20 Countries, The EU Report*, York: European Observatory on National Family Policies, EU/University of York.

Bradshaw, J. and E. Mayhew (2006), 'Family benefit packages', in J. Bradshaw and A. Hatland (eds), *Social Policy, Employment and Family Change in Comparative Perspective*, Cheltenham, UK and Northampton, MA, USA: Edward Elgar.

Bradshaw, J. and D. Piachaud (1980), *Child Support in the European Community*, London: Bedford Square Press.

Ditch, J., H. Barnes and J. Bradshaw (1996), *A Synthesis of National Family Policies in 1995*, York: European Observatory on National Family Policies, CEC.

Ditch, J., H. Barnes, J. Bradshaw, J. Commaille and T. Eardley (1995), *A Synthesis of National Family Policies in 1994*, York: European Observatory on National Family Policies, CEC.

Ditch, J., H. Barnes, J. Bradshaw and M. Kilkey (1998), *A Synthesis of National Family Policies*, York: European Observatory on National Family Policies, EC/University of York.

Forster, M. and M. D'Ercole (2004), 'Income distribution and poverty in OECD countries in the second half of the 1990s', OECD Social, Employment and Migration working papers, Paris.

Kuivalainen, S. (2002), 'How to compare the incomparable: an international comparison of the impact of housing costs on levels of social assistance', *European Journal of Social Security*, **5**(2), 128–49.

OECD (2004), 'Purchasing power parities, main economic indicators', April 2004, accessed at www.oecd.org/std/ppp.

APPENDIX

Case 1 (1 Earner on Half Average National Earnings)

Lone parent + 1 child aged 2 years 11 months × 2
Lone parent + 1 child aged 7   × 2
Couple +1 child aged 7
Couple + 2 children aged 7 and 14
Couple +3 children aged 7, 14 and 17

Case 2 (1 Earner on Average National Earnings)

Lone parent + 1 child aged 2 years 11 months × 2
Lone parent + 1 child aged 7   × 2
Couple + 1 child aged 7   × 2
Couple + 2 children aged 7 and 14   × 3
Couple + 3 children aged 7, 14 and 17   × 2

Case 3 (2 Earners, 1 on Half Average, 1 on Average National Earnings)

Couple + 1 child aged 7   × 2
Couple + 2 children aged 7 and 14   × 3
Couple + 3 children aged 7, 14 and 17   × 2

Case 4 (2 Earners, Both on Average National Earnings)

Couple + 1 child aged 7
Couple + 2 children aged 7 and 14
Couple + 3 children aged 7, 14 and 17

Case 5 (Social Assistance Case)

Lone parent + 1 child aged 2 years 11 months
Lone parent + 1 child aged 7
Couple + 1 child aged 7
Couple + 2 children aged 7 and 14

Total: 32 cases

5. Paying for the costs of children in eight North European countries: ambivalent trends

Ulla Björnberg

INTRODUCTION

How should the responsibility for financing the costs of raising and caring for children be divided between society and parents? This political problem is gaining increasing importance in contemporary societies. A major reason for this is that women increasingly spend more time in the labour market when they have small children, and have less time for family care. It is increasingly acknowledged that children have rights as citizens, which means that societies have to recognise that children need societal protection and provision. In recent literature children are seen as investments for the future; children represent prospective human capital, and a potential for economic growth and competitive advantage in the contemporary global knowledge society (see also Jenson, Chapter 2, and Lister, Chapter 3, in this volume). Societies need to rely on a well educated labour force for economic growth.

The logics of these kinds of developments imply that children are no longer regarded as an exclusive private matter and a matter of concern for parents only. It is not only parents who must look after the welfare of their own children but increasingly, it seems, this is a political concern as well.

This chapter addresses child welfare from the perspective of policy discourses and national policies in eight North European countries. Special focus is on how economic support for children is institutionalised in the countries and on the developments and trends in approaching the costs of children.[1] I start with a brief overview on family policies in the eight countries. I then discuss the implications of the institutional arrangements in family policies for child welfare, and their implications for parental choices from a gender perspective.

FAMILY POLICY TRENDS AND DEBATES[2]

Figure 5.1 displays trends in expenditure on families and children as percentages of the total social expenditure from 1992 to 2001 in the eight countries. From the middle of the 1990s, due to a sudden and sharp economic recession in the economy, Sweden and Finland had to make large cuts in family policies in terms of both transfers and services. Also in the United Kingdom and the Netherlands, the share of family policy spending decreased, whereas in Germany there has been a sharp increase since 1995. In the Netherlands spending on family policy is far below the other studied countries, which is related to the fact that children and families are not given high priority in public policy. However the figures for the United Kingdom do not reflect all spending since a large share of expenditures

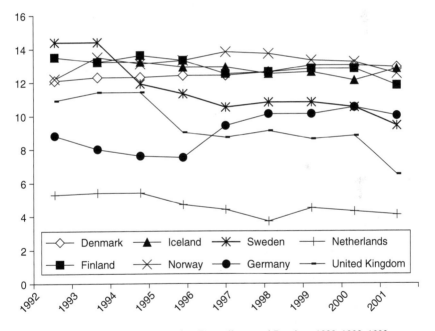

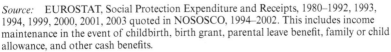

Source: EUROSTAT, Social Protection Expenditure and Receipts, 1980–1992, 1993, 1994, 1999, 2000, 2001, 2003 quoted in NOSOSCO, 1994–2002. This includes income maintenance in the event of childbirth, birth grant, parental leave benefit, family or child allowance, and other cash benefits.

Figure 5.1   *Expenditure on families and children as percentages of the total social expenditure in the Nordic countries, Germany, the Netherlands and United Kingdom, 1992–2001*

within this area are indirect and based on tax credits, which is not the case for the other countries. Both the United Kingdom and Germany have launched 10-year plans for improvements of the living conditions of children and their families.

The overarching drivers for family policy in all the countries, except for the UK, are centred on fertility and the employment of women. This focus has been strengthened over the decade, with the decline in the fertility rate. Female employment is regarded as a positive development since the presence of women in the contemporary workforce is regarded as a necessary investment for the future economic prospects of society. There is a need for an educated workforce and women now tend to be as educated or even more educated than men (Björnberg et al. 2006). Concomitant with women's increasing labour force participation, childbirth is being postponed and even forgone. In addition, the quality of life of children is gaining great attention in all eight countries. Anxieties about the welfare of children are connected to the changing family situations for bringing up children. Divorce and separations, less childcare in the home, lone motherhood, absent fathers and low-income families are highlighted as family matters that might bring lower quality of life for children. Childcare costs pose problems for parents in all the countries. Problems associated with child poverty and socialisation are also emphasised.

In all countries, the reconciliation of work and family is widely discussed and the role of employers in establishing family-friendly policies at the workplace has gained a lot of attention. Options for flexibility in combining work and family is institutionalised in different ways in different countries, in particular in respect of leave schemes for parents. Further, the role of fathers in taking care of children has been highlighted through parental leave schemes and regulations after divorce.

The Nordic countries have a fairly well developed social infrastructure adapted to an adult worker model family, and high employment rates for women. Still, a shortage of childcare places and the high cost of childcare remain problems in these countries as well. Privatisation of childcare has not however been a big issue. Rather, making childcare more flexible in terms of devoting more public money to supporting parental care in the home has been an issue for debate in these countries. Reforms centring on 'cash for care' have been introduced, with arguments that parents should have a free choice to care for their children at home. In addition, this could also solve problems of the shortage of childcare and unemployment to some extent. Parental leaves enable someone else to enter the labour market.

In West Germany, since the 1990s, state policies have been geared towards strengthening the employability and education of mothers. The arguments are described as instrumental in that a move away from the male breadwinner family has been driven by the need of society to guarantee a continuous and well educated labour force for the future. Income from work is necessary in order to provide children a decent standard of living. So far childcare has been mainly based on part-time provision and on the informal care provided by relatives and friends. In order to improve the quality of life of children and to accomplish a goal of more education within the childcare system, voucher systems and more private sector provision have been promoted.

At the end of the 1990s, the Labour government in the UK made a commitment to end child poverty. Basically, income from work rather than targeted benefits was seen as the most effective way of increasing the incomes of families. Following this agenda, more emphasis has been placed on how to combine work and family by promoting childcare services. In 2005, a 10-year childcare strategy was announced by the government, including the extension of paid maternity leave and the right of fathers to claim part of this entitlement as paternity leave if the couple so wish. Also (the very high) costs for childcare will be reduced for parents.

In contrast, Dutch family policy has tried to avoid supporting adult worker families as a state responsibility. In the Netherlands the ideal adult worker model consists of one-and-a-half earners, care at home being provided preferably by women. People in general are in favour of role sharing and against full-time work of mothers. Policy discussions have been centred on promoting more by way of services to families and less by way of cash transfers – an approach that has translated into reductions in expenditure on cash transfers to families. However, children are increasingly seen as 'investments' and childcare provision has been strongly debated. The solution has been to rely on the private expansion of childcare provision, with means-tested support for childcare fees.

THE ECONOMIC WELFARE OF CHILDREN

Child Benefits

Child benefits are paid in all countries for all children. Payments are universal and not means-tested. Only in Iceland are child benefits related to income. The rules vary slightly regarding payments according to the age of the children or the number of children. Income supplements for the number of children are paid in Sweden and Norway. The general trend is to extend the cut-off for child benefits from 16 years to 18–19 years, depending in some countries on whether the child is in full-time education.

In the UK and Germany the amount paid per child increases with the number of children, whereas in Denmark and the Netherlands the amount paid per child increases with the age of the child. The amount paid for the first child varies from €99–104 in the UK, Finland and Sweden, to €154 in Germany, €134 in Norway and €115 in Iceland (MISSOC 2004).

After the child finishes school and/or reaches the age of maturity, parents are no longer obliged to provide support and consequently child benefits are no longer paid to parents. However, if the youngsters are unemployed or studying, different rules apply regarding the parent's obligations to maintain them. In the UK, an Educational Maintenance Allowance has been institutionalised, which aims at encouraging children from low-income families to stay on in education to improve their skills and qualifications and to enhance their future employability. It is a means-tested weekly allowance paid to the young person. Another aim is to recognise the young person as an independent young adult and promote financial maturity.

During the last decade the transition into stable work has become prolonged, partly due to the nature of the educational systems in the different countries.[3] A common trend is that short-term jobs and part-time work are a general route into more stable employment (Gangl et al. 2003). This pattern has implications for parents in terms of the financial support they may feel they owe to their adult children, but policies are not addressing this problem as a public concern, rather it is kept at the level of private arrangement.

Supporting Lone Mothers

Economic deprivation and poverty among children is an important target for family policy reforms in all the countries. Measures of poverty or economic deprivation give a fairly consistent picture as to the kind of families that are at risk for economic deprivation or fall below the poverty line:[4] lone mother families, and families with small children are particularly vulnerable.[5] In Denmark, Iceland, the Netherlands and the UK around one third of lone parent families have very low incomes (Skevik 2006; Bradshaw and Ritakallio 2006). In response to the relatively low standard of living among lone mother families, all countries have introduced policy measures to support lone parents (mainly mothers) and low-income households.

These institutional arrangements have tended to take the form of supplements to income earned through employment. Norway and the Netherlands are the only countries that provide adequate state support for mothers with small children. In the other countries, state benefits do not guarantee lone parent families an adequate standard of living, and the policies there aim to increase the rate of employment of lone mothers, with the idea that they should support themselves and their children, thus forming autonomous households. Most countries also give priority for childcare to lone parents, although in Sweden and in Denmark it is discretionary (Finch 2006). However childcare has to be paid for. State provision rarely guarantees a full day of care, and only in Finland, Denmark and Sweden do children have a legal right to after-school care. So even if lone mothers are supposed to be working, childcare is likely to be an obstacle. In most countries lone mothers are encouraged financially to engage in education in order to increase their employability and earnings from paid work. The UK and Norway display the most differentiated systems of support.

Institutionalisation of Maintenance Paid by Non-resident Parents

Another response to the economic disadvantages of the children of low-income lone parents is to promote a more stable and secure system for maintenance.

Minimum amounts of maintenance on the part of the absent parent are regulated in all countries except for the Netherlands. Where child maintenance is guaranteed by the state (all countries except for the Netherlands and the UK), it is regarded as a form of minimum benefit to children living with a lone parent. The state advances payments and often institutionalises measures to collect or recover the money from the liable parent.

Guaranteed child maintenance has to be applied for by the custodial parent, who has to provide the name of the liable parent, but it is not an absolute obligation. In general, this means that governments have responded to increased rates of divorce and separation, and to births to single women, by relaxing the conditions for divorce and by introducing more regulation of the parental relationship in separated families, especially in respect of conditions for paying maintenance. Maintenance agreements between the divorced parents are subject to control and authorisation by the public authorities. This is the case in all the countries except for Denmark. In the UK, however, payments are only paid to the parent caring for the child if they are collected from the non-resident parent by the Child Support Agency. State involvement depends on the parent caring for the child drawing social assistance, or initiating a claim. In such cases a standard formula is applied.

Not only are the economic responsibilities of biological parents towards children regulated, but increasingly in some countries, also arrangements regarding residence and contact. In all but the UK and Iceland, joint legal custody has been introduced as the norm after divorce.[6] Visitation rights are more strictly regulated in Finland and Sweden, because joint custody and stricter rules for paying maintenance are the norm. Fathers' groups have been mobilising in all the countries, partly as a response to more stringent obligations to pay maintenance by absent fathers (Hatland and Mayhew 2006).

PAYING FOR THE COSTS OF CHILDCARE

In addressing the issue of paying for care, I differentiate between measures directed towards parental care and care of children at home involving different forms of leave allowances, public support for out-of-home childcare (normal institutional public and private care), and support for informal care.

Leave Schemes for Parents

Since the beginning of the 1990s all countries have introduced decommodifying schemes for parents who leave the labour market to take care of children. All countries have separate rules for mothers and fathers plus gender-neutral schemes.[7] Maternity leave (only for mothers) tends to be more generously paid than paternity leave (leave only for fathers). Only in Iceland, Norway and Sweden are replacement rates similar for mothers and fathers (80–100 per cent). Paternity leave exists in all countries except for Germany, although the available time is more limited for fathers than for mothers. In addition, paid parental leave (gender-neutral scheme) is now available for fathers in all eight countries, but with big variations in terms of generosity.

The leave schemes that have been developed in the eight countries are complex, with different conditions in respect of entitlements, length of leave, and levels of replacement payments, which may vary depending on the gender of the parent and the duration of leave. Most important is the recognition that caring for children entails a cost, which means that people who fulfil certain conditions regarding employment are entitled to leave and will receive some income replacement. Economic support is also available for the non-employed, who receive benefits as income support. It is also recognised that caring for children is a legitimate reason for regulating work hours, either by making provision for unpaid leave or by introducing flexible work hours. In all leave schemes there is an element of recognition that childcare, or care for dependants in general, is not only a responsibility of women, but also of men. Some countries, such as Norway, Sweden, Finland and Iceland, have introduced extended individual rights for fathers and mothers, meaning that entitlements are forgone if not used, thus encouraging a change of behaviour on the part of fathers in respect of care responsibilities. To ensure that fathers use their rights, income replacements are set at fairly high levels in these countries. However in Germany and the Netherlands parental leave for fathers is paid, but at fairly low levels, and in the UK it is unpaid. But in all the countries women are using their rights to take leave to care for their children far more than men are, which is due to a dominant gender order based on perceptions that care is the task of women (Björnberg 2002).

Care Allowances

In Norway, Finland and Germany, governments have introduced schemes that allow parents to continue to stay at home to care for their children after the parental leave period expires. Parents are offered an allowance or benefit to care for their children themselves at home. In Finland, after parental leave, a benefit can be paid for three years to those parents who do not use public daycare for their children. Two periods of leave are available for both parents, paid at 40–60 per cent of income replacement. Unpaid leave can be taken part time for six months in some cases. In Norway similar rules apply for the parents of children under three years. The benefit is paid from the child's second year for two years and is conditional on public childcare not being used. It is paid at a maximum of €427 per month and is reduced according to the number of hours the child is in public childcare. As in Finland, it thus replaces state sponsored childcare. However, parents do not have to take care of the child themselves. They might choose to ask grand-parents to do this and pay the allowance to them. In Denmark, from 2002, municipalities have been able to pay parents of children under five who do not have income from the labour market care allowances rather than pro-viding institutional care (Pylkkänen and Smith 2004). The German scheme covers the first three years of the child's life and can be used by both parents. The benefit attached to the leave is means-tested and can be com-bined with part-time work.

The arguments in favour of these home care allowances are partly linked to the issue of providing choice to parents in respect of working or caring, and partly to demands from parents for more time to spend with their chil-dren. The allowances are, compared to earning an income, quite low. However in all five countries the option to stay at home for a longer period than that granted via parental leave has been widely recognised and utilised – by women. In Sweden a similar scheme to those in the other Nordic coun-tries was introduced at the beginning of the 1990s, in response to arguments about the importance of free choice. It was popular despite the low rate of benefit. The Left parties in Sweden were very much against the reform because its gendered take-up posed a threat to gender equality and for cost reasons. However from 2005 the Swedish government introduced a sabbatical period of 3–12 months compensated at 85 per cent of the unemployment benefit rate. Applications must be made to the employer, who must give consent and hire an unemployed or disabled person to replace the person on leave. This leave can be (and has been) used for taking care of children, but also for other purposes. The reform is a labour market policy measure and can only be used by a maximum of 12 000 people.

The different ways of paying parents to care have different implications for gender equality. In general, the combination of long leave schemes and low replacement rates (the case of Germany, the UK and the Netherlands) do not give incentives for men to take leave. Men in general earn more money than women do and the loss of income for the household will be larger if the father takes leave. Long leave can be detrimental to career prospects – a risk that more women are prepared to take. The outcome for children of long parental leave has not been studied, but it is generally assumed to be the best alternative. In large measure, long leave policies result from a complicated mixture of 'gendered moral rationalities' whereby women are assumed to want to care (Duncan and Edwards 1999), and the lack of availability of alternative solutions.

Paying for Out-of-Home Childcare

In all five Nordic countries public childcare has been made available for working parents. Only Sweden, Finland and Denmark guarantee formal childcare provision for children under three. All Nordic countries also offer after-school care, where provision has increased to a large extent since the 1990s. Only in Sweden and Finland is after-school care mandatory.

The financing of childcare is a mixture of public financing via taxes and parental fees. None of the Nordic countries offer childcare free of charge to working parents. However in Finland no fees are charged to low-income families. Fees are means-tested, according to the parents' level of income and the number of children they have enrolled in childcare. Fees also vary regionally, in some instances there can be large differences between how much parents have to pay in different municipalities. In Sweden and Denmark governments have set maximum rates for fees, which means that parents do not pay fees above a certain limit.

In all Nordic countries the institution of public daycare has been driven by labour market concerns and the need to offer working parents a place for their children while they are working. In addition, it seems that more and more emphasis is being placed on the educational aspects of childcare, at least for children who are not attending after-school care. Childcare in most countries is the responsibility of the Ministry of Education: there are curricula for childcare in Sweden, Finland and Germany. The concern with early years learning is also visible in the trend to give children some access to childcare irrespective of the needs of parents to work outside the home. The staff in Nordic childcare centres are well qualified. In Sweden the word 'childcare' has been officially replaced by the word 'pre-school' in order to emphasise the educational pedagogical aspect of institutional childcare. In Iceland the development of day-care was deeply connected with the idea of education from the start. In Denmark it is emphasised in public documents that education is an important element in day-care. Staff are highly trained and it is argued that they should be empowered in their position as educators. By contrast, in Norway the educational element of childcare is contested. Those arguing against it emphasise children's right to play on their own terms and argue that socialisation and learning should take place via play rather than an educational curriculum.

In all Nordic countries the expansion of childcare has meant that the number of children per teacher has increased. This tendency is prevalent for all age groups, but mostly for children in after-school care. The implication of this deteriorating staff–child ratio for early years learning has not been evaluated in the Nordic countries, but it has been the subject of discussion and worry among parents, pre-school teachers and politicians.

In Germany, since 1995, children over age three have been granted a right to publicly funded or subsidised childcare. The Federal Legislation recommends that the states and municipalities finance childcare and consider the needs for care of children under three years. As in the Nordic countries, the fees that parents pay are regulated according to their ability to pay and the number of children they have attending daycare. Furthermore, fees vary regionally. The heterogeneity of state and municipal regulations for provision makes it hard to present a coherent overview of provision. Evidence suggest that coverage for children above three years is close to 100 per cent, but there are regional variations. As in the Nordic countries, the staff–child ratio is an issue of concern threatening the quality of care. As in Norway, German parents feel that quality lies more in play and good care than in education and learning. However, recently discussions in Germany have taken into account the 'social investment' aspect of early childhood and the need for human capital development. It has been argued that quality could be improved by strengthening market supply of childcare, which would open up more diverse provision. In Sweden there were similar discussions during the early 1990s. However in Sweden the market supply of pre-schools has not grown.

In contrast, the Netherlands is moving strongly in the direction of exclusively market provision. The same trend is visible in the UK. The market solution for childcare is driven by the very high demand for childcare places and a considerable shortage in supply. In both countries, increasing numbers of women are employed, both part time and full time. In the UK, the demand for day-care or nursery provision is also driven by the government's 1998 National Child Care Strategy, which aims to make childcare more accessible for working parents. This means more available and more affordable places. Here a distinction is made between early years education and childcare. Part-time nursery places are free, whereas childcare – when it is formal (registered and approved by the municipal authorities) – is subsidised through tax credits.

Efforts have been made to ease the burden that lack of childcare represents for working parents. Both in the UK and in the Netherlands special rules make it easier for lone parents, unemployed and immigrant parents to access childcare. Childcare provision of good quality is of great concern for parents and children in both these countries. The low supply has driven prices to ever increasing levels. In the UK a typical place in day nursery costs €171 a week, which is about 23 per cent of an average household income, but the cost is much higher in London. In the Netherlands, fees for parents using publicly authorised childcare centres are regulated, in contrast to those for private and informal childcare centres. In the UK the childcare component of the working tax credit can cover up to 70 per cent of childcare costs below €275. The childcare used must be formally registered and approved and includes a variety of forms. A recent investigation revealed that there is a general lack of knowledge about the childcare tax credit. In general parents pay three quarters of the costs of childcare, and only 13 per cent use formal childcare services (Woodland et al. 2004).

The large demand has driven the expansion of many alternative forms of childcare, for instance care by relatives, neighbours, migrants. This represents the largest source of childcare in both the UK and the Netherlands. In both countries parental use of childcare is becoming polarised. High quality childcare centres are developing that offer good professional care but at high prices, in contrast to the varied and often lower quality care provided by childminders, which is used by a majority of poorer parents.

In the Netherlands a new 2005 law regulates childcare centres, in terms of costs and quality, but it does not guarantee parents a right to childcare. The development of places is to be market driven and public provision will be phased out altogether. Childcare policy is regarded as a shared responsibility between parents, employers, labour unions and the state. However the state will act only to stimulate the development of childcare, rather than to provide finance. At present the fees that parents pay vary greatly. One of the consequences is that immigrant children, and children from low-educated and low-income families are under-represented. The municipalities have to approve of new private sector childcare providers, but informal childcare is not included in these regulations. In the UK plans to extend affordable childcare were announced at the end of 2004. By 2008 local authorities will be obliged to secure a sufficient supply of childcare. The year 2010 is set as the date for achieving the goals of a huge expansion in the supply of child-care for all children and, indeed, in other services for children.

Ambiguous Trends

In contemporary societies the dominance of male breadwinner families is losing ground in practice and in terms of cultural legitimacy (see for instance Castells 1997; Crompton 1999; Leitner et al. 2004; Therborn 2003; Esping-Andersen et al. 2002). Children's living conditions depend on how conditions for paid employment are changing and the extent to which poli-cies are responding to the needs of children in the context of an adult worker model family. The fragility of family forms also has important implications for the living conditions of children, particularly regarding their financial support and care. In order to adapt to the new circumstances of families, policymakers are facing challenges in how to elaborate policies that combine ideological assumptions about what they themselves and female and male voters regard as 'best' family functioning on the one hand, and economically feasible solutions for care and support of children on the other. The policy developments in the eight countries addressing these matters are contradictory, and institutional regulations reflect the contra-dictions and ambivalent approaches in respect of economic concerns, equal opportunities for women and social citizenship of children.

Almost all countries in the world have ratified the UN Convention on the Rights of the Child, which means that the states have committed them-selves to protect the welfare and the well-being of children. Children are to be regarded as social citizens and as such they have in principle the right to make claims on the state. This also constitutes a new frame of understand-ing in discussions on how to redistribute resources within a more general welfare state discourse. The new perspective is reflected in a shift in focus at the level of discourse and practice from supporting 'the nuclear family with a housewife and the children' to the financial support of the children. In the national policy reports recurrent themes in the national policy discourses are that children are investments for the future, thus children should be offered early education, and child poverty must be reduced in order to avoid the long-term social consequences of economic deprivation. At the level of discourse at least, the cost of children (accompanying the investment in education thesis), and even the rights of children as citizens have been brought more to the fore than was the case 15 years ago (Goldson et al. 2002; Hendrick 2003; Esping-Andersen et al. 2002; Eydal and Satka 2004).

There has been something of a mental shift in ideas about how the responsibility for supporting and educating children should be divided between the state and parents, which contradicts the powerful ideology that children are best educated by mothers at home, and implies that children will pose greater costs in welfare budgets for care and education.

In all eight countries child benefits are universal and have for many years represented the recognition that the costs of children should be shared by society and parents. In addition, most countries have developed various measures to deliver income support to low-income households. More and more governments encourage or oblige lone mothers to support their families through paid work. However, experiences suggest that employment is not sufficient to keep children out of risk of economic deprivation in lone mother families (Skevik 2006). The share of economically deprived children living in households at 60 per cent and 50 per cent below the median disposable income is lowest in the Nordic countries in comparison with all OECD countries. Several studies suggest that financial transfers to families with children have a positive effect on economic deprivation and explain why economic deprivation among children is lower in the Nordic countries. It is also suggested that the extent of subsidised services to families with children has a positive effect on the living conditions of children (Batljan 2004).

In addition, more emphasis is placed on the maintenance obligations of non-custodial parents, who are usually fathers. Maintenance agreements are increasingly being supervised by public authorities and standardised. Authorities take measures to enforce payments by non-resident parents (fathers). An important measure applied by an increasing number of countries is to advance the maintenance payments to the custodial parent and then to collect the money from the absent parent. These measures act to strengthen the financial aspects of parenthood (fatherhood). The regulation of financial parenting after divorce has also been accompanied by more rights for non-resident fathers to have access to their children. This means that in most countries, paying for children is in principle not separated from contact with the non-resident parent. These rights have been strengthened in the Nordic countries and in Germany, although sanctions for refusing access are only enacted against the parent who denies access, not against the parent who refuses to visit the child. This focus underlines the assumption that the main caring responsibility rests with the mother, who is also the person with the duty to orchestrate the parental relationships of the child. This contrasts with the view that children have an absolute right to have, or to refuse to have, relationships with either parents regardless of what the parents themselves want.

In all eight countries the policy response to an ever increasing number of women who help to support their families by earning has been to increase the availability of public childcare and to take steps to introduce parental leave and other forms of care leave. In general, care is necessary work normally carried out in families and does not have a market value. The defamilialisation of care consists of moving care from unpaid work in the family, usually provided by women, into the formal labour market (where it is also provided by women). This means that care of dependent children and of other dependants is dragged into the logic of 'commodification' in several different ways (Knijn and Kremer 1997; Lister 2003). 'Defamilialisation' (Lister 2003) measures mean that care work becomes paid in the public arena, whether in the state or market sector.

In his work on welfare regimes Esping-Andersen (1990) employed the concepts of commodification and decommodification. In his understanding, commodification is a basic condition for making a living in contemporary market societies. To be commodified is to be able to give work a market value. His notion of decommodification is about the degree to which market work can be replaced by public transfers in periods when citizens cannot work for money because, for example, of old age, sickness, unemployment or care responsibilities.

It is possible to analyse the implications of different measures to secure decommodification in the eight countries in relation to the logic of commodificaton. Economic transfers that replace forgone income from work are tied to the individual and can be regarded as an individual right as opposed to household entitlements. Now, if we summarise the principles underpinning payments for care that have been developed in the eight countries, we see that all countries have applied the principle of (more or less generous) income replacement, particularly for women, in the form of maternity leave and/or parental leave. Women in general have been granted longer periods of leave on this basis than men, which means that the economic incentives are stronger for women to be decommodified in order to do care work. Maternity leave recognises employed women as mothers/ workers. This is an important step in strengthening the social citizenship of mothers. In order to engage fathers in care, all the Nordic countries have introduced a father quota, whereby rights to paid leave are forgone if they are not used.[8]

Flat-rate benefits for doing care work, usually for prolonged periods, are generally set at lower levels than leave providing a fixed proportion of income, and can be regarded as economic incentives to women rather than men to do care work, since men generally earn more and the household would lose more income were men to take advantage of the benefit. Flat-rate or means-tested benefits for doing care work are applied in five countries, in combination with compensation based on income replacement. These kinds of measures reflect the ambivalence in policies regarding the care of small children. They are attractive to women with a weak attachment to the labour market, women with low education and low income. In fact, my conclusion is that for these women the policies support the male bread winner model family rather than an adult worker model, at least during the years where there are small children in the families. They also bring a class dimension into parental care policies, which is potentially in conflict with the political emphasis on childcare as investment in the education of all young children.

The demand for out-of-home childcare is very high in all countries, and the supply of childcare is inadequate (except for Sweden and Denmark). In all countries a large part of out-of-home childcare is commodified in the sense that it must be paid for by the users, even when it is subsidised. The prices that people have to pay are posing big problems for many parents. They also bring inequalities in provision in respect of quality. Due to high costs, low-income families have difficulties in purchasing childcare provided by the market.

Measures to control the costs of formal childcare have been taken in all eight countries, but they take different forms. Public subsidisation of fees on a means-tested basis is common in the Nordic countries, Germany and the UK. Means-tested childcare tax credits exist in the UK. In Sweden and Denmark a maximum fee level has been set for everybody. However, in the Netherlands it seems that no regulation of prices or fees exists at present.

The needs for childcare in the Netherlands and the UK and Germany are mostly met through informal childcare, by grandparents, friends, neighbours and (legal and illegal) migrant women. When it comes to the protection of the well-being of the children and the quality of care, it is left to parents to take the responsibility when using informal care. However, with publicly supplied childcare or vouchers or tax credits, the kind of childcare used must reach the standards set by the paying authority, which brings some control of quality. Parents who can afford it prefer to rely on high quality childcare through market provision in the Netherlands and Germany, even though the fees have become quite high. In all countries, however, there are concerns over the quality of childcare, not only regarding the cost for parents, but also concerning group sizes, the number of children per childminder and the qualifications of the childcare workforce.

The diverging quality and costs of childcare result in unequal use of childcare (and unequal income for mothers). A British study compared women's income over a lifetime in relation to education levels. The data from the study showed the lifetime income gap between low and high skilled women to be very high. The high skilled woman made around £1 million over her working life, whereas the low skilled made £59 000 (Joshi and Davies 2002, p. 120): 'whatever their source, differences in earning power are magnified by the different strategies each woman uses to combine motherhood and paid work. The woman with low earning power provides her own childcare until her children go to school. The high-earner probably pays for someone else to help' (p. 121). Joshi and Davies concluded that the low skilled mother could not afford to pay for childcare and the high skilled woman could not afford *not* to pay for childcare.

In general women pay most for the care of children in terms of forgone earnings and in terms of dependence on a husband or partner, even in a country like Sweden with strong public support for gender equality. In the budget proposal delivered by the Swedish government in 2004, a special study was devoted to the economic consequences of parenthood for women and men. Over the period 1994–2003 in a couple family with average male and female earnings, it was calculated that the loss of income amounted to €32 903 for women and €108 for men. Eighty-two per cent of the income loss for women was due to part-time work. The loss of accumulated pension entitlement worked out at €5412 for women and €108 for men, as compared with the case without parenthood (Budget proposal 2005).

The Nordic countries have a generally high commitment to gender equality. Against this background it is interesting that in Finland and Norway policies have been introduced to increase 'free choice' in childcare through the introduction of childcare allowances paid to parents (mothers) who do not utilise public childcare services, but rather organise childcare on their own. The 'free choice' argument is understood as giving parents more time for children but also as a measure to address the problem of the shortage of public childcare (as was also the case in Norway).[9] The case for 'free choice' in childcare is largely argued by right-wing parties and is geared towards couple families. The allowances paid are to enable a lone mother to take advantage of them.

The introduction of home care allowances in Norway and Finland (possibly also to a certain extent Denmark), means that these countries join Germany, the Netherlands and the UK in providing policies that still give impetus to the male breadwinner model for couple families, especially to those on low incomes. The measures contrast with the arguments in favour of 'welfare-to-work'. The willingness to pay benefits to parents (mothers) who take care of children at home can be interpreted as a measure to reinforce a traditional division of labour because it is regarded as best for children but also for the economy, since subsidised institutional childcare is more expensive than paying flat-rate allowances for home care. It is a low cost alternative for the state but a high cost alternative for those who do it.

Transfers of cash to parents to pay for care may also constitute public support for the development of a market for care work, underpinned by a large demand for and supply of women who in many instances cannot find

any other jobs. This amounts to a reappearance of a private domestic workforce that is partly made up of legal or illegal immigrants (Ehrenreich and
Hochschild 2003; Sassen 2003; Gavanas and Williams 2004). Gavanas and
Williams (2004) have reviewed the research on domestic work and drawn
attention to the implications of the commodification of care work in
general. They stress that the acceptance of domestic care workers differs
between countries and also between social classes and political parties
within countries. For instance in Sweden, Social Democratic public policy
is resistant to supporting private domestic service work, whereas Liberals
and Conservatives favour it. However, in private households there is a
growing acceptance of this kind of work. The issue is much debated.
Gavanas and Williams stress that there are many kinds of driving forces
behind the development: demand for care, lack of time, lack of money to
pay for quality care, and the need for 'quality time' with children of
mothers who want to buy time to be with their children. There are several
problems involved in this development, in particular the rewards given for
the care work and the hierarchical relationships involved. They emphasise
the risk of reproducing the gendered dimension of care work as work being
carried out by women at low cost. This trend contradicts the growing
support given to the role of the caring father and poses a threat to the feminist endeavour to create more equitable family life.

A further issue that Gavanas and Williams do not consider is the diversity
in quality of childcare that private domestic childcare brings. When an
investigation of the experiences of childcare arrangements (Samhällets
barntillsyn-barnstugor och barnstugor 1967) revealed the low quality and
high turnover of private childminding arrangements in Sweden during the
1960s, political determination to invest in public and professional childcare
in Sweden followed. The Swedish model might not suit everybody since
people have different views regarding what constitutes quality in childcare.
The lesson to be learned, however, is that parents need support in controlling
the quality of childcare, primarily for the sake of the welfare of children.

CONCLUSION

Broadly, the eight countries seem to have pursued similar goals, in that the
promotion of the adult worker family model form is central to contemporary family policies. In particular there is an agenda whereby women, lone
mothers included, are identified as working mothers. This is highlighted by
the fact that substantial economic support is geared towards the employed,
underlining that work is to be encouraged among all mothers. Fathers'
caring responsibilities are also recognised in all countries, at least in so far

as they have some right to leave from work to take care of children. This, together with changes in family law, emphasising joint custody and the visiting rights of non-resident parents (alongside maintenance obligations), all speak to increased state determination to support and enforce the right of children to receive care from both parents. The Nordic countries, albeit with some ambivalence, keep a high profile in pursuing measures for equality between women and men in family life and in work. The Nordic countries also follow a welfare tradition of equalising living conditions for children, at least in so far that they keep children out of poverty. Childcare policies have a high priority, although costs to parents and quality for children have been questioned. However, in the other countries there is clear national ambivalence around the measures applied to achieve equal opportunities for mothers and fathers. Since in general mothers have more attractive conditions for paid parental leave, these policies underline the basic assumption that mothers are the main carers. Despite different policies this also characterised many of the developments in the Nordic countries. Childcare policies are important for the economic well-being and quality of life of children. Measures are applied to reduce economic deprivation and to enhance early education and care among children, but there is a clear tendency towards polarisation among social classes in terms of childcare provision. Means-testing is far more prevalent in Germany, the UK and the Netherlands, representing a kind of 'path dependency' in terms of the general welfare regimes in these countries. In all countries involvement in paid work (that is, commodification) is a major aim. However, the incentives for full commodification are not equal for all women due to expensive childcare and poor job opportunities. There must be major concerns regarding inequality among children and women in the context of the march towards the adult worker model.

NOTES

1. I draw on results from a comparative study covering Denmark, Finland, Iceland, Norway, Sweden, Germany, the Netherlands and the United Kingdom on developments until about 2003, with the project title 'Welfare policy and employment in the context of family change' (Bradshaw and Hatland 2006).
2. The following text, if not otherwise referenced, draws on the national policy reports published at http://www.york.ac.uk/inst/spru/research/summs/welempfc.htm, 15 May 2003.
3. Young persons in countries with apprenticeships and training built into the education systems are more easily integrated into the labour market (Gangl et al. 2003).
4. Generally defined at 50 per cent below the median income.
5. Workless households, single earner families, families with many children, and immigrant families also belong to the risk groups for economic deprivation.
6. Whereas joint legal custody refers to parents' responsibilities to take decisions on behalf of the child, practical custody is about the parental care and everyday commitment to the

child. In Sweden and Finland visitation rights and shared practical custody can also be regulated by the courts.
7. For a detailed overview of the rules see Finch (2006).
8. In Denmark only ten days are available.
9. For further reading on cash benefits for care I recommend Leira (2002) who gives an elaborated analysis, with references to countries beyond those included in this chapter.

REFERENCES

Batljan, I. (2004), *Ekonomiskt utsatta barn*, Swedish governmental report DS 2004:4, Stockholm: Ministry of Health and Social Affairs.

Björnberg, U. (2002), 'Ideology and choice between work and care: Swedish family policy for working parents', *Critical Social Policy*, **22**(1), 33–52.

Björnberg, U., S. Olafson and G. Eydal (2006), 'Education, employment and family formation: differing patterns', in J. Bradshaw and A. Hatland (eds), *Social Policy, Employment and Family Change in Comparative Perspective*, Cheltenham,UK and Northampton, MA, USA: Edward Elgar.

Bradshaw, J. and A. Hatland (eds) (2006), *Social Policy, Employment and Family Change in Comparative Perspective*, Cheltenham, UK and Northampton, MA, USA: Edward Elgar.

Bradshaw, J. and M. Ritakallio (2006), 'Family poverty in the European Union', in J. Bradshaw and A. Hatland (eds), *Social Policy, Employment and Family Change in Comparative Perspective*, Cheltenham, UK and Northampton, MA, USA: Edward Elgar.

Budget proposal for Sweden (2005), Ministry of Finance 'Distribution of economic resources between women and men', Prop.2004/05:1 Appendix 4, Stockholm.

Castells, M. (1997), *The Power of Identity. Vol II: The Information Age: Economy, Society and Culture*, Cambridge, MA: Blackwell.

Crompton, R. (ed.) (1999), *Restructuring Gender Relations and Employment. The Decline of the Male Breadwinner*, Oxford: Oxford University Press.

Duncan, S. and R. Edwards (1999), *Lone Mothers, Paid Work and Gendered Moral Rationalities*, Basingstoke: Macmillan.

Ehrenreich, B. and A. Hochschild (2003), *Global Women. Nannies, Maids and Sex Workers in the New Economy*, London: Granta Books.

Esping-Andersen, G. (1990), *The Three Worlds of Welfare Capitalism*, London: Polity Press.

Esping-Andersen, G., D. Gallie, A. Hemerijcke and J. Myles (2002), *Why We Need a New Welfare State*, Oxford: Oxford University Press.

EUROSTAT (1980–1992, 1993, 1994, 1999, 2000, 2001, 2003), Social Protection Expenditure and Receipts.

Eydal, G. and M. Satka (2004), 'The history of Nordic welfare states for children', in H. Bremebeck, B. Johansson and J. Kampmann (eds), *Beyond the Competent Child. Exploring Contemporary Childhoods in the Nordic Welfare Societies*, Roskilde: Roskilde University Press.

Finch, N. (2006), 'Child care and parental leave', in J. Bradshaw and A. Hatland (eds), *Social Policy, Employment and Family Change in Comparative Perspective*, Cheltenham, UK and Northampton, MA, USA: Edward Elgar.

Gangl, M., W. Müller and D. Raffe (2003), 'Conclusions: explaining cross-national differences in school-to-work transitions', in M. Gangl and W. Müller (eds),

Transitions from Education to Work in Europe. The Integration of Youth into EU Labour Markets, Oxford: Oxford University Press.

Gavanas, A. and F. Williams (2004), 'Eine Neue Variante des Herr-Knecht-Verhältnis?', in S. Leitner, I. Ostner and M. Schratzenstaller (eds), *Wohlfartsstat und Geschlechterverhältnis im Umbruch. Was kommt nach dem Ernärhermodell?*, Wiesbaden: VS Verlag für Sozialwissenshaften.

Goldson, B., M. Lavalette and J. McKechnie (2002), *Children, Welfare and the State*, London: Sage Publications.

Hatland, A. and E. Mayhew (2006), 'Parental rights and obligations', in J. Bradshaw and A. Hatland (eds), *Social Policy, Employment and Family Change in Comparative Perspective*, Cheltenham, UK and Northampton, MA, USA: Edward Elgar.

Hendrick, H. (2003), *Child Welfare. Historical Dimensions, Contemporary Debate*, Bristol: The Policy Press.

Joshi, H. and H. Davies (2002), 'Women's incomes over a synthetic lifetime', in E. Ruspini and A. Dale (eds), *The Gender Dimension of Social Change. The Contribution of Dynamic Research to the Study of Women's Life Courses*, Bristol: The Policy Press.

Knijn, T. and M. Kremer (1997), 'Gender and the caring dimension of the welfare state: towards inclusive citizenship', *Social Politics*, **5**, 328–61.

Leira, A. (2002), *Working Parents and the Welfare State: Family Change and Policy Reform in Scandinavia*, Cambridge: Cambridge University Press.

Leitner, S., I. Ostner and M. Schratzenstaller (eds) (2004), *Wohlfartsstat und Geschlechterverhältnis im Umbruch. Was kommt nach dem Ernärhermodell?*, Wiesbaden: VS Verlag für Sozialwissenshaften.

Lister, R. (2003), *Citizenship. Feminist Perspectives*, 2nd edn, New York: New York University Press.

MISSOC (2004), 'Comparative tables on social protection in the member states', Europa European Commission, Employment and Social Affairs.

National policy reports (2003), accessed 15 May at www.york.ac.uk/inst/spru/research/summs/welempfc.htm.

NOSOSCO (1994–2002), 'Social protection in the Nordic countries. Scope, expenditure and financing', Nordic Social-Statistical Committee report series xx, Copenhagen.

Pylkkänen, E. and N. Smith (2004), 'Career interruption due to parental leave: a comparative study of Denmark and Sweden', OECD Social, Employment and Migration working papers no 1, Paris.

Samhällets barntillsyn-barnstugor och barnstugor (1967), *Förslag av familjedaghemsutredningen*, Swedish Government Official Report Series SOU 1967, Stockholm: Ministry of Health and Social Affairs.

Sassen, S. (2003), 'The feminisation of survival. Alternative global survuits', in M. Morokvasic-Müller, U. Erle and K. Shinozaki (eds), *Crossing Borders and Shifting Boundaries. Vol. 1: Gender on the Move*, Opladen: Leske & Budrich.

Skevik, A. (2006), 'Working their way out of poverty? Lone mothers in policies and labour markets', in J. Bradshaw and A. Hatland (eds) (2006), *Social Policy, Employment and Family Change in Comparative Perspective*, Cheltenham, UK and Northampton, MA, USA: Edward Elgar.

Therborn, G. (2003), *Between Sex and Power: Family in the World 1990–2000*, London: Routledge.

Woodland, S., M. Miller and S. Tipping (2004), '*Repeat Study of Parents' Demand for Childcare*', National Centre for Social Research, research report no 348, London.

6. Paying for children: current issues and implications of policy debates

Fran Bennett

Parents . . . have the primary responsibility for the upbringing and development of the child . . . States Parties shall render appropriate assistance to parents . . . in the performance of their child-rearing responsibilities. (Article 18, United Nations Convention on the Rights of the Child, 1989)

INTRODUCTION

As MISSOC (Mutual Information System on Social Protection in the European Union) states, in the European Union (EU) 'all countries provide for a series of cash benefits, tax allowances and benefits in kind' for children and families (2002, p. 6). As this statement makes clear, support for children includes not only social security payments but also support through tax relief (for example, family benefits being exempt from taxation) and in addition, in a number of countries, reduced tax liability relating to size of family, as well as help in kind through services, and so on. This chapter focuses on the principles underlying financial support for children and examines some current debates about policy issues relating to such support.

Of course support for children must be seen in the context of broader family policy within each country. Traditionally some countries have been more interventionist in relation to the family, while others (such as the UK, at least prior to the late 1990s) have adopted a 'hands off' approach to what are considered private matters (Hantrais 2004). Moreover, some European countries have a long history of pronatalism and social solidarity (such as France), while others have favoured more traditional forms of the family, especially privileging marriage, and are committed to enabling family obligations to be fulfilled (such as Germany) (O'Neill 2005). In some countries, perhaps particularly those in Southern Europe, 'paradoxically [as] in Italy the family is given excessive importance and yet at the same time none' – with the result that in practice family solidarity can act as a multiplier of poverty (Conti and Sgritta 2004, pp. 299–300).

Commentators have detected recent moves in some European countries towards more family-oriented welfare state policies. Seeleib-Kaiser et al. (2005), for example, argue that in Austria, Germany and the Netherlands family policy has become much more important. Germany's recent history makes it likely to see the family as private, and pronatalist policies as taboo (Jurczyk et al. 2004). But Bleses and Seeleib-Kaiser (2004) argue that Germany has moved from a wage-earner centred social policy to being more family oriented. By 2000:

> it had become the hegemonic interpretative pattern among policy-makers that families need more support from the state . . . The question today is no longer whether social policy in the Federal Republic of Germany will become increasingly family-oriented, but how fast it will happen. (Bleses and Seeleib-Kaiser 2004, p. 139)

Hantrais (2004) also argues that both Austria and Germany have developed an increasingly explicit family policy, although Germany's main organising principle is still, in her view, 'conjugal' (favouring marriage) (p. 161).

These differences between countries mean that the justifications for supporting children, and the key debates about the shape and amount of transfers for children, are refracted through different lenses. Hantrais (2004), in her overview of recent family policy in Europe, suggests that although the objectives of changes in different countries seem to be converging, they are still markedly different in timing and the pace of change. Reactions to socio-demographic change cannot necessarily be predicted from statistical data. She argues (p. 137) that in terms of family policies, 'governments in European Union member states have sought to meet three main policy objectives, reflecting different rationales underlying their welfare regimes: income redistribution, pronatalism and equal opportunities', and some have pursued all three goals together. A different 'policy logic' (Lewis 1997) operates in each country, even though all may be subject to similar demographic, economic and ideological pressures. The result is a rich mix, shifting and coalescing in different ways.[1]

This chapter examines family support in European countries in this context, and in particular explores the implications of some current debates about financial support for children through social security and the personal taxation system. The main focus of the chapter is on support for the *direct costs* which those bringing up children incur for food, clothing and other similar goods.[2] After discussing the preliminary issue of the balance between such transfers to children and other possible forms of support (such as service provision or reductions in outgoings), the chapter gives an overview of the broad debates about the justifications for giving support to children. Then some current policy debates concerning support for children are highlighted – including the increasing link with parental responsibilities, the best form and method of payment of transfers to children, and whether or how to increase payments with family size. The conclusions consider several issues in policy debates about payments for the direct costs of children that are likely to be key in the future.

The indirect costs of bringing up children (in particular the forgone earnings of parents, usually mothers) are of course also significant – in fact, usually much more significant in terms of amount than direct costs.[3] Issues about these indirect costs, and about care work, are dealt with elsewhere in Part III of this volume. Most of the recent debates about the family in EU and OECD circles have also concentrated on these issues (see, for example, OECD 2005); and other authors (for example Leitner 2003) have analysed such topics as the degree and type of 'familialism' within different EU member states, by examining parental leave and other measures related to the care of children. The danger is that the prominence given to these (important) debates relegates those concerning transfers for the direct costs of children to the sidelines. Yet debates about support for direct costs also involve issues that are critical for children and their well-being.

The main focus of this chapter is therefore payments towards the direct costs of children, and, within those, the transfers 'explicitly labelled as being child-related' (such as child benefit/family allowances and so forth), rather than 'any transfer that an otherwise-equivalent household without children would not receive' (such as an additional allowance in a payment for housing costs) (Adam and Brewer 2004, p. 1).

However, even in the use of payments to meet the direct costs of children, some complex issues arise in terms of boundaries. For example, children may benefit from transfer payments and other income intended not for them but for their parent(s), and/or from the pension income of grandparents living in the household (UNICEF 2005). Sutherland (2005) finds that the countries with the lowest child poverty rates are those in which children benefit from other transfers that are not necessarily directed to them but are given to the households in which they live.

Many families with children also receive support in cash or kind from other households than their own, in particular from extended family members such as grandparents. Hirsch (2005) notes that children's financial circumstances depend not only on state provision but also on other factors that vary across families, including support from non-resident parents and the extended family (as well as differences in costs facing families and take-up of entitlements). This support is important (Middleton et al. 1997), and 'family solidarity' is called on increasingly (Hantrais 2004, p. 130). Another vital element of income may be children's own income, either pocket money or payment for work done (Mayhew et al. 2004). While recognising that all these forms of private support may be vital for children's well-being, this chapter does not discuss them in detail, but limits itself to public forms of support. Within this, the focus is on the principles underpinning such support and current policy issues. Detailed information about the structure and amount of support for children in different countries of the EU is available elsewhere.[4] In this chapter concrete examples from across the EU are used, drawing particularly on the UK, to illustrate some of the debates about the future direction of financial support for children.

BALANCE BETWEEN CASH PAYMENTS AND OTHER FORMS OF SUPPORT

Benefits in kind, service provision, subsidies and reductions in outgoings can be equivalent to paying cash benefits towards the costs of children – and can be critical to the exercise of children's agency and autonomy. For example, if public transport is expensive, the mobility of children in low-income families can be drastically curtailed; if leisure facilities are costly, such children will have very unequal opportunities for maintaining social relations with their peers (Mayhew et al. 2004, p. 412). And increasingly children need to travel between the homes of divorced or separated parents as well (Jensen et al. 2004b). Most studies of income and wealth do not include the distributional impact of such policy instruments; but they can be as valuable as increases in income. And as Matsaganis et al. (2004) argue, 'family services and cash benefits are complements, not substitutes' (p. 16).

The balance between services and benefits in particular countries may depend on the political situation. Bulgaria, for example, like other transition countries, has a range of subsidised goods for children, including school meals and public transport (Raycheva et al. 2004) – an inheritance from former regimes. Alternatively, as Hantrais (2004) points out, where governments are not trusted to deliver services, cash benefits may be more acceptable because they appear to give greater choice. This is the case, for example, with the trend towards supporting parents directly in paying childcare costs, in preference to giving subsidies to childcare providers (OECD 2004). However, when benefits in kind or subsidies for costs related to children are under discussion, arguments about choice are often overridden by concern about children's welfare on the one hand and uncertainties about the relationship between parental income and child outcomes on the other (Adam and Brewer 2004, p. 5). The end result is the expansion of services, goods or subsidies for items or activities considered important for children, in preference to higher cash transfers.

The balance between benefits and services may also be a party political issue. Seeleib-Kaiser et al. (2005), for example, contrast Christian
Democrat views favouring benefits and tax credits with Social Democrat
views favouring public services. Hantrais (2004) cites Finland as an
example of a country where parties of the right tend to prioritise
monetary benefits and those of the left prefer services. However, as she
also points out, in practice the most 'defamilialised' European countries
tend to provide high levels of both benefits *and* services for families.
Analysis by the OECD of spending on services, cash payments and fiscal
measures exclusively for families in a selection of countries in 2001
supports this judgement (Adema and Ladaique 2005). This chapter of
course focuses on benefits and allowances provided through the
social security and tax systems, while recognising that this can give only
a partial picture of the total amount of support being provided for
children.

JUSTIFICATIONS FOR SUPPORTING CHILDREN

'How governments should direct money to families with children seems to
be a constant part of the political and policy debate' (Adam and Brewer
2004, p. 1).

The United Nations Convention on the Rights of the Child (1989)
declares that children have a right to 'a standard of living adequate for the
child's physical, mental, spiritual, moral and social development' (Article
27). This statement does not suggest that such a standard of living has to
be achieved solely through transfer payments. But it does assert that there
is a wider social interest in the welfare of children above and beyond the
parents' own interest.

Hirsch (2005), in a recent paper for a Commission on Families
and the Wellbeing of Children in the UK, aims to clarify the 'basic
principles' determining how responsibilities are divided between parents,
the state and others. He starts from the perspective of basic human
rights as defined by international agreements to set out underlying
principles:

- there should be a transfer from non-parents to parents, regardless of
  income, which should be maintained in value, as an act of social solidarity;
- there should be sufficient provision to keep children out of poverty,
  based on robust conclusions about what minimum living standard
  for children the state will support; and

- a reasonable degree of choice for families about time spent on paid work and caring should be facilitated, with a fair relationship between payments in and out of work.

He argues in addition that the end of childhood is not fixed, but may cover a period of transition in which resources from the state as well as parents can play a role.

Adam and Brewer (2004, p. 5), in more pragmatic vein, suggest several possible rationales which may justify support for all children:

- to compensate households for the extra costs associated with having children;
- to help redistribute income from rich to poor while avoiding disincentives;
- to improve children's life chances, thus benefiting the whole of society; and
- to influence fertility decisions.

They also set out possible principles that may justify support related to income (which gives higher payments to those with lower incomes):

- to target child poverty, because children cannot control their own circumstances; and
- to help ease the market failure of lifecycle problems of matching income and needs.

In a comprehensive treatment of the issues, Ridge (2003) discusses seven possible aims of social security support for children: the relief of poverty; investment in children; recognition of the costs of children; redistribution of resources; replacing or enforcing parental support; citizenship and children's rights; and incentive payments.

Such aims provide a useful framework of principles. But what has happened in practice? In the 1980s, at least in the UK, children seemed to be seen by many as equivalent to a private consumption choice of their parents, and therefore no more deserving of public support than other such choices (Dilnot et al. 1984). This view has been countered by several arguments. One is that payments for children are largely a form of redistribution over the lifecycle, as the vast majority of us have children at some point in our lives (Brown 1988). This argument may be seen as losing some of its force when fertility is declining and childlessness increasing, however. Another argument is about horizontal equity or social solidarity – that those bringing up children are bearing additional costs, which should be shared by society as a whole (Brown 1988). Hirsch (2005) adds that having children cannot be seen as equivalent to a consumption decision in any case, because even if a voluntary choice is made at the beginning of a child's life, this becomes a long-term commitment.

This social solidarity argument for support for children rests on them being seen as benefiting society as a whole and so meriting public support (Folbre 1999): 'If children can be viewed, at least partly, as a public good, then shifting some of their cost to the society at large can be seen as promoting distributional justice' (Matsaganis et al. 2004, p. 16).

This does not hold true throughout Europe, however, even today. One study, for example, argues that in Italy 'the child is not a "public good" but a private one' (Conti and Sgritta 2004, p. 298). And in post-War (West) Germany, benefits for children have been paid separately from the state administration, to avoid any hint that the state was intervening in family life (Jurczyk et al. 2004). In Denmark, on the other hand, children can be described as the focus of a shared project between parents and the welfare state (Kampmann and Nielsen 2004). Norway is the only country in a recent collection of profiles by a European network (Cost Action 19) to emphasise that savings are put aside as a matter of policy for future generations (Jensen et al. 2004a). But Folbre (1999) argues that if we accounted for intergenerational flows properly, 'instead of describing expenditures aimed at young children as a transfer, we would describe them as a loan which they are required to pay back' (p. 25).

Indeed, as described in more detail in Part I of this volume, children can be seen as an investment (Esping-Andersen and Sarasa 2002). This is rapidly becoming received wisdom, as Lister (Chapter 3, this volume) describes. There is an obvious danger of instrumentalism, however, unless this view is supplemented or countered by a rights focus. (The same was of course true of the view of children as a private consumption good, which did not accord them the status of rights bearers.)

There is also an argument, often deployed in favour of support to prevent or relieve child poverty in particular, that children did not ask to be born, and/or that their parents' supposed 'undeservingness' should not be visited on them (Brown 1988). However, this does not necessarily always override governments' conflicting policy priorities. Indeed, it could be argued that recently in some countries there has been more focus on developing justifications for *not* supporting children. For example, in the UK the children of asylum-seekers may not receive financial or other support in some circumstances (Mayhew et al. 2004). This would seem to come about because the government accords more importance to its goal of deterring 'bogus' asylum-seekers than to its principle of 'every child matters'. More broadly, the reduction or withdrawal of financial support in order to influence behaviour seems to have become more common recently; this is discussed in a later section in terms of its potential impact on the welfare of children.

This chapter goes on to focus on some current policy debates about support for children. The first of these concerns the increasing focus on responsibilities in relation to parenting.

PARENTING RESPONSIBILITIES: AN INCREASING FOCUS

Most commentary about the increasing focus on responsibilities within European transfer systems concerns the 'activation' strategies of governments in relation to employment. In-work benefits and tax credits can be 'employment conditional' (OECD 2004); this means that the additional income can only be accessed by those who have paid employment, and thus rewards those who fulfil their responsibility to participate in the labour market. There has been a trend in recent years towards greater emphasis on these forms of transfer, with some countries newly introducing them and others refining or reinforcing existing schemes (OECD 2004, and see above). They are not always confined to families with children. Belgium introduced a wider tax credit in 2002 and increased its generosity in 2004. France introduced a tax credit in 2001, which unlike Belgium's depends on family income. From 2003, Germany, however, no longer provides additional family benefit supplements to low-paid employees with children, having replaced this with more general help to those in work; and Belgium has recently decided to replace its tax credit with other forms of subsidy to 'make work pay'.

Such payments are indeed intended to 'make work pay' – and thus to bolster the requirement to seek and take employment. The Chancellor of the Exchequer in the UK explicitly links increased conditionality for those out of work with higher rewards for those in work: there is no excuse not to try to obtain a job if additional subsidies are available to 'make work pay' for (almost) everyone. More conditionality for those out of work – often known as 'activation' – has also affected families with children in many other European countries in recent years. In the Netherlands from 1996, for example, lone mothers were expected to be prepared to take paid employment once their child reached five years of age, although Knijn and van Wel (2001) argued that this measure had met considerable resistance from both lone mothers and the caseworkers who were meant to implement it, and so had not been very successful. However, lone mothers with younger children are now in principle included within the scope of 'activation' measures by municipalities as well (Davidse and Kraan, forthcoming).

This example illustrates the power of officials – for good or ill. In Portugal, as elsewhere, many social benefits in kind or in cash are awarded to families through the discretionary decisions of welfare workers (Ferreira 2005). In the UK, while social assistance has traditionally been largely nondiscretionary, in principle, the more recent idea of personalised services leaves room for more discretion, and therefore potentially for more discriminatory treatment (Wright 2003). This may be particularly likely in the context of a greater emphasis on conditionality, and hence deserving/undeservingness.

This increasing emphasis on conditionality and activation has implications for parents among others, of course (although conditions of availability for paid work may be applied differently to them). And Lister (Chapter 3, this volume) points to the potential tension between a government on the one hand emphasising the obligation to take paid work, and on the other stressing the importance of attentive and responsible parenthood. But here we are more concerned not with demands on parents to participate in the labour market but with injunctions to *parent* responsibly, which may result in the withdrawal or reduction of payments made to meet the direct costs of children if they are not fulfilled. In the UK, this forms part of a broader proactive strategy of attempting to affect personal behaviour as a key aspect of government activity (Halpern et al. 2004).

It is possible that as children are increasingly seen as more of a shared project and investment, sanctions are more likely to be exacted if parents are not seen to be cooperating satisfactorily in this mutual endeavour (Kampmann and Nielsen 2004). In Finland, for example, despite the recent improvement in children's welfare, and the small number of children with negative outcomes, a new discourse is said to have emerged that concerns the 'responsibilization' of parents; the key public debate is therefore about parental negligence and disregard of children's needs (Alanen et al. 2004). Folbre had already noted in 1999 that the issue of 'pay for performance' had been raised, in terms of linking financial support to child outcomes; on the positive side, if children had done much better than expected, it was suggested that parents might get extra rewards for 'value added'.

In Bulgaria, families with a low monthly income receive a child allowance, but only on condition that their children of school age actually attend school (Raycheva et al. 2004). In the UK, educational maintenance allowances to encourage older children from low-income families to stay on at school are paid direct to the young people themselves, on condition that they fulfil an attendance contract. Hirsch (2005) argues that because children cannot have as much control over their circumstances as adults, conditionality is not appropriate for them, but in the UK at least, this principle is sometimes modified in relation to older children/young people. It has also arguably been implemented, albeit in a gentler form, with the linking of education for financial capability in schools to the introduction of the child trust fund, which gives lump sums to every child born since a certain date, to be invested on their behalf and withdrawn in adulthood.[5]

In general, if governments sanction parental behaviour in relation to other responsibilities (such as failing to actively seek employment, for example), they often reduce or remove only the payment for the adult(s), leaving payments intended for children untouched (or they establish a minimum – perhaps on a discretionary basis – below which benefit payments cannot fall).[6] It is of course difficult to believe that this does not affect the amount of resources available for the children, especially as we know that low-income parents, especially mothers, often deprive themselves to safeguard their children's welfare (Women's Budget Group 2005), presumably digging into their own allowances to do so.

But in any case, in relation to sanctioning parental behaviour that fails to fulfil the responsibilities of parenthood, it may be precisely the payment for the needs of the children that is reduced or withdrawn, rather than the payment for the adult(s). In the UK, for example, award of the maternity payment for low-income mothers has in the last few years been made conditional on their making contact with a health official;[7] this is intended to safeguard their own health and that of their baby, but non-payment is likely to result in some goods for the child's birth not being purchased. In addition, the UK prime minister in 2002 suggested taking child benefit away from parents of children persistently truanting from school. This was an odd proposal, as it seemed to represent not so much the punishment of a parent but the deprivation of a child, given the wealth of evidence that child benefit is seen as specifically for the child/ren and is spent on them. The proposal was withdrawn in response to criticism. This may have been in part because, as with many such ideas, the extension of conditionality is in practice likely to affect the parent who is already taking the main responsibility for looking after the child, since the person (in intact or separated families) who receives the benefit to meet the direct costs of children is likely to be the main carer.[8] Already a lone parent may in some areas in the UK be evicted from social housing because of their child/ren's 'antisocial behaviour'. While there has also been greater emphasis in recent years on the responsibility of non-resident parents to pay child support, including tougher sanctions for those who do not cooperate, it seems ironic that it is the resident parent/main carer who often seems to bear the brunt of the increased emphasis on conditionality in terms of fulfilling parenting responsibilities.

Of course private intra-household and/or inter-household transfers can also often be conditional; Jensen et al. (2004a), for example, note that grandparents may make their gifts to family members contingent on various forms of behaviour.

FORM OF TRANSFERS AND METHOD OF PAYMENT

The amount of support for children is of critical importance; to cite one example, financial support for children increased in the UK by over 50 per cent between 1999 and 2003 (Adam and Brewer 2004). Sutherland (2005) asks what fraction of the additional household needs arising from the presence of children are met by elements of the tax and transfer systems directed explicitly to them. She finds considerable cross-country variation, but support amounts to more than 30 per cent of these additional needs in two-thirds of the 15 EU countries she studied. This can be key to the well-being of children.

But it is not just the amount of support that is crucial, but also the form this takes. The source, labelling, recipient and management of income also seem to be important for children's well-being (Goode et al. 1998). The next section discusses the form of transfers and the method of payment. In particular, it examines the debates about using the tax system to deliver support; means-tested versus universal provision; and the appropriate recipient of support for children.

Using the Tax System

Perhaps the clearest policy change in support for children in recent years has been the increasing use of the tax system to deliver financial support for children. Analyses by Eurostat have not usually included tax relief and allowances in their analyses of cash transfers for children (Abramovici 2005), but Matsaganis et al. (2004) and Sutherland (2005) argue that it is vital to include them to obtain a complete picture. This is becoming increasingly difficult to deny, as payments through the tax system for children become more common.

Traditionally some countries have in any case relied on the tax system as a major part of their redistributive policies for families (Adema and Ladaique 2005). France, for example, still retains the quotient system in its personal income tax system (Hantrais 2004), by which the tax paid is a function of a formula taking account of the number of children as well as adults, in combination with total income.[9] Bradshaw and Finch (2002), in their study of 22 countries' packages of financial support for children/families, also noted a shift over the 1990s towards using the income tax system. Anglo-American countries have used the tax system to administer benefits for children and/or low-paid workers for many years (Whiteford et al. 2003); but there has been an expansion of these payments among other EU countries besides the UK recently.

Overall, the treatment of children by the income tax system in Southern European countries, at least in the late 1990s, tended to be regressive, with cash benefits being better targeted both vertically and horizontally than tax reliefs and allowances; and since then, better-off families in Italy and Spain have gained more through recent changes (Matsaganis et al. 2004). However, in 2002 tax reform in Cyprus resulted in the abolition of exemptions for children, with a shift towards benefits instead, though the universal child benefit is not very generous (Kouloumou 2004). In Greece, non-refundable child tax credits reduce tax bills for those eligible at a flat rate; but in 2002 a new refundable tax credit was also introduced, targeted at low-income families with children at school. Italy provides an income tax credit for dependent children. Spain replaced child tax deductions with a child tax allowance in 1999, and added a refundable tax credit (for working women with children under three) in 2003; in Portugal, tax credits for dependent family members offset certain amounts against gross tax liability.

The first trend identified by Adam and Brewer (2004) for the system of 'child-contingent support' in the UK since 1975 is 'a fall, and then resurgence, in the role of the tax system' (p. 17).[10] The way in which the tax system in the UK supports children has changed from tax allowances to tax credits over this period, however. 'New' tax credits, introduced in 2003, can now provide significant amounts of support; Hirsch (2005) writes that in the UK 'recent increases in the level of in-work income supplements have meant that even some working families can have most of their income provided by the state' (executive summary). The UK government's argument has been that routing payments via the tax system reduces stigma because taxation affects almost everyone, and connects financial support with paid work, improving take-up (HM Treasury 1998). It is not clear, however, whether these arguments apply with as much force to child tax credit, which is paid to families in and out of work, as to working tax credit, which is only available to those in paid work of 16 hours per week or more.

The exclusion of payments via the tax system from 'social benefits' as categorised by Eurostat (Abramovici 2005) has the paradoxical effect of making it appear as though those EU countries who pay significant proportions of their transfers to children via the tax system are not as generous as others. Increases in support will not be recorded as such, making them appear as laggards. On the other hand, one of the arguments for moving to tax credits for transfers to children is that politically it may be easier to increase such payments because at least in part they do not count as public expenditure in accounting terms.[11] Which of these effects is dominant in governments' minds may depend on how much they are playing to international or domestic audiences, and/or how important it is to them to boast of their generous support to families on the one hand or their fiscal rectitude on the other.

Means-tested versus Universal Provision

The recent moves to making more use of the tax system to assess and pay transfers for children have in several cases, as noted above, involved in effect a continuation and/or expansion of (a form of) means testing. This is true of the introduction of child tax credit in the UK, for example. According to Hantrais (2004, p. 137): 'progressively the emphasis in welfare systems has been on helping children at risk, rather than the family unit, in line with the child-centred approach adopted in the 1990s'. She argues that this shift in emphasis from horizontal redistribution (family benefits policies) to vertical redistribution and safety net provision (income maintenance policies) has reopened debates about the relative advantages and disadvantages of targeted and universal provision.

One way in which fiscal pressures on family benefits were translated into policy was that several countries made means-testing of family benefits more systematic before 1999 (OECD 2004), and these changes were generally retained after that date. However, the OECD does cite some counter-examples, including the Slovakian Republic, and other countries became concerned about the adverse impact of means-tested benefits on incentives, and therefore introduced mitigating measures (including a higher income disregard for working lone parents in Poland).

In the UK in recent years 'child-contingent support programmes have been increasingly means-tested and decreasingly based on past contributions' (Adam and Brewer 2004, p. 27). Child tax credit, which – although it is paid at least in part to the vast majority of families with children – is dependent on a test of income, is now the main vehicle of direct financial support for children, having overtaken child benefit in expenditure. Adam and Brewer state that child benefit fell from 79 per cent of total support for children in 1979 to 42 per cent in 2003.[12] Hantrais (2004), however, asks whether the recent emphasis on means-tested benefits and tax credits in the UK is more a general development of social policy rather than family policy.

A study of social security changes from 1990 to 2002 in the Czech Republic, Hungary and Poland (Fultz and Steinhilber 2004), while it focuses on gender equality, includes an examination of family benefits, as well as maternity benefits.[13] It describes reform of family benefits as 'incremental and continuous' (p. 254). By the end of the 1990s, there had been a sharp decline in spending on family benefits as a proportion of GDP, especially in Poland and Hungary. Benefits were concentrated on low-income families, which softened some of the shocks associated with transition, but this could have adverse effects on work incentives, and is also described as bringing about a shift in status for claimants 'from holders of personal rights to petitioners of the state' (Fultz and Steinhilber 2004, p. 260). Now, however, Hungary at least is planning to change its system of cash transfers and fiscal support for children in the opposite direction (Ferge et al. 2005). The reform envisages the amalgamation of three different systems of support for children – universal family allowances, means-tested child assistance and tax allowances – into one, universal, benefit. The change would, according to these writers, 'make the system more predictable, strengthen social rights, and would abolish some inequalities' (p. 15).

The potential of a change in this direction – to put more emphasis on universal benefits – was explored for Southern European countries by Matsaganis et al. (2004). Here, the role of the state in matters of family policy has traditionally been subsidiary to the family, and 'familialism' has meant that family resources are expected to be used to help relatives at risk of poverty, so the impact on child poverty of family transfers[14] (analysed in the late 1990s) was weak and their value was very low. However, they argue that there is at the same time extensive, and politically 'unproblematic', reliance on tax benefits in several of these countries. The combination of limited social assistance, regressive tax benefits and contributory family benefits often results in uneven and fragmented coverage for families with children (Matsaganis et al. 2004).[15] However, Greece does stand out for having a lower risk of poverty for children than for the population as a whole; and Cyprus is similar in this respect (Kouloumou 2004).

Introducing universal child benefit schemes (as in the UK, Denmark and Sweden) in Southern European countries would have a considerable impact on child poverty, in part because currently many children in low-income families receive little or no support.[16] They would also of course incur a significant cost, but combining a universal benefit with targeted policies could be a more effective way to reduce child poverty at reasonable cost (Matsaganis et al. 2004).[17] UNICEF (2005) finds that higher government spending on family and social benefits is clearly associated with lower child poverty rates (though there is still variation between countries with similar spending levels). Similarly, Sutherland (2005) finds that in one set of European countries with low child poverty rates, child-contingent payments make a large contribution to poverty reduction – and these are mainly universal benefits and tax concessions. Those countries 'targeting' income only to children in poverty, on the other hand, have similar levels of spending, but higher child poverty rates.

Universal benefits such as child benefit reach more children living in poverty than any of the benefits specifically 'targeted' to them, because of problems with take-up, administration, and so on. Adelman et al. (2004) have suggested that times of transition (in parental relationships and/or employment status) seem to be associated with severe or persistent child poverty. Universal benefits such as child benefit tend to 'follow the child' more successfully than so-called 'targeted' payments, which may stop and need to be reclaimed on changes of partnership and/or employment (Women's Budget Group 2005).

Folbre (1999) argues that 'in principle, universal programs make sense, supplemented by some extra targeted provisions for the poor' (p. 26). Indeed, 'targeting' does not have to involve means testing, but can involve focusing additional resources on certain population groups that may be more at risk of poverty because of their situation, such as large families and/or lone parent families, and so on.

THE RECIPIENT OF SUPPORT

Another interpretation of 'targeting' might link it to success in ensuring that money given for children reaches them. The first point of debate involves asking whether parents spend money intended for children on them. And there are two further current debates, about the recipient of support: whether this should be the 'main carer', or whether there should be alternative arrangements; and whether the child him or herself rather than the parent should in some cases receive the benefit.

As Adam and Brewer (2004, p. 5) suggest, 'a complication in using cash transfers to help children is that money is given to parents, not directly to children'. There is evidence that parents try to protect their children from the worst impact of child poverty, although this is not always possible in situations of severe or persistent poverty (Adelman et al. 2004). Gregg et al. (2005) suggest that low-income families who received additional financial help with the costs of children in the UK between 1996/97 and 2000/01 did spend more money on items that benefited their children, and that material deprivation among these families fell.

MISSOC (2002) describes the beneficiary of family allowances or child allowances, with a note clarifying that 'in most . . . cases it is the mother' (p. 7). The case for paying benefits for children to mothers is that they are more likely to spend money on children, and evidence suggests that this is the case. There is some concern that identifying a 'main carer' may not facilitate a more equal sharing of gender roles (Goode et al. 1998); but this has usually been overridden by the opposing arguments. There are usually arrangements for paying benefits in full or in part to someone else in special cases. But in the UK, payment of benefits for children to the 'main carer' is increasingly being challenged in principle by fathers, especially those who are separated from their partners but who care for their children for part of the time (Baker 2005).

If a 'non-resident' parent in the UK looks after the child/ren for a certain minimum number of nights per year, the private child support (maintenance) they have to pay for their child/ren is reduced. In Norway, a regulation of 2003 also means that non-resident parents pay less child support the more time they spend with their child/ren. According to the authors of one study, 'it may be argued that children's time has been commodified in the process' (Jensen et al. 2004a, p. 366) – child/ren's time is now given a monetary value, because spending time with them reduces the amount of child support that needs to be paid. A similar split is now being demanded for state benefits in some countries. In the UK, this would include child benefit, income support, housing benefit/council tax benefit and child tax credit/ working tax credit (O'Sullivan 2005).[18]

Baker (2005) argues that 'the most widespread examples of indirect sexual discrimination are those which allocate all benefits for the support of children to one parent irrespective of how the care and costs are shared' (p. 1).[19] He suggests various ways of deciding the allocation between separated parents. O'Sullivan (2005) puts forward the advantages of splitting benefit payments between separated parents, but also the disadvantages – for example: 'Suddenly, a resident parent would have a financial incentive to cut the time that children spent with an ex-partner'. The splitting of benefits could result in lower total support for the child/ren if the benefit/tax credit is means-tested, because non-resident fathers are more likely to be well-off than resident mothers, and therefore may not qualify for much, if any, payment. The UK government argues that its strategy to tackle child poverty is the reason for continuing to pay benefits for children in full to the main carer (House of Commons *Hansard*, Written Answers 2 December 2004, col 199W).

In Ireland, if families are separated, child-dependent allowances in social welfare payments are usually paid to the person with care of the children, but other options do exist (sometimes set down through mediation, or by the courts).[20] In Sweden, the Social Insurance Office is reviewing gender issues in the child benefit system (Burgess 2005). In Denmark, child benefit is attributed to the child according to where they are reported to be living in the population register if parents are separated or divorced. But in the Netherlands, benefit is divided equally between the two parents (Hantrais 2004).

As these examples suggest, this is an issue that is not going to disappear. However, it has no straightforward solution. And Koopmans et al. (2004)

argue that all elements of a tax and benefits system become problematic if two parents share the care of children – and that this applies whether they are separated or not. In the UK, the upcoming statutory duty on public authorities from 2007 onwards to promote gender equality may be used by fathers' groups to push these issues higher up the agenda. And if so, the implications for intact families, as well as separated families, are likely to come under the spotlight.

The other, less pressing, policy issue about who is paid any financial support for children is whether the children should be considered as potential recipients. One analysis of childhood in Austria describes child benefit as a basic income for minors, even though in practice the parent receives it (Beham et al. 2004). In Northern Europe, according to Hantrais (2004, p. 122), where the child is thought of as the intended recipient, the main cash transfer for children is more likely to be called 'child benefit'; but in French-speaking and Southern European countries, such payments are regarded more as a contribution to family income; the family unit is seen as the beneficiary and payments are more likely to be called 'family allowances'. (Interestingly, in the UK, many parents still describe their child benefit as their 'family allowance', even though the name and form of the payment were changed almost 30 years ago.)

But does a child-centred approach logically imply that benefits for children are a legal right of the child (Ridge 2005) and should be paid to the child? In the UK, educational maintenance allowances, while means-tested on parental incomes, are paid direct to young people. So far, this involves only young people of an age where they could otherwise be in the labour market and earning an income themselves. But it is possible that the growing emphasis on the autonomy and agency of children may move this issue up the agenda as well.

STRUCTURE OF PAYMENTS FOR CHILDREN: THE ISSUE OF FAMILY SIZE

There are several issues currently under debate about the structure of payments for children, of which one of the most pressing is whether and how they should vary according to family size. Given the topicality of debates relating fertility to family policy in some quarters, it might be thought that policies on relating transfers to family size would be starting to converge. On the contrary, however, they seem to differ considerably across Europe, and the OECD (2004) notes varying policy moves recently, rather than a consistent trend. For example, Sweden's universal child benefit scheme rises in value with family size (Matsaganis et al. 2004). In Austria, low-income families with three or more children receive an additional allowance for the third and subsequent children (Beham et al. 2004). In Belgium, France, Italy, Germany and Luxembourg, benefits increase with each additional child, or are larger for later children (such as the fourth or fifth child) (Kamerman 2003). In France, family allowances are not paid for the first child (Hantrais 2004), but the third and subsequent children count for double the usual amount in the 'quotient familial' in the income tax system.

There can be different reasons for providing bigger payments for larger families, which may include preventing or relieving poverty, in addition to trying to encourage higher fertility. The example of the UK below shows that a rationale can also be advanced for providing proportionately bigger payments for smaller families. There has long been an argument that larger families are more at risk of poverty, and some countries have attempted to counter this via transfer payments. In Norway, however, there is no linear connection between the number of children and low income, with a link only for those families with five children or more (Jensen et al. 2004a). Thus the link between family size and poverty risk is not inevitable.

The High Level Expert Group (2004), in its report on the future of social policy in an enlarged European Union, suggested that among the three key components of future EU social policy would be policies to allow people to have the number of children they want. The Group carefully did not label this proposal 'pronatalism'. But several countries have recently given incentives for larger families because of their concern about population decline.

The CEE countries have been particularly keen on measures to promote fertility in recent years (Hantrais 2004). Estonia doubles child benefit for second and subsequent children, and from 1998 onwards introduced a new supplementary child benefit for families with four or more children, as well as relating tax relief to the number of children. But one study argues that Estonia's government is in a double-bind, as it is concerned about low fertility but is also keenly aware that each extra child increases the risk of family poverty, and it has not put enough money into benefits to affect fertility rates (Kutsar et al. 2004). And in practice, it is in the area of indirect rather than direct costs – the forgone earnings of women in particular, and problems with the reconciliation of work and family life – that the concern about population decline is likely to prove a more obvious catalyst for policy change (see, for example, Esping-Andersen et al. 2002).

Hantrais (2004) argues that there has been a rejection of pronatalism in Southern European countries recently. But analysis using Euromod (based on 1998 figures) showed that family transfers in four of these countries – Italy, Spain, Portugal and Greece – were more effective at taking children out of poverty, and at reducing the 'poverty gap', if they were living in large

families. Greece has traditionally given substantial assistance to large families, and since 2002 this is no longer income tested. This may in part explain
why the risk of poverty among children in Greece is lower than for the
population as a whole, although the recent change has increased the benefit
to better-off families (Matsaganis et al. 2004). The amounts exempt from
income tax in Croatia rise with the number of family members supported,
with a regressive effect (Raboteg-Saric 2004). Italy introduced a benefit for
large families (with three or more children) in 1999, tested on household
income, although, despite the improvement this brought about, it is still
mostly larger families who are in poverty (Conti and Sgritta 2004). On the
other hand, Spain's child tax deductions, which used to rise more than proportionally with the number of children, were replaced in 1999 with a child
tax allowance that rises only proportionally (Matsaganis et al. 2004).

In the UK, however, 'the last 28 years have seen structural changes to
child-contingent support programmes that place more weight on whether
a family has *any* children than on *how many* it has' (Adam and Brewer 2004,
p. 24, emphasis added). The then Conservative government in the UK cited
the larger differential between the resources of those with one child and no
children (compared with the difference between families with one child and
those with more children) as the rationale for the introduction of a higher
payment for the first or eldest eligible child in child benefit. But this was
examined and found wanting (Ditch et al. 1992). Political motivations were
more obvious than valid intellectual justifications, since the amount
involved did not approach the 'opportunity cost' of having a child/children.
This was the main element in the differential between people with no children and people with one child or more, and was used as the justification
by the government for its policy change. Thus, as with the concern about
poverty described above, it is likely to be the indirect costs of large families – the barriers to employment for parent(s), and mothers in particular –
that cause the difference in living standards, rather than the additional
direct costs of having more children. To try to solve this problem via the
payments to help with the direct costs of children seems contradictory
(though perhaps better than not trying to solve it at all).

CONCLUSIONS

Despite the demographic reality of ageing populations in EU countries,
there has been a welcome emphasis in recent years on support for children,
and the EU itself is being urged to take on increasing responsibility for policies on children in future (Ruxton 2005). It is difficult to draw up a balance
sheet of recent developments in financial support for the direct costs of

children across the EU, in part because of differences in what is included in 'family benefits',[21] and in part because the focus of analysis is often specific – for example, policies to tackle child poverty – rather than about support for children more broadly. In addition, data, especially those necessary for cross-national comparisons, are often out of date. But there is some indication in recent analyses (see, for example, Abramovici 2005) that there have been real increases in social protection expenditure on families and children in the past few years, notwithstanding the fall in the number of children.

Policy issues relating to financial support for the direct costs of children that may emerge as key for the future include fertility, responsibility and the recipient of support. Demographic concerns have led to heightened sensitivity to the birthrate in various European countries. Measures to encourage higher fertility will be likely primarily to involve compensation for the indirect costs of childrearing, especially parental loss of income. But concern about the birthrate may also result in proposals to increase payments towards the direct costs of children. It is difficult for advocates of improved financial support for children to resist such moves whatever their justification. But instrumentalist views of children run counter to the growing emphasis on their rights as citizens and will not be able to provide a durable foundation for a sustainable commitment to supporting children for their own sake.

Countries as far apart in terms of their traditions of family policy as Finland and the UK have begun to put significantly more emphasis on parental responsibilities. The increasing focus on investment in children was always likely to lead in this direction. And parents in the UK subject to parenting orders – under which because of their child's behaviour they are obliged to attend parenting classes – have largely welcomed these classes (perhaps as an opportunity to share experiences as well as learning new parenting techniques). However, to go further than this and to implement reductions in payments for children in response to parents' perceived failures to fulfil their responsibilities, would be a step too far.

The failure to pursue an EU directive on the individualisation of benefits in the 1980s was in part due to the difficulty of deciding what to do about payments for children. Who benefits and tax credits for children are paid to appears to be a non-issue in some countries; in others, it is highly controversial. Challenges from the fathers' lobby to the receipt of benefit by the woman, or by the 'main carer', will be likely to be a theme of policy debates of the future, and will prove difficult to resolve. While it may sometimes appear that most attention is paid to the indirect costs of childrearing, this chapter has tried to demonstrate that many of the most lively current policy debates in EU countries today also concern how best to meet the direct costs of children.

NOTES

1. Gauthier (2002) investigated the development of family policies between 1970 and 1999 in a selection of industrialised countries, and concluded that the evidence points to divergence (including between countries within the European Union) rather than convergence. However, the family policies she examined are wider than transfer payments alone, including support for working parents as well.
2. A summary overview of the usual characteristics of transfers for direct costs is given by Kamerman (2003).
3. Childcare costs can be seen as either direct or indirect costs. Support for childcare costs is not discussed in detail here, though some measures of financial support for children include it.
4. Publications that contain an overview of financial provisions for families across different countries include Abramovici (2003 and 2005); MISSOC (2002) (and annual tables comparing provisions across different member states, as in MISSOC 2004); OECD (2004).
5. Higher payments are given for the children of low-income families.
6. Willem Adema, OECD, personal communication, October 2005.
7. The level of the maternity payment has also been increased significantly.
8. See below (pp. 124–126) for discussion about the recipient of benefit payments for children.
9. Hantrais (2004) describes variations on this, which are noted in relevant later sections of this chapter.
10. The other trends in the UK since 1975 are: a rise in means-testing; a steady decline in the role of contributory benefits; and a continuing important role for non-contributory, non-means-tested benefits (especially child benefit).
11. For international accounting purposes, the amount of tax credits paid to people who would have no tax liability is usually counted as the equivalent of public expenditure, whereas the amount that offsets a tax liability is usually counted as revenue forgone rather than public expenditure. This is not the same as the EU's categorisation of social benefits, which ignores all payments via the tax system.
12. It is possible to calculate 'total support' in a different way, but the main point remains valid.
13. In Hungary, family benefits are also paid through the tax system.
14. Like this chapter, Matsaganis et al. (2004) restrict their definition of family transfers to those specifically labelled as being for children, rather than including the additions to various benefits (including pensions) for households that have children. They consider Greece, Italy, Spain and Portugal, and examine the situation primarily in 1998.
15. The reference year for comparison was, however, 1998, since when various programmes of family support have been introduced and/or amended in the Southern European countries examined in the study.
16. This benefit would substitute for existing family transfers, as analysed in 1998.
17. As Matsaganis et al. (2004) argue, taking account of (non)-take-up of income-tested benefits – which is seldom done in distributional analyses – significantly increases the attractions of universal benefits.
18. One legal case (*Guardian*, 2 February 2005), taken by a separated father called Hockenjos, resulted in a judgement that both parents should be given the allowances for children; but this solution would be expensive. Allowances for children within this particular benefit (jobseeker's allowance) are also being replaced in the near future by child tax credit in the UK, although this is currently delayed.
19. These benefits are not usually being paid for care work, but to meet the direct costs of children. Allowances for children in out-of-work benefits in the UK have previously been paid to the claimant (usually the man in couples), but child tax credit is paid to the 'main carer' instead.
20. Personal communication from Helen Johnston, Combat Poverty Agency, September 2005.
21. For example, tax measures may be included or excluded; family support may include payments to meet indirect costs (such as the impact of childrearing on parental incomes).

REFERENCES

Abramovici, G. (2003), 'Social protection: cash family benefits in Europe', in *Statistics in Focus: Population and Social Conditions: Theme 3 – 19/2003, Population and Living Conditions*, Brussels: Eurostat, European Commission.

Abramovici, G. (2005), 'Social protection in the European Union', in *Statistics in Focus: Population and Social Conditions 14/2005*, Brussels: Eurostat, European Commission.

Adam, S. and M. Brewer (2004), *Supporting Families: The Financial Costs and Benefits of Children Since 1975*, Bristol: The Policy Press.

Adelman, L., S. Middleton and K. Ashworth (2004), *Britain's Poorest Children: Severe and Persistent Poverty and Social Exclusion*, London: Save the Children.

Adema, W. and M. Ladaique (2005), '*Net social expenditure, 2005 edition: more comprehensive measures of social support*', OECD Social, Employment and Migration working paper no 29, Paris.

Alanen, L., H. Sauli and H. Strandell (2004), 'Children and Childhood in a Welfare State: the Case of Finland', in A.-M. Jensen, A. Ben-Arieh, C. Conti, D. Kutsar, M. Nic Ghiolla Phadraig and H. Warming Nielsen (eds), *Children's Welfare in Ageing Europe*, vols I & II, Trondheim: Norwegian Centre for Child Research.

Baker, J. (2005), 'Discrimination and social entitlements and benefits', Families Need Fathers position statement, London.

Beham, M., H. Wintersberger, K. Worister and U. Zartler (2004), 'Childhood in Austria: cash and care, time and space, children's needs and public policies', in A.-M. Jensen, A. Ben-Arieh, C. Conti, D. Kutsar, M. Nic Ghiolla Phadraig and H. Warming Nielsen (eds), *Children's Welfare in Ageing Europe*, vols I & II, Trondheim: Norwegian Centre for Child Research.

Bleses, P. and M. Seeleib-Kaiser (2004), *The Dual Transformation of the German Welfare State*, Basingstoke: Palgrave Macmillan.

Bradshaw, J. and N. Finch (2002), 'A comparison of child benefit packages in 22 countries', Department for Work and Pensions research report 174, Corporate Document Services, Leeds.

Brown, J.C. (1988), *Child Benefit: Investing in the Future*, London: CPAG Ltd.

Burgess, A. (2005), 'State intervention and parental responsibility: child support in Australia', *Public Policy Research*, **12**(1), 49–55.

Conti, C. and G.B. Sgritta (2004), 'Childhood in Italy: a family affair', in A. M. Jensen, A. Ben-Arieh, C. Conti, D. Kutsar, M. Nic Ghiolla Phadraig and H. Warming Nielsen (eds), *Children's Welfare in Ageing Europe*, vols I & II, Trondheim: Norwegian Centre for Child Research.

Davidse, E. and A. Kraan (forthcoming), 'Back to work! First results of a new system of social assistance for the Netherlands', *Benefits*.

Dilnot, A., J. Kay and C.N. Morris (1984), *The Reform of Social Security*, Oxford: Oxford University Press.

Ditch, J., S. Pickles and P. Whiteford (1992), *The New Structure of Child Benefit: A Review*, London: Coalition for Child Benefit and Child Poverty Action Group.

Esping-Andersen, G. with D. Gallie, A. Hemerijck and J. Myles (2002), *Why We Need a New Welfare State*, Oxford: Oxford University Press.

Esping-Andersen, G. and S. Sarasa (2002), 'The generational conflict reconsidered', *Journal of European Social Policy*, **12**(1), 5–21.

Ferge, S. with L. Bass and A. Darvas (2005), 'Social policy in Hungary at a glance', in European AntiPoverty Network, *Network News*, **114**, 15.

Ferreira, S. (2005), 'The past in the present: Portuguese social security reform', *Social Policy and Society*, 4(3), 331–8.

Folbre, N. (1999), 'Public support for parents', in M.S. King (ed.), *Squaring Up: Policy Strategies to Raise Women's Incomes in the United States*, Ann Arbor, MI: University of Michigan Press.

Fultz, E. and S. Steinhilber (2004), 'Social security reform and gender equality: recent experience in central Europe', *International Labour Review*, 143(3), 249–73.

Gauthier, A.H. (2002), 'Family policies in industrialized countries: is there convergence?', *Population*, 57(2), 447–74.

Goode, J., C. Callender and R. Lister (1998), *Purse or Wallet? Gender Inequalities and Income Distribution Within Families on Benefits*, London: Policy Studies Institute.

Gregg, P., J. Waldfogel and E. Washbrook (2005), 'That's the way the money goes: expenditure patterns as real incomes rise for the poorest families with children', in J. Hills and K. Stewart (eds), *A More Equal Society? New Labour, Poverty, Inequality and Exclusion*, Bristol: The Policy Press.

Halpern, D., C. Bates, G. Mulgan and S. Aldridge with G. Beales and A. Heathfield (2004), *Personal Responsibility and Changing Behaviour: The State of Knowledge and its Implications for Public Policy*, London: Prime Minister's Strategy Unit, Cabinet Office.

Hantrais, L. (2004), *Family Policy Matters: Responding to Family Change in Europe*, Bristol: The Policy Press.

High Level Expert Group (2004), *On the Future of Social Policy in an Enlarged European Union*, Brussels: European Commission.

Hirsch, D. (2005), 'Financial support for children – defining responsibilities and adequacy', National Family and Parenting Institute report to the Commission on Families and the Wellbeing of Children, London.

HM Treasury (1998), *Work Incentives: A Report By Martin Taylor – The Modernisation of Britain's Tax and Benefit System No. 2*, London: HM Treasury.

Jensen, A.-M., A. Ben-Arieh, C. Conti, D. Kutsar, M. Nic Ghiolla Phadraig and H. Warming Nielsen (eds) (2004b), *Children's Welfare in Ageing Europe*, vols I and II, Trondheim: Norwegian Centre for Child Research, for COST A19.

Jensen, A.-M., A. Trinekjorholt, J. Qvortrup and M. Sandboek with V. Johansen and T. Lauritzen (2004a), 'Childhood and generation in Norway: money, time and space', in A.-M. Jensen, A. Ben-Arieh, C. Conti, D. Kutsar, M. Nic Ghiolla Phadraig and H. Warming Nielsen (eds), *Children's Welfare in Ageing Europe*, vols I & II, Trondheim: Norwegian Centre for Child Research.

Jurczyk, K., T. Olk and H. Zeiher (2004), 'German children's welfare between economy and ideology', in A.-M. Jensen, A. Ben-Arieh, C. Conti, D. Kutsar, M. Nic Ghiolla Phadraig and H. Warming Nielsen (eds), *Children's Welfare in Ageing Europe*, vols I & II, Trondheim: Norwegian Centre for Child Research.

Kamerman, S.B. (2003), 'A social security for everyone: child well-being, family allowances, and social services', paper for International Social Security Association Regional Meeting for the Americas Social Services and Family Allowances: Social Security for Everyone, San Jose, Costa Rica, 27–29 January.

Kamerman, S.B. and A.J. Kahn (1997), 'Investing in children: government expenditures for children and their families in western industrialized countries', in A.G. Cornia and S. Danziger (eds), *Child Poverty and Deprivation in the Industrialized Countries*, Oxford: Oxford University Press.

Kampmann, J. and H.W. Nielsen (2004), 'Socialised childhood: children's childhoods in Denmark', in A.-M. Jensen, A. Ben-Arieh, C. Conti, D. Kutsar,

M. Nic Ghiolla Phadraig and H. Warming Nielsen (eds), *Children's Welfare in Ageing Europe*, vols I & II, Trondheim: Norwegian Centre for Child Research.

Knijn, T. and F. van Wel (2001), 'Careful or lenient: welfare reform for lone mothers in the Netherlands', *Journal of European Social Policy*, **11**(3), 235–51.

Koopmans, I., T. Jaspers, T. Knijn and J. Plantenga (2004), 'Balancing care and security: an international comparison of care components in pension systems', in N. van de Hallen, T. van de Lippe and J. Schippers (eds), *Diversity in Lifecourses: Consequences for the Labour Market*, Tilburg: Organisation voor Strategisch Arbeids-markfonderzoek, Institute for Labour Study, pp. 137–54.

Kouloumou, T. (2004), 'Children's welfare and family life in Cyprus: a family affair with intergenerational implications', in A.-M. Jensen, A. Ben-Arieh, C. Conti, D. Kutsar, M. Nic Ghiolla Phadraig and H. Warming Nielsen (eds), *Children's Welfare in Ageing Europe*, vols I & II, Trondheim: Norwegian Centre for Child Research.

Kutsar, D., M. Harro, E.-M. Tiit and D. Matrov (2004), 'Children's welfare in Estonia from different perspectives', in A.-M. Jensen, A. Ben-Arieh, C. Conti, D. Kutsar, M. Nic Ghiolla Phadraig and H. Warming Nielsen (eds), *Children's Welfare in Ageing Europe*, vols I & II, Trondheim: Norwegian Centre for Child Research.

Leitner, S. (2003), 'Varieties of familialism: the caring functions of the family in comparative perspective', *European Societies*, **5**(4), 353–75.

Lewis, J. (1997), *Lone Mothers in European Welfare Regimes: Shifting Policy Logics*, London and Philadelphia: Jessica Kingsley Publishers.

Matsaganis, M., C. O'Donoghue, H. Levy, M. Coromaldi, M. Mercader-Prats, C. Farinha Rodrigues, S. Toso and P. Tsakloglou (2004), 'Child poverty and family transfers in southern Europe', University of Essex Euromod working paper noEM2/04, Colchester.

Mayhew, E., E. Uprichard, B. Beresford, T. Ridge and J. Bradshaw (2004), 'Children and childhood in the UK', in A.-M. Jensen, A. Ben-Arieh, C. Conti, D. Kutsar, M. Nic Ghiolla Phadraig and H. Warming Nielsen (eds), *Children's Welfare in Ageing Europe*, vols I & II, Trondheim: Norwegian Centre for Child Research.

Middleton, S., K. Ashworth and I. Braithwaite (1997), *Small Fortunes: Spending on Children, Childhood Poverty and Parental Sacrifice*, York: Joseph Rowntree Foundation.

MISSOC (2002), *Family Benefits and Family Policies in Europe*, Brussels: European Commission Directorate-General for Employment and Social Affairs.

MISSOC (2004), *Social Protection in the Member States of the European Union, of the European Economic Area and in Switzerland – The Situation on 1 May 2004*, Brussels: European Commission Directorate-General for Employment, Social Affairs and Equal Opportunities.

OECD (2004), *Benefits and Wages: OECD Indicators 2004*, Paris: Organisation for Economic Co-operation and Development.

OECD (2005), *Reconciling Earning and Caring: Social Policies for Working Families*, Paris: Organisation for Economic Co-operation and Development.

O'Neill, R. (2005), *Fiscal Policy and the Family: How the Family Fares in France, Germany and the UK*, London: Institute for the Study of Civil Society (Civitas).

O'Sullivan, J. (2005), 'The gender gap', *Guardian*, 2 February.

Raboteg-Saric, Z. (2004), 'Children's welfare in the context of social and economic changes in Croatia', in A.-M. Jensen, A. Ben-Arieh, C. Conti, D. Kutsar, M. Nic

Ghiolla Phadraig and H. Warming Nielsen (eds), *Children's Welfare in Ageing Europe*, vols I & II, Trondheim: Norwegian Centre for Child Research.

Raycheva, L., K. Hristova, D. Radomirova and R. Ginev (2004), 'Bulgaria: childhood in transition', in A.-M. Jensen, A. Ben-Arieh, C. Conti, D. Kutsar, M. Nic Ghiolla Phadraig and H. Warming Nielsen (eds), *Children's Welfare in Ageing Europe*, vols I & II, Trondheim: Norwegian Centre for Child Research.

Ridge, T. (2003), 'Benefiting children? The challenge of social security support for children', in J. Millar (ed), *Understanding Social Security: Issues for Policy and Practice*, Bristol: The Policy Press, pp. 167–88.

Ridge, T. (2005), 'Supporting children? The impact of child support policies on children's wellbeing in the UK and Australia', *Journal of Social Policy*, **34**(1), 121–42.

Ruxton, S. (2005), *What About Us? Children's Rights in the European Union: Next Steps*, Brussels: Euronet.

Seeleib-Kaiser, M., S. van Dyk and M. Roggenkamp (2005), 'What do parties want? An analysis of programmatic social policy aims in Austria, Germany and the Netherlands', University of Bremen Centre for Social Policy Research working paper 01/2005, Bremen.

Sutherland, H. (2005), 'The impact of tax and transfer systems on children in the European Union', UNICEF Innocenti Research Centre working papers 2005–04, Florence.

UNICEF (2005), 'Child poverty in rich countries, 2005', UNICEF Innocenti Research Centre report card no 6, Florence.

Whiteford, P., M. Mendelson and J. Millar (2003), *Timing it Right? Tax credits and How to Respond to Income Changes*, York: Joseph Rowntree Foundation.

Women's Budget Group (2005), *Women's and Children's Poverty: Making the Links*, London: Women's Budget Group.

Wright, S. (2003), 'The street-level implementation of unemployment policy', in J. Millar (ed.), *Understanding Social Security: Issues for Policy and Practice*, Bristol: The Policy Press.

PART III

Caring for children

7. Cultures of childhood and the relationship of care and employment in European welfare states

Birgit Pfau-Effinger

INTRODUCTION

Women have been integrated into European labour markets to a higher degree in recent decades, and to some extent in more equal positions. At the same time, childcare has been formalised by transfers from the family to other institutions in the public sector, the non-profit sector or the markets. These policies have helped to create new opportunities for caregiving women to integrate into the labour markets, and new types of social integration for children. Informal childcare has, however, survived everywhere in Europe, and a substantial proportion of care is still provided informally in the family.

Often, a relatively high proportion of informal care in a country is taken to be an indicator of a more 'traditional' welfare state that is lagging behind the more advanced 'women-friendly' welfare states, which substantially support the integration of women into employment by providing a high level of public childcare. However, this argument does not adequately take into account some important elements of change that have taken place. On the one hand, informal care provided by parents within the family has, to a substantial degree, undergone changes in forms and significance, and is different from traditional informal care within the framework of a 'housewife marriage'. Moreover, welfare state policies and the behaviour of parents and mothers are related in part to cultural models of what is a 'good childhood', which are based on assumptions that elements of childcare provided by parents are an important part of a 'good childhood'.

The aim of this chapter is to depict the main features of change in informal care and to show how these changes can partially be explained by changes in welfare state policies on the one hand, and by cultural values on the other, which interact in different ways in different welfare states.

In addition, it points to the contradictory nature of care arrangements in private households.

DEVELOPMENT OF INFORMAL CARE

The relationship between formal and informal 'care' receives widespread attention in international comparative social policy research nowadays. The degree to which the formalisation of childcare and care of the elderly has advanced – which is usually measured by the extent of paid involvement on the part of women and the public infrastructure for childcare – is regarded as the key indicator of 'women-friendliness' in welfare states (e.g. Siim 2000). Formal and informal care work are often seen as opposites. Formalised 'care' is classified as modern and women-friendly because it relieves women of care work in the home, while informal childcare and care for the elderly tend to suggest backwardness and the social exclusion of those who provide it (see also Cousins 1998). Hence, informal care work is linked to the traditional model of the housewife marriage and is essentially characterised by the fact that it is unpaid, takes place in the family household out of the public eye and results in the marginalisation or exclusion of those who provide it. In contrast, paid work is seen as the core of social integration and is also seen as the key factor determining social recognition, the earning of income and the acquisition of prestige.

In this way informal care work is associated with traditional backwardness and is regarded as a relic of housewife marriage and the male breadwinner family model. That is why those family policy instruments that are intended to assist those who provide informal care work also tend to be regarded as backward and as obstacles on the road towards equality of the sexes (Hofaecker 2003; Leira 2002).

However, the conceptual dualism of formal and informal care work does not really do justice to the processes of change. After all, some informal care work has taken place in an intermediate area and has resulted in an erosion of the boundary between the two types of work. Therefore it is necessary to analyse the different developments and reciprocal relationships with regard to formal and informal care work in the context of welfare state policies on the one hand, and cultural attitudes towards childhood on the other.

There are essentially three main trajectories in the development of informal care (Figure 7.1). All involve a formalisation of 'care': (1) a shift towards the area of formal paid work, (2) the creation of new semi-formal types of paid care work, and (3) a 'commodification' of care without it having been formalised in the form of undeclared work.

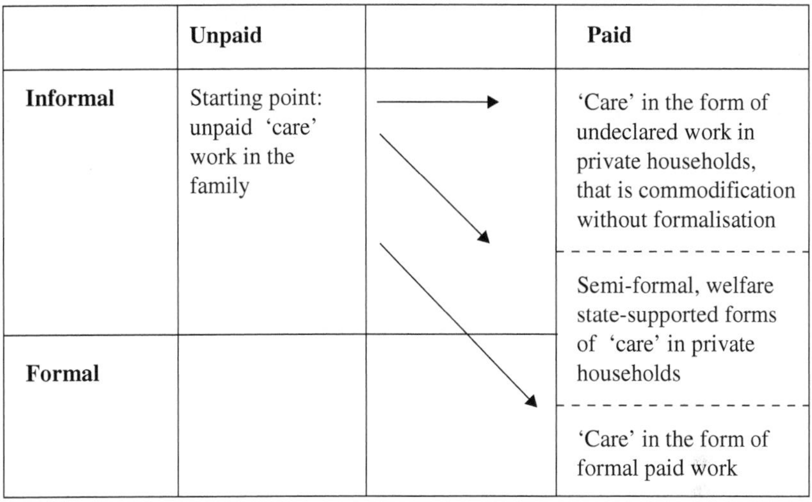

	Unpaid		Paid
Informal	Starting point: unpaid 'care' work in the family		'Care' in the form of undeclared work in private households, that is commodification without formalisation
			Semi-formal, welfare state-supported forms of 'care' in private households
Formal			'Care' in the form of formal paid work

Figure 7.1   Trends of change in unpaid care work

Formalisation of Informal Work and Changes in the Welfare Mix

In the system of formal paid work, large proportions of childcare and care of the elderly have been organised as part of the social services sector, or the education and healthcare sectors, and often professionalised on the basis of occupational training courses. In this way care work has been transferred from the family household to institutions outside the family and thus made visible (Geissler 2002). The processes taking place may not all run in the same direction, thus care may become both more formalised and more informal at the same time, although this kind of development has not predominated so far, at least with regard to developments in Western Europe.

New Semi-formal Types

Nevertheless, a substantial proportion of informal care work is still being provided by parents and caregiving relatives in private households, essentially by women. The nature of the gendered division of paid and unpaid work and hence also the amount of informal carework varies considerably in a comparison of Western European countries (EC 1998). The informal work now performed by parents and relatives is to some extent different from when it was integrated in the traditional housewife marriage. New, welfare state-supported forms have come into being, which I refer to as 'semi-formal' types of work (Pfau-Effinger 2001, 2005a). They are based on a new connection between the caring/nursing relationship in the family and the welfare state. Examples are 'parental leave' and the 'nursing care insurance scheme' in the German welfare state. Parental leave is based on release from the duties of an employment contract or from the obligation to take on work in the case of those receiving state transfer payments. In the German parental leave arrangement, parental work is often financed by state subsidies, which may be a kind of compensation (as in the German nursing care insurance scheme), a subsistence allowance (as during the parental period), or a substitute for income (as in the case of parental leave in Norway and Sweden, for example). In addition, caregivers are usually integrated into the social security systems in some way. Entitlements in the case of parental leave are always designed to be temporary, for a limited period of care, while in the case of nursing care they usually cover the remainder of the patient's life.

In addition, the social importance of this type of work has also changed – nowadays it tends to be defined as part of a temporary phase in the life of the parent, which is oriented mainly towards paid work. General reference to care work provided by parents and relatives within the family as being 'unpaid' and 'informal' has thus effectively become obsolete.

Commodification Without Formalisation

In many countries there is also a growing tendency for middle-class households to employ domestic staff, who support the family in handling the 'care' responsibilities. This often involves unemployed women or female migrants who tend to be socially marginalised and who are employed as cheap, flexible labour to solve the problems of reconciling the family and paid work (Hillmann 2005). This care work is undeclared, which means that it is paid but not formally known to the authorities. The conversion from unpaid informal work to paid informal work in the form of undeclared employment can also be termed 'commodification'; that is, inclusion in the market without formalisation.

THE IMPORTANCE OF WELFARE STATE POLICIES: NEW SOCIAL RIGHTS

The changes in welfare state policies with regard to 'care' have had a major contribution in changing and transforming care (Geissler 1997; Lewis 1992, 1998; Lewis and Ostner 1994; Ostner 1998; Pfau-Effinger 1999; Sainsbury 1994).

Changes in welfare state policies have exerted considerable influence in determining the importance of formalisation processes and new semi-formal types of care work. Policies have responded to the transition in family structures and their cultural basis by tending to adopt an 'adult worker model' (Lewis 2002, 2003), and also a new type of social rights has been established for parents and children (Pfau-Effinger 2005a; Pfau-Effinger and Geissler 2005).

The term 'social rights' originates from the theory proposed by T.H. Marshall (1950) concerning the historical development of citizenship. In this context the history of modern societies is regarded as a process during the course of which people have been able to expand their civil, political and, finally, social rights. Social rights, which were established during development of the welfare states in the second half of the twentieth century, were linked to paid work and provided employees with social security during those periods when they would not be in paid work ('decommodification', according to Esping-Andersen 1990, 1999).

Within the scope of recent welfare state restructuring, new types of social rights have been established that are no longer primarily oriented towards paid work but towards 'care', in response to the changes in family structures and their cultural basis (Knijn and Kremer 1997). The basic principles can be described as follows:

1. *Social rights to claim for childcare or care of the elderly*: First there is the social right of children or of parents to public childcare or publicly financed childcare and a corresponding expansion of the public infra-structure. Generally speaking, one view, which constitutes part of the 'European model', is that childcare – like education – is a public good so it falls within the responsibility of the welfare state, or of the non-profit organisations appointed and financed by the state. In the UK, the only country that has historically left childcare up to the market, the state has recently also begun to finance more childcare with public funds. A comprehensive range of public childcare is a key requirement for enabling women and parents to engage in paid work to the extent they desire.

2. *Social rights to care for one's own children in one's own household on a temporary basis*: In the housewife marriage women took responsibility for childcare in the private family household on an unpaid, 'hidden' basis, and were not expected to participate in the labour market. Changes in family structures and culture, however, have led to new social rights becoming established in connection with the informal childcare provided by parents. These are rights to temporary release from existing employment for parents, the beginnings of payment for

parental work and its integration into social security systems. Consequently, family childcare has been made visible and recognised by
society as a type of 'work'. This can also be interpreted as the welfare
state extending the predominant notion of 'work' beyond paid work.

On balance, welfare state policies reflect cultural trends in the population,
but they may either lag behind cultural transitions or attempt to influence
them (Pfau-Effinger 2005a). All in all, it is evident that in the recent politics of Western European welfare states a 'dual' path of change towards
childcare policies has been chosen, in which both types of social rights – to
childcare provision and to leave – have been considerably extended
(Hofaecker 2003; Pfau-Effinger 2005a; Pfau-Effinger and Geissler 2005;
Ungerson 2005). As a result, options have also been created for parents,
enabling them to choose between different types of childcare. The options
available are maximised when, on the one hand, the supply of public childcare and its quality are high, and when, on the other hand, parents' social
rights to provide temporary childcare in their own household are such that
care providers retain their right to re-enter the labour market and are
financially independent while they engage in 'active care'. The extension of
social rights has been largest in Scandinavian welfare states and in France,
where the two types of entitlement in respect of childcare offer the best
quality, so that parents' options are broadest (Daune-Richard 2005;
Anttonen and Sipilä 2005; Fagnani and Letablier 2005; Pfau-Effinger
2004a, 2005b). In the conservative welfare regimes of continental Europe,
there are signs of a general trend towards the much more highly developed
care policies of the social democratic model.

At this point brief mention should be made of the fact that with regard
to the second type of social rights – to provide care in one's own home on a
temporary basis – some welfare states have also established separate rights
for fathers ('daddy months') because programmes that are formulated neu-
trally in terms of gender have proved to be relatively ineffective in securing
gender equality. In the Scandinavian welfare states, reserving a portion of
parental leave for use by the father has contributed to a significant rise in the
involvement of fathers in family childcare (Eydal 2005).

Thus a new type of parent or relative has emerged: someone who looks
after his or her own children (or nurses elderly relatives) in his or her own
home, is released from paid employment, full time or part time, receives
some kind of payment and is integrated into the social security system in
some way.

Within the family household the responsibilities for care work have
started to be redistributed between women and men, but the extent of
men's involvement in this work varies considerably in an international

comparison. Nowhere does it even approximately reach the number of hours that women spend on this work (Blossfeld and Drobnic 2001; Künzler et al. 1999).

THE IMPORTANCE OF CULTURAL MODELS FOR A 'GOOD CHILDHOOD' WITH REGARD TO INFORMAL CHILDCARE

The fact that informal childcare is still as or more important than formal childcare provision in a fair number of European countries can be explained not only by welfare state policies but also by cultural models as to what constitutes a 'good childhood' in each country. These have a specific relationship with the general attitudes towards women's paid work, which are sometimes contradictory. This in turn influences the way in which care policies differ internationally and contributes to the fact that different behaviour patterns for mothers and parents in dealing with informal care exist in countries with similar policies and political instruments.

In the 1950s and 1960s the family model of the housewife marriage provided the cultural basis for the organisation of the family and 'care' in most European societies (although certainly not in all; Pfau-Effinger 2004b). The model was based on the assumption of a fundamental separation of the 'private' sphere from the 'public' sphere and a complementary positioning of the two genders in the two spheres. The public sphere of paid work was regarded as the husband's place, while the wife was regarded as responsible for the private household and the tasks of childcare (and care of the elderly), financially protected by her husband's income. This involved certain notions of what a 'good childhood' should be.

These notions prompted the idea that caring by parents/family members in the private household was the type of care work that would guarantee the best quality of care, because it was provided out of a feeling of responsibility and moral obligation, rather than on the basis of financial interest.

This model has increasingly been replaced by a new, modernised family model based on the concept of involving both genders in paid work. Jane Lewis describes this new model as the 'adult worker model' (Lewis 2002, 2003). However, it does not wholly correlate with a shift in cultural models with regard to what is believed to make a 'good childhood'. In a number of countries the majority of the population believe that children should be cared for by a parent at home, usually the mother, at least so long as they are pre-schoolers. Table 7.1 indicates that a majority of the population in some European countries still feels that employment for the mothers of pre-school children runs counter to children's well-being. At the same time,

Table 7.1   Attitudes towards the well-being of pre-school children and waged work of mothers

	A pre-school child is likely to suffer if his or her mother works (strongly agree/agree)	Work is best for women's independence (strongly agree/agree)
Austria	64.6	82.1
Switzerland	58.9	77.4
Poland	56.8	75.3
West Germany	55.6	77.7
Spain	52.2	80.4
France	42.4	80.7
Netherlands	39.8	56.8
Great Britain	38.4	55.3
East Germany	32.7	83.8
Denmark	31.4	80.2
Sweden	23.7	62.5

Source: ISSP (2002).

however, the majority of the population everywhere hold the opinion that paid work by women is essential for their independence. The majority of the population in all countries expect mothers of pre-school children to make compromises with regard to their paid work in the interests of their children, by remaining at home temporarily, working part-time, or combining the two.[1]

In the first six countries in Table 7.1, more than 40 per cent of respondents think that 'a pre-school child is likely to suffer if his or her mother works', yet at the same time, a large majority of the respondents in these countries believe that waged work 'is best for women's independence'.[2] Clearly, consideration for the well-being of children conflicts with attitudes about what is necessary to secure women's quality of life. What most people expect, therefore, is that mothers' behaviour will somehow balance the needs of children with waged work.

On the other hand, there is a group of countries that includes East Germany, Denmark and Sweden,[3] where less than one third of the population believe that a pre-school child suffers when the mother is employed, and there is therefore little conflict between ideas regarding what best promotes children's and women's welfare.[4] We know from other studies that in countries where conflict is particularly pronounced mothers will tend to take extended family leave and be employed part time. Where conflict is low, mothers tend to work full time. Only in Poland among the first group of six countries in Table 7.1 is part-time work for mothers relatively rarely regarded as a solution, which might be due to the relatively low average household incomes and the tradition of mothers being employed full time.

There is an interesting pair of countries that fall somewhere between these two groups with regard to ideas about children's well-being: Great Britain and the Netherlands. In these countries, the proportion of respondents who believe that a pre-school child suffers when its mother actively pursues waged work is lower than in the first group and higher than in the third group. However, this view does not conflict to the same degree with attitudes about the well-being of mothers as is the case in many other countries, because the proportion of those who think that waged work is particularly important for the independence of women is lowest in these two countries.

The notions of a 'good childhood' play an important role with regard to the differences between the pattern of relatively continuous full-time paid work for mothers/parents on the one hand, and either paid work based on a lengthy interruption in employment or part-time employment for mothers/fathers, on the other. Other dimensions that differ in the new family models are financial autonomy and financial dependence of care providers, and the role of fathers with regard to childcare.

Broadly, there are three new cultural models used as family models:

1. *Dual breadwinner/external care model*: This model predominates in countries such as Denmark, Finland, Sweden (where although part-time work for mothers plays a major role, the number of hours worked is only slightly less than full-time employment), France and post-socialist countries such as East Germany and Poland.
2. *Male breadwinner/female part-time care provider model*: This model predominates in countries such as West Germany and the UK.
3. *Dual breadwinner/dual care provider model*: This model predominates at the cultural level in the Netherlands and in Norway, even though in practice a male breadwinner/female part-time care provider model prevails.

In countries where models 2 and 3 predominate the modernised model for the phase of 'active motherhood' provides for a – more or less lengthy – interruption to employment, and after that part-time work for mothers because it is believed that a 'good childhood' is best guaranteed by at least partial family care. However, even in countries with a dual breadwinner/external care provider model more or less lengthy family leave for the mother is regarded as important for a 'good' childhood.

In all countries the predominant model more or less offers a combination of informal childcare by parents and external childcare provision, but in

Caring for children

very different combinations and with different points of emphasis. Formal childcare is usually provided by the public sector, although in the UK the market plays an important part in the provision of care and in Southern European and Eastern European countries such as Spain and Poland, extended family networks are important (Pfau-Effinger et al. 2005).

More than one model can exist in a country. For example, Switzerland is divided approximately between the German-speaking area, where a male breadwinner/female part-time care provider model predominates, and the French-speaking area, where a dual breadwinner/state care model predominates (Buehler 2002; Pfau-Effinger 2006). In Germany there is a split between the dominance of a male breadwinner/female part-time provider model in West Germany, and a dual breadwinner/state care model in East Germany.

A historical, comparative study has demonstrated that these differences tend to be path dependent. In Western Europe alone (except for the Mediterranean countries) there are two different paths of family development and two different cultural models of a 'good childhood', the roots of which go far back in history (Pfau-Effinger 2004b). In countries where a good childhood is held to depend in large measure on care provided by the mother at home, we find ideas about the importance of a 'private' childhood, the roots of which are historically embedded and are associated with the cultural predominance of the housewife marriage model, which is most likely to guarantee this type of childhood.

However, today the cultural importance of care work provided by parents in the private household differs from that of the informal care provided within the traditional housewife marriage, amounting to a new concept of active parenthood for a specified period in an adult life that is otherwise devoted to paid work. Indeed, the time that parents spend with their children is regarded not so much as a duty but as an important part of self-fulfilment.

West Germany as an Example

West Germany is a good example of this modernised model of informal care. Children have gained in importance for the lives of their parents. Parents have significant expectations that their children will bring them personal happiness, and children are of central importance within a family. The relationship is regarded as unique since, by contrast with other social relationships, it cannot be terminated. Bühler-Niederberger (1999) argue that children are given a value that is primarily associated with fulfilment in life, with the meaning of life, with personal hopes concerning happiness, and also with symbolic prolongation of one's own existence. This, however, also involves higher demands on parental care and solicitude:

The idea propagated by the public, and also by science, that for their emotional and cognitive well-being children require constant attention, stimulation, and socialisation, contributes to parents' desire to take care of their children more intensively than ever before, especially younger ones. (Schutze 1988, p. 104)[5]

This also increases the demands placed on parents' time, usually on the mother. It seems paradoxical that while the role of the housewife and mother has lost its social appreciation, esteem for children and the demands on mothers have increased significantly.

Part-time work enables mothers to be gainfully employed without giving up their fundamental responsibility for their children. A shift towards temporary part-time employment with pro-rata entitlement to social security benefits was therefore a major component of modernising the cultural model of the family and gender arrangements during the transition to a service society (see Pfau-Effinger and Geissler 1992, 2002). But mothers' decisions to interrupt employment and work part time for a shorter or longer period were also influenced by institutional factors, such as inconvenient opening hours of kindergartens and schools.

The results in Table 7.2 show the extent to which preferences for modernised cultural models of motherhood and childhood underpin the widespread orientation of women towards part-time employment.

Despite all the burdens, women seem to have hopes for personal gains from a lifestyle in which they have an individualised existence in the

Table 7.2   Working time preferences in formal employment according to the age of children in West Germany (in per cent)

	Small children (below 3 years)	Pre-school children (3–6 years)	Children at elementary school (6–10 years)
Both partners full time	7	5	6
Both partners not employed full time but more than half time	9	9	9
Both partners half time	7	6	9
One partner employed full time, the other half time	63	64	65
One partner employed full time, the other not employed	14	16	11

Source: Engelbrech and Jungkunst (2001) (Representative attitude survey by the Institut für Arbeitsmarkt- und Berufsforschung, Bundesanstalt für Arbeit 2001, Adults 18–68 years old).

working world and a care role in respect of their children and the family. As Table 7.2 shows, even at the beginning of the twenty-first century the most popular cultural model of the family is based on marriage between a male breadwinner and a female part-time carer. In all age groups of children up to 10 years only a small proportion of the respondents preferred a model with both partners working full time. The traditional housewife model did not receive much support either. Instead, the majority opted for a model of one partner being employed full time (usually the man), while the other works part time (usually the woman).

Cultural change has also affected men and there are indications that critical economic developments and changes in companies' employment policies have led to an erosion of the standard male career biography. However, this development has resulted in men focusing more on their children and on childcare only to a very limited extent (see Künzler et al. 1999).

CONTRADICTIONS IN CARE ARRANGEMENTS AND THE ROLE OF UNDECLARED WORK

The provision of informal care work often takes place in a complex area of conflict. It is frequently characterised by contradictions between mothers' belief in and wish to pursue the ideal of a 'good childhood' on the one hand, and their own paid work on the other. In many cases it also takes place in a network of tensions or conflicts between various institutions, between demands made by the family and the employment system on the one hand and between the family and welfare state mechanisms on the other. Insofar as informal care is practised within a male breadwinner model, there are also contradictions because informal care is underpinned by the woman's financial dependence on her husband, who, according to the principle of family subsidiarity, is held to be responsible for earning a living. However, this concept contradicts the model of personal autonomy, which is of key importance to post-industrial society. In my opinion it is not sufficient to describe this area of conflict in terms of 'reconciling family and work' or 'work life balance'.

In the welfare regimes other than the social democratic states, households with small children are in many respects left alone to manage as best they can, even though considerably more legislative change has taken place in all these welfare states. Private households often endeavour to solve their problems related to childcare by using close family networks. Undeclared work also plays a crucial role in bridging the gap between family and employment. Cross-national comparative research has indicated that this strategy is common in middle-class households in Poland, Spain, Great

Britain and Germany.[6] Undeclared work helps to bridge the gap between the time demands of the employment system on the one hand and the limitations of the welfare state's childcare services on the other. In countries such as West Germany, where the role of the mother as a caregiver for her own children is given considerable weight culturally, undeclared work is sometimes used more to reduce the burden of domestic chores than that of childcare. There are some indications that this type of undeclared work in private households has increased because a large pool of labour has been created as a result of both mass unemployment and the arrival of immigrants without a work permit, who are unable or unwilling to work in the formal labour market.

By contrast, undeclared work in private households is very uncommon in the childcare and domestic work sector in Scandinavian countries. The difference can be explained by two factors in particular. First, the public childcare services are much more comprehensive and flexible in these countries, and are supplemented by free or low-cost municipal childminder services that parents can fall back on. Second, there is no established personal service culture in Scandinavian countries in the context of profoundly egalitarian values, while in other countries this has historical roots. For example, while this cultural tradition was lost in Poland during the communist period, it was relatively easy to establish again in the cultural vacuum after the introduction of the market economy (Pfau-Effinger et al. 2005).[7]

In general it seems that a combination of different types of informal and semi-formal care is part of the new lifestyle of middle-class households, which they adopt to balance their cultural values towards childhood with interests in and commitments to their various activities beyond the household, and as a means of realising their shift towards a dual-earner family model. The main types include informal and semi-formal, state-supported forms of childcare provided by adults in the household, mainly mothers; informal childcare provided in close family networks, mainly by grandparents; and undeclared housework and childcare.

CONCLUSION

Thus informal care has substantially changed in form and significance. In part as a consequence of new welfare state policies, which have established new social rights in relation to care, new semi-formal types of care have been established within private households. In those countries where informal care still plays a substantial role and is supported by welfare state policies, it should not necessarily be seen as a product of a traditional or backward-oriented welfare state policy that hinders the formalisation of social care. Instead, the care policies of welfare states have developed in such a way as to reflect the fact that informal care also plays an important role in the modernised cultural concept of childhood, the family and gender equality. However, informal and semi-formal care takes place in a field of contradictory cultural values and in institutional contexts which mean that it is precarious. The development of high-quality social rights associated with informal care, in addition to social rights associated with extensive, flexible public care provision, are of major importance for 'progressive' care policy.

NOTES

1. Unfortunately, the questions in the ISSP are relatively vague concerning the time span for which mothers of pre-school children should stay at home and/or work part time. The period may vary between two months after the birth of a child and five years in different countries. Such differences are particularly important when explaining cross-national differences in the labour market behaviour of women.
2. However, we do not know how the value of 'independence' is generally weighted in relation to values that stress social bonds. Independence might generally be of less importance as a value in societies where social integration is still strongly based on family networks and where individualisation is not so strongly developed, e.g. in Spain and Poland.
3. East Germany is included here as a different type of society because it experienced a very different development with regard to the culture and structure of the family until the beginning of the 1990s (see Pfau-Effinger and Geissler 2002).
4. In Sweden, there is even less contradiction since the share of those who think that work is important for women's independence is considerably lower than in the other two countries (62 per cent in Sweden compared to 80.2 in Denmark and 83.8 in East Germany). This can be explained by the fact that parents who are temporary care providers in Sweden are often financially independent because parental leave schemes have relatively high rates of compensation.
5. The original reads: Die durch die Öffentlichkeit und nicht zuletzt die Wissenschaft propagierte Idee, daß das Kind für sein emotionales und kognitives Gedeihen ständiger Zuwendung, Anregung und kindgerechter Umfangsformen bedarf, wirkt als verstärkendes Moment, sich intensiver denn je mit den Kindern, vor allem den jüngeren, zu beschäftigen.
6. 'Formal and Informal Work in Europe. A Comparative Analysis of their Changing Relationship and their Contribution to Social Integration', EU FP5 Programme, coordinated by the author.
7. The basis in each case was 35 partially structured interviews in middle-class households with children below the age of six in major cities and their suburban regions in Finland, Denmark, Great Britain, Germany, Poland and Spain.

REFERENCES

Anttonen, A. and J. Sipilä (2005), 'Comparative approaches to social care: diversity in care production modes', in B. Pfau-Effinger and B. Geissler (eds), *Care and Social Integration in Europe*, Bristol: Policy Press.

Blossfeld, H.-P. and S. Drobnic (eds) (2001), *Careers of Couples in Contemporary Society. From Male Breadwinner to Dual Earner Families*, Oxford: Oxford University Press.

Buehler, E. (2002), *Frauen- und Gleichstellungsatlas Schweiz. Reihe 'Gesellschaft Schweiz'*, Zürich: Seismo Verlag.

Bühler-Niederberger, D. (1999), 'Minorität und moralische Instanz – der öffentliche Entwurf von Kindern', *Zeitschrift für Soziologie der Erziehung und Sozialisation*, **19**, 128–50.

Cousins, C. (1998), 'Social exclusion in Europe: paradigms of social disadvantage in Germany, Spain, Sweden and the United Kingdom', *Policy and Politics*, **26**(2), 127–46.

Daune-Richard, A. (2005), 'Women's work between family and welfare state: part-time work and childcare in France and Sweden', in B. Pfau-Effinger and B. Geissler (eds), *Care and Social Integration in Europe*, Bristol: Policy Press.

Engelbrech, G. and M. Jungkunst (2001), *Erwerbsbeteiligung von Frauen: Wie bringt man Beruf und Kinder unter einen Hut?*, IAB-Kurzbericht 7, Nürnberg: Institut für Arbeitsmarkt- und Berufsforschung.

Esping-Andersen, G. (1990), *The Three Worlds of Welfare Capitalism*, Cambridge: Polity Press.

Esping-Andersen, G. (1999), *Social Foundations of Postindustrial Economies*, Oxford: Oxford University Press.

European Commission (EC) (1998), *Care in Europe. Joint Report of the 'Gender and Employment' and the 'Gender and Law' Groups of Experts*, Brussels: European Commission.

Eydal, G.B. (2005), 'Child care policies of the Nordic welfare states. Equal rights of mothers and fathers to parental leave in Iceland', in B. Pfau-Effinger and B. Geissler (eds), *Care and Social Integration in Europe*, Bristol: Policy Press.

Fagnani, J. and M.T. Letablier (2005), 'Social rights and care responsibility in the French welfare state', in B. Pfau-Effinger and B. Geissler (eds), *Care and Social Integration in Europe*, Bristol: Policy Press.

Geissler, B. (1997), 'Netz oder Sieb? Generationenkonflikt und Geschlechterkonflikt in der aktuellen Krise des Sozialstaats', *Kritische Justiz*, **1**(30), 1–14.

Geissler, B. (2002), 'Die (Un-)Abhängigkeit in der Ehe und das Bürgerrecht auf care. Überlegungen zur gender-Gerechtigkeit im Wohlfahrtsstaat', in K. Gottschall and B. Pfau-Effinger (eds), *Zukunft der Arbeit und Geschlecht*, Opladen: Leske und Budrich.

Hillmann, F. (2005), 'Migrants' care working private households, or the strength of bilocal and transnational ties as a last(ing) resource in global migration', in B. Pfau-Effinger and B. Geissler (eds), *Care and Social Integration in Europe*, Bristol: Policy Press.

Hofaecker, D. (2003), 'Towards a dual earner model?', Globalife working paper 49, University of Bamberg, Bamberg.

Knijn, T. and M. Kremer (1997), 'Gender and the caring dimension of welfare states: toward inclusive citizenship', *Social Politics*, **5**, 328–61.

Künzler, J, H. Schulze and S. van Hekken (1999), 'Welfare states and normative orientations towards women's employment', in A. Leira (ed.), *Family Change: Practices, Policies and Values. Comparative Social Research*, Vol. 18, Stamford, CT: JAI Press.

Leira, A. (2002), *Working Parents and the Welfare State: Family Change and Policy Reform in Scandinavia*, Cambridge: Cambridge University Press.

Lewis, J. (1992), 'Gender and the development of welfare regimes', *Journal of European Social Policy*, **2**, 159–73.

Lewis, J. (1998), *Gender, Social Care and Welfare State Restructuring in Europe*, Aldershot: Ashgate.

Lewis, J. (2002), 'Gender and welfare state change', *European Societies*, **4**(4), 331–58.

Lewis, J. (2003), 'Erwerbstätigkeit versus Betreuungsarbeit', in U. Gerhard, T. Knijn and A. Weckwert (eds), *Erwerbstätige Mütter. Ein europäischer Vergleich*, Munich: C.H. Beck.

Lewis, J. and I. Ostner (1994), 'Gender and the evolution of European social policy', Centre for Social Policy Research working paper 4, University of Bremen.

Marshall, T. (1950), 'Citizenship and social class', reprinted in T.H. Marshall and T. Bottomore (1992), *Citizenship and Social Class*, London: Pluto Press.

Ostner, I. (1998), 'The politics of care policies in Germany', in J. Lewis (ed.), *Gender, Social Care and Welfare State Restructuring in Europe*, Aldershot: Ashgate.

Pfau-Effinger, B. (1999), 'Change of family policies in the socio-cultural context of European Societies', *Comparative Social Research*, **18**, 135–69.

Pfau-Effinger, B. (2001), 'Wandel wohlfahrtsstaatlicher Geschlechterpolitiken im soziokulturellen Kontext', *Kölner Zeitschrift für Soziologie und Sozialpsychologie*, **41**, 488–511.

Pfau-Effinger, B. (2004a), *Development of Culture, Welfare States and Women's Employment in Europe*, Aldershot: Ashgate.

Pfau-Effinger, B. (2004b), 'Historical paths of the male breadwinner family model – explanation for cross-national differences', *British Journal for Sociology*, **55**(3), 177–99.

Pfau-Effinger, B. (2005a), 'Welfare state policies and development of care arrangements', *European Societies*, **7**(3), 321–47.

Pfau-Effinger, B. (2005b), 'Culture and welfare state policies: reflections on a complex interrelation', *Journal of Social Policy*, **34**(1), 1–18.

Pfau-Effinger, B. (2006), 'Care im Wandel des wohlfahrtsstaatlichen Solidaritätsmodells – Deutschland und die Schweiz im Vergleich', in E. Carigiet, U. Mäder, M. Opielka and F. Schulz-Nieswand (eds), *Wohlstand durch Gerechtigkeit? Deutschland und die Schweiz im sozialpolitischen Vergleich*, Zürich: Rotpunkt Verlag.

Pfau-Effinger, B. and B. Geissler (1992), 'Institutionelle und sozio-kulturelle Kontextbedingungen der Entscheidung verheirateter Frauen für Teilzeitarbeit. Ein Beitrag zu einer Soziologie des Erwerbsverhaltens', *Mitteilungen aus der Arbeitsmarkt- und Berufsforschung*, **25**, 358–70.

Pfau-Effinger, B. and B. Geissler (2002), 'Cultural change and family policies in East and West Germany', in A. Carling, S.S. Duncan and R. Edwards (eds), *Analysing Families: Morality and Rationality in Policy and Practice*, London & New York: Routledge.

Pfau-Effinger, B. and B. Geissler (2005), 'Change of European care arrangements', in B. Pfau-Effinger and B. Geissler (eds), *Care and Social Integration in Europe*, Bristol: Policy Press.

Pfau-Effinger, B., S. Sakac-Magdalenic and A. Schüttpelz (2005), 'Formal and informal work in Europe: a comparative analysis of their changing relationship and their impact on social integration', final report of the 5th EU Framework Programme research project FIWE, contract no. HPSE-CT-2002-00126, University of Hamburg, Hamburg.

Sainsbury, D. (ed.) (1994), *Gendering Welfare States*, London: Sage.

Sainsbury, D. (1996), *Gender Equality and Welfare States*, Cambridge: Cambridge University Press.

Schutze, Yvonne (1998), 'Zur Veraenderung in Eltern-Kind-Verhaeltnis Seit der Nachkriegzeit', in R. Nave-Herz (ed.), *Wandel und Kontinuitaet der Familie in der Bundesrepublik Deutschland*, Stuttgart: Enke.

Siim, B. (2000), *Gender and Citizenship: Politics and Agency in France, Britain and Denmark*, Cambridge: Cambridge University Press.

Ungerson, C. (2005), 'Gender, labour markets and care work in five European funding regimes', in B. Pfau-Effinger and B. Geissler (eds), *Care and Social Integration in European Societies*, Bristol: Policy Press.

8.   From a childcare to a pedagogical discourse – or putting care in its place

Peter Moss

'Childcare' is high on the social policy agenda in many countries and with many international organisations. One of the most striking features of the New Labour government that swept to power in the United Kingdom in May 1997 was its ready espousal of a strong public policy discourse of childcare, following decades of official indifference or distaste. In March 2002, the European Union, at a presidency Conference in Barcelona, agreed that 'Member States [should strive] to provide childcare by 2010 to at least 90% of children between 3 years old and mandatory school age and at least 33% of children under 3 years of age' (European Council of Ministers 2002). Yet at the same time that many countries are grappling with how to increase the availability of 'childcare' and with where 'childcare' fits within the welfare state, a second transition is occurring in a number of countries: what I would term a move from a 'childcare discourse' to a 'pedagogical discourse'; an attempt to move beyond childcare as a way of conceptualising and structuring policy to a broader concept – pedagogy or education in its broadest sense – and a set of structures that integrate a range of policy objectives.

In this chapter, I consider these two discourses in more detail, going back to the origins of the childcare discourse and considering examples of countries that have adopted – conceptually and structurally – a pedagogical discourse. I look in more detail at one country, the United Kingdom, currently in the throes of attempting a transition, a process that illuminates some of the obstacles to change in 'liberal' welfare regimes. I also reflect on the concept of care in policy and provision for children, in particular when it no longer forms a distinct field for policy, provision and practice: does moving to a pedagogical discourse mean throwing care out with the childcare bathwater?

Central, then, to my argument is that the current heightened interest in many countries in services for children, exemplified by widespread policy attention to 'childcare', raises issues that go beyond responsibility, delivery and technical practice. It also provokes, or should do so, critical political and ethical questions about meaning and understanding. What do we mean by 'care' and 'education'? How do we understand – socially construct – institutions for children and families? What is our image of the child? And permeating the whole area, though not often acknowledged, is the question of instrumentality. Welfare states and their institutions for children will always be concerned with governing through the achievement of predetermined outcomes and goals. But to what extent can and should they go beyond a narrow, calculative relationship between means and ends? Do they recognise, value and enable unanticipated possibilities? Do they leave space for the unexpected and for experimentation, for wonder, amazement, joy, enthusiasm and passion? Can they go beyond envisaging children primarily as vehicles for investment in the future – the image of a redemptive agent – to also seeing them as people living an important part of life? (For further discussion of these questions and issues, see Dahlberg et al. 1999 and Dahlberg and Moss 2005.)

This chapter focuses on early childhood services, that is for children below compulsory school age. What I do not have space to consider is the larger issue of the relationship between compulsory schooling and 'school-age childcare' (another part of the childcare discourse) and what a pedagogical discourse might mean for this relationship. Nor is there space to consider another relationship brought to prominence by the development of early childhood services – the relationship between these services and the compulsory school. While policy in many countries today dwells on the theme of how early childhood services can 'prepare children for school', and one rationale for the expansion of early childhood services is because of their supposed benefit to school performance, some voices question this relationship.

The first report of a major review of early childhood education and care (ECEC) by the Organisation for Economic Co-operation and Development (OECD) expresses concerns about 'a risk that increased co-operation between schools and ECEC could lead to a school-like approach to the organisation of early childhood provision'. The report adds that 'downward pressure on ECEC to adopt the content and methods of the primary school has a detrimental effect on young children's learning'. Instead it urges the development of a 'strong and equal partnership', in which 'early childhood is viewed not only as a preparation for the next stage of education (or even adulthood), but also as a distinctive period where children live out their lives' (OECD 2001, p. 129). (In the light of Mahon's discussion in Chapter 9 in this volume about the two faces of the OECD, this should be considered *a* voice of OECD, not *the* voice.)

What that partnership might look like and how schools as well as early childhood services might need to change to achieve it are important questions. So as well as the relationship between care and education in early childhood, which is the focus of this chapter, other relationships between institutions for children are increasingly at issue within the welfare state, as well as how these institutions are structured, delivered and understood.

SPLIT SYSTEMS: A NINETEENTH-CENTURY LEGACY

The so-called developed world has recently faced growing demand both for more childcare and for more early education, experienced by different countries at different times since the 1960s. In determining how to respond, they have had to start from a widespread legacy of the nineteenth-century origins of formal early childhood services: one set of services developed for the care of children of poor working families (nurseries, crèches) and another set of services for the education of children of middle-class families (kindergartens, nursery schools). Today, that legacy is still apparent in the split systems found in many countries, in which services for young children are divided between 'childcare' services, usually located in the welfare system, and 'early education' services, usually located in the education system. Each system has its own rationale, principles and distinctive structures including different types of provision, funding, staffing and admission criteria.

Within split systems, there are some differences in the balance between 'childcare' and 'early education'. In systems with universal full-time nursery schooling spanning at least three years (France being a classic example), the early education system dominates. While in other systems (the USA or the UK being good examples), where nursery education is less extensive because of lower coverage and/or shorter periods of attendance, childcare services have relatively more significance.

Even in still split systems, the rigid distinction between childcare and education has been breaking down to some degree. 'Childcare' services are recognised as having some developmental or educational functions; while some children attending nursery school are recognised to need childcare, this 'out of school childcare' – also for older children – being mostly provided on school sites (Petrie 2003). Yet the split systems remain in place, apparent both conceptually and structurally. Indeed, the extent to which they dominate becomes even more apparent when contrasted with those countries that have gone beyond the 'childcare discourse' to a 'pedagogical discourse', or else are well into the transition process. But before considering some examples, I need to define what I mean by these two discourses.

THE CHILDCARE AND THE PEDAGOGICAL DISCOURSES

The discourse of childcare speaks about the necessity of providing substitute care for children because their parents are unavailable through participation in the labour market. The rationale for childcare is, first and foremost, to enable parental employment, although this may be extended somewhat, for example to promote gender equality in the labour market and to support children and families deemed to be 'in need'. The childcare discourse is most obvious in the recurring suggestion by government (and others) in the UK that employers should support childcare for their employees, encouraged by measures to stimulate employers to assume this role (see HM Treasury 2004, para. 7.20). Such an approach renders a service for children into one of a range of supply side inducements available to employers for ensuring an adequate labour supply.

Despite my use of 'parents' here, the childcare discourse usually assumes that the need for substitute care arises from mothers' employment. This assumption is reproduced by politicians and policymakers, who often refer to 'childcare' being needed because of, or to further encourage, employment among *mothers* rather than, for example, because mothers are joining fathers in the labour market; and by researchers who continue to frame research questions in terms of the consequences for children of *maternal* employment rather than, for example, the consequences for children of various patterns of parental employment (for recent UK examples see Joshi and Verropoulou 2000; Gregg et al. 2005). While the discourse is framed in terms of the needs of parents/mothers, it is often ambivalent in its attitudes towards parental/maternal employment; 'childcare' may be viewed as the lesser of two evils, as a second best to parental/maternal care and best undertaken, if unavoidable, in home-like conditions by carers deemed to be as close as possible to parents/mothers (for example, relatives, childminders). Singer (1993) has referred to this as 'attachment pedagogy', the idea that mother care is needed for secure development and that, in its absence, non-maternal care needs to be modelled on a dyadic mother–child relationship.

This discourse, therefore, is closely linked to wider discourses about the upbringing of children and to the 'maternalist assumption': 'that the mother's primary and natural duty is to look after her child, and that as an extension childcare is and should be a "women's issue"' (Randall 2000, p. 183). It generates a particular set of understandings: of services as substitute homes, meeting a particular need of a particular group of families; of children as 'passive' dependants, placed at risk by the disruption of natural forms of private upbringing; and of workers in services as substitute mothers, who require qualities and competences that are either innate

to women ('maternal instinct') or else are acquired through women's practice of domestic work ('housewife skills'). Within a liberal welfare regime,
'childcare' has further been understood as the commodification of a discrete household task, a private responsibility to be met in the main through
local 'childcare' markets, with a limited state role confined to regulating the
market and facilitating participation.

The 'childcare discourse' takes its most extreme form, constructing
'childcare' services as simply domestic care transferred to the market, in the
perspective of economists and labour market specialists. Anxo and Fagan
(2001), for example, speak in terms of how 'public policies promoting the
development of employment in social services (health, education) and the
*outsourcing of female domestic tasks into the market (childcare in particu-
lar)* may accelerate women's labour market integration by *transferring some
tasks from the domestic sphere to the labour market*' (p. 109, emphasis
added). Early childhood services clearly do have the effect of reducing the
care undertaken by parents by increasing the care given elsewhere; more
contestable, however, is the assumption in the discourse that children's
experience and relationships in early childhood services are equivalent to
those in the home and whether these services should attempt to replicate
the home or create a different though complementary environment.

The 'childcare discourse' is most prominent in liberal, English-speaking
welfare states where, as already suggested, nursery schooling has a less
dominant role than in countries such as France. It is in marked contrast to
what I would term the 'pedagogical discourse', which is most apparent in
the Nordic countries, with their 'social democratic' welfare regimes. This
discourse is about the provision of a service for all young children and families, irrespective of parental employment status. The service is understood
as a complement to, not a substitute for, the home, offering children quali-
tatively different experiences and relationships. The members of the workforce are viewed as reflective and researching practitioners, and as such
many are graduates with a similar status to school teachers. Children are
active subjects and citizens with rights, able to participate with ease and
enjoyment from an early age in both private and public spheres, a view
vividly expressed by Loris Malaguzzi about the experience in the Italian
city of Reggio Emilia, world famous for the pedagogical theory and practice of its early childhood centres for children from birth to six years:[1]

> [The children in Reggio] understood sooner than expected that their adventures
> in life could flow between two places. [In the nurseries] they could express their
> previously overlooked desire to be with their peers and find in them points of ref-
> erence, understanding, surprises, affective ties and merriment that could dispel
> shadows and uneasiness. For the children and their families there now opened
> up the possibility of a very long and continuous period of [children] living

together [with each other], 5 or 6 years of reciprocal trust and work. (Malaguzzi 1993, p. 55)

These services, it is recognised, do provide care for children while their parents are at work: this function is an almost taken for granted requirement in a modern society where parental employment is normative. But in addition they have broader purposes, meeting a wide range of child, parent and community needs, and are for all children and families, irrespective of whether or not parents are in paid work. Rather than a substitute home (or indeed an enclosure for applying technologies to children to achieve predetermined outcomes, another common understanding of services today), they can be viewed as a children's space:

> The concept of 'children's space' does not just imply a physical space, a setting for groups of children. It also carries the meaning of being a social space, 'a domain of social practices and relationships' (Knowles 1999, p. 241); a cultural space, where values, rights and cultures are created; and a discursive space for differing perspectives and forms of expression, where there is room for dialogue, confrontation (in the sense of exchanging differing experience and views), deliberation and critical thinking, where children and others can speak and be heard. (Moss and Petrie 2002, p. 9)

It is this holistic approach to both the child and the public provision that names the discourse pedagogical. Pedagogy is a long-established and strong tradition in Continental Europe but virtually unknown in the English-speaking world where 'pedagogy' is often translated, incorrectly, as 'the science of education' and the 'pedagogue' as 'teacher' (the meanings given, for example, in my Chambers dictionary). Pedagogy is a relational and holistic approach to working with people. The pedagogue sets out 'to address the whole child, the child with body, mind, emotions, creativity, history and social identity. This is not the child only of emotions, the psycho-therapeutical approach, nor only of the body, the medical approach, nor only of the mind, the traditional teaching approach' (Moss and Petrie, 2002, p. 143). For the pedagogue, learning, care and upbringing (*erziehung* in German, a typically pedagogical term) are indivisible activities; these are not distinct fields that must somehow be joined up, but inter-connected facets of life that cannot be envisaged separately. The approach is also broad in another way: pedagogues can work in a range of settings, not just early childhood services (for fuller discussions of pedagogy and the pedagogue see Moss and Petrie 2002; Moss and Korintus 2004).

The profession of pedagogue is perhaps most fully developed in Denmark. Here pedagogues undertake a 3½ year degree course, typically starting in their mid-20s, and are qualified by this education to work, as some put it, with people from birth to 100 years of age (Jensen and Hansen 2003). Indeed, pedagogues are the main group in the workforce across a wide range of areas, including early childhood services, free-time services (school-age childcare), residential child and youth care, other youth services and services for adults with severe disabilities (Jensen and Hansen 2003). Danish pedagogues have considerable scope for mobility, both vertical (for example, into management or training) and horizontal (for example, between working with young children and working with young people or adults) (Moss and Korintus 2004).

A pedagogical discourse, therefore, does not reject the importance of and need for care, but neither does it treat care as a distinct field or commodity. Rather, it treats care as an inseparable part of any work with people, of whatever age or in whatever setting, which cannot be extracted and treated as a separate field of policy, provision or practice or as a commodity that can be packaged and sold on the market. In this it is close to the proposition, informed by feminist scholarship on the ethic of care (see Tronto 1993; Sevenhuijsen 1999), that the place of care in services should be envisaged as an ethic: 'Care as ethic moves us from care as a task performed by adults on children. Rather care is inscribed in all relationships – not only between adults and children (understood as an interactive and reciprocal relationship), but also between adults (parents, workers and others) and between children themselves' (Moss 2003, p. 39).

ADOPTING THE PEDAGOGICAL DISCOURSE: THE FIRST WAVE

The adoption of the pedagogical discourse began earliest and its implementation in practice is most complete in the Nordic countries, in particular Denmark and Sweden.[2] Both have had fully integrated early childhood services for several decades, since the key policy decision was taken in the 1960s to merge separate systems (for a fuller discussion of this process of integration in Sweden and of the previous split system of services, see Holmlund 2003 and Lenz Taguchi and Munkhammar 2003). Both integrated systems now offer an entitlement to a place to all children from about 12 months of age, children before that age being assumed to be at home with parents taking paid leave. Both are administered by one department at national and local levels. Both have a single system of funding, mainly tax-based supply funding, with some parental fees; this entails a major investment of public funds, amounting to about two per cent of GDP (Organisation for Economic Co-operation and Development 2002). Both have a fully integrated workforce, about half of whom are graduates. Also, both have

a decentralised system of administration, which gives considerable autonomy to local authorities and individual institutions with respect to the interpretation of curriculum and more general application of practice.

There are, however, some important distinctions. The Swedish system is
very largely based on one type of provision, an age-integrated centre
(*forskola* or pre-school) for children from 12 months until they start at
school, usually at six years of age. The Danish system has age-integrated
centres, but also age-segregated services, nurseries for children under three
years and kindergartens for children from three to six years, the legacy of
its formerly split system; childminding is also more widespread, especially
for children under three years. But the most striking difference is that
Denmark's integrated early childhood service remains within the welfare
system (as is the case for Finland and Norway), while Sweden's (like
Iceland's) is within education, following transfer from welfare in 1996.
While the possibility of transfer into education was discussed for many
years in Sweden, the rationale for the move when it took place was Sweden's
need as a 'knowledge society' for lifelong learning, with early childhood services as the first step in that process.

The Swedish transfer to education provides an interesting contrast to
England, where 'day-care services' were transferred to education shortly
after in 1998 and which is considered in more detail below (within the UK,
a similar transfer has occurred in Scotland, but not in Northern Ireland or
Wales). The Swedes transferred a system that was already highly developed
and fully integrated, and based on a strong pedagogical tradition: 'for a long
time pre-schools in Sweden had been recognised as having a progressive
pedagogical approach, emphasising play, children's natural learning strategies and their overall holistic development' (Korpi 2005, p. 10). But following transfer, Swedes have built on these foundations by applying educational
principles to the system. Entitlement to provision, already available to
employed and studying parents, was extended to all Swedish children who
now have the right to a place in a pre-school from 12 months of age: the link
with parental employment has been cut. A curriculum was introduced for
pre-schools, spanning the full pre-school age range, a short framework
document similar in orientation to that for compulsory school. A free
period of provision was introduced for four- and five-year-olds and a ceiling
placed on remaining parental fees, as initial steps towards the educational
principle of free attendance (for a fuller account, see Cohen et al. 2004).

In some respects, the most radical post-transfer change concerns the
workforce. Prior to transfer, there were three main professional groups in
pre-schools, schools and *fritids* or free-time services (the Swedish term
for what in England, with its stronger childcare discourse, is termed
'school-age childcare'): respectively pre-school teachers, school teachers

and free-time pedagogues. Each profession had its own identity and separate education, though all were qualified at graduate level. Since 2001,
however, there is one common educational framework for all wanting to
work in these services professionally, comprising 18 months undertaken in
common by all students (whether they plan to work with 18-month-olds or
18-year-olds) and 24 months of specialised courses. Students no longer
have to decide in which field they want to specialise before they enter their
education, but do so once on the course. All qualify as teachers, though
with differing 'profiles' (Johansson 2003).

The transition to a pedagogical discourse in Denmark and Sweden is
not limited only to policymakers and practitioners. It is apparent too
among parents, whose views about upbringing have changed as services
have developed and become established as an integral and well regarded
feature of everyday life. Two Danish researchers describe:

> a tendency [among Danish parents] towards regarding early childhood care and
> education as part of lifelong learning which means that parents more and more
> want their children to attend a childcare facility, not only for the reason that they
> are being taken care of when parents are working, but as a place for play, social-
> isation and community . . . [T]he policy that childcare is an offer to all children
> and not dependent on their parents' attachment to the labour market has meant
> an increase in demand. *It has become more of a cultural norm that children from
> one or two years are attending a public facility.* (Jensen and Hansen 2002, pp. 8,
> 38; emphasis added)

Two Swedish researchers, in a review of recent developments in Sweden,
describe a similar process in their country:

> [D]uring the 1990s, early childhood education and care became the first choice
> for most working and studying parents. . . . Enrolling children from age one in
> full-day pre-schools has become generally acceptable. What was once viewed as
> either a privilege of the wealthy for a few hours a day or an institution for needy
> children and single mothers has become, after 70 years of political vision and
> policy making, *an unquestionable right* of children and families. Furthermore,
> parents now expect a *holistic pedagogy* that includes health care, nurturing and
> education for their pre-schoolers . . . [A]cceptance of full-day pre-schooling and
> schooling has complemented the idea of lifelong learning and the understand-
> ing of education as encompassing far more than imparting basic skills such as
> reading, writing and mathematics. (Lenz Taguchi and Munkhammar 2003,
> p. 27; emphasis added)

As this shows, moving beyond the childcare discourse to a pedagogical discourse means a fundamental shift in understanding by all involved, not
only of the role and purposes of services, but also of upbringing, childhood
and parenthood. It also involves a conceptualisation of all services as

public goods, akin to schools, and, as such, a universal entitlement. Last, but not least, moving beyond childcare frees up space for other discussions, about for example the meaning of education and the relationship between pre-school and school. Thus, in Sweden, the transfer of responsibility for early childhood services to education has been accompanied by a discussion about how the relationship between pre-school and school can be based on equality and reciprocity, and how 'schoolification' of pre-schools can be avoided:

> Announcing the transfer to education, prime minister Göran Persson stated that early childhood education and care should be the first step towards realising a vision of lifelong learning. He added that the preschool should influence at least the early years of compulsory school. Initiatives taken since have sought to build closer links between pre-school, free-time services (school-age childcare) and school, treating all as equal parts of the education system. Development work is focusing on the integration of pre-school pedagogy into primary schools and creating pedagogical 'meeting places' between all three services. (Korpi 2005, p. 10)

ADOPTING THE PEDAGOGICAL DISCOURSE: THE SECOND WAVE

The Nordic countries began the development of their pedagogical discourse about early childhood services in the third quarter of the last century by integrating responsibility for all of these services within their welfare systems – even though two countries, Sweden and Iceland, subsequently transferred responsibility for services from welfare to education. But other countries have started the process of transition to a pedagogical discourse by locating overall responsibility for all early childhood services within education, transferring responsibility for 'childcare' services from welfare to education. The first country to do this was New Zealand in 1986, followed by Spain (1990), Slovenia (1993), England and Scotland (1998).

Of these, New Zealand has gone furthest. Unlike Denmark and Sweden, but like the UK, New Zealand has a complex and fragmented system of provision, with different types serving different purposes and groups: 'childcare centres' usually provide all-day provision for all ages, with some developed by and for Pacific Island communities; 'kindergartens' usually provide half-day sessions for three- and four-year-olds; 'playcentres' are parent-led, parents often staying; *kōhanga reo* (literally 'language nest') are Maori language immersion centres; while 'home-based services' provide for children in the homes of carers. New Zealand, too, has a substantial for-profit sector, less than in the UK but far in excess of the Nordic countries where this sector is negligible.

However, like Sweden, New Zealand has followed through the logic of 'educationalising' its early childhood services. A highly innovative national curriculum for early childhood, covering birth to five years of age, has been introduced: *Te Whāriki*, a Maori word meaning mat, to indicate how the curriculum is woven from various principles, strands and goals (Carr and Rameka 2005). An early years teacher, specialising in work with children from birth to five years, has also been introduced, with the government setting an ambitious target of all staff being early years teachers by 2012 (New Zealand Ministry of Education 2002). If achieved, this ambitious target will exceed the levels of professionalisation in the Nordic early years workforce. A common system of funding has been applied across all services, based mainly on supply funding provided direct to services, and structured so that services do not need to pass on to parents the increased costs arising from an increasingly well qualified workforce and other quality improvements. Twenty hours per week of free attendance is being introduced for three- and four-year-olds from July 2007 – though only for children attending 'community-based' (meaning not for-profit) services, thus targeting public funds to encourage more non-profit providers at the expense of for-profit providers.

Underpinning these structural reforms is a broad conceptualisation of early childhood services as universal provision serving a multitude of purposes. Significantly New Zealand refers to 'early childhood education' (not 'education and care' or 'childcare'), indicating a broad, pedagogical view of education – what might be termed 'education in its broadest sense' (perhaps the nearest translation in English for 'pedagogy').

If we consider those few countries that have made a substantive transition from a childcare to a pedagogical discourse, it can be seen that what they have in common has been a combination of a broad and integrative way of thinking – pedagogy or education in its broadest sense – with a range of structural changes that have created a common framework for all services. This framework encompasses legislation, administration, regulation (including curriculum), access, staffing and funding. Re-forming, therefore, has involved re-thinking and re-structuring, to shape a new system that creates a new, inclusive relationship between young children, their families and the welfare state.

ENGLAND: A COUNTRY IN TRANSITION?

As already noted, the New Labour government broke with the past in putting early childhood services high on its social policy agenda. Blair (2004) has emphasised how 'a full-employment economy in tandem with the profound changes in family life poses an entirely new challenge for us as a government and a society. One which puts childcare and work/life balance centre-stage'. A range of policy measures have resulted.

A universal entitlement to part-time early education has been introduced for three- and four-year-olds; a large-scale intervention programme – Sure Start – has been developed in the most disadvantaged areas of the country, with over 500 local schemes now in operation; an ambitious programme of Children's Centres is being implemented, with 3500, one in every community, scheduled for 2010; while a national childcare strategy promises 'for all families with children aged up to 14 who need it, an affordable, flexible, high quality childcare place that meets their circumstances' (HM Treasury 2004, p. 1), with proposed legislation to place a duty on local authorities 'to secure sufficient childcare to meet the needs of their areas' (Department for Education and Skills 2005a, para. 15).

This attempt to increase access to services has been accompanied by an emphasis on a more integrated approach to services. A new children's agenda has been created, which seeks to develop a common framework for all children's services, including early childhood services and schools. National responsibility for all services for children, except health, is now located in the Department for Education and Skills, while at local level responsibility is brought together in new Departments of Children's Services. The government has defined five key outcomes for children, which will apply across all services: being healthy; staying safe; enjoying and achieving; making a positive contribution; and economic well-being. In addition to the range of services offered by Children's Centres for children under age five and their families, all schools by 2010 will have to deliver extended services, including 'high quality "wraparound" childcare . . . [A] varied menu of activities . . . [P]arenting support . . . [S]wift and easy referral to a wide range of specialist support services. . . . [And] wider community access to ICT, sports and arts facilities' (Department for Education and Skills 2005b, p. 8). At the same time a 'Children's Workforce Strategy' is being developed, again to encompass a wide range of services, and a 'common core of training' is proposed for all those who work, either solely or occasionally, with children and families.

This agenda to bring the whole gamut of children's services into closer and more coherent relationship is arguably the most wide-ranging in the world today. Within this general framework, there are indications of some movement towards a more pedagogical discourse for early childhood services. Integration of administrative responsibility within the education department has been matched by the integration of inspection of childcare and early education under the auspices of OFSTED, the national educational inspectorate. Early years education can be delivered either by schools or childcare services, both being publicly funded to do so and required to follow the same curriculum, the Foundation Stage. The Children's Centre programme supports the development of a form of service that integrates care, education and other services: 'the aim is for a network of centres across the country, offering information, advice and support to parents/carers, as well as early years provision (i.e. integrated childcare and early learning), health services, family support, parental outreach and employment advice for disadvantaged families' (Sure Start Unit 2005, p. 3).

There are also signs that government is grappling conceptually with the relationship between childcare and education, increasingly emphasising their inter-connectedness, the educational role of childcare services and the care role of schools. There is recognition of the value of integrating child-care, education and other services for young children and their families. The English Department for Education and Skills (2005a) reiterates that 'research has shown that integrated settings which fully combine education with care, along with nursery schools and classes, promote better intellec-tual and social development in children . . . The Ten Year [Childcare] Strategy, therefore, made the commitment to create a single framework for early education and childcare services for children from birth to the end of the Foundation Stage [that is, six years]' (para. 50). The government has pro-posed 'a new legal framework that removes the current distinction between care and education' (para. 54). This will involve the creation of what is termed an 'Early Development and Learning Framework' (EDLF), includ-ing a single regulatory system for all services up to the end of the current Foundation Stage (that is when children are six years of age) and a 'new quality framework which will take an integrated approach to care and edu-cation and will bring together *Birth to Three Matters* and the Foundation Stage and incorporate elements of the national standards for under-eight's day care and childminding' (para. 55). The government's aim is 'to create a system that ensures the experience for the child is of the same high quality, irrespective of the setting or sector' and that 'all settings offering care for more than two hours to children up to the end of Foundation Stage (that is, the end of the school year in which the child turns five) will be required to deliver the EDLF and inspected against it' (para.61), which will include day nurseries, pre-schools, playgroups, childminders, and schools.

At the same time, a major structural split remains. Early childhood services continue to be divided between school-based services, mainly nursery and reception classes for three- and four-year-olds, but also a rela-tively small number of nursery schools; and 'childcare services', mainly for-profit private nurseries and self-employed childminders. Between them come 'Children's Centres', mainly targeted by government at poorer areas where the private market is weak and the needs of children and families are perceived to be greater. Together with local Sure Start projects, Children's Centres are intended to spearhead the government's early intervention policy aimed at reducing a wide range of social problems associated with poverty and inequality and heavily concentrated in these areas. In due course Children's Centres are also planned for the 70 per cent 'more advantaged areas', but here they will only be required to provide support and information services; by contrast, centres in the most disadvantaged 30 per cent of areas must provide 'integrated early learning and childcare for babies and children until they are five years old [and] childcare suitable for working parents/carers for a minimum of five days a week, 48 weeks a year, 10 hours a day' (Sure Start Unit 2005, p. 9). Outside poorer areas, therefore, most families will have to rely on a private market in childcare, and no attempt is being made to build up a community alternative to for-profit services (as in New Zealand).

Nor, unlike in New Zealand, is there any movement to an integrated funding system, applied across the board. Schools are funded direct by government, while 'childcare' services rely on parental fees, with an element of demand funding for parents through the tax credit system. Even Children's Centres will, after an initial period, have to rely on demand funding and fees.

Nor, again unlike in New Zealand, has the workforce divide been addressed. Indeed, the whole edifice of 'childcare services' funded by parental fees and limited tax credits depends for its viability on an ever growing workforce of 'childcare workers' whose training and pay is far lower than that of teachers. The government's aim may be 'to create a system that ensures the experience for the child is of the same high quality, irrespective of the setting or sector', but this is to be achieved by two separate groups of workers, the great majority of whom earn little more than the minimum wage and have qualifications at level three or below. Even the Children's Centre programme is premised on relatively low qualified staff: centres providing integrated childcare and early learning need only initially employ one early years teacher on a half-time basis, and though this is a minimum, the goal is just one full-time teacher within 12–18 months of designation (Sure Start Unit 2005). In stressing this low level of teacher input, I am not proposing that the current UK teacher qualification is a panacea for early childhood services, the question of what sort of professional is needed in early years services being very much up for discussion. Rather, I am emphasising how the transition from childcare to pedagogical discourse has yet to grapple with the central issue of the workforce, unlike not only Denmark and Sweden but also New Zealand.

These glaring structural divisions reflect a continuing conceptual problem. Some in government, including the authors of most recent key policy documents, clearly understand the need to remove the current distinction between care and education, since 'there is no sensible distinction between good early education and care' (Department for Education and Employment 1998, para. 1.4). Yet the childcare discourse seems to maintain a strong hold on politicians, policymakers, media and the general public alike. The continuing high profile use of the term 'childcare', with its connotations of a service specifically for working parents to provide substitute parental care, is telling – 'Childcare Strategy', 'Childcare Bill', 'childcare element of the working tax credit', 'employer supported childcare', 'childcare services' and so on. Underlying a continuing split structure lies a way of thinking that constructs care as a separate and distinct field and childcare as a private commodity: the childcare discourse proves resistant to change.

CAN LIBERAL WELFARE STATES MAKE THE PEDAGOGICAL TURN?

This language of 'childcare', and the understanding of services that lies behind it, is highly significant. A pedagogical discourse, to be achieved, requires a reconceptualisation of services – as pedagogical (an alien concept, so far, in the UK, but appearing recently for the first time in a government document published by the Department for Education and Skills 2005c, Chapters 3 and 4), or as educational (but education understood in a broad and holistic sense, unlike the narrowly standards-based interpretation currently dominant in the United Kingdom). Once this has been achieved – as in Denmark, Sweden or New Zealand – it becomes possible to decentre 'childcare' in the sense of treating safe and secure attention for children while parents are working as just one of a cluster of possibilities that services may provide, rather than a primary function around which a whole system of services should be centred. It becomes possible too to envisage 'care' as an ethic pervading practice and relationships in work with children, whether or not their parents are employed, rather than some commodified product that parents buy when they cannot supply enough themselves.

This does not mean that parental employment is marginalised as an issue (services need to take working hours into account in many aspects of their operations, from opening hours to promoting parental participation), or that there is no recognition of parental employment in the funding regime (it is possible to imagine extending the idea of a free entitlement to a specified period of attendance for three-, four- or five-year-olds to all pre-school age children from say 12 months of age, while expecting parents using a service for a longer period to pay an additional fee related to income). It simply means that a new form of social institution for children and families has been recognised as an important feature of contemporary life – like school.

The recent history of early childhood services in England illustrates the resistance to making a pedagogical turn within a liberal welfare regime. The last ten years have seen unprecedented policy priority given to early childhood services, greatly increased funding and major changes. Yet at the same time, there are major continuities with what went before: targeted public provision, 'childcare' treated as a market commodity and private responsibility, a large private for-profit 'childcare' sector, reliance on a poorly paid 'childcare' workforce, and a restricted early education sector based on part-time attendance and ended by early (at least in international terms) school entry (for a fuller discussion of change and continuity pre- and post-1997, see Cohen et al. 2004).

This history suggests that the adherence of liberal welfare regimes to values such as markets, targeting, and individual responsibility constrains change. The rationale for current changes – a deeply instrumental 'social investment' logic (discussed further in Chapters 2 and 3 by Jenson and Lister in this volume), which argues for targeting resources on selected policy areas that are thought to provide high returns and improve national competitiveness, does not in itself guarantee a shift from a childcare to a pedagogical discourse; it can equally produce a refinement of what already exists. For it seems to be the case that 'care' in liberal regimes – whether 'childcare', 'eldercare', 'social care' – is understood first and foremost as a private responsibility and a discrete and gendered activity. To make the pedagogical turn means having a different understanding of care, as part of a larger whole – pedagogy or education in its broadest sense, for instance – which in turn legitimises its provision as a public good and collective responsibility (the implications of a turn from a 'social care discourse' to a 'pedagogical discourse' in the case of elderly people are vast and largely unexplored).

The turn to a pedagogical discourse by countries such as Denmark and Sweden has, by contrast, been facilitated by a longstanding culture of pedagogy in work with children, drawing on a Continental European tradition with deep historical roots, and a social democratic welfare regime whose values are in accord with that culture and with an understanding of early childhood services as a universal public entitlement for children and their families. These and other Nordic countries have, of course, been influenced by labour market requirements and notions of social investment (as, for example, the lifelong learning rationale for recent Swedish reforms). But there has also been space for other, less instrumental, rationales to flourish, not least about children's rights and the importance of childhood in its own right (the child as a being as well as a becoming).

As ever in comparative work, exceptions mar attempts to delineate neat patterns. Recent developments have taken New Zealand far along a process of transformation. The extent to which this country has turned towards the pedagogical discourse is all the more surprising given that this process was initiated against the backdrop of the introduction of neo-liberal economics, which have had a major impact on the welfare state and led to a rapid and large-scale deterioration in the general position of children as measured, for example, in terms of child poverty (Blaiklock et al. 2002). Gray (1998) observes that 'only in New Zealand, where neo-liberal policies were even more radical and the egalitarian inheritance more pronounced, did inequality grow faster [than in the UK]' (p. 32) during the 1980s and early 1990s.

The shift towards a pedagogical discourse in New Zealand is not complete and could yet be reversed by changes in government, which did in fact make the reform process stutter in the 1990s. But a lot has already been achieved, not only conceptually but structurally also. This may mean that there have been special circumstances at work in New Zealand, leading to an increasing need for childcare being channelled into a transformation of early childhood services. These circumstances may have included growing pressure to make amends to the Maori population for past injustices, which has introduced a strong emphasis on diversity into policy and practice; and a strong group of women academics who have had a clear and coherent vision of the direction services should take and have played an influential part in policy development. Or perhaps it means that liberal welfare regimes can make a turn away from a childcare discourse if certain conditions occur.

There is an important story still to be told about the New Zealand experience, which will help clarify what happened in that country and why. But more generally, it is important for welfare state studies to devote more attention to researching current changes in early childhood services (as well as in the role of schools and the relationship between early childhood and compulsory schooling) to understand better the nature of change – of concept, structure and practice; the forces (historical, social, economic, cultural) shaping change; and the institutions that are emerging to parallel schools as universal public spaces for children and families. Lumping what seem increasingly complex and varying services under broad headings such as 'childcare' or 'daycare' no longer (if it ever did) matches reality.

NOTES

1. The pedagogical theory and practice of the Italian city of Reggio Emilia has been influential in the Nordic states, as well as in many other countries. For more on Reggio and its understandings of early childhood services and young children, see Edwards et al. (1998); Giudici et al. (2001); Rinaldi (2005).

2. While there are some strong similarities, there are also significant differences between the Nordic states in early childhood policy. Some differences between Denmark and Sweden are considered above. Others involve differences in parental leave, with Finland providing a three-year period, which reduces use of services in this age group; funding parents of children not using public services (Finland and Norway); and lower levels of graduate workers in Iceland and Norway.

REFERENCES

Anxo, D. and C. Fagan (2001), 'Service employment: a gender perspective', in D. Anxo and D. Storrie (eds), *The Job Creation Potential of the Service Sector in Europe*, Luxembourg: Office for Official Publications of the European Communities.

Blaiklock, A.J., C.A. Kiro, E. Davenport, I. Hassell, M. Belgrave and W. Low (2002), 'When the invisible hand rocks the cradle: New Zealand children in a time of change', UNICEF Innocenti working papers, no. 93, Florence.

Blair, T. (2004), Speech made to the annual conference of the Daycare Trust, 11 November, Queen Elizabeth Conference Centre, London.

Carr, M. and L. Rameka (2005), 'Weaving an early childhood curriculum', *Children in Europe*, **9**, 6–7.

Cohen, B., P. Moss, P. Petrie and J. Wallace (2004), *A New Deal for Children? Reforming Education and Care in England, Scotland and Sweden*, Bristol: Policy Press.

Dahlberg, G. and P. Moss (2005), *Ethics and Politics in Early Childhood Education*, London: RoutledgeFalmer.

Dahlberg, G., P. Moss and A. Pence (1999), *Beyond Quality in Early Childhood Education and Care: Postmodern Perspectives*, London: Falmer Press.

Department for Education and Employment (1998), *Meeting the Childcare Challenge*, London: Stationery Office.

Department for Education and Skills (2005a), *Childcare Bill Consultation*, London: Department for Education and Skills.

Department for Education and Skills (2005b), *Extended Schools: Access to Opportunities and Services for All. A Prospectus*, London: Department for Education and Skills.

Department for Education and Skills (2005c), *Children's Workforce Strategy: A Strategy to Build a World-class Workforce For Children and Young People*, London: Department for Education and Skills.

Edwards, C., L. Gandini and G. Forman (ed.) (1998), *The Hundred Languages of Children*, 2nd edn, Norwood, NJ: Ablex.

European Council of Ministers (2002), Presidency conclusions from the Barcelona European Council 15–16 March, paragraph 32, accessed at http://ue.eu.int/ueDocs/cms_Data/docs/pressData/en/ec/71025.pdf.

Giudici, C., C. Rinaldi and M. Krechevsky (eds) (2001), *Making Learning Visible: Children as Individual and Group Learners*, Reggio Emilia: Reggio Children.

Gray, J. (1998), *False Dawn: The Delusions of Global Capitalism*, London: Granta Books.

Gregg, P., L. Washbrook, C. Popper and S. Burgess (2005), 'Effects of a mother's return to work decision on child development in the United Kingdom', *Economic Journal*, **501**, 1–6.

HM Treasury (2004), *Choice for Parents, the Best Start for Children: A Ten Year Strategy for Childcare*, London: Stationery Office.

Holmlund, K. (2003), 'Governing new realities and old ideologies: a gendered, power-based and class-related process', in M. Bloch, K. Holmlund, I. Moqvist and T. Popkewitz (eds), *Governing Children. Families and Education: Restructuring the Welfare State*, New York: Palgrave Macmillan.

Jensen, J.J. and H.K. Hansen (2003), 'The Danish pedagogues – a worker for all ages', *Children in Europe*, **5**, 6–9.

Johansson, I. (2003), 'Teaching in a wider perspective', *Children in Europe*, **5**, 14–17.

Joshi, H. and G. Verropoulou (2000), *Maternal Employment and Child Outcomes*, London: Smith Institute.

Knowles, C. (1999), 'Cultural perspectives and welfare regimes', in P. Chamberlayne, A. Cooper, R. Freeman and M. Rustin (eds), *Welfare and Culture in Europe: Towards a New Paradigm in Social Policy*, London: Jessica Kingsley.

Korpi, B.M. (2005), 'The foundation for lifelong learning', *Children in Europe*, **9**, 10–11.

Lenz Taguchi, H. and I. Munkhammar (2003), *Consolidating Governmental Early Childhood Education and Care Services Under the Ministry of Education: A Swedish Case Study*, Unesco Early Childhood and Family Policy Series no 6, Paris: UNESCO.

Malaguzzi, L. (1993), 'History, ideas and basic philosophy', in C. Edwards, L. Gandini and G. Forman (eds), *The Hundred Languages of Children*, Norwood, NJ: Ablex.

Moss, P. (2003), 'Getting beyond childcare: reflections on recent policy and future possibilities', in J. Brannen and P. Moss (eds), *Rethinking Children's Care*, Buckingham: Open University Press.

Moss, P. and M. Korintus (2004), 'Work with young children: a case study of Denmark, Hungary and Spain (consolidated report)', accessed 21 April 2005 at http://144.82.31.4/carework/reports.pdf.

Moss, P. and P. Petrie (2002), *From Children's Services to Children's Spaces: Public Policy, Children and Childhood*, London: RoutledgeFalmer.

New Zealand Ministry of Education (2002), 'Pathways to the future: a 10 year strategic plan for early childhood education', accessed at www.minedu.govt.nz/web/downloadable/dl7648_v1/english.plan.art.pdf.

Organisation for Economic Co-operation and Development (OECD) (2001), *Starting Strong*, Paris: OECD.

Organisation for Economic Co-operation and Development (2002), *Starting Strong*, Paris: OECD.

Petrie, P. (2003), 'School-age children: services in development', *Children in Europe*, **3**, 2–3.

Randall, V. (2000), *The Politics of Child Daycare in Britain*, Oxford: Oxford University Press.

Rinaldi, C. (2005), *In Dialogue with Reggio Emilia*, London: RoutledgeFalmer.

Sevenhuijsen, S. (1999), *Citizenship and the Ethics of Care: Feminist Considerations on Justice, Morality and Politics*, London: Norton.

Singer, E. (1993), 'Shared care for children', *Theory and Psychology*, **3**(4), 429–49.

Sure Start Unit (2005), '*A Sure Start children's centre for every community. Phase 2 planning guidance (2006–08)*', accessed at www.surestart.gov.uk/_doc/P0000457.doc.

Tronto, J. (1993), *Moral Boundaries: A Political Argument for the Ethics of Care*, London: Routledge.

9. The OECD and the work/family reconciliation agenda: competing frames

Rianne Mahon

Across advanced capitalist countries, welfare state restructuring has come to include a 'farewell to maternalism' – that is, the other side of the male breadwinner state, variously providing support for mothers' domestic caregiving role – albeit one proceeding at different speeds (Orloff 2004). For some, the 'farewell' may be identified with the withdrawal of support for mother-caregivers, especially in the form of the shift from 'welfare to workfare' for lone parents. Yet it also involves the prescription of 'reconciliation of family and work' policies designed to support mother-wage earners. Just like the earlier maternalist policies, these new policies can take different forms, with quite different consequences for women's equality and for children's rights. As welfare regime theory suggests, these differences will likely reflect the impact of social policy legacies, institutionalised at the national level. Yet channels of policy learning are increasingly multi-scalar, including an important role for transnational flows of ideas or 'fast policy', packaged as a set of transferable 'best practices' (Peck 2002; Jessop 2003).

The shift from maternalism to reconciliation thus cannot be understood as simply the effect of structural changes (for example, the shift to post-industrial employment), demographics (ageing societies), or even the impact of second wave feminism, although all of these have contributed. As Mazy argues, 'ideas rarely enter the policy-making process without conscious effort on the part of interested actors, who construct new policy frames based upon scientific knowledge and/or particular values and belief systems in an attempt to bring about policy change' (2000, p. 338). While actors in national settings continue to play an important role here, the idea that new measures to help reconcile family and working life are necessary is also being actively promoted by influential supra- and international organisations such as the Organisation for Economic Co-operation and Development (OECD). The OECD operates as an important source of transnational policy knowledge construction and dissemination. It is therefore of interest to ask, how does it frame the issue?

Throughout the 1980s and for much of the 1990s, that advice bore a marked neo-liberal stamp (McBride and Williams 2000; Armingeon and Beyeler 2004). As the twentieth century drew to a close, however, the OECD's social policy prescriptions began to reflect a 'third way' or 'inclusive liberalism' perspective,[1] with a (liberal) feminist twist. It is this perspective that dominates the new social policy agenda announced in *A Caring World* (OECD 1999), and which carries through the important series dealing with reconciliation policies, *Babies and Bosses* (OECD 2002a, 2003a, 2004a, 2005). As will be argued in this chapter, this set of prescriptions promotes a shallow version of gender 'equity' and does little for the rights of children. The key concern is the formation of 'flexible' labour markets and households for a globalised economy. As Morth (2000) reminds us, however, international organisations like the OECD are complex and thus capable of harbouring competing frames. This is the case here. *Starting Strong*, the special thematic review of Early Childhood Education and Care (ECEC), frames the issue quite differently, starting as it does from children's needs. Moreover, *Starting Strong* eschews the 'fast policy' model of policy transfer, in favour of contextualised learning.[2] This chapter will explore the differences between these frames.

FAREWELL TO MATERNALISM, HELLO?

Feminists have rightly argued that the welfare states, begun in the late nineteenth century and consolidated in the twentieth, focused on the male breadwinner and the risks – unemployment, injury, old age – he faced. Yet it was never just about the male breadwinner; welfare regimes also supported in various ways the role of women as wives and thus providers of (unpaid) care in the household. This component could take the form of joint (family-based) taxation, spousal allowances in male breadwinner social insurance programmes or child/family benefits paid directly to caregivers. In many countries, moreover, mothers were exempted – for greater or lesser periods – from the necessity of turning to paid work in the absence of the male breadwinner. While they varied in the degree of generosity and in who was designated beneficiary,[3] in none of these variants was the domestic caregiver on a par with the male breadwinner. Rather, as Orloff points out, 'nowhere did the programs of modern social protection instituted in the late nineteenth and early twentieth centuries . . . embody feminist ideals of women's individuality and independence. Instead, gender difference was linked to gender inequality and women's lack of independence' (2004, p. 6).

While the workfare turn in the USA, the UK and Canada has focused attention on the softening, and at times outright repeal of the right of lone mothers to assistance as domestic caregivers (Bashevkin 2002), it is actually the whole gamut of maternalist policies that are in question today. The end to maternalism is not just about retrenchment, moreover, as the (partial) termination of women's domestic caregiving role generates the need for alternative care arrangements (Jenson 1997; Daly and Lewis 2000; Mahon 2002b). In other words, the end of maternalism has given rise to pressures for new state initiatives such as public support for non-parental childcare, parental leave arrangements, 'flexitime' and the like. Yet, just as there were different ways of sustaining maternalism, so, too, are there different ways of supporting mother-wage earners. These differences have consequences for equality – among women, between men and women, and among children.

In North America, attention has understandably focused on the neo-liberal model, for which the USA, at the national and state level, constitutes the paradigm exemplar. In the USA women's labour force participation rate is amongst the highest in the world, while the solution to the resulting need for extra-parental care is largely found in the existence of a large pool of low-wage workers (Esping-Andersen 1999). In care work, this labour force is usually female and often racialised (Glenn 1992). National state involvement comes in the form of neo-liberal labour market (and immigration) policies, as well as the turn to workfare, but state and local level experimentation play an important part (Peck 2001). The national government also offers tax deductions, for corporations as well as individuals, which has encouraged the extension of corporate (or 'private') welfare to 'reconciliation' needs – for those well-positioned in the labour market (Michel 1999).

The US model also includes important feminist elements, however. Thus feminists have secured employment equity rights (O'Connor et al. 1999), as well as the right to freedom from sexual harassment in the workplace (Zippel 2000). As Orloff notes, this has contributed to a labour market in which 'women with good education or training are able to take advantage of many employment opportunities, and have . . . penetrated the upper echelons of private business and the professions and masculine working-class occupations to a greater degree than their Nordic or European counterparts' (2004, p. 24). These feminist gains are, however, not sufficient to challenge the dominance of the neo-liberal model in the USA. Consequently, this version of reconciliation comes at the price of greater (class) inequality among women and the 'care solution' – via low-wage labour of some – does little to contribute to the growth of good post-industrial jobs (Esping-Andersen 1990).

Children do not figure large in neo-liberal discourse, as they are seen as the responsibility of their families. Yet there is some – albeit limited – room for remedial state action to 'save' children from the 'cycle of poverty', through targeted programmes like Head Start. For the most part, parental market power determines the quality of childcare to which children have access. While children of middle- and upper-class families are more likely to have access to better quality childcare, those from lower income families 'are found predominantly in the lowest-quality, least-regulated programs' (Morgan 2005, p. 225).

In Europe, three other blueprints have attracted more attention than the neo-liberal: the neo-familialist, third way, and egalitarian. The neo-familialist draws on, while seeking to modernise, traditional views of gender difference. It is more likely to be found among the conservative welfare regimes of continental Europe, but there are also signs of this approach in 'social democratic' Finland.

Neo-familialism shares with neo-liberalism an emphasis on 'choice', but here the choice is understood not in terms of markets for care but as women's right to choose between a temporary housewife–mother role and labour force participation, with the balance tipped in favour of the former. This is underpinned by the neo-familial view of child development: maternal care in the early years is understood to be in the best interests of the child. While this position was supported in the 1950s and 1960s by child development experts like Bowlby (Michel 1999), the dominant view today sees an important role for quality childhood education and care.[4] The neo-familial model nevertheless hews to the earlier view. Thus the hallmark of the neo-familialist model is publicly supported long childcare leave (two to four years) – and little, if any, public support for non-parental childcare for children aged three and under. Women are encouraged to return to work, but rarely to their former job, and usually on a part-time basis, when the child enters public pre-school. This model does little for gender equality and, its typically low rate of reimbursement means that it operates primarily as an incentive for working-class, not professional, women to withdraw from the labour market.

Whereas neo-familialist reconciliation policies would preserve the older gender difference model, third way advocates favour a gender sameness view, in which equality of the sexes is defined as encouraging women to remain in the labour market. Ignoring the unequal division of care work within the home, third way advocates focus on short ('to preserve their human capital'), but funded, parental (in name, maternal in practice) leave and public support for childcare. Consistent with the 'new public management' theory on which third way, like neo-liberal, thinking draws (Giddens 2003, p. 14), the state is not to play the role of provider. Rather, in the name of efficiency and equity, the public role should be limited to supporting the choices of consumer-citizens through demand-side subsidies, improving the flow of information, and/or regulation. States work thus work in 'partnership' with the private (commercial and non-profit) sector, usually at the local level. This form of reconciliation is found in hybrid regimes like those of Britain and Canada (liberal with social democratic elements) or the Netherlands (conservative-social democratic).[5]

The third way should not be confused with neo-liberalism, although there are shared elements. Rather it should be seen as part of the attempt to 're-embed' the globalising market economy set in train by the neo-liberalism of the 1980s. As Porter and Craig note:

> For nations, this means adopting world trade rules and conservative fiscal policies, removing trade barriers and opening capital markets . . . For individuals, this primary inclusion is inclusion in labour markets, or in training for these, a preparation which now begins in social investment made all the way from (before) the cradle to the community to the (global) workplace and economy. (2004, p. 392)

In contrast to Thatcherism, such re-embedding involves recognising 'the social', but seeks to establish new rules – 'responsibilities (to work or to train) as well as rights'. Earlier social democratic/social liberal visions of equality of condition are abandoned, for post-industrialism has supposedly rendered equality 'in the here and now' no longer feasible, due to the productivity gap that exists between the goods and service sectors. As net job growth occurs in the latter sector, politicians will have to choose between inequality (the US model) and un- or low employment (arguably the continental European choice).[6] In the name of liberal inclusiveness, third way advocates are thus prepared to accept the formation of a market for personal and social services as low wage, low skill jobs. There is a role for the state here, in 'making work pay' via targeted tax credits and the like, and in providing training and other supports designed to help people move above the poverty line (Esping-Andersen 1999).

In other words, equality in the here and now is abandoned in favour of equality of opportunity over the life course. What this overlooks is that women, as well as racialised minorities, hold a disproportionate share of non-standard jobs. Moreover, women's continued primary responsibility to provide care creates barriers to their moving above the poverty line. Although third way advocates reject long periods of care leave as destructive of (women's) human capital, they see part-time work as a good 'bridge' back into the labour market. In this sense, they share with their neo-familial counterparts an acceptance of a one-and-a-half-earner model. In addition, in the third way model, children are viewed instrumentally, as adults-in-the-making. Public expenditure for quality childcare is thus seen as an investment in the labour force of the future. In his recent work, Esping-Andersen highlights the normative dimension underlying this perspective:

> If childcare policy were nothing more than a response to women's demands for greater compatibility, there would be a priori, no reason why the welfare state should assure uniform high quality standards. . . . The key point is that a policy of universal access to high quality day care for the zero to six-year-olds kills two birds with one stone. It obviously helps resolve the incompatibility problem that working mothers face, and it is arguably an effective tool in the war against social inheritance . . . it is a productive investment in children's life chances and in society's future productivity. (2003, p. 117)

Investment in quality childcare thus links concerns about the constitution of flexible and competitive labour markets, now and in the future, with the discourse on equality of opportunity over the life cycle.

There is a fourth 'egalitarian' blueprint, which might incorporate the following features:

1. Parental leave structured to foster an equitable sharing of domestic childcare between mothers and fathers, with additional supports offered to lone parent wage-earners.
2. Provision of universally accessible, affordable childcare and non-parental care services.
3. Children have the right to age-appropriate early childhood education and care, whether or not their parents are working or involved in some form of training.
4. Care is provided by skilled providers and the value of their skills is recognised through equitable wages, good working conditions and in-service opportunities to improve their skills.
5. Provision is made for democratic control, including a strong element of parental and community voice.

Sweden and Denmark, countries with 'social democratic' welfare regimes, come the closest to this ideal.

This model does better than all the others in terms of equality of the sexes, in that it promotes equal sharing of the remaining domestic caregiving. It contributes to the continued abatement of class inequality in that, by supporting the development of quality childcare, provided by caregivers whose skills are duly recognised, it contributes to the growth of good post-industrial jobs. In fact, one of the strengths of Esping-Andersen's earlier (1990) work, is that it showed the connection between differences in social policy regimes and the important variations in the structure of post-industrial labour markets. While the liberal (American) model yields a polarised 'good jobs, bad jobs' labour market, a social democratic regime produces a lot of decent jobs and far fewer bad ones. With regard to the child, an egalitarian view would seek to balance the third way emphasis on the future payoffs to be gained from early childhood education and care, with concern over children as beings in the here and now (Lister 2004). Cohen et al. (2004) would take this further, arguing that children need to be seen as active citizens, with rights of their own, including voice. It is this approach that permeates the important work on quality in childcare services produced by the European Commission Network on Childcare (CRRU 2004).

TRANSNATIONAL POLICY LEARNING: THE OECD

The end of maternalism and the concomitant embrace of reconciliation policies are not simply the spontaneous response to a set of common challenges. Rather, the change is occurring through a (contested) process of policy learning (and unlearning), in which new ideas or ways of framing the issues come into play. The national state remains an important locus of such policy learning and contestation. Yet, as Peck notes, 'channels of policy learning, transfer, and networking are increasingly being structured in transnational . . . terms as new knowledge communities, intermediary agencies, global consultancy houses, and multilateral partnerships are established to facilitate and foster the process of fast policy transfer' (2002, p. 349). Peck focuses on the role played by such cross- and transnational networks in the shift from welfare to workfare. Similar dynamics come into play in the broader field of reconciliation policies where supra- and international organisations and advocacy networks are contributing to national policy learning processes.

Some work has been done on the role of the European Union in this regard.[7] This chapter focuses, however, on the role played by the OECD, an important international organisation whose membership includes the United States and other key advanced capitalist countries.[8] It functions as a key source of economic, and more recently, social policy analysis and prescription. Its advice is likely to be especially important in situations such as that with which this chapter is concerned, when states are involved in a process of 'unlearning' old policies (maternalism), and learning new ones (reconciliation). In this context, the OECD contributes a new way of framing social policy problems, and marshals its moral authority behind a new paradigm.

The OECD's standard modus operandi makes it a good example of the process of transnational 'fast policy transfer'. In contrast to contextualised policy learning,[9] fast policy transfer involves the development and circulation of 'essentialized readings of effective local [and national] programs in which a small number of supposedly decisive (and potentially replicable) design features are privileged and promoted. In the process, complex and locally embedded interventions are rendered as simplified, disembodied and reproducible administrative routines' (Peck 2002, p. 349). Sahlin-Andersson's (2000) examination of the OECD's role in propagating 'New Public Management' (NPM) corroborates Peck's thesis. For her, this involved a process of editing in which 'national experiences and reforms tend to be presented to others in terms of existing templates, examples, categories, scientific concepts, theoretical frameworks and widespread classifications that are familiar. These concepts, references and frameworks form the infrastructure of editing and they restrict and direct how the accounts are given' (Sahlin-Andersson 2000, p. 13).

Editing tends to be most pronounced in certain parts of the reports – the executive summaries, introductions and conclusions – which are most likely to be read by time-pressed policymakers. Thus in the case of NPM, 'the final and summarizing chapters . . . downplayed the differences and uncertainty; they presented a reform agenda which embodied the principle features of the national reforms. . . . The reforms were described and justified as responses to a common set of problems facing all OECD countries, and they were labelled as a coherent and consistent package' (Sahlin-Andersson 2000, p. 16). As Porter and Webb underline, such editing 'helps to define economic and social reality, not just measure what already exists, using objective categories' (2004, p. 11). In other words, what is transmitted is not pure research results, but the very definition of common problems and prescribed solutions.

What kind of frame does the OECD employ in its editing processes? In the broadest terms, the frame stems from its mandate – defining 'standards of appropriate behaviour for states which seek to identify themselves as modern, liberal, market-friendly, and efficient' (Porter and Webb 2004, p. 10). Yet liberalism, especially its technical underpinnings in economics, has undergone a series of important modifications since the OECD was formed in 1961.

Initially, the OECD functioned within a Keynesian policy paradigm. In fact, during the 1960s it operated as an important source of transmission of 'Keynes plus' prescriptions. For instance, when Gösta Rehn, co-inventor, with Rudolf Meidner, of the famous Swedish solution to the unemployment/inflation tradeoff (Martin 1979), was seconded to the OECD, the organisation became a promoter of active labour market policy as a solution to the Phillips curve inflation–unemployment tradeoff. In the 1970s, however, it became an early convert to the neo-liberal supply-side paradigm (Serré and Palier 2004, p. 111). With the publication of the

McCracken report (1977), demand management was seen as no longer able to solve problems of unemployment but rather to fuel inflationary expectations. Neo-liberal nostrums continued to shape its country reviews throughout the 1980s and 1990s (Armingeon and Beyeler, 2004), and underpinned its 1994 Jobs Strategy (McBride and Williams 2000). All of these documents were produced by its powerful Economic Secretariat, however.

Yet just as the European Commision is composed of different directorates that 'sponsor different ways of conceptualizing issues' (Morth 2000, p. 174), so too is the OECD a complex organisation, capable of harbouring different frames. Thus McBride and Williams admit that the Directorate for Employment, Labour and Social Affairs (DELSA)[10] had staked out a more moderate line than the Economic Secretariat, one that, in fact, rebutted the Jobs Strategy's core arguments. This represents a shift in orientation from the neo-liberalism that marked DELSA's social policy stance in the 1980s (Deacon et al. 1997). The turn seems to have begun in 1991, when the Council commissioned a new round of social policy studies by the Directorate (Deacon et al. 1997, p. 71). The *New Orientation for Social Policy* (OECD 1994) was perhaps the first to articulate the emergent 'social investment' paradigm, which seeks to align the member states' social policies with flexible labour markets. On this, the 'new social policy agenda' announced in 1997 was clear:

> A new approach to social protection will have a stronger emphasis on interventions earlier in life and more preventive (and less remedial) measures. The goal would be to re-define equity and security in terms of barriers towards life-course flexibility, and to avoid definitions which suggest that the goal of social policy is to provide protection against flexibility . . .
>
> Employment opportunities are likely increasingly to favour people who show flexibility, whether through being from a household with other earners (so that short-term fluctuations in income are supportable) or because of their own adaptability. (Pearson and Scherer 1997, p. 7)

These themes are further developed in *A Caring World* (OECD 1999), produced under the direction of Mark Pearson and Willem Adema, who would later be responsible for *Babies and Bosses*.

In the introduction to *A Caring World*, the Secretary General celebrated the new paradigm that was beginning to catch on among member states: 'The new social policy agenda is how to achieve social solidarity through enabling individuals and families to support themselves' (OECD 1999, p. 4). The new frame accords well with the third way's (economically) active, 'empowered' citizens, and its emphasis on 'welfare to work'. It accepts a greater role for the state than is admitted in neo-liberal discourse but, in the new social policy agenda, states need to operate within the strict fiscal parameters established by globalisation (OECD 1999, p. 35). Expanding employment is important, but this is to be done through the use of supply-side measures. 'Making work pay' is to be achieved, not by focusing on job quality, but rather by (directly or indirectly) subsidising low-wage employment ('welfare in work'). The new social policy agenda is also informed by NPM's concern to promote the formation of markets – or quasi-markets – as a solution for governments concerned 'to do less with more', by counter-acting the power of budget-maximising bureaucrats. It also reflects NPM's emphasis on decentralisation. As *A Caring World* notes, the economic case for decentralisation concerns the capacity of local authorities to tailor poli-cies to local needs and their sensitivity to financial pressures, which will induce them to invest in reducing social assistance rolls (1999, p. 103).

The OECD's new social policy frame has gender and generational dimensions. Thus *A Caring World* announces:

> Social policies based on the male-breadwinner model of family relations have become outmoded. . . . First, the growth of female labour market participation provides a forum of self-insurance to households, with the income risks attached to involuntary non-employment reduced. Second, working women become enti-tled to insurance-based benefits in their own right. Third, demands increase for some sorts of social support (in particular, childcare and maternity and pater-nity leave). (1999, pp. 14–15)

In other words, dual-earner families constitute an important complement to the flexible labour markets long recommended in OECD economic policy documents. They also make pension reform easier, a theme that has run through its recommendations since the 1980s.[11] This new family requires public support, of course, but in different ways from that accorded the male breadwinner/female caregiver family of the past. Lone parents, and the poverty to which their children are exposed, are of particular concern. Here, high quality early intervention programmes can help break the cycle of poverty, but as these are seen as costly, such programmes should be narrowly targeted on the most disadvantaged families (OECD 1999, p. 86). The best way to address the poverty of lone parents is seen as welfare-to-work programmes.

The intellectual foundations of this new view of families were laid in an earlier study commissioned by the OECD, *Sustainable Flexibility* (Carnoy and Castells 1997). Here Martin Carnoy and Manuel Castells linked their analysis of the flexibility requirements of the new economy to a view of the family as an 'investment–production partnership':

> The family in a flexible work system is . . . a hub of productive and reproductive activity. When it is potentially 'strong' (with two highly educated adults at its

core) it serves as a risk hedge against periods of unemployment, as a source of child development for its offspring, of investment capital for adult and child education and training, and of personal security and growth. (1997, p. 41)

The state's role is to 'enhance the household partnership's capacity to invest in learning'. This includes 'helping the family acquire education for its children even as parents are on flexible work schedules; [and] giving parents new possibilities to take further education and training themselves' (1997, p. 49).

In 2003–4, the generational emphasis seems to have shifted somewhat, from the child as investment in the future, to the child as solution to the problem posed by ageing. This time women's labour force 'activation' is presented as part of the solution to ageing – along with other under-represented groups in the labour market.[12] Again this requires reconciliation measures. As the *2003 Employment Outlook* notes, 'financial incentives are not enough. Subsidised childcare services, promoting flexibility for workers with family responsibilities and expanding part time work can be effective ways of facilitating access to employment, notably among women' (OECD 2003b). The reconciliation message was reiterated in the 2004 Employment Outlook, which noted that, while some have succeeded in boosting employment levels, 'governments must consider a range of issues including the need to boost employment levels and meet individuals' needs for job security and work-life balance' (OECD 2004d).

Such broad policy documents certainly contribute to shaping the social policy paradigm of member states. It is through the publication of country-specific assessments, however, that the OECD is able to employ benchmarking and the 'name and shame' instrument of peer review to press 'laggards' to learn, much as the European Union does via Open Method Coordination. In the next sections, therefore, we focus on two such reviews: *Babies and Bosses* and *Starting Strong*. The first, produced under the direction of those involved in the framing documents discussed above, consists of four volumes that analyse the full gamut of reconciliation policies in Australia, Austria, Canada, Denmark, Finland, Ireland, Japan, New Zealand, Portugal, Sweden, Switzerland and the United Kingdom. *Babies and Bosses* (OECD 2002–2005) counsels the rejection of maternalism in favour of supports for the new dual-earner (or lone-parent earner) family. Not surprisingly, it shares the third way view of how to support such a family with *A Caring World*. As we shall see, while the detailed chapters do recognise 'anomalies', the power of the social investment frame prevails. The prescriptions thus fall short of 'helping both mothers and fathers'. In other words, this way of framing reconciliation does not include measures designed to ensure men and women equally share the unpaid care work. Where children appear, moreover, they are treated in an instrumental way.

This is in marked contrast to the frame employed in the *Starting Strong* (OECD 2001) project, which examines the early child education and care practices of more than half the member countries, placed in their wider economic, social and policy context.[13] Located in the Education Directorate, this thematic review came under the Education and Training Policy Division, headed by Abrar Hasan, with Michelle Neuman and John Bennett as project managers. Drawing on a different epistemic community, *Starting Strong* works from a 'broad and holistic' view of children as individuals and as active members of their families and communities. It also sees providers as skilled workers whose skills should be properly valued and this, too, is in marked contrast to *Babies and Bosses*.

BABIES AND BOSSES: THE FAMILY-FRIENDLY OECD?

Babies and Bosses clearly presents women's increased labour market participation as a solution to common problems (if to a different degree) of poverty, low fertility and ageing. It recognises, moreover, that replacing maternalist with a new, 'reconciliation'-oriented, 'family friendly' policy may involve the 'potential escalation of public intervention' but 'this may not be a bad thing' (2002a, p. 13). Echoing Carnoy and Castells (1997), it is argued that having two earners:

> the family becomes richer; it becomes less vulnerable to labour market shocks (i.e. if one partner loses their job, the family still has income from work); family dissolution is less catastrophic for the partner who becomes the main carer for the children if she has income from work. . . . It is incumbent on governments to eliminate barriers to work, so that families can realise these gains. (OECD 2002a, p. 22)

The country studies contain useful information, and those prepared to read the chapters that provide detailed analyses of various aspects will find observations that suggest the limitations of its third way frame. Nevertheless, the three volumes (2002–2004) stand as good examples of the 'fast policy' approach, in which a third way analytic grid is used to edit (and criticise) national experiences.

Thus member states should eliminate the remaining vestiges of maternalism. Australia, Austria, Ireland, Japan and the Netherlands are chided for not having done more to break with maternalism, while in the volume dealing with Austria, Ireland and Japan, all three countries are warned that more needs to be done: 'current labour supply is less than it could be, and human capital is underused. This result is not an efficient use of labour market resources, and were this situation to be perpetuated, it will limit economic growth relative to potential. At the same time, the declining number of children also has obvious implications for the shape of future society' (OECD 2003a, p. 10).

In some countries, the solution involves the elimination of spousal allowances from government and employer social insurance schemes (Japan, for example). Other countries are encouraged to move to individual, rather than family, taxation (such as the Netherlands and Austria). Of greater concern, however, is the special treatment of lone parents as exempt from the obligation to seek work. The 'welfare to work' orientation is to be embraced by all. Accordingly, the Swiss are admonished to 'avoid negative effects on financial incentives to work', when implementing supplementary family benefits (OECD 2004a, p. 14). Similarly, the New Zealand government is encouraged to modify its Domestic Purposes benefit to 'make work pay' and to enforce mutual obligations 'requiring sole parents to seek work actively' (OECD 2004a, p. 12). Ireland is asked to 'reduce long term benefit expectations' among recipients of one parent family benefits and to develop 'a comprehensive employment support approach' to ensure that the family income supplement 'becomes a more effective tool in helping single parents back to work' (OECD 2003a, p. 12).

The authors of the *Babies and Bosses* series favour 'choice', but not the neo-familial choice between parental (maternal) care and childcare services. Parental leave is seen as constituting an important part of the new family-friendly policy kit, but familialism's long leaves are rejected as destructive of mothers' human capital and weakening their labour market attachment. Thus Austria is encouraged to 'introduce higher Childcare Benefit payment rates for those who return to work at an earlier stage, for example, upon one year of parental leave' and to 'ensure parents are fully aware of the different durations of Childcare Benefit (30/36 months) and the employment-protected parental leave period (up to the child's second birthday), to reduce the risk of parents not returning to work when the parental leave period is over' (OECD 2003a, p. 11).

After a leave of suitable length, parents/mothers should be in paid work. The *Babies and Bosses* studies do make some attempt to address labour market and workplace barriers to women's labour force integration. Japan, in particular, is criticised for the highly gendered split between regular and irregular employees, and the Japanese government is encouraged to 'enforce more actively gender equity and equal pay for equal work legislation' (OECD 2003a, p. 13). Nevertheless, the series recommends the expansion of part-time work to Austria, Ireland and Portugal as a 'women-friendly' development (OECD 2003a, 2004a). It does this despite its recognition that part-time work contributes to channelling women into low-paid, non-standard jobs. Thus, for instance, the first volume notes that 'many households in Australia and the Netherlands distribute paid work along a "one and one half" earner model in terms of hours of paid employment, while in terms of contribution to household income a "one and one quarter" model appears a better description' (OECD 2002a, p. 28). The second volume admits that 'the gender gap in terms of job quality is larger than that in employment rates' (OECD 2003a, p. 14).

Moreover, the *Babies and Bosses* volumes recognise that it is women whose lives are being changed in this new 'family-friendly' world, not men. The first volume notes that 'men do not appear to have changed their behaviour markedly. . . . Indeed male behaviour remains largely traditional in all three countries: take up rates of parental leave among men are low, and although the gender gap in unpaid housework is smaller in Denmark than in the other two countries, caring remains primarily a female activity' (OECD 2002a, p. 14). In the second volume, it is noted that there is a long hours culture for male workers in all three countries, leaving men little time to make a contribution to daily housework (OECD 2003a, p. 15). In this context, the vision of shared care through the reduction in working time for both parents, which has been on the agenda in the Netherlands, 'is likely to remain illusory for the near future, as it would require a fundamental change in male labour market behaviour, evidence for which is lacking' (2002a, p. 15). Despite this, reconciliation does not include measures to change men's work patterns.[14]

What happens when mothers are at work? Clearly non-parental child-care arrangements are needed and here the *Babies and Bosses* advocates parental choice in the form of a (subsidised) childcare market. Public sector 'monopolies' are not recommended, even though the *Babies and Bosses* authors recognise that wage rates and employment conditions in the Danish system, which are mainly municipally run, are much better than in the countries relying on private sector provision (OECD 2002a, p. 91). Private provision is to be preferred as it 'is geared towards serving customer demand . . . and may also be conducive to innovative practices' (OECD 2002a, p. 88). Here and elsewhere in the reports there is also the suggestion that private provision is to be preferred when there is need for rapid expansion to 'exploding public budgets and tax rates' (OECD 2002a, p. 88). Thus recent Australian (since 1990), Dutch and Japanese policy decisions, which support the growth of private, including commercial, provision, get the stamp of approval.

At the same time, *Babies and Bosses* acknowledges that in the Netherlands, choice 'is severely constrained by very limited childcare capacity' (OECD 2002a, p. 97). In other words, markets are not capable of delivering the number of spaces needed, at a price parents can afford. There is a role for government to compensate for the failure of markets to generate adequate supply. For the authors of the *Babies and Bosses* volumes, however, demand-side subsidies are to be preferred to subsidising the supply side. Part of the rationale is 'equity', the logic here being that, in the context of scarcity, supply-side subsidies only benefit those who are able to get a place, and do nothing for parents who cannot find one. If governments subsidise parents, then the latter presumably can find some form of care, even if in the informal sector (OECD 2003a, p. 149). The main reason, however, has to do with 'efficiency': demand-side subsidies put pressure on providers to keep costs low and to meet parental demands, such as for more flexible opening hours. Cleveland and Krashinsky (2003) suggest, however, that 'the debate over demand-side and supply-side is often really a debate over what kind of quality will be provided and what kind of standards will be set' (OECD 2003b, p. 42). In other words, demand-side subsidies usually cost less because they are set at levels that are too low for many parents to purchase high quality care.

What, then, of quality? *Babies and Bosses* certainly recommends that public subsidies only be used for quality childcare, including that provided by childminders. Yet how is quality to be assured? This is where *Babies and Bosses'* economistic, or public choice, view of childcare providers as a group pursuing its own self-interest, potentially at the expense of children and parents unless checked by market-like mechanisms, comes through strongly. Thus the first volume notes the important role allocated to parents in the Danish system but raises the concern that 'without any external bench-marking, the system leaves local professionals in a very powerful position, relative to parents' (OECD 2002a, p. 108). The Australian quality assurance system, introduced after the way was opened to subsidising commercial provision, is discussed in considerable detail. Caution is needed even here, however: 'Although this system appears to be working well at the moment, care is needed to avert the risk that over-reliance on other child-care professionals may create a profession more concerned about defining its collective interests, rather than promoting wider social objectives' (OECD 2002a, p. 21). In other words, the authors of the *Babies and Bosses* reports are concerned parents and governments will be held hostage by self-interest optimising professionals. It is this that underlies their emphasis on demand-side subsidies as well as the call for external benchmarking.

Babies and Bosses thus does lay out a post-maternalist vision of 'family-friendly' policies, but it is one informed by the same third way approach mapped out in the frame documents. As such it refrains from advocating for the full sharing of care and paid work (the Dutch ideal, but not the practice) as between parents. Instead, governments should make it easier for mothers to care for their child during its first year, and then to choose part-time work while their children are young. Children figure in this series as potential impediments to parental/maternal labour market participation and, to a lesser extent, as human capital to be developed by prudent social investments. Although the issue of the quality of non-parental childcare is raised, *Babies and Bosses* favours demand-side subsidies to private providers over public investment in the development of a high quality early child and education system. The expansion of childcare should thus occur within the fiscal parameters (low tax, low spend) consistent with 'making work pay'. Pressure will be kept on 'childcare professionals' to keep costs down, while meeting parent demands for flexibility. As we shall see, this is a very different approach from that taken in the *Starting Strong* reviews.

EARLY CHILD EDUCATION AND CARE: POLICY FOR CHILDREN

Although the *Starting Strong* thematic review started in DELSA, it was set in motion by the 1996 meeting of Education Ministers which focused on 'life long learning'. This was part of the broader shift from neo- to inclusive liberalism. In this case, it involved moving from the preoccupation with technology (ICT) and growth (the 'knowledge economy') to the social (and human capital) prerequisites for a 'knowledge society' (Larner et al. 2006, p. 10). In adopting the goal of making life-long learning accessible to all, the Ministers of Education recognised that this involved 'strengthening the foundations for learning throughout life, by improving access to early childhood education, particularly for disadvantaged children' as well as revitalising schools and supporting adult learning (OECD 1996, p. 1). Although the Ministers' communiqué reflected a liberal concern to target 'disadvantaged' children, the Early Childhood Education and Care (ECEC) Policy Branch of the Division of Education and Training interpreted its mandate in terms more consistent with the egalitarian model.

Starting Strong drew on a different epistemic community – experts in early child development rather than economists – than *Babies and Bosses*. As might be expected, then, rather than being treated primarily as potential impediments to their mothers' labour force participation, children occupy a central place in this project. Thus all children should have access to quality ECEC, irrespective of their parents' labour market status. This is as true for under-threes as it is for pre-schoolers, though in most countries, infant and toddler care is still treated as a babysitting service for working mothers. More broadly, *Starting Strong* rejects the narrow 'child as human capital-in-the-making' focus found in other third way writing and practice (OECD 2001, p. 41). Clearly ECEC can and should help lay strong foundations for future learning, but children must also be seen as active learners and citizens in the here and now – just as they are in the UN Convention on the Rights of the Child. The ECEC review thus recognises that 'children not only have their own culture, but also their own rights and "voice"' (OECD 2001, p. 42). This means using appropriate pedagogies and the rejection of didactic teaching methods, narrowly focused on laying the foundations for literacy and numeracy. It also means that children participate in the ongoing quality assessment process.

A second important difference between *Starting Strong* and *Babies and Bosses* is the view of staff. For the former, care providers are seen as self-interest maximising agents who are inclined to use their professional knowledge to fend off principals (parents, governments). Moreover, although their detailed analyses show that, while no childcare staff are well-paid, those in publicly owned centres fare better – they prefer a competitive market for care, and subsidies targeted at parent-customers to keep providers efficient. In contrast, *Starting Strong* argues the importance of appropriate training and working conditions to quality ECEC:

> Quality ECEC depends on strong staff training and fair working conditions across the sector. Initial and in-service training might be broadened to take into account the growing educational and social responsibilities of the profession. There is a critical need to develop strategies to recruit and retain a qualified and diverse, mixed-gender workforce and to ensure that a career in ECEC is satisfying, respected and financially viable. (OECD 2001, p. 11)

In personal services like ECEC, quality not only depends on the skills of the providers but also is fostered by fair wages and good working conditions, which are crucial for recruitment and retention.

Although *Starting Strong* recognises the skills required to deliver quality ECEC, it also recognises the importance of quality assessment. For *Starting Strong*, however, this is envisioned as a dialogical, democratic process: 'defining, ensuring, and monitoring quality should be a participatory and democratic process that engages staff, parents and children' (OECD 2001, p. 11). In support of this dialogical and ongoing process, governments have a role to play in ensuring the collection and availability of good data and supporting ongoing research and innovative practice.

A third important distinction between *Starting Strong* and *Babies and Bosses* is the former's approach to parental leave and its remuneration. Compared to the six months or so leave found in several other countries, the leave recommended in *Starting Strong* is at least one year, in deference to the needs of young children. The Swedish model is often invoked – that is, a one year entitlement, remunerated according to employment status, which includes a guaranteed right to return to the same level of work.

Through the introduction of 'daddy months', Swedish parents are encouraged to share in the care of children, in recognition of the need to promote greater bonding of male partners of their children and, in the future, a more equitable sharing of childrearing. The public attitudes thus formed, and the link between employment insurance and the funding of the leave, serve to lessen employers' tendency to avoid employing women of childbearing age. Parental leave is closely linked to an entitlement to early childhood services from 18 months, and includes out-of-school provision for children 6–12 years, so as to enable women to avoid part-time jobs, which tend to be less-well paid and reduce pension rights at the end of career.

Starting Strong does not take a clear position on public versus private provision, though it does note that most OECD countries favour public delivery, at least for pre-schoolers (OECD 2001, p. 90). The Irish *Country Note*, moreover, brings out the disadvantages of commercial care:

> Without public management and sustainable public funding, market-led child-care provision remains fragmented and inequitable. For this reason, governments in English-speaking countries are obliged to intervene constantly by increasing childcare allowances, reviewing quality supervision and even directly funding parts of the system, such as Head Start (US) . . . that are aimed at targeted groups. Although competition can lead to some good programmes, these are often confined to parents who can pay high fees. When dominated by private, for profit interests, profits are often derived from high fees, increasing numbers of children per staff and/or low staff wages. There is a tendency to employ untrained staff at the bottom end of the market, where modest and disadvantaged families are the clients. (OECD 2004b, p. 46)

Starting Strong does not explicitly come out in favour of supply-side subsidies. It does, however, underline the fact that, again, in systems which rely on demand-side subsidies, it is difficult for low-income families to gain access to quality ECEC (OECD 2001, pp. 57, 94, 130). It goes on to spell out the key conditions for developing a quality ECEC system, laying particular emphasis on the need for substantial levels of public investment, including in the infrastructure, and coordination, both horizontal and vertical (OECD 2001).[15]

Clearly, this kind of system requires substantial public backing and resources that the low tax states favoured by *Babies and Bosses* would find difficult to marshal. In contrast, in several country reviews, *Starting Strong* underlines that countries that invest in early childhood services of high quality reap many benefits in terms of child development, the prevention of future inequalities in education, more equal opportunities for women and significant savings in welfare dependency. Direct provision of the service by the state is not considered a necessity when appropriate private partners are available. *Starting Strong* underlines, however, that the state has every interest in supplying strong funding and policy direction, and high levels of training and support to educators and parents to achieve and maintain high quality.

Its preferred system of governance certainly allocates an important coordinating role to national states. At the same time, it stresses the democratic involvement of children, parents and their local (and ethnic) communities in the co-determination of the aims and methods, as well as in quality assessment. It also eschews the 'fast policy' approach in favour of contextualised learning. This is clear throughout its studies. Thus while Sweden and Denmark may stand out as especially strong examples, the recommendations for other countries, like Ireland and Canada, build on textured and dynamic analyses of their particular situations. This approach reflects its conception of ECEC as systems that develop through an ongoing, dialogical process, in which different values and perspectives are at play, a conception that has much in common (and not by accident) with that developed by the European Commission's Childcare Network in the 1990s (CRRU 2004).

Starting Strong thus has many of the elements of the egalitarian model outlined in the first section. It counsels the establishment of an ECEC system that would offer quality care to all children, irrespective of the labour market status of their parents. Its recommendations would also contribute to the development of good post-industrial jobs, and thus would help counteract the emergence of a polarised labour market. Women would continue to hold many of these jobs, and thus would benefit from improved wages and career possibilities. Ideally, however, there would be a better gender balance among staff, reflecting a view that men are carers too.

Yet *Starting Strong* does not come to grips sufficiently with the unequal distribution of unpaid care work in the home, which contributes to gender inequality in the labour market. The low value placed on women's domestic care responsibilities, moreover, feeds into a system that systematically undervalues care work in the market place. In this sense it shares the strengths and weaknesses of the European Commission's Network, on whose foundations it builds. For the latter, it was important to make the needs and interests of children central:

Whilst the Network has been established as part of an Equal Opportunity Programme, and retains a strong commitment to supporting equal treatment for women in employment, it has emphasized that the needs and interests of children must also be a major concern. . . . However, the Network has not seen the two interests . . . as in opposition. Both can be met and are indeed interdependent, since services that are adequate in quantity but poor in quality will be a major obstacle to employment for many women. (CRRU 2004, p. 1)

In this respect, both the Network and *Starting Strong* have an important contribution to make to realising the egalitarian vision. Yet as we have seen, gender equality is easily subordinated to 'primary' goals such as growth and competitiveness. For gender and generational equality and social justice, the child-centred vision needs to be incorporated into a broader strategy for 'sharing' work and family life.

CONCLUSIONS

The OECD is an active participant in framing the issue of reconciling work and family life. It thus contributes to the establishment of 'family/work reconciliation' as the new common sense, especially for conservative regimes in Europe and Asia and 'laggard' liberal regimes like Ireland. Yet the OECD has not one but (at least) two ways of framing the issue – one informed by third way thinking, the other by a vision that is consistent with the egalitarian blueprint. These differences are important. Framing is a deeply political process. Frames direct attention to particular issues and policy options while obscuring other alternatives. They can also empower certain actors while marginalising others. The reconciliation frame deployed in *Babies and Bosses* depicts women as a reserve army of labour whose time has come to be deployed in order to meet the labour market needs resulting from declining fertility and rapid ageing. Its way of framing the reconciliation agenda draws on the economistic language it shares with neo-liberalism and its benefits are 'tied to participation in the globalizing economy for both men and women' (Larner et al. 2006, p. 6). Its implementation would do little to advance equality between the sexes or across generations.

The ECEC unit's perspective represents more of a challenge to the status quo. It is not as well-placed as the 'family-friendly' unit in DELSA, however. It reports to a smaller, more narrowly focused (education) directorate than DELSA (labour markets and social policy). More importantly, it is but a small unit of the Education and Training Division, where it pales by comparison with the unit charged with the division's main business, the national education reviews. What strength it may have comes from the way the review process was structured. *Starting Strong* carried out its work in such a way as to draw *in* and develop a transnational network of early childhood specialists and advocates. It thus blurred the boundary between epistemic communities, made up of experts linked by cognitive and professional ties (Haas 1992), and transnational advocacy networks – 'networks of activists, distinguishable largely by the centrality of principled ideas or values in motivating their formation' (Keck and Sikkink 1999, p. 89). In this it has built on, and extended, the earlier work of the European Commission's Childcare Network. Just as the latter forged links among childcare advocates operating at different scales – local and national – adding the European, the ECEC branch has done the same across the OECD. Its success, of course, will depend on the capacity of advocates to make good use of these reports in their struggles in diverse national contexts. Part of the hope may lie, as Cohen et al. conclude, in countries where 'the long default position of the child located in the private sphere of the family is being disturbed by some glimmerings of the "public child", replete with voice, rights and citizenship' (2004, p. 211). Yet this 'new child' will need allies. These might be found in part in recharged feminist movements.

NOTES

1. I follow Porter and Craig (2004) in seeing the 'third way' as a form of 'inclusive liberalism', fashioned in the 1990s in response to the limitations of 1980s-style neo-liberalism.
2. On fast policy, see Peck (2002, p. 349); on contextualized learning, see Zeitlin 2003, p. 15).
3. See Sainsbury (1996), especially Chapters 3 and 4.
4. See for example the work McCain and Mustard (1999).
5. Mahon (2002a) on the UK and the Netherlands; Lister (2004), on Canada and the UK.
6. This is the argument put forward by Iversen and Wren (1998) and Esping-Andersen (1999). See Mahon (2000) for a critique of the logic underpinning this.
7. See in particular Ross (2001), Mahon (2002a); and Stratigaki (2004).
8. The original 20 included the United States, Canada, Austria, Belgium, Denmark, France, Germany, Greece, Iceland, Ireland, Italy, Luxemburg, the Netherlands, Norway, Portugal, Spain, Sweden, Switzerland, and the United Kingdom. Japan joined in 1964 , Finland in 1969, Australia 1971 and New Zealand, 1973. Over the last decades, the Czech Republic, Hungary, Poland, the Slovak Republic, Mexico, and South Korea have been admitted.
9. The latter involves 'careful examination of both the institutional environment from which a given policy solution originated and the local conditions surrounding its proposed implementation elsewhere' (Zeitlin 2003, p. 15).
10. Established in 1974 as the Directorate for Education, Employment, Labour and Social Affairs (DEELSA), it became DELSA, when Education was split off to form its own directorate. For simplicity's sake, I will simply refer to it as DELSA.
11. Looking back on the OECD's achievements, Pearson (2004) noted that 'overgenerosity' of some provisions had been reduced and sources of retirement income 'diversified'.
12. The others are older workers, migrants and the low-skilled.
13. These are: Australia, Austria, Belgium, Canada, Czech Republic, Denmark, Finland, France, Germany, Hungary, Ireland, Italy, Korea, Mexico, the Netherlands, Norway, Portugal, Sweden, the United Kingdom and the United States.
14. The 'policy brief' prepared for the 2005 meeting of Social Affairs Ministers, heralded a sudden shift on this question. Here it stated that 'nowhere is it suggested that mothers rather than fathers should provide personal care throughout this period. Nevertheless, gender inequality in care-giving within families remains widespread' (OECD 2005, p. 4). Later in the text, potential solutions are noted – Sweden's introduction of two 'daddy months' and Iceland's one-third allocation for each parent and one-third shared leave (OECD 2005, p. 6). This about-shift, likely the fruit of Janet Gornick's five-month secondment to the programme in 2003, was echoed in the Social Affairs Ministers' final communiqué: 'The importance of both mothers and fathers to the long term

development of children should be recognized and both should be encouraged to play a full and active role in family life', available at www.oecd.org/documentprint/0,2744,en_2649_201185_34668207_1_1_1_1,00.html. It stopped short of recommending the introduction of daddy-months, however.

15. Like *Babies and Bosses*, *Starting Strong* recognises that decentralisation can bring some real advantages, but this needs to be balanced by the 'need to limit variation in access and quality' (OECD 2001, p. 9).

BIBLIOGRAPHY

Armingeon, K. (2004), 'OECD and national welfare state development', in K. Armingeon and M. Beyeler (eds), *The OECD and European Welfare States*, Cheltenham, UK and Northampton, MA, USA: Edward Elgar.

Armingeon, K. and M. Beyeler (eds) (2004), *The OECD and European Welfare States*, Cheltenham, UK and Northampton, MA, USA: Edward Elgar.

Bashevkin, S. (2002), *Welfare Hot Buttons: Women, Work and Social Policy Reform*, Toronto: University of Toronto Press.

Carnoy, M. and M. Castells (1997), *Sustainable Flexibility: A Prospective Study in Work, Family and Society*, Paris: OECD.

Childcare Resource and Research Unit (CRRU) (2004), *Quality in Early Learning and Child Care Services: Papers from the European Commission Childcare Network*, Toronto: Childcare Resource and Research Unit.

Cleveland, G. and M. Krashinsky (2003), '*Financing early childhood education and care services in OECD countries*', accessed at oecd.org/dataoecd/55/59/201.23665.pdf

Cohen, B., P. Moss, P. Petrie and J. Wallace (2004), *A New Deal for Children: Reforming Education and Care in England, Scotland and Sweden*, Bristol: Policy Press.

Daly, M. and J. Lewis (2000), 'The Concept of social care and the analysis of contemporary welfare states', *British Journal of Sociology*, **51**(2), 281–98.

Deacon, B. with M. Hulse and P. Stubbs (1997), *Global Social Policy: International Organisations and the Future of Welfare*, London: Sage.

Esping-Andersen, G. (1990), *The Three Worlds of Welfare Capitalism*, Princeton, NJ: Princeton University Press.

Esping-Andersen, G. (1999), *Social Foundations of Postindustrial Economies*, New York: Oxford University Press.

Esping-Andersen, G. (2003), 'Against inheritance', in A. Giddens (ed.), *The Progressive Manifesto: New Ideas for the Centre Left*, Oxford: Polity Press.

Giddens, A. (2003), 'Introduction: the new progressivism: a new agenda for social democracy', in A. Giddens (ed.), *The Progressive Manifesto: New Ideas for the Centre Left*, Oxford: Polity Press.

Glenn, E.N. (1992), 'From servitude to service work: historical continuities in the racial division of paid reproductive labor', *Signs*, **18**, 1–43.

Haas, P. (1992), 'Introduction: epistemic communities and international policy coordination', *International Organisation*, **46**(1), 1–36.

Iversen, T. and A. Wren (1998), 'Equality, employment and budgetary restraint: the trilemma of the service economy', *World Politics*, **50**, 507–46.

Jenson, Jane (1997), 'Who cares? Gender and welfare regimes', *Social Politics*, **4**(2), 182–7.

Jessop, Bob (2003), *The Future of the Capitalist State*, Oxford: Polity Press.

Keck, M. and K. Sikkink (1999), 'Transnational advocacy networks in international and regional politics', *International Social Science Journal*, **51**(159), 89–101.

Koven, S. and S. Michel (1993), *Mothers of a New World: Maternalist Politics and the Origins of Welfare States*, New York: Routledge.

Larner, W., R. LeHeron and N. Lewis (2006), 'Co-constituting "after Neo-Liberalism": globalizing governmentalities and political projects in Aotearoa New Zealand', in K. England and K. Ward (eds), *Neo-Liberalism: States, Networks, People*, Oxford: Blackwell.

Lister, R. (2004), 'New policy directions in OECD countries: the emergence of the social investment state', paper presented at the Policy Research Initiative workshop on Exploring New Approaches to Social Policy.

McBride, S. and R. Williams (2000), 'Globalization, the restructuring of labour markets and policy convergence: the OECD jobs strategy', *Global Social Policy*, **13**, 281–309.

McCain, Margaret and Fraser Mustard (1999), '*Reversing the brain drain: the early years study final report*', accessed at www.childsec.gov.on.ca.

McCracken, P.W. (1977), *Towards Full Employment and Price Stability: Report to the OECD by a Group of Independent Experts*, Paris: OECD.

Mahon, R. (2000), 'Death of a model? Swedish social democracy at the end of the twentieth century', *Studies in Political Economy*, **63**, 27–60.

Mahon, R. (2002a), 'Child care policy: toward what kind of social Europe?', *Social Politics*, **9**(4), 343–79.

Mahon, R. (2002b), 'Gender and welfare state restructuring: through the lens of child care', in S. Michel and R. Mahon (eds), *Child Care Policy at the Crossroads: Gender and Welfare State Restructuring*, New York: Routledge.

Marcussen, M. (2004), 'Multilateral surveillance and the OECD: playing the idea game', in K. Armingeon and M. Beyeler (eds), *The OECD and European Welfare States*, Cheltenham, UK and Northampton, MA, USA: Edward Elgar.

Martin, A. (1979), 'The dynamics of change in a Keynesian political economy', in C. Crouch (ed.), *State and Economy in Contemporary Capitalism*, London: Croom Helm.

Mazy, S. (2000), 'Introduction: integrating gender – intellectual and "real world" mainstreaming', *Journal of European Public Policy*, **7**(3), 333–45.

Michel, S. (1999), *Children's Interests/Mothers' Rights: The Shaping of America's Child Care Policy*, New Haven, CT: Yale University Press.

Morgan, K. (2005), '*Gender, states and social policy: the politics of mothers' employment in four nations*', draft manuscript.

Morth, U. (2000), 'Competing frames in the European Commission – the case of the defence industry and equipment issue', *Journal of European Public Policy*, **7**(2), 173–89.

OECD (1994), *New Orientations for Social Policy*, social policy studies no 12, Paris: OECD.

OECD (1996), 'Making life long learning a reality for all', draft communique for the meeting of the Education Committee at the ministerial level.

OECD (1999), *A Caring World: The New Social Policy Agenda*, Paris: OECD.

OECD (2001), *Starting Strong*, Paris: OECD.

OECD (2002a), *Babies and Bosses: Australia, Denmark and the Netherlands, Volume 1*, Paris: OECD.

OECD (2002b), '*Data needs in early childhood education and care*', compiled by John Bennett, accessed at www.oecd.org/dataoecd/25/54127858604.pdf.

OECD (2003a), *Babies and Bosses: Austria, Ireland and Japan, Volume 2*, Paris: OECD.

OECD (2003b), *2003 Employment Outlook*, Paris: OECD, accessed at www.oecd.org/documentprint/02744,en-2649-33729-14753163_1_1_1_1_1,00.html.

OECD (2004a), *Babies and Bosses: New Zealand, Portugal and Switzerland, Volume 3*, Paris: OECD.

OECD (2004b), *Country Note for Ireland*, Paris: OECD.

OECD (2004c), *Starting Strong: Curricula and Pedagogies in Early Childhood Education and Care*, Paris: OECD, accessed at www.oecd.org/dataoecd/23/3631672150.pdf.

OECD (2004d), *2003 Employment Outlook*, Paris: OECD, accessed at www.oecd.org/document/37/02340,en_2649_33927_3176485_1_1_1_1,00.html.

OECD (2005), 'Babies and bosses: balancing work and family life', *OECD Policy Briefs*, March, accessed at oecd.org/dataoecd/12/2/34566853.pdf.

O'Connor, J., A.S. Orloff and S. Shaver (1999), *States, Families, Markets: Gender, Liberalism and Social Policy in Australia, Canada, Great Britain and the United States*, Cambridge: Cambridge University Press.

Orloff, A.S. (2004), 'Farewell to maternalism? State policies and mothers' employment', paper presented at 2004 meeting of Research Committee 19, Paris, 2–5 September.

Palier, B. (2003), 'The Europeanisation of welfare reform', paper presented at RC 19, 22–24 August, Toronto, Canada.

Pearson, M. (2004), 'New directions in social policy', paper presented at workshop on Exploring New Approaches to Social Policy, sponsored by the Policy Research Initiative, Ottawa, December, accessed at www.policyresearch.gc.ca/page.asp?pagenm=social_approaches1204_slides.

Pearson, M. and P. Scherer, (1997), 'Balancing security and sustainability in social policy', *OECD Observer*, **215**, April/May.

Peck, J. (2001), *Workfare States*, New York: Guilford Press.

Peck, J. (2002), 'Political economies of scale: fast policy, interscalar relations and neoliberal workfare', *Economic Geography*, **78**(3), 331–61.

Peng, I. (2004), 'Postindustrial pressures, political regime shifts and social policy reform in Japan and Korea', paper presented at RC 19 meetings, Paris, 2–5 September.

Porter, D. and D. Craig (2004), 'The third way and the third world: poverty reduction and social inclusion in the rise of "inclusive" liberalism', *Review of Radical Political Economy*, **11**(2), 387–423.

Porter, T. and M. Webb (2004), 'The role of the OECD in the orchestration of global knowledge networks', paper prepared for the annual meeting of the International Studies Association, March, Montreal.

Ross, G. (2001), 'Europe: an actor without a role', in J. Jenson and M. Sineau (eds), *Who Cares? Women Work and Welfare State Redesign*, Toronto: University of Toronto Press.

Sahlin-Andersson, K. (2000), 'National, international, and transnational construction of new public management', Stockholm University SCORE report series 2000:4, Stockholm.

Sainsbury, D. (1996), *Gender, Equality and Welfare States*, Cambridge: Cambridge University Press.

Serré, M. and B. Palier (2004), 'France: moving reluctantly in the OECD's direction', in K. Armingeon and M. Beyeler (eds), *The OECD and European Welfare States*, Cheltenham, UK and Northampton, MA, USA: Edward Elgar.

Skocpol, T. (1992), *Protecting Soldiers and Mothers: Political Origins of Social Policy in the United States*, Cambridge, MA: Harvard University Press.

Stratigaki, M. (2004), 'The cooptation of gender concepts in EU policies: the case of reconciliation of work and family', *Social Politics*, **11**(1), 30–56.

Wade, R.H. (2002), 'The United States and the World Bank: the fight over people and ideas', *Review of Radical Political Economy*, **9**(2), 215–43.

Zeitlin, J. (2003), 'Introduction: governing work and welfare in a new economy: European and American experiences', in J. Zeitlin and D. Trubek (eds), *Governing Work and Welfare in a New Economy: European and American Experiences*, Oxford: Oxford University Press.

Zippel, K. (2000), 'Policies against sexual harassment: gender equality policy in Germany, in the European Union and in the United States in comparative perspective', PhD dissertation, University of Wisconsin-Madison.

PART IV

Children and the search for a work–life balance

10. Childcare in a changing world: policy responses to working time flexibility in France

Marie-Thérèse Letablier

In a context of far-reaching changes in family life and labour markets, childcare has become a major issue for welfare states. The nature and extent of these changes are of such importance that they call for new approaches to the social provision of care and for new thinking about care work. These same changes have coincided with a period of welfare state restructuring and with increasing government concern about employment. In all countries, activation policies are being implemented to raise employment rates. The shift from social support to social inclusion via labour market participation is characteristic of these trends and is driven by the aim of promoting competition and growth. In most European countries, attempts to promote active welfare have focused on employment, with little attention being paid to the question of care.

In France, as in most other EU member states, the emphasis on employment has been underpinned by high unemployment rates in a context where the length of working life has been reduced for both men and women by later labour market entry and earlier labour market exit. Meanwhile, childcare has become a central issue for family policy. Not only have childcare services been extensively developed, but childcare benefits have also been provided for families, especially for families with very young children, either to encourage parents – primarily mothers – to look after their young children, or to help reduce the cost of childcare. Childcare provision has increased significantly since the early 1980s, although supply still does not match demand. An important aim in developing childcare services has been to promote women's work and improve the well-being of children (Letablier and Jönsson 2005). Today, the quality of childcare services is, however, uneven, since the market remains highly segmented between public collective provision and private individualised childcare by childminders in the home.

The ability of parents to balance work and family life is not only determined by the provision of childcare services, but also by the distribution of time: the well-being of children depends in part on the time parents devote to work and care. Whereas flexible working time arrangements can provide an opportunity for parents to manage work and family life – at least when they can choose their working schedule – flexible working hours may become a nightmare if they are imposed on parents, especially on parents with young children. Harriet Presser (2000, 2004) has drawn attention to the development of a '24-hour economy', which poses a threat to family life and the well-being of children. And Arlie Hochschild (1998) has shown how family life in the USA has become more and more dependent on the organisation of working life, especially for working parents with young children. The French context differs profoundly from the American context with regard to the development of family-friendly policies, which are examined in this chapter. Policy responses to increases in working time flexibility are explored, together with their impact on childcare arrangements. How are childcare services being adapted in response to flexible working hours, and what is the impact of flexibility on childcare workers and the work organisation of childcare services? To what extent should childcare services be adapted to suit the 24-hour economy? What are the parameters of 'a normal family life', and how can parents avoid their family life becoming entirely subjugated to the requirements of companies?

WORK–LIFE BALANCE: A MATTER OF TIME

The amount of time that people spend at work differs considerably across Europe. Compared with the West, in Eastern Europe, both men and women spend longer at work, and fewer people work part time. This tradition of full-time work for both men and women contrasts with most West European countries where vestiges of the male breadwinner model remain, even though dual earner families are becoming the norm. The Netherlands record the shortest working hours: according to Eurostat's Labour Force Survey for 2002, Dutch men work on average 35.6 hours a week and women 23.9 hours. Figures were lower still for men and women employees, at 34 hours and 23.7 hours respectively. Figures for France were 40.6 hours for men (all workers) and 33.9 hours for women, and 38.6 hours for male employees and 33.1 for female employees. The average number of hours worked by employees in the EU 15 was 38.7 hours for men and 31.4 for women (Eurostat 2003). Surveys carried out by the Dublin Foundation on gender, employment and working time preferences in Europe indicate that workers, men and women, state that they would like to work less, on average 37 hours per week for men and 30 hours for women (Fagan and Warren 2001). Similar findings are obtained from a survey conducted in a selection of East and West European countries, conducted by Claire Wallace (2003). According to this survey, 28 per cent of the respondents stated they would like to reduce their working hours, the main reason being to spend more time with the family. Surprisingly, men rather than women were more interested in reducing their working hours, especially well-educated men in West European countries who have the longest working hours.

While the average number of working hours has progressively decreased over the past century, the number of women in the labour market has grown substantially, thereby increasing the amount of time families spend in paid work and limiting the time they can devote to care. It is not, therefore, surprising that when parents with young children are questioned about their use of time in France, the great majority report feeling a time squeeze. Considering the time-use patterns of employed women in France, the hours devoted to gainful work per day are among the longest in Europe: 4 hours 32 minutes per day, while the time devoted to domestic work is about the European average: 3 hours 40 minutes per day (Eurostat 2004a). Time pressure is more strongly felt by workers with long working hours, particularly in professional occupations, and by workers with irregular working schedules (Chenu 2002). The laws reducing the length of the working week from 39 hours to 35 hours in France (passed between 1996 and 2000) did not change this perception of time pressure, although average working time has decreased for most workers. Whereas according to the law, the working week should not exceed 35 hours, the effective working week is 40.8 hours for all full-time workers and 38.8 hours for full-time employees (the self-employed work longer hours). Average working time for full-time workers in France is slightly below the average in Europe, higher than in Germany and the Netherlands and lower than in Sweden and the UK (Table 10.1).

However, working patterns over the life cycle show that paid work is concentrated between the ages of 25 and 49 in France, whereas younger and older people have low employment rates in comparison with other EU member states, which illustrates the heavy burden on adults during the parenting phase of their lives. This working time profile, which can also be found in Southern European countries, makes it difficult to balance paid work and family life: time pressures in family and working life occur simultaneously. In addition, only 16.6 per cent of the labour force worked part time in France in 2004, and 29 per cent of part-timers reported that they wanted to work longer hours. The French working-time regime offers little flexibility for parents to accommodate family responsibilities. According to a survey carried out in 2002–2003 for the Ministry for Social Affairs (Garner et al. 2005), almost 39 per cent of workers reported difficulty in combining their work schedule with family life. These problems increased with the number of children: with three children, 45 per cent of fathers as well as mothers find it difficult to combine paid work and family life. The problems seem to decrease as children grow older. Some jobs appear to be more difficult than others to combine with family life, for instance professional workers with long working hours, or employees in the service sector or retailing who are exposed to 'atypical' hours, who work on Saturdays and Sundays or at night, are most likely to say they suffer from time pressure.

Impact of the Reduction of Working Time on the Work–Family Balance

The reduction in working time imposed by law was a central plank of public employment policy in France between 1996, under the *loi Robien*, and 2002, under the Aubry Laws, which progressively extended the implementation of the '35 hours' week. If the impact of these laws has been relatively limited (and rather controversial) in terms of job creation, which was the primary policy objective, the impact on the bargaining process in the workplace and on family life has been more marked (Estrade et al. 2001). Studies show that employees whose legal working time was reduced to 35 hours a week are most likely to have irregular or non-standard working patterns (Afsa and Biscourps 2004). The complexity of the implementation process – a compromise between flexibility and work reorganisation, funded jointly by employees, employers and the state – has produced a variety of outcomes.

Moreover, policy measures encouraging part-time work have not produced the expected effect:[1] part-time work increased from 11.9 per cent in 1990 to 16.5 per cent in 2002. Since state support for part-time recruitment was withdrawn in 2002, part-time work has not increased and remains at under 17 per cent of the labour force. Thus policies to promote part-time work were abandoned before the level of part-time work reached the level in the UK (25 per cent of the labour force). Part-time hours are also, on average, four hours longer in France than in Sweden, Denmark, Germany or the Netherlands. In 2004, 30 per cent of women in employment worked part-time in France, a lower proportion than the EU average and much lower than in Germany (40.7 per cent), the UK (43.1 per cent) and the Netherlands (74.4 per cent). In France where full-time work remains the norm, part-time work is not a major means of reconciling work and family life; indeed slightly over 30 per cent of those working part time say that they would like to work longer hours.

By limiting working time to 35 hours per week, the Aubry Laws should have provided an opportunity for working parents to devote more time to family life, leisure and other activities. But such effects have not been widely observed among parents with young children. Research on the arrangements made by parents with young children underlines the fact that it is not sufficient to reduce working time to improve the reconciliation of paid work with family life (Fagnani and Letablier 2004). Of 700 respondents, 42 per cent of parents reported that the 35-hour week has not made reconciliation any easier than before the reduction of working time. Reasons given for the lack of improvement were the poor organisation of working hours and the problem of combining parents' hours of work with children's hours of care or schooling. Irregular working schedules and non-standard working hours (Saturdays or Sundays, working at night or early in the morning), make it difficult for parents with young children to arrange childcare and to have a 'normal' family life.

Similar findings were produced by a survey carried out in 2000 for the French Ministry of Labour and Social Affairs (Méda and Orain 2002). Parents who report that the reduction of working time has had a positive impact on family life generally work standard and regular hours. In addition, they have had the opportunity to choose how they reduce their working time: daily, weekly or annually. In workplaces where employees have had their work schedules imposed on them without being able to negotiate flexibility, the reduction of working time has not brought any real improvement in the balance between paid work and family life. According to the same survey, 59 per cent of respondents report that the reduction in working hours has helped to improve their daily life, whereas 13 per cent claim to have experienced a 'deterioration' and 28 per cent were not aware of any change (Estrade et al. 2001). The figures vary according to gender and level of education, and also to the way in which the reduction has been implemented by companies. The higher the level of education, for example, the greater has been the perception of the improvement in everyday life. For almost 50 per cent of parents with children under 12, fathers as well as mothers reported that, since the reduction in working hours, they spend more time with their children: well-educated employees take more days off work to spend with their children, whereas employees with a low level of education tend to reduce the length of their working day and thus devote more time to caring for their children on a daily basis. About a third of the parents questioned claim that the reduction in working hours has made it easier to combine paid work with family life, and 57 per cent reported no change in this respect.

An unexpected outcome of the laws was to promote the sharing of parental responsibilities between parents. In situations where employees can choose their working schedules, they sometimes arrange working hours so that they can take turns in caring for their children and, thus, avoid the cost of childcare (Fagnani and Letablier 2003). These findings are in line with the results of American research showing that fathers who are 'bad' for employees when considering work–life balance. 'Good flexibility' is when people have control over their working time schedules and is usually associated with a high level of job satisfaction. It is more often found among middle-class workers, many of whom have regular and secure jobs in the public sector. 'Bad flexibility' is associated with lack of control over hours, place of work and working conditions, low job satisfaction, as experienced by low-skilled workers in services, retail, hotels and catering. In Western Europe, women are more exposed than men to bad flexibility because they are most likely to be in these sectors. Bad flexibility is often linked to insecure forms of work, irregular and atypical jobs. The individualisation of working hours helps to increase employee-led flexibility for workers with secure jobs and open-ended working contracts, who are in a position to negotiate their working schedules, compared with workers faced with employer-led flexibility. The European survey on households, work and flexibility coordinated by Wallace (2003) shows that employees' control over working schedules was greater in the Netherlands than in most other European countries. The Netherlands appears to be the EU member state where employees are the most satisfied with their working time arrangements. Not only do workers have a high degree of control over flexibility through the collective bargaining system, but the development of part-time work also increases their satisfaction. In the Netherlands, part-time work is viewed as a means of combining work and care, whereas in France it is considered to be a form of bad flexibility, because this working time arrangement is used mainly by women but does not contribute to gender equity in the workplace, nor does it stimulate shared carework between parents at the household level. Also, part-time work means part-time wages and limited social rights, especially with regard to pensions.

In 2001, more than two out of three employees had similar working schedules every day and every week in France, while slightly more than 10 per cent had regular working schedules that vary week by week, and 20 per cent had irregular working schedules that varied during the day or during the week, or both (Biscourps 2004). Comparison of the 1995 and 2001 Institut National de la Statistique et des Etudes Economiques (INSEE) surveys on working time reveal little change in working schedules when laws reducing the hours of work were adopted. Although women's working schedules have remained more regular than those of men, the gap has tended to reduce as a growing number of women work in retail, services and catering, where hours of work are often irregular and 'atypical' (that is, a non-standard working week).[2] Research on working time indicates that the standard working week is less common than supposed in France (Table 10.3). The reduction of working time has led to a reorganisation of working patterns: flexibility has, in general, been increased, but 'bad

Table 10.3   Proportion of employees with different working arrangements

	Men	Women	Total
Number of hours of work changes every day	37.4	32.6	36.6
Number of working days changes each week	23.3	20.2	21.9
Flexible working hours	30.1	25.8	28.2
Non-standard working day	10.7	9.3	10.1
Shift work	23.0	20.7	22.0
Two shifts	9.1	10.1	9.5
Three shifts	8.8	5.0	7.2

Source: Boisard et al. (2002, p. 25).

flexibility' for low-skilled workers, and especially women, has reinforced differences between workers. Four in ten employees working full time continue to have regular and predictable working hours, whereas two in ten have experienced an increase in the variability of their working schedules (Estrade and Ulrich 2003). Employees with 'atypical working hours', having to work at times otherwise devoted to family activities, rest or leisure, have difficulty in reconciling work and family life and in accessing childcare services.

However, as Hantrais and Ackers (2004) have shown from interviews conducted in France, Spain and Poland, it is difficult to understand how women make their choices about their work–life balance. Choice is a complex, contingent and relative concept, which is both facilitated and constrained by public policies and working regulations. In France, attitude surveys consistently indicate that women give a medium or high value *both* to work and to family life, and do not expect to have to choose between the two. Compared to other European countries, external constraints on choice are minimised: the French state is highly supportive of family life (and more especially of working mothers), and in addition to working time policies, benefits and services are provided to families to facilitate the reconciliation between work and family life (Letablier 2004). But, even in France, where the supply of childcare services is relatively generous, crèches are open at regular or standard working times, from 7.30 or 8.00 in the morning to 18.00 or 18.30 in the evening, Mondays to Fridays. Outside of these opening hours, it is difficult to find childcare. As yet, very few countries offer 24/7 childcare services.

Surveys of the impact of atypical working hours on family life show that time flexibility is less developed in France compared with most other EU member states. In addition to being one of the countries where working hours are relatively short, France is also a country where the symbolic value attached to working time remains strong, and where the gender gap with regard to working time is relatively small. Nevertheless, the debate about the possible effects of imposed flexibility is still very current, especially with regard to work–life balance issues. For a number of years, family and child-care policy has aimed to take account of the needs of working parents, and to adapt childcare services to match the extension of parents' working hours. A compromise has been sought between the interests of working parents and the interests of children. Extending the opening hours of child-care services to 24/7 is not, however, considered to be a reasonable solution or one likely to contribute to the well-being of children. Rather, support for private childcare by childminders appears to be the main trend in childcare policy. This type of care allows the kind of flexible arrangements between parents and carers that are more difficult to achieve with collectively provided public services.

HOUSEHOLD ORGANISATION OF TIME: CARE, CHILDREN AND EMPLOYMENT

The vast majority of children in France under the age of six (91 per cent) live in families composed of a couple with children. The proportion is higher still for children under the age of three (Avenel 2001). However, 10.3 per cent of children aged three to five live with only one parent. The proportion is 7.6 per cent for children under three. Irrespective of the age of children living in lone-parent families, in most cases the lone parent is the mother. Lone mothers are more often economically active than mothers living in couples, unless they have children under three, when they are eligible for lone-parent allowances. Whereas 47 per cent of children under six live with two parents who are in paid work, only 14 per cent have at least one parent who is unemployed. Nearly 62 per cent of mothers with children under six living in couple households work full time, compared with 30 per cent who have chosen to work part time (Table 10.4).

The structure of households in the 25–40 age category in respect of work organisation, varies across countries: the proportion of full-time dual-earner families is larger in France than in Italy, Germany and the UK, where childcare facilities have not been a political priority (Table 10.5).

Childcare: The Time Challenge

Combining work with family responsibilities has become a challenge in most western societies. Even though women are engaged in the labour market, they continue to do most of the care work, and lone mothers face

Table 10.4   Children under six according to the work status of parents in France (per cent)

Occupational status	1990	2000
Two parents employed	45.1	47.1
One parent employed, other non-employed	34.9	30.3
One parent employed, other unemployed	8.0	8.3
Two parents unemployed	1.1	0.9
One parent unemployed, other non-employed	2.7	3.2
Two parents non-employed	1.2	1.3
Lone parent employed	3.8	4.4
Lone parent non-employed	1.7	2.9
Lone parent unemployed	1.5	1.6
All children (%)	100.0	100.0
Number	4 458 000	4 216 000

Source: Avenel (2001), from INSEE (1990, 2000).

Table 10.5   Work organisation of couples aged 25–40 with at least one partner in employment in selected EU member states (% of couples)

	EU 25	France	Italy	Germany	UK
Both partners working full time	45	52	38	37	44
Only man working	29	25	45	26	21
Man full time/woman part time	19	16	13	28	30
Both part time or woman full time and man part time	2	2	2	2	2
Only woman working	5	5	2	7	3
Total	100	100	100	100	100

Source: Eurostat (2004b).

more difficulties than other mothers because they have to act as both bread-winner and carer. The French model of providing childcare rests on the principle of parents' 'freedom of choice' between public collective childcare services on the one hand, and private individualised services by childminders or employees in the home on the other, both subsidised by the state. The childcare issue is mainly a concern for children under the age of three, since 98 per cent of children aged three to six attend nursery school (*écoles maternelles*), although it is not compulsory. Pre-schools are free of charge and open Monday, Tuesday, Thursday and Friday from 8.30 to 16.30 and until noon on Saturdays. At lunchtime, in the evening until 18.00, on Wednesdays and during holidays, most – but not all – children are offered childcare services by local authorities. *Écoles maternelles* are not part of the childcare system but are under the control of the Ministry for Education; they are organised and regulated on the same basis as primary schools.

Children under three may be cared for in public collective childcare services (*crèches*) by trained and qualified employees, in the private home of a registered childminder, or at their parents' home by a family employee. Childcare supply is thus highly segmented between the private and public sectors, and between collective and individual arrangements. Collective childcare services are subsidised by the family policy fund, and charges for parents are income related. Whereas collective provision is the cheapest form of childcare service for low-income families, most parents using such services belong to the middle classes or are working in the public sector. When they are interviewed, parents claim that they prefer collective childcare for their children, mainly because of the high quality of the service, but only 11 per cent of children under three are cared for in *crèches*. Not only is the supply limited, but the distribution of *crèches* across the country is uneven: most are in large cities. Since the mid-1980s, governments have given priority to individual childcare services in the context of high unemployment, the objective being to create family-care jobs. Since the 1980s, various allowances and tax deductions aimed at lowering costs for parents have been implemented (Fagnani and Letablier 2005). Childminders have to be registered: they must be approved by local authorities and are obliged to undergo a minimum of 60 hours of training. Their work status is kept under review, mainly with the objective of upgrading the professional skills required by the job.

More than half of all children under three (54 per cent) are cared for at home by their mothers, some of whom are on parental leave and in receipt of a parental leave allowance; 26 per cent are cared for by a childminder or a family employee; and 37 per cent of two–three year olds already attend pre-school. According to a large survey carried out by the Ministry of Social Affairs, children who are cared for more than 30 hours per week belong to families with the highest incomes and to parents who are working the longest hours (Méda and Orain 2002). Some of these families employ a nanny in their own home to care for their children and to do the housework, with financial support from the state. Although the reform of childcare services in 2003 brought a reduction in the cost of childminding, it is still higher than the cost of public collective services for low-income parents. However, the choice of childcare services is not made simply on the basis of cost, but also according to parents' approach to childcare and education. Qualitative surveys on childcare choices show that preference for a childminder is often related to the family environment provided for the child, as opposed to the standardisation of the *crèches*. The contrast between private and public childcare services reflects the opposition between two different ways of conceptualising quality of care and the well-being of children (Odena 2005). In *crèches* there are high standards of childcare, with the emphasis on education, pedagogy, psychology and developmental activities. Staff are not substitutes for mothers as are child-minders. Instead, they are teachers, who are practitioners trained in peda-gogical methods. The demand for collective public childcare is greater than the supply and much of the demand goes unsatisfied.

If choices with regard to childcare services are socially constructed, opin-ions about what is the best form of childcare tend to be contradictory: the interests of parents are best served by childminders because of their greater flexibility compared with collective childcare services, but when the inter-ests of children are prioritised, the preference is for *crèches* (Crédoc 2003). Parents increasingly expect more flexible childcare services, better suited to their needs. The development of atypical hours of work has resulted in new constraints for parents with young children, who have to find a way of mixing and matching a variety of possible childcare arrangements. When the formal childcare supply does not fit with working time flexibility, parents have to rely on informal networks, and especially on grandparents or friends. Finding suitable childcare arrangements can become such a nightmare that some mothers abandon their job and stay at home to care for their young children. Mothers who cannot reconcile work with caring responsibilities tend to be the less well educated and are more often in inse-cure jobs with unsocial hours of work, often part time.

In a context where women are being encouraged to be in the labour market, working time flexibility is a new challenge for childcare policies. Working parents are demanding extended childcare services as well as emer-gency childcare to deal with family crises, usually among lone mothers. These demands correspond to two different logics, implying that there are political choices to be made.

WORKING FLEXIBILITY AND CARING ARRANGEMENTS

The issue of policy responses to working time flexibility has not received the same amount of attention everywhere, and in those countries where it is considered to be an important social issue, policy responses tend to vary according to the conceptualisation of the role of the state in childcare arrange-ments, the strength of working time norms, and the conceptualisation of the well-being of children. The issue is not so important in Mediterranean countries, for example, where caring arrangements still rely heavily on informal care by kin or on private services provided by immigrant women. In France, where childcare services have been promoted by the state through a wide variety of provisions in kind and in cash, childcare policies are expected to meet the needs of parents.

Between 2002 and 2005, several studies were carried out for the National Family Allowance Fund (*Caisse nationale des allocations familiales* – CNAF) to identify family needs, to locate and analyse innovative schemes and to investigate the impact on childcare services and on childminders' patterns of work. These studies have found that family needs with regard to atypical hours of work of parents and the availability of childcare services vary according to particular working arrangements and employers' attitudes towards the caring needs of employees, which are partly determined by the characteristics of the private sector. In their study of the difficulties and the childcare needs of parents with atypical hours of work, Martin et al. (2005) have found that atypical working hours are not matched by the opening hours of public and private services. They argue that it is crucial whether working hours are predictable, because parents need to be able to anticipate childcare needs, and whether working schedules can be negotiated or not (see also Le Bihan and Martin 2005).

In fact, atypical working hours are not necessarily seen as negative from the parents' perspective and with regard to work–life balance. When associated with short working hours, they can provide opportunities for childcare arrangements between parents. Negotiation and predictability are crucial for caring arrangements, two criteria that law does not cater for.

The needs of families also vary according to family structures, networks, and income. Lone mothers with atypical working hours experience more difficulty in combining work and care than mothers living with a partner. Their difficulties increase if they cannot rely on family networks – on resources offered by grandparents for instance – and if their income is not sufficient to buy services on the market. The fact is that lone mothers are over-represented among employees with atypical hours of work (Bué 2002). Most of them work part time but more under constraint than by choice. In general, they report more difficulties than other working mothers in combining work and family life unless they work short hours (Garner et al. 2005). Qualitative surveys of low-qualified women in the retail sector, social care services and hotels and restaurants show that flexible working hours do not mean more autonomy for employees, but rather more constraints for mothers with regard to childcare (Gadrey et al. 2005; Fagnani 1999). Most of them cannot overcome the work–family conflict and give up work to care for their children (Méda et al. 2003).

'Shift' Parenting

As already mentioned, one of the impacts of the 35-hours legislation on family life has been to increase the involvement of fathers in childcare and to promote shift arrangements between parents. In fact, 'shift' parenting has long been widespread among low-paid workers in the UK, because childcare services at reasonable costs were not available (Gregory and Windebank 2000). In fact, non-standard working hours offer an opportunity for the sharing of care responsibilities within dual-earner families. Preferences for 'flexitime' sometimes reflect a parental strategy aimed at limiting childcare expenses. This strategy was observed in American families (Glass 1998; Presser 1994) as well as in English families (Perrons 1998) and French families (Fagnani and Letablier 2003). Atypical working hours generate the opportunity to share caring responsibilities between parents who take turns with children at home. The negotiation takes place within the family. According to our survey on the nature of reconciliation between paid work and family life, more than 25 per cent of mothers reported that this organisation was the result of a choice: parents take advantage of the opportunity to devote more time to care while saving money. One third of all parents with no overlapping working hours stated their preference for this form of parental organisation. These findings were confirmed by Boyer and Nicolas (2006) in their study of childcare arrangements, highlighting the positive correlation between mothers with non-standard hours of work and fathers' participation in caring duties. Although the aim is not clearly to improve gender equality, the fact is that the use of atypical working hours increases fathers' participation in childcare.

Although the reduction in working time has not greatly changed daily hours of work (less than 25 per cent of employees have experienced a daily reduction of their working time), rhythms of work during the week or during the year have been modified: 36 per cent of employees reduced their working time by taking days or half days off from time to time, 35 per cent preferred to take more vacation, and 20 per cent had renegotiated their working hours. If in general the 35-hour legislation has given parents more time to devote to parental duties, the use of time varies according to level of education: low qualified parents have reduced their working day so as to limit expenses for childcare services, while middle-class parents have reduced their working week in order to spend more time with children during the weekend (cleaning and other domestic tasks being done during the week). Highly educated parents prefer to have more vacation with their children. However, parents' appreciation of the impact of the 35-hour legislation on their family life depends on their work schedules and on their ability to negotiate their working time with the employer. Nevertheless, there has been a reduction in childcare expenses, because the need for complementary childcare has been reduced, and there has been an increase in family care for children. The participation of fathers in childcare has also grown, although they still do not take primary responsibility. Since their working time has been reduced, 52 per cent of fathers with children under 12 state that they spend more time with their children. The figure for mothers is 63 per cent (Estrade et al. 2001).

POLICY RESPONSES TO PARENTS' DEMAND FOR FLEXIBLE CHILDCARE PROVISIONS

Since the 1980s, state support has given priority to private individualised childcare by childminders or family employees to the detriment of public collective services. Notwithstanding the fact that these forms of childcare are subsidised by the state through allowances and tax deductions for employers, this has led to a privatisation of childcare. This policy orientation can be explained both by the lower costs for the state and by the wish to create jobs in a context of high unemployment. Childcare policy has also tried to involve firms in developing childcare services; tax deductions are now offered to businesses participating in the development of childcare services.

However, family policy has also supported innovative childcare services, either by providing encouragement to *crèches* to open at non-standard hours, early in the morning and late in the evening for parents with atypical, but regular, hours of work. This means that there have been changes in the work patterns of childcare services and the introduction of shift work. Moreover, family policy has supported other forms of childcare services aimed at responding to specific, irregular demands. These services are organised at the local level in partnership with municipalities and with voluntary associations. In a study of innovation in childcare services, Eydoux (2005) examined how childcare structures are being reorganised to respond to flexible needs of working parents. The survey was conducted among care services with extended hours or atypical time schedules, such as collective childcare services, emergency services at the parent's home or childminders caring for children at atypical hours. The study confirms that the demand for childcare during non-standard hours is due to various factors: professional (for example, very long hours of work, evening or night work), family (for example, lone parents), or temporary problems in managing work and family life (for example, health problems, violence). It examined the impact on workers in childcare services and highlighted the work–family balance dilemma they are facing themselves when they have children, contributing as they now do to the development of a '24-hour economy'. While responding to the demand from parents with atypical hours of work, the extension of flexible childcare services also means an extension of atypical hours for an increasing number of workers and for children, thus raising the crucial question: what kind of society do we want for our children?

NOTES

1. A law passed in 1992 made it possible for companies hiring part-time workers to benefit from a 30 per cent deduction to their social insurance contributions.
2. Defined as a week of five working days, with 35–44 hours of work and no night work.

REFERENCES

Afsa, C. and P. Biscourps (2004), 'L'évolution des rythmes de travail entre 1995 et 2001: quel impact des 35 heures?', *Economie et statistique*, **376–377**, 173–213.

Avenel, M. (2001), 'Les enfants de moins de six ans et leurs familles en France métropolitaine', *Drees: Etudes et résultats*, **97**,1–4.

Biscourps, P. (2004), 'Les rythmes de travail entre 1995 et 2001: faible progression de l'irrégularité', *Insee Première*, **994**, 1–4.

Boisard, P., D. Cartron, M. Gollac and A. Valeyre (2002), *Temps et travail: la durée du travail*, Rapport pour la Fondation européenne pour l'amélioration des conditions de vie et de travail, Luxembourg: Office des publications officielles des Communautés européennes.

Boyer, D. and M. Nicolas (2006), 'La disponibilité des pères: subordonnée aux contraintes de travail des mères?', *Recherches et prévisions*, **82**(forthcoming).

Bué, J. (2002), 'Temps partiels des femmes: entre choix et contraintes', *Dares: Premières informations et premières synthèses*, 08.2, 1–7.

Chenu, A. (2002), 'Les horaires et l'organisation du temps de travail', *Economie et statistique*, **352–353**, 151–67.

Crédoc (2003), 'Enquête d'opinion sur les modes de garde des jeunes enfants', *L'Essentiel*, **11**, CNAF.

Estrade, M.A., D. Méda and R. Orain (2001), 'Les effets de la réduction du temps de travail sur les modes e vie: qu'en pensent les salariés un an après?', *Dares: Premières informations et premières synthèses*, 21.1, 1–8.

Estrade, Marc-Antoine and Valérie Ulrich (2003), 'Réduction du temps de travail et réorganisations des rythmes de travail', in *INSEE: Données sociales*, 301–8.

Eurostat (2003), *Enquête sur les forces de travail*, Luxembourg: Commission européenne, Office des publications officielles des Communautés européennes.

Eurostat (2004a), *How Europeans Spend their Time, Everyday Life of Women and Men, Data 1998–2002*, European Commission: theme 3: population and social conditions, Brussels: Pocket books.

Eurostat (2004b), *L'emploi en Europe 2003*, Luxembourg: Commission européenne, Office des publications officielles des Communautés européennes.

Eydoux, A. (2005), 'Les métiers de la petite enfance à l'épreuve des horaires atypiques', *Recherches et Prévisions*, **80**, 41–54.

Fagan, C. and T. Warren (2001), *Gender, Employment and Working Time Preferences in Europe*, Dublin: European Foundation for the Improvement of Living and Working Conditions, accessed at www.eurofound.ie.

Fagnani, J. (1999), 'Politique familiale, flexibilité des horaires de travail et articulation travail/famille. L'exemple des employées de la grande distribution en France et en Allemagne', *Droit social*, **3**, 244–9.

Fagnani, J. and M.T. Letablier (2003), 'Qui s'occupe des enfants pendant que les parents travaillent?', *Recherches et Prévisions*, **72**, 21–35.

Fagnani, J. and M.T. Letablier (2004), 'Work and family life balance: the impact of the 35-hour laws in France', *Work, Employment and Society*, **18**(3), 551–72.

Fagnani, J. and M.T. Letablier (2005), 'Social rights and care responsibility in the French welfare state', in B. Pfau-Effinger and B. Geissler (eds), *Care and Social Integration in European Societies*, Bristol: Policy Press.

Gadrey, N., F. Jany-Catrice and M. Pernod-Lemattre (2005), 'Les conditions de travail des employés non qualifiés', in D. Méda and F. Vennat (eds), *Le travail non qualifié*, Paris: La Découverte.

Garner, H., D. Méda and C. Sénik (2005), 'Conciliation entre vie professionnelle et vie familiale, les leçons des enquêtes auprès des ménages', *Travail et Emploi*, **102**, 57–68.

Glass, J. (1998), 'Gender liberation, economic squeeze, or fear of strangers: why fathers provide infant care in dual-earner families?', *Journal of Marriage and the Family*, 60, 821–34.

Gregory, Abigail and Jan Windebank (2000), *Women's Work in Britain and France. Practice, Theory and Policy*, Basingstoke: Macmillan.

Hantrais, L. and P. Ackers (2004), 'Women's choices in Europe: striking the work–life balance', *European Journal of Industrial Relations*, **11**(2), 197–212.

Hochschild, Arlie R. (1998), *The Time Bind: When Work Becomes Home and Home Becomes Work*, New York: Metropolitan Books.

Institut National de la Statistique et des Etudes Economiques (1990), *Enquêtes emploi*, Paris: INSEE, accessed at www.insee.fr.

Institut National de la Statistique et des Etudes Economiques (2000), *Enquêtes emploi*, Paris: INSEE, accessed at www.insee.fr.

Le Bihan, B. and C. Martin (2005), 'Atypical working hours: consequences for childcare arrangements', in T. Kröger and J. Sipila (eds), *Overstretched. European Families Up Against the Demands of Work and Care*, Oxford and Malden, MA: Blackwell.

Letablier, M.T. (2004), 'Work and family balance: a new challenge for policies in France', in J. Zollinger Giele and E. Holst (eds), *Changing Life Patterns in Western Industrial Societies*, Oxford: Elsevier; Advanced Life Course Research, Vol. 8.

Letablier, M.T. and I. Jönsson (2005), 'Caring for children: the logic of public action', in U. Gerhard, T. Knijn and A. Weckwert (eds), *Working Mothers in Europe. A Comparison of Policies and Practices*, Cheltenham, UK and Northampton, MA, USA: Edward Elgar.

Martin, C., B. Le Bihan, A. Campeon and G. Gardin (2005), *Petite enfance et horaires atypiques, analyse de quatre sites expérimentaux*, Dossier d'études no 73, Paris: CNAF.

Méda, D. and R. Orain (2002), 'Transformations du travail et du hors travail. Le jugement des salariés', *Travail et emploi*, **90**, 23–38.

Méda, D., M.O. Simon and M. Wierink (2003), 'Pourquoi certaines femmes s'arrêtent-elles de travailler à la naissance d'un enfant?', *Dares: Premières informations et premières synthèses*, 29.2, 1–8.

Odena, S. (2005), 'Les modes de garde de la petite enfance: facteurs de reproduction sociale et sexuée', Thèse pour le doctorat de sociologie, Université Aix-Marseille – Université de Provence (sous la dir. de T. Bloss).

Organisation for Economic Co-operation and Development (2004), *Employment Outlook 2004*, Paris: OECD, accessed at www.oecd.org.

Perrons, D. (1998), *Flexible Working and the Reconciliation of Work and Family Life, Or a New Form of Precariousness. Equality between Men and Women*, final comparative report, Brussels: European Commission (Employment and Social Affairs).

Presser, H.B. (1994), 'Employment schedules among dual-earner spouses and the division of household labour by gender', *American Sociological Review*, **59**, 348–64.

Presser, Harriet, B. (2000), 'Towards a 24-hour economy', *Science*, **284**, 1778–9.

Presser, H.B. (2004), *Towards a 24-hour Economy: Nonstandard Work Schedules and America's New Families*, New York: The Russell Sage Foundation.

Wallace, Claire (ed.) (2003), 'Households, work and flexibility', survey comparative report 4, vol 2, accessed at www.hwf.at.

11. Work life balance from the children's perspective

Ute Klammer

INTRODUCTION

Work life balance has been a topic in the academic as well as in the political debate for many years now. The main focus of the debate has been on the reconciliation between work and care, in particular from the perspective of working mothers (for example, Gerhard et al. 2005; Ludwig et al. 2002). In the context of the trend towards an adult worker family model the need to combine work with care obligations has become even more urgent in most European welfare states. The flexibilisation of work contracts and working times has sometimes eased work life balance for people with care obligations, but has also led to new challenges and problems in this field. At the same time many programmes and initiatives have been launched to enable mothers (parents) to reconcile work with care, not least inspired by the political intention to reverse negative demographic trends, as well as by the European Union's policy – in the Lisbon strategy – to increase women's labour market participation rates to at least 60 per cent before 2010.

Whereas mothers' (parents') work life balance has been broadly discussed, the children's perspective on (their parents') work life balance, on their own time use and preferences has remained a neglected issue so far.[1] This chapter picks up and discusses some of the relevant aspects. What are the implications of the trend towards an adult worker model, and in particular towards mothers' increasing labour market participation, for the children? Are there 'good' and 'bad' combination scenarios from the perspective of children? Do parents' opinions about what is a 'good' solution go along with their children's opinions? Does family policy, do companies and do parents take children's needs into account sufficiently?

The chapter reviews some of the literature dealing with the topics mentioned above. It also draws on two qualitative research projects conducted by the WSI[2] in which parents and (in one project) children were interviewed about their daily lives, their work life balance and their opinions about it.[3] Additionally the chapter presents some of the findings of two quantitative surveys conducted by the WSI in 2002 and 2003 on working time arrangements and family-friendly measures in companies, as well as on parents' demands for family-friendliness in their companies. Finally the chapter scrutinises recent trends and programmes of family policy in Germany. The analysis centres on the initiative Alliance for the Family, which was launched in 2003 by the German family ministry in cooperation with the Bertelsmann Foundation, and in particular on its two sub-programmes Audit Career and Family and Local Alliances for Families. The question is whether this new approach can be expected to improve the conditions for work life balance from the perspective of children.

THE INCREASE OF MOTHERS' LABOUR MARKET PARTICIPATION AND THE FLEXIBILISATION OF WORKING TIMES – NEW CHALLENGES TO WORK LIFE BALANCE

The Increase in Mothers' Labour Market Participation in Germany

For a long time, social policy and family policy in (West) Germany were focused on the breadwinner model of married couples. This was based on the expectation that women, in particular married women with children, would withdraw from the labour market at least temporarily. This model was (and partly still is) promoted and subsidised by state family policy, in particular through the instruments of matrimonial tax splitting, premium-free health and long-term care insurance of non-employed spouses, the derived system of survivors' pensions, and numerous other individual regulations in the tax and transfer system. In contrast, the expansion of the childcare infrastructure was neglected and has progressed only very slowly compared to the situation in many other countries of Europe (Klammer et al. 2000, pp. 336–40; Daly and Klammer 2005). Concern over the demographic trends and in particular the low birth rate[4] have refocused attention on family policy in recent years, and it has now become a key field of debate and policy. While family policy has been concentrated on monetary benefits for families for a long time (Schratzenstaller 2002, p. 129), the Red-Green government in its second period in office (2002–05) has geared its policy towards making it easier for mothers to reconcile work with family. The emphasis was on facilitating and increasing the attraction of the 'modified breadwinner model' (with the wife working part time).

Although the family type living the 'strong breadwinner model' still exists, it is no longer the norm for the majority today. On average, the activity rate of women in Germany now reaches almost 65 per cent, a quota which is slightly above the European average (61.5 per cent) and which places Germany 11th among the 25 EU countries (Eurostat data for 2003). The actual employment rate of women (which does not take the unemployed into account) is currently about 59 per cent, almost reaching the target of 60 per cent set by the EU's Lisbon strategy for 2010. Although the employment gap between mothers and women without children is still bigger in Germany than the EU 25 average (Eurostat 2005), the rise in mothers' employment has been considerable in recent years. The activity rate of mothers with children below 12 years in the household is now in the region of 60 per cent, with considerable differences between West and East Germany (Table 11.1).

If one looks at the household level at couples with children, a broad range of working time combinations can be found. The 'traditional' full-time breadwinner/housewife model is still not unusual in West German family households with small children, and 'involuntary' breadwinner combinations due to unemployment (for example, full-time–unemployed) are currently widespread in East Germany; a high share of households, however, consist of two earners, either in a full-time–part-time combination or in a full-time–full-time combination. Among West German married couples with children below 14 years, the share of families with a male full-time/female part-time model is currently about 42 per cent and in another 7 per cent of these family households both parents are working full time. In East Germany almost 40 per cent of married couples with children below 14 have a full-time–full-time model, and another 20 per cent a full-time–part-time model. In most other cases in East Germany one of the partners is unemployed, only one couple out of ten has a one earner/housewife model (GSOEP data for 2003, see Schneider 2005, pp. 29–31). If we add up the working hours of couples, a steady increase over time has taken place.

Table 11.1   Employment rate* of German mothers according to region and age of children 2004, in per cent

Age of youngest child	West Germany			East Germany		
	Total	Full time	Part time	Total	Full time	Part time
0–2	29	10	19	44	27	17
3–5	54	12	42	67	38	28
6–9	65	15	50	69	41	28
10–14	71	21	50	73	51	22

Note: *Working at least 1 hour per week.

Sources: German Statistical Office, Microcensus; Bothfeld et al. (2005, Chapter 3.6).

A comparison of the actual and desired situations shows, however, that parents in Germany are still far from able to achieve their preferred working time combinations. According to the 'Employment Options of the Future Survey' (Bielensky et al. 2002), still many more couples with children below the age of six are in households where the 'husband is full-time/wife not employed' than actually want to live in this way. Under the current conditions, there appear to be a majority in favour of a model in which mothers work part time and fathers full time – at least in cases where small children need to be cared for. Four in five mothers whose children were born after 1991 are voicing a preference for this set-up – in both West and East Germany (Engelbrech and Jungkunst 2001; Klammer and Klenner 2004).

New Problems of Work Life Balance in a Flexible Working World With Two-earner Households

While the share of two-earner families is rising, additional challenges arise from the flexibilisation and pluralisation of working times. What can be seen is a polarisation of working times with rising shares of both jobs with very short, and jobs with very long, working hours. The polarisation occurs along the gender and qualification lines: more and more women (and mothers) are in the workforce, but a rising share work in short part-time and flexible jobs, while most men are still working full time. As far as qualifications are concerned, highly qualified workers tend to work longer hours, whereas people with low qualifications tend to work fewer hours (Lange 2004a, p. 5). Overtime work is widespread among both sexes, however – in 2003, 46 per cent of all employed women (41 per cent of all employed mothers with a child below 13 years in the household) and 62 per cent of all employed men (67 per cent of all fathers with a child below 13 years in the household) reported regular overtime work over and above their contractual working time (Bauer et al. 2004, p. 48).

The flexibilisation of working times is a multi-faceted phenomenon. One of the most characteristic trends is that working times more and more often deviate from the 'standard working week' (defined as daytime work, Monday to Friday). In 2004, about 41 per cent/22 per cent/32 per cent of all employed women and 47 per cent/27 per cent/44 per cent of all employed men in Germany worked on Saturdays/Sundays/evenings (Bauer et al. 2004; Bothfeld et al. 2005). Other aspects of flexibilisation that affect family life include irregular and predictable working times (Presser 2003).

The economy has become the most important institution dictating families' time structures. Flexible and irregular working times have to be reconciled with the 'temporal design' of other institutions such as the time schedules of kindergartens and schools, but also with opening times of administrative institutions, schedules of public transport, and so on. These institutions often follow different, less flexible rhythms. The increasing inclusion of children in childcare institutions in Germany therefore brings along new chances for mothers' employment, but also new challenges for the organisation of family time.

How Do Parents Actually Cope and What Are Their Wishes?

If we look at the everyday lives of working parents with young children, we find a wide range of amazingly complex patterns and arrangements, and hardly any two are the same. There are not only differences in the specific conditions, but also there is no generally accepted model for 'how to live with children'. Individualisation and pluralisation lead to differing basic 'family arrangements' (Klenner et al. 2002, pp. 49–51). These arrangements are influenced by many factors – such as individual attitudes towards partnership, child raising and family life, different ideas on the scope of employment that is appropriate for the two partners, career ambitions, the sharing of housework, childcare preferences, and so on. Externally dictated rhythms are combined with some autonomy to arrange family times. The end result is based on the decisions and actions of the family members (above all the parents) and is constantly adapted in response to changes in external conditions. As a result, each family arranges its life in its own specific way (Jürgens 2001).

Nearly all parents make use of and combine elements of state family policy (parental leave, public childcare facilities, etc.), company-level services and options (above all in the area of flexible working time arrangements), and private support networks to create their own individual welfare mix. With a great deal of effort and planning, they put together the various resources to form tailored time and childcare 'packages' that change as their children become older (Knijn et al. 2005). Data from the children panel of the German Youth Institute (DJI) reveals more about parents' present care arrangements in Germany (Deutsches Jugendinstitut 2005; BMFSFJ 2005):

- at age five–six, only a minority of children (4 per cent of children, of mainly from a poor economic background) do *not* attend a kindergarten, but at the same time in West Germany only 18 per cent of all children at age five–six have a full-time place including a mid-day meal at kindergarten (East Germany 76 per cent).[5]
- About two-thirds of all couple households and almost three-quarters of all single parent households have at least one regular care arrangement for their children in addition to kindergarten, in about

25 per cent of all couple households and 20 per cent of all single parent households three or more additional care arrangements are in place.

- Grandparents are still the most frequent additional carers. They are involved in the care mix in about 34–39 per cent of all families, depending on the mother's labour market participation.
- Families from poor areas/living in poor conditions have fewer care arrangements. The higher the social status, the lower the share of care arrangements with family members and the higher the share of other care arrangements.

These time and childcare packages are often fragile and prone to disruption; many of them need to be rejigged with a great deal of improvisation or using 'emergency plans' when minor irregularities arise – such as the cancellation of school lessons, the illness of daycare help, or the obligation of the mother to work unscheduled hours at short notice.

A central problem is the still inadequate public childcare infrastructure, particularly in West Germany. Although there has been a right to a nursery place for children above the age of three since 1996, this right does not extend to full-day care places and the system is, moreover, still not implemented all over Germany. When it comes to children below the age of three who attend childcare facilities, West Germany is still near the bottom of the European league. In autumn 2004 a new law (*Tagesbetreuungsausbaugesetz*) encouraged the further extension of public childcare for children below the age of three, with a focus on places for children who need particular support and on children with working parents; however, the law did not introduce a *right* to a childcare place for children below the age of three.

In West Germany, working parents complain that the opening hours of childcare facilities have in no way kept pace with the flexibilisation of working times. Many of the parents surveyed in Project One and Project Two said that they did not want to put their children in infant or day care for longer overall but that they would welcome the opportunity to make use of these facilities at different times and for varying periods of time when the need arises. The increasing complexity and fragility of family arrangements when children make the transition to school has been described frequently (for example Ludwig et al. 2002, pp. 110–12; Klenner et al. 2002, pp. 124–33). Short and unreliable school hours, long holidays, and the lack of afternoon care provisions for schoolchildren has made full-time employment for both parents almost an impossibility up to the present time without the wide-scale use of other resources. As far as school children are concerned, there are still two different realities in Germany: a predominantly half-day school without lunch in West Germany, and predominantly full-time arrangements (including a mid-day meal and the so-called *hort* for afternoon care) in East Germany (80 per cent) (Deutsches Jugendinstitut 2005; BMBFSJ 2005). Full-day care arrangements are most widespread for middle-class children in East Germany, whereas in West Germany it is in the main middle-class children who attend only a 'traditional' half-day school. Parents in West Germany often spend much time in the afternoon taking their children from one side of town to the other to different schools, nurseries and leisure facilities and picking them up again afterwards. This makes the time-based arrangements of many parents additionally complex (Ludwig et al. 2002, pp. 30–40; Klenner et al. 2002, pp. 100–1).

Where both parents are in employment, problems often arise that necessitate wide-ranging family time management. During the school holidays, parents frequently make use of what can only be described as 'emergency solutions', such as parents taking their holidays separately, or a combination of different solutions that children are by no means always willing to accept (Project Two). In some cases, school holidays are 'bridged' by making use of short sabbaticals and longer holidays drawn from working time accounts to enable the parents to spend time with their children above and beyond the annual family vacation.[6]

Even if childcare obligations are generally unevenly distributed, some of the mothers and fathers do today share the responsibility for looking after children and organise their time accordingly. Surveys show an increase in the prevalence of attitudes that deviate from the traditional stereotypes regarding gender-specific roles. Today, more than two in three fathers believe in a concept of fatherhood that primarily emphasises their social role ('fathers as child raisers', Fthenakis and Minsel 2001, p. 7); less than 30 per cent see themselves primarily as breadwinners. Fthenakis and Minsel (2001) have used the term 'co-parenting' to describe a form of 'joint responsibility, shared obligations' based on allocation of tasks and assignment of care periods. In this system of alternating care of children by mothers and by fathers, the work-related absence of the one parent is filled by the other. The surveys on the day-to-day activities of working parents (Project Two) show that the higher the overall working time of the couple, the greater the desire for partnership-based structuring of working and caring time – and the greater the need for the asynchronous organisation of working times to allow optimum distribution of family-related tasks. In such cases, time planning in the family is based on a staggered system of childcare (the partner who isn't working at a particular time takes care of the child). Mothers and fathers use any flexibility for organising their working hours to ensure equal division of childcare times (and, in some cases, of housework) to the greatest extent possible. This is sometimes achieved by reducing working time by a few hours – and by organising working hours so that partners take care of the children on 'short' working. Parents also make use of flexi-time or the reduction of time credits on working time accounts to create time for family-related needs. Sometimes there are informal arrangements permitted by the employee's manager that allow deviation from the regulations, particularly in respect of core working hours. Longer work-free periods resulting from shift schedules or working time accounts and options like sabbaticals are also used to create the necessary time in phases that parents deem to be important (helping children to get started at school, for example).

When care times are divided up like this, the time schedules of the two partners need to fit in with one another exactly and reliably to enable a 'flying changeover' of children. This makes parents less able to react to short-notice changes in the schedule at the workplace, particularly when it comes to working overtime. Parents who share care responsibilities and schedules make productive use of flexible working times in the interests of their family life – but they also have to have reliable schedules and a degree of stability in the area of working time patterns, as working times have to be synchronised a certain extent to permit family life. Many interviews (Project One and Two, for example, Ludwig et al. 2002, pp. 75–83) confirmed that parents are not generally opposed to the flexibilisation of working times, and working times that deviate from the norm can by no means be generally described as 'family-unfriendly'. The key factor is the degree of fit between the specific time needs of the parents on the one hand and the widely varying company-level flexibilisation needs on the other.

In fact parents and other carers regard family-friendly working time schemes to be the most important task for companies to support family life. This is the result of a survey conducted by the WSI on behalf of the German family ministry (BMBFSJ 2004). Some 36 per cent of all women and 28 per cent of all men with children or eldercare obligations said this was their first priority. The next most important were financial support by the company and (additional) leave schemes (Table 11.2).

A majority of employees with care obligations can already make use of flexible working time schemes, such as a flexible beginning and end of the working day (48 per cent of male and 40 per cent of female respondents with care obligations), or of free time in exchange for overtime work (60 per cent of both sexes). Most respondents to the survey mentioned in particular working time accounts as a positive instrument for work life balance.[7] At the same time, however, four out of ten employees mentioned that their changing or flexible working times sometimes led to problems for work life balance and childcare. They particularly complained about Sunday work (but not generally about weekend and evening work). On the whole about two-thirds of the parents interviewed regarded their company to be

*Table 11.2   What do parents/carers need and expect from their companies?
Areas in which companies' engagement is most urgent
according to parents/carers (Germany 2003)*

Measure	Women (%)	Men (%)
Family-friendly working time schemes	35.6	27.7
Financial support	14.0	21.7
Leave schemes for care work	13.4	16.5
Support for finding external care options	11.4	6.7
Family-friendly atmosphere in the company	10.7	11.6
Offers during parental leave	7.6	9.1
None of these measures	7.3	6.7

Sources: WSI survey 'Family-friendly company', Nov/Dec 2003 ($n = 1.976$);
BMBFSJ (2004).

family-friendly, but almost one-third said the family-friendliness of their company was not sufficient. This shows that flexible working time models can be used to adapt working times to suit the family, but can be used just as easily to flexibilise working times to meet the specific requirements of the employer. It appears that the 'working culture' within the company is more important than any particular company-level provision.

HOW ABOUT THE CHILDREN'S PERSPECTIVE?

The Rights of Children According to the UN Charter

Do children have a voice when it comes to these time (and care) arrangements? Or are they victims of the flexibilisation of the working world and the trend towards an 'adult worker model'? Before reviewing some of the empirical findings, it makes sense to have a look at the international agreements concerning children's rights and well-being as laid down in the UN Convention on the Rights of the Child in 1989. This convention, which is in force in all but two countries,[8] highlights and defends the children's perspective as well as the family's role in children's lives. In the preamble and in Articles 5, 10 and 18, the convention specifically refers to the family as the fundamental group of society and the natural environment for the growth and well-being of children. Under the convention, states are obliged to respect parents' primary responsibility for providing care and guidance for their children and to help parents in this regard, providing material assistance and support programmes.

The convention confirms that children have a right to express their views and to have their views taken seriously – although children also have a responsibility to respect the rights of others, especially those of parents. The convention emphasises the need to respect children's 'evolving capacities'; this is rooted in the idea that the child's path from total dependence to adulthood is gradual. In Article 3, the convention states that the best interests of the child shall be a primary consideration in all actions concerning children, whether undertaken by public or private social welfare institutions, courts of law, administrative authorities or legislative bodies. In each and every decision affecting the child, the various possible solutions must be considered and due weight given to the child's best interests. Such an approach prevails at all levels – from direct interventions by states in their jurisdictions to the private context of family life, where states may intervene indirectly – through to local authorities, for example. Article 3 also demands that the institutions provided for childcare and so on have to meet certain standards, and that there has to be adequate and sufficiently educated staff.

'Best interests of the child' means that legislative bodies must consider whether laws being adopted or amended will benefit children in the best possible way. Courts and others settling conflicts of interest should base their decisions on what is best for the child. When administrative authorities intervene, actions should be on behalf of children and should safeguard their best interests. In the allocation of budgets, special attention should be given to children's policies and to the impact that policies will have on children's lives. Parents have the main responsibility for the children's development and they should try to achieve the best for their child (Article 18, para. 1). The state has a supportive role, in particular by providing public childcare facilities (Article 18, para. 2). The state is obliged to make sure that there are enough childcare places for children of working parents (Article, 18 para. 3).

Several provisions in the Convention on the Rights of the Child reflect children's right to participation. According to Article 12 children have the right to express their views and to have their views taken seriously and given due weight. The principle of participation affirms that children are persons who have the right to express their views in all matters affecting them and requires that those views be heard and given due weight in accordance with the child's age and maturity. It recognises the potential of children to enrich decision-making processes and to share perspectives as participative actors. The convention therefore envisages a changed relationship between adults and children. Parents, teachers, caregivers and others interacting with children are seen no longer as mere providers, protectors or advocates, but also as negotiators and facilitators. Adults are expected to create spaces and promote processes designed to enable and empower children to express views, to be consulted and to influence decisions. The 'survival and development' principle (Article 6) is in no way limited to physical well-being; rather, it further emphasises the need to ensure the full and harmonious development of the child, including spiritual, moral and social aspects. In that regard, states assume deeper obligations: ensuring that children will be able to develop talents and abilities to their fullest potential, that children will be prepared for a responsible life in a free society and that they will feel solidarity with the world they live in.

The convention obliges both the parents and the state to pay attention to children's needs and wishes. Other actors, such as the companies, and their (potential) role are not directly addressed, however; the role of the market forces and the working world therefore remains vague. What does this mean for children's interests in an 'adult worker society'? The following sections will shed some light on the changed context of childhood and children's attitudes towards their parents' work and family arrangements.

Childhood Today

If we want to discuss the perspective of children on their parents' arrangements concerning work and family life, we must reflect on how children live today. Out of the broad literature on childhood today – in particular the 'new social studies of childhood' (James et al. 1998) – this chapter can only refer to some selected findings that might be relevant to this question.

To take the children's point of view seriously means first of all seeing them as capable agents of their own lives. This premise, which is in line with the Convention of the rights of the child, is frequently stressed in the new literature on childhood (e.g. Kaltenborn 2001; Morrow 2003). Children are no longer seen as passive creatures in a given framework, but as agents with an interest in the families' (time) arrangements (Thorpe and Daly 1999). Anne Solberg concluded in her study on Norwegian children: 'In my account children are responsible, independent and "big"; to some extent they are adultlike' (Solberg 1990, p. 142). But children have to face new challenges and contradictions. Childhood today is closely connected to new family forms, but also to new rhythms and time structures that prevail in societies (Zeiher and Zeiher 1998; Zeiher 2000; Lange 2001, 2004b; Kirchhöfer 2001):

- Autonomy (creativity, authenticity) is expected from children at an ever earlier age. At the same time structural time control has grown and children increasingly have to follow strict time schedules and targeted activities. Children often have diminished obligations to help their parents, but they have new, dense schedules of their own. This implies that there are new contradictions between dependency and autonomy.

- Not only parents' flexible working times, but also children's full agendas complicate the organisation of everyday family life.
- At the same time, similarities between adults' and children's time structures are obvious: children's weekdays are much more pre-structured than their weekends; this is a consequence of adults' structuring of children's times.
- Children need more competence today to organise their own times and to cope with a variety of options and contradictions.
- Children are directly involved in the market economy. They are consumers themselves whose chances of participation depend strongly on their parents' position and resources.

To sum up, children have to develop the ability to 'give sense' to an increasingly complicated, contradictory world, and they have to learn to cope with ambiguities, uncertainties and time pressure. This requires some assistance and guidance.

The rapid changes that occurred in East Germany after re-unification can – to a certain extent – serve as an example of the new challenges children are exposed to. Kirchhöfer (2001) has shown the extent to which children's lives have changed in East Germany after re-unification. While the former GDR was changing from a socialist society to a market economy, insecurities for children were growing and formerly regular rhythms were dissolved. Parents' working times became more and more unpredictable and the private networks of families became increasingly unreliable. On the one hand children gained more freedom and autonomy. On the other hand they have to face more challenges: they have to cope with new inconsistencies; they have to define their own goals; they have to balance different, sometimes contradicting demands. Kirchhöfer noticed an erosion of time discipline and more non-rational behaviour among East German children in the 1990s. Many of them had difficulty in using the new freedom. They tended to give up a part of their autonomy and tried to seek stability in the company of like-minded contemporaries, such as by joining fan clubs or political groups (often right-wing groups). Interestingly two-earner families were the norm in the former GDR. This shows that it is not only the trend towards higher labour market participation of mothers that has increased the demands for children's self-organisation; children's life is increasingly influenced by new options, and also new insecurities.

What Do Children Think about Their Parents' Work Life Balance and Use of Time?

What do children actually think about their parents' work and about the way their parents combine work and family life? How do they cope with their families' time arrangements and with the limited amount of time many working parents can spend with their children?

In fact there are relatively few studies about children's perspectives on working parents and their perceptions of their parents' use of time,[9] and the results are controversial. Lange (2004a) illustrates this convincingly by juxtaposing the results of two American studies on the topic: Galinsky's encompassing quantitative study 'Ask the Children: What America's Children Really think About Working Parents' (1999) and Polatnick's qualitative study 'Quantity Time: Do Children Want More Time with Their Full-time Employed Parents?' (2002). In a representative sample of children with working parents ($n = 1023$) Galinsky found that for the majority of the children having more time with their parents was *not* the priority. Only 10 per cent said it was their top wish to have more time with their mothers; 15.5 per cent wished in particular to spend more time with their fathers. Galinsky came to the conclusion that working parents much more often regarded the time they spent with their children as being insufficient than did their own children. One could assume – and the US media repeatedly did so (Lange 2004a, p. 16) – that working parents' concern about the well-being of their children and the lack of time for family life was exaggerated, and that children were more able to cope with the actual arrangements than many adults believed.

But Polatnick (2002) in a smaller qualitative study (22 in-depth interviews with children of working parents) showed that things are not that simple. Her interviewees revealed a much more ambivalent attitude towards their parents' work and absence; their feelings about more time with their parents were complex and contradictory. While most children still said the absence of their parents was all right with them, their language and nonverbal communication (signs of hesitation or nervousness) often made it clear that their feelings about the issue were more ambiguous. Sometimes children obviously did not allow themselves to ask for more time with their parents because they had learned the social message that they should not press for more time. In other cases they put such considerations as the financial needs of the family and their parents' well-being first. As Polatnick found, children seemed reluctant to express negative emotions about their parents' long working hours. Instead they used the same argument as many of their parents: it's not the quantity, but the quality of the time spent together that counts. In this study, children (in the middle phase of childhood) simultaneously wished to have more time on their own and more quality time with their parents.

Due to the continuing dominant system of the half-day school, children in Germany still have a considerable amount of time that is not pre-structured by compulsory institutions.[10] As Roppelt (2003), who inter-viewed 130 children in South Germany, found, children enjoyed having time on their own, but also suffered when there were no reliable arrangements, when they were not able to reach their parents at the workplace, or when they had to 'bridge' long hours waiting for their parents. Children beyond a certain age preferred a balance between close contact with and distance from their parents. In particular they wanted to have reliable arrangements. Roppelt also found that children appreciated family and time arrangements that ensured they saw both parents. Some children were dissatisfied because their parents worked very much, but others were dissatisfied because their mothers did not work; children whose parents had a 'middle' workload seemed to be most content (see also Lange 2004a, pp. 27–31).

As our own interviews with children (and parents) reveal (Project Two, see also Klenner et al. 2002, 2003), children can obviously cope with a lot of different work and care arrangements as long as some basic rules are followed. If this is not the case, labour market flexibility and parents' labour market participation *do* pose problems for family life. Children not only depend on regular schedules; it is also essential that they can experi-ence certain times as 'family times' – in particular late afternoon and evening (before going to bed) and Sundays.[11] Meals and family rituals, as well as watching TV with their parents, and at weekends outdoor activities, are important during these times. One aspect of 'quality time' is obviously that parents need to have 'time at the right time'. The younger the children, the greater the interest of families with tight time schedules to achieve evenly distributed working time commitments over each working day.

Flexible working times are therefore an important precondition for coordination processes between working parents. But flexible working times can also have an adverse impact if the times to be worked fluctuate excessively, if employees have insufficient influence on working times, or if they are given insufficient notice of extra work (Project Two). When working time flexibilisation is accompanied by a blurring of the borders and frequent overtime; when the working climate is characterised by com-petitive pressure, the 'compression' of work-related duties and the like; and when the 'zero-drag' employee (Hochschild 2002, pp. xxvii–viii) – employees who let nothing prevent them from placing their time fully and unreservedly at the disposal of the company – becomes the norm, then combining working life and family needs becomes a difficult and exhausting business, and often does not take children's needs adequately into account.

One of the key findings of our qualitative surveys was that, from the point of view of parents and their children, family-friendly working must above all address the following requirements:

- provide the leeway necessary for employees to address family-related needs (for example via self-regulated withdrawals from working time accounts);
- predictable and reliable working times;
- options in the area of working time duration (permitting change between full-time and part-time work, as well as different hours for part-time employees);
- life course-specific time planning (for example, 'time-out' phases for the busy periods in an individual's life);
- minimisation or avoidance of weekend and evening work, as these are the most important communal times for parents and children;
- limits on the duration of working times, above all, avoidance of forms of overtime that do not create some kind of 'time credit'.

As the interviews have shown, not all working parents had a clear opinion about their children's time needs and wishes; very often parents expressed a feeling of guilt because they believed they did not spend enough time with their children. On the other hand parents not only took their children's 'strict' schedules (for example, school times) into account, but also often gave their children's special time wishes a high priority. They frequently failed, however, because the requirements and expectations of the working world were opposed to family needs.

Various kinds and levels of provisions that could ease work life balance are already in place in Germany. The most important regulatory instrument for working time is the sectoral collective agreement. Additionally company-level arrangements are playing an ever-greater role. Company-level agreements need to be negotiated to ensure that 'decentralisation' does not automatically translate into 'deregulation'. Only in a minority of cases, however, are the existing collectively agreed provisions explicitly geared towards reconciling work with family, in the interests of working parents and of children. This is an area in which the collective bargaining parties and the players at company level still need to make up lost ground.

RECENT DEVELOPMENTS IN GERMAN FAMILY POLICY: FOR THE BETTER OR FOR THE WORSE FROM THE CHILDREN'S PERSPECTIVE?

The New Approach: 'Alliance for the Family'

German family policy recently witnessed a shift, when the new initiative 'Alliance for the Family' was launched by the German family ministry (in cooperation with the Bertelsmann Foundation) in summer 2003. A broad range of different measures and activities intended to improve the work life balance in Germany were brought together under the roof of the Alliance for the Family.[12] The basic idea is to create a new awareness among the different actors about the importance of the family for the whole society, and an awareness about the need to support families. The initiative is therefore not restricted to the family policy of the state, but unites the activities of different actors, such as the employers' associations and the trade unions, local governments, voluntary associations, companies, and so on. The focus of interest is on family-friendliness of the 'company culture', work organisation, working time regimes, the recruitment and development of personnel, and on the company level that support families.

Activities include regular meetings and exchange of experiences and material between actors on different levels. Bi- and multilateral projects of the partners involved have been launched. Representatives of the institutions involved have built a so-called 'competence group for balance' to work towards achieving a common view. A network of scientists supports the actors involved. The whole process is organised and moderated by the family ministry and the Bertelsmann Foundation.

Two central elements of the Alliance for the Family are the Local Alliances for Family and the Career and Family Audit. The Local Alliances for Family initiative aims to build local round-table alliances that could help to improve the context for family life in the municipality. Members may include local government members and offices, employers and their associations, trades unions, churches, and third sector organisations. Last but not least families (parents) are encouraged to engage themselves in the process of debate and finding solutions. In November 2004 – only 11 months after the start of the initiative – the family minister was able to announce the founding of the 100th Local Alliance for the Family.[13] By Autumn 2005, more than 130 local alliances had been formed. The family ministry has set up an office to support local authorities interested in starting a Local Alliance for Family and to assist the parties to find their own, locally appropriate strategies.[14] Different local alliances are focusing on different aspects of family life and work life balance. The topics treated range from the organisation of public childcare and eldercare to flexible working time arrangements, family-friendly opening hours of public services and adjusted timetables for public transport and so on.

The Career and Family Audit has been introduced to give private sector firms as well as public sector establishments incentives and ideas to develop family-friendly strategies in accordance with their particular situation and goals. The audit is a management instrument serving as a means to improve the awareness of family obligations in companies' human resource management. Companies in Germany can apply for this audit and get support to develop firm-specific strategies. Within the auditing process existing family-friendly measures are scrutinised and the firm-specific potential to develop additional family-friendly activities is analysed. The underlying philosophy is that the introduction or improvement of family-friendliness can turn out to be a win–win strategy, helping employees to realise a satisfactory work life balance and thereby increasing the company's profit through content, reliable and motivated employees.[15] Working time arrangements, company-level childcare facilities, and measures that refer to the location of work and work organisation are included among more than 140 items checked within the auditing process (Schmidt and Mohn 2004, pp. 183ff.).

What Can Be Expected for Work Life Balance from the Children's Perspective?

So far there are no exact evaluation data that could give information about outcomes of the Alliance for the Family initiative. It only started in summer 2003, and brings together a range of diverse projects and activities that are mostly of a qualitative nature and not easy to evaluate in quantitative terms.

What can be said is that the Local Alliances for the Family have a high level of approval among the German population. According to a survey conducted in March 2004, 86 per cent of all respondents (and 89 per cent of women) agreed that an alliance of strong partners at the local level was a promising approach to improve living conditions for families (Schmidt and Mohn 2004, pp. 179f.).

As far as the Career and Family Audit is concerned, 80 companies and public sector establishments covering more than 220,000 employees obtained the basic certificate between 2000 and 2003 (Schmidt and Mohn 2004, p. 184). Although in absolute numbers the success of the audit is modest so far, the impact of this exemplary behaviour may be more important than the absolute number of certified companies as a percentage of all companies. According to a survey of firms that participated in the audit, 80 per cent of respondents said that the satisfaction and motivation of employees had increased considerably due to more recognition being given to their family responsibilities. In about 70 per cent of the certified companies the quality of work improved, and about 90 per cent of the firms said that their ability to attract qualified personnel had improved thanks to the audit (Schmidt and Mohn 2004, p. 184).

But what can be expected from the child's perspective? The overall analysis of recent trends reveals that in many respects children's needs only play a minor role when it comes to new services that claim to facilitate work life balance. The creation of highly flexible childcare services ('all-round 24-hour carefree service'), for example, could further underpin the norm of the employee who is available at all times rather than increasing acceptance for time-based needs outside the workplace. The rise of 24-hour care institutions might increase parents' disposability at their workplace in a flexible 24/7 economy, but raises questions about the minimum standards for work life balance from the children's perspective.

The main goals of the 'Alliance for the Family' have been laid down in a consensus paper (BMBFSJ 2003). The central aim is the development of a 'sustainable family policy' based on three assumptions: 1) that (German) society needs a higher fertility rate, 2) that the economy needs qualified workers and higher labour market participation by women, and 3) that children need (better) education and guidance in their early years, even before they start school.

The first two goals result from the concern about the foreseeable demographic and labour market developments. The last goal relates to the findings of the international PISA tests and other empirical evidence, which has shown that many children in Germany only reach a relatively poor level of skills and knowledge, compared to other developed countries. In addition their educational chances depend largely on the educational level and professional position achieved by their parents. It is obvious that the first two goals do not (directly) take children's own interests and needs into account, whereas the third goal focuses on children, although there is clearly an economic motive here too.

In spite of the fact that children's interests are not the main focus of the 'Alliance for the Family', the endeavours to facilitate mothers' labour market participation and parents' work life balance (foe example, by an extension of public childcare) can bring two positive effects for children:

1. During recent decades the risk of poverty has shifted from the elderly population to children in Germany. More than one million children today live on social assistance, the main reason being the joblessness or insufficient labour market income of one or both parents. Lone mothers and their children are a particularly disadvantaged group: due to the insufficient childcare facilities, many lone mothers are not able to take

up employment and have to live on social assistance. Whereas in 2003 3.7 per cent of households received social assistance, the figure for lone other households was 26.3 per cent (Bundesregierung 2005, p. 87). More than 35 per cent of all lone mothers and their children live below the poverty line (p. 85).[16] A policy enabling more mothers, in particular lone mothers, to take up a job or increase their working hours can improve children's chances to get out of poverty, and to get a better education.

2.   As has become clear from the international PISA tests during recent years, the educational skills of German children are at best moderate when compared internationally, and there are particular problems in the education of children from vulnerable and disadvantaged families (such as migrants and social assistance recipients). The extension of public childcare – now an explicit goal of the government – could improve the educational chances of children from disadvantaged families. This, however, will only occur if the quality of childcare (and not just the quantity) is improved.

CONCLUSION

Most Western European countries are seeing a shift from the so-called 'breadwinner-model family' to an 'adult worker model' in which all adults are expected to do paid work. This will – to a certain extent – render women's labour market participation more 'normal' and improve their chances to earn their own income. At the same time this poses new challenges to work life balance and family life. 'Family' is no longer a self-evident, 'natural' structure, but has the character of a project that has to be 'produced' again and again in everyday life (Lange 2004a). 'Doing family' can only be successful if the different needs and wishes of all family members are taken into account. Where the rhythms of children and of family life are dictated by increasingly flexible and irregular working times of the parents, the risk of neglecting children's needs is obvious.

Children's perception of time and their wishes concerning the family's time (and care) arrangements are deeply embedded in the expectations, attitudes and 'temporal ecologies' (Levine 1998) of their societal context. But although they are changing, there is obviously a need for time together in families, and a need for stability and regular rhythms that is staunchly in opposition to the labour market ideal of the flexible worker. At the same time parents' time input in the family can be regarded as a contribution to children's education and socialisation. Consequently it has to be acknowledged that the overall norm in the labour market cannot be the '(male) full-time worker without any obligations beyond work' any more. What is needed is a paradigm shift in companies, creating a situation in which each employee is automatically also seen as a caregiver, whether they care for their own children or relatives or are involved in other socially relevant activities. Family-friendliness in this sense means that companies automatically take into account that all employees potentially bear responsibility in the 'other sphere' of societal activity and no longer base their planning concepts on a norm of an employee – particularly the qualified employee – who is freed from the full range of household duties.

NOTES

1. For an international overview on the (relatively few) studies on children's time use and activities see Ben-Arieh and Ofir (2002).
2. WSI = Institute for Economic and Social Research, Düsseldorf – the research institute the author worked for until September 2004.
3. Ludwig et al. (2002), referred to as 'Project One', and Klenner et al. (2002), referred to as 'Project Two'. The information taken from these projects focuses on the reconcilability strategies of couples with young children.
4. The German birth rate currently ranks 181st worldwide out of 191 surveyed countries.
5. The school starting age in Germany is seven years.
6. Working time account arrangements allow greater freedom in the determination of working-time duration, location and distribution. The basic form of account defines fluctuating margins within which the actual day may vary, and a time period over which the contractual duration of working time must be reached.
7. Overall, 37 per cent of all female and 45 per cent of all male employees have working time accounts today (data for 2003, Bauer et al. 2004). The crucial question is whether the employer or the employee has the 'time sovereignty' to decide about the distribution of working time. As an investigation of German working time accounts has shown that the majority of highly qualified (in particular male) white collar workers can decide on the distribution of their working time, whereas working time accounts of low qualified blue collar workers are often an instrument by which the employer distributes working time according to the company's needs.
8. In Germany since 5 April 1992.
9. As Wehr (2004) has shown, children in the 'middle phase' of childhood already have a differentiated understanding of time.
10. As Lange (2004a, p. 4) points out, the interest in children's activities and time use in German research on childhood is closely connected to the fact that children in the past had more free time than in most other European countries.
11. For the importance of the early evenings and weekends as family times see also Kleine (2003) and Lange (2004a).
12. The following description of the 'Alliance for the family' is primarily based on the official information provided on the website of the family ministry (www.bmfsfj.de) and on Schmidt and Mohn (2004).
13. www.bmfsfj.de, press information from 22 November 2004.
14. The project is evaluated scientifically by the German Youth Institute, Munich.
15. The positive effects of family-friendliness in the company have been confirmed by a research study carried out by Prognos on behalf of the German family ministry. This cost–benefit analysis of the economic effects of family-friendly measures in 10 German companies showed an average return on investment of +25 per cent. According to the study, family-friendly policies in the company prevented over 50 per cent of the costs incurred as a result of the lack of reconcilability of work with family, in particular

bridging (costs of a temporary worker), fluctuation (costs of recruitment) and reintegration costs (Prognos 2003).
16. Poverty line: 60 per cent of net equivalent household income (median).

REFERENCES

Bauer, F., H. Groß, K. Lehmann and E. Munz (2004), 'Arbeitszeit 2003', Arbeitszeit, Arbeitsorganisation und Tätigkeitsprofile Berichte des ISO, Köln.
Ben-Arieh, A. and A. Ofir (2002), 'Time for (more) time-use studies: studying the daily activities of children', *Childhood*, **9**(2), 225–48.
Bielensky, H., G. Bosch and A. Wagner (2002), *Working Time Preferences in Sixteen European Countries*, Luxembourg: Office for Official Publications of the European Communities.
BMBFSJ (ed.) (2003), *Balance von Familie und Arbeitswelt. Allianz für die Familie*. Grundlagenpapier der Impulsgruppe, Berlin: BMBFSJ.
BMBFSJ (ed.) (2004), *Erwartungen an einen familienfreundlichen Betrieb. Erste Auswertung einer repräsentativen Befragung von Arbeitnehmerinnen und Arbeitnehmern mit Kindern oder Pflegeaufgaben*, Berlin: BMBFSJ.
BMBFSJ (ed.) (2005), *Monitor Familiendemographie. Ausgabe Nr. 2: Wer betreut Deutschlands Kinder?*, Berlin: BMBFSJ.
Bothfeld, S., U. Klammer, C. Klenner, S. Leiber, A. Thiel and A. Ziegler (2005), *WSI-FrauenDatenReport 2005*, Berlin: Sigma Verlag.
Bundesministerium für Familie, Senioren, Frauen und Jugend, www.bmfsfj.de.
Bundesregierung (2005), Lebenslagen in Deutschland. Der 2. Armuts- und Reichtumsbericht der Bundesregierung (Anhänge), Berlin.
Daly, M. and U. Klammer (2005), 'Women's participation in European labour markets', in U. Gerhard, T. Knijn and A. Weckwert (eds) (2005), *Working Mothers in Europe: A Comparison of Policies and Practices*, Cheltenham, UK and Northampton, MA, USA: Edward Elgar.
Deutsches Jugendinstitut (2005), DJI-Kinderbetreuungsstudie 2005. Erste Ergebnisse, accessed 25 August at www.dji.de.
Deutsches Jugendinstitut, Lokale Bündnisse für Familie, Bündnis-Datenbank, www.dji.de/lokale-buendnisse.de.
Engelbrech, G. and M. Jungkunst (2001), 'Wie bringt man Beruf und Familie unter einen Hut?', IAB Kurzbericht 7, Nürnberg.
Eurostat (2005), Pressemeldung 49/2005, Luxembourg.
Fthenakis, W.E. and B. Minsel (2001), *Die Rolle des Vaters in der Familie*, Berlin: Bundesministerium für Familie, Senioren, Fraven und Jugend.
Galinsky, E.A. (1999), *Ask the Children: What America's Children Really Think about Working Parents*, New York: William Morrow.
Gerhard, U., T. Knijn and A. Weckwert (eds) (2005), *Working Mothers in Europe: A Comparison of Policies and Practices*, Cheltenham, UK and Northampton, MA, USA: Edward Elgar.
Hochschild, A.R. (2002), 'Keine Zeit. Wenn die Firma zum Zuhause wird und zu Hause nur Arbeit wartet', Opladen:
James, A., C. Jenks and A. Prout (1998), *Theorizing Childhood*, Oxford: Polity Press.
Jürgens, K. (2001), 'Familiale Lebensführung. Familienleben als alltägliche Verschränkung individueller Lebensführungen', in Günter G. Voß und Margit

Weihrich (eds), *Tagaus – tagein. Neue Beiträge zur Soziologie Alltäglicher Lebensführung*, München and Mehring: Reiner Hampp Verlag, pp. 33–60.

Kaltenborn, K. (2001), 'Aufwachsen mit familialen Übergängen. Expertenwissen und kindliche agency in posttraditionalen Gesellschaften', in I. Behnken and J. Zinnecker (eds), *Kinder. Kindheit. Lebensgeschichte. Ein Handbuch*, Seelze: Kallmeyer, pp. 502–21.

Kleine, W. (2003), *Tausend gelebte Kindertage. Sport und Bewegung im Alltag der Kinder*, Weinheim: Juventa.

Kirchhöfer, D. (2001), 'Kindliche Lebensführung im Umbruch', in Günter G. Voß and M. Weihrich (eds), *Tagaus – tagein. Neue Beiträge zur Soziologie Alltäglicher Lebensführung*, München and Mering: Reiner Hampp Verlag, pp. 61–85.

Klammer, U. and C. Klenner (2004), 'Geteilte Erwerbstätigkeit – gemeinsame Fürsorge. Strategien und Perspektiven der Kombination von Erwerbs- und Familienleben in Deutschland', in S. Leitner, I. Ostner and M. Schratzenstaller (eds), *Wohlfahrtsstaat und Geschlechterverhältnis im Umbruch. Was kommt nach dem Ernährermodell*, Wiesbaden: VS Verlag für Sozialwissenschaften.

Klammer, U., C. Klenner, C. Ochs, P. Radke and A. Ziegler (2000), *WSI-FrauenDatenReport*, Berlin: Sigma.

Klenner, C., S. Pfahl and S. Reuyß (2002), 'Arbeitszeiten – Kinderzeiten – Familienzeiten. Bessere Vereinbarkeit durch Sabbaticals und Blockfreizeiten?', Projektendbericht an das MASQT NRW, Düsseldorf, accessed at www.arbeitszeiten.nrw.de/pdf/SABBATI2.PDF.

Klenner, C., S. Pfahl and S. Reuyß (2003), 'Flexible Arbeitszeiten aus der Sicht von Eltern und Kindern' ['Flexible working times seen by parents and children'], *Zeitschrift für Soziologie der Erziehung und Sozialisation*, **23**(3), 268–85.

Knijn, T., I. Jönsson and U. Klammer (2005), 'Care packages: The organisation of work and care by working mothers', in U. Gerhard et al. (eds.), *Working Mothers in Europe: A Comparison of Policies and Practices*, Cheltenham, UK and Northampton, MA, USA: Edward Elgar.

Lange, A. (2001), 'Zur Lebensführung von Kindern und Jugendlichen. Chancen und Risiken raschen und widersprüchlichen sozialen Wandels', in Bundesvereinigung kulturelle Jugendbildung (ed.), *Kulturelle Bildung und Lebenskunst*, Remscheid: Bundesvereinigung Kulturelle Jugendbildung, pp. 51–62.

Lange, A. (2004a), 'Arbeits- und Familienzeiten aus Kinderperspektive, Expertise für den 7', Familienbericht, München, unpublished manuscript.

Lange, A. (2004b), 'Kindsein im Übergang von der fordistischen zur postfordistischen Gesellschaft. Eine soziologische Skizze', *Merz Thema*, **6**(47), 7–17.

Levine, R. (1998), *Eine Landkarte der Zeit. Wie Kulturen mit Zeit umgehen*, München: Piper.

Ludwig, I., V. Schlevogt, U. Klammer and U. Gerhard (2002), *Managerinnen des Alltags. Strategien erwerbstätiger Mütter in Ost- und Westdeutschland*, Berlin: Sigma.

Morrow, V. (2003), 'Perspectives on children's agency within families', in L. Kuczynski (ed.), *Handbook of Dynamics in Parent–Child Relations*, Thousand Oaks, CA: Sage.

Polatnick, M.R. (2002), '*Quantity time: do children want more time with their full-time employed parents?*', Center for Working Families working paper 37, Berkeley, CA.

Presser, H. (2003), *Working in a 24/7 Economy: Challenges for American Families*, New York: Russel Sage Foundation.

Prognos (2003), 'Betriebswirtschaftliche Effekte familienfreundlicher Maßnahmen – Kosten-Nutzen-Analyse. Im Auftrag des Bundesministeriums für Familie, Senioren, Frauen und Jugend', Köln.

Roppelt, U. (2003), *Kinder – Experten ihres Alltags?*, Frankfurt a.M.: Peter Lang.

Schmidt, R. and L. Mohn (eds) (2004), *Familie bringt Gewinn. Innovation durch Balance von Familie und Arbeitswelt*, Gütersloh: Bertelsmann.

Schneider, J. (2005), 'Wie verbreitet ist das männliche Ernährermodell heute noch?', unpublished manuscript.

Schratzenstaller, M. (2002), 'Familienpolitik – wozu und für wen? Die aktuelle familienpolitische Reformdebatte', *WSI-Mitteilungen*, **3**, 127–32.

Solberg, A. (1990), 'Negotiating childhood: changing constructions of age for Norwegian children', in A. James and A. Prout (eds), *Constructing and Reconstructing Childhood. Contemporary Issues in the Sociological Study of Childhood*, Basingstoke: The Falmer Press.

Thorpe, K. and K. Daly (1999), 'Children, parents, and time: the dialectics of control', *Contemporary Perspectives on Family Research*, **1**(1), 199–223.

Wehr, Laura (2004), 'Zeit ist das Leben', *Uni Nova*, **96**, 19–20.

Zeiher, H. (2000), 'Familienalltag und Kindheit', in Alois Herlth et al. (eds), *Spannungsfeld Familienkindheit. Neue Anforderungen, Risiken und Chancen*, Opladen: Leske + Budrich; pp. 121–135.

Zeiher, H.J. and H. Zeiher (1998), *Orte und Zeiten der Kinder. Soziales Leben im Alltag von Großstadtkindern, 2. Auflage*, Weinheim and München: Juventa Verlag.

12. Squeezed between two agendas: work and childcare in the flexible UK

Diane Perrons

A defining feature of contemporary societies is the increase in the proportion of women taking paid employment while retaining their traditional primary responsibility for domestic work and caring. This trend is almost universal but the context in which this altered practice materialises varies cross-nationally. All states are constrained in their freedom to manage their economies and finance social policy by the growing supremacy of neo-liberalism, characterised by economic deregulation, privatisation, and fiscal discipline. Likewise firms are compelled to operate within the intensely competitive global market, which shapes their internal working patterns and practices. Even so, states operate within this common global framework in different ways.

Working practices, employment regulations, childcare support and social expectations regarding the respective roles of women and men vary considerably across Europe, reflecting the continued existence of different welfare states, gendered welfare regimes and varieties of capitalism. These differentiated contexts affect the relative positioning of women and men in the labour market and the ease with which paid work and caring can be combined. This chapter focuses on the UK but the discussion is contextualised within the European Union whose policies have shaped and in turn are shaped by the UK, especially as other European countries are looking towards the high employment, flexible UK as a possible model for moving towards a competitive knowledge-based society.[1]

This chapter explores some of the implications of the flexibility agenda for working parents and their children in the UK. In particular it questions the claim that flexibility enhances economic *and* social objectives, more specifically increased productivity, enhanced work life balance and lower child poverty. The primary concern is that these objectives are conflated in thought and policy, and that insufficient attention is given to the socially differentiated practical outcomes. With reference to Figure 12.1, an

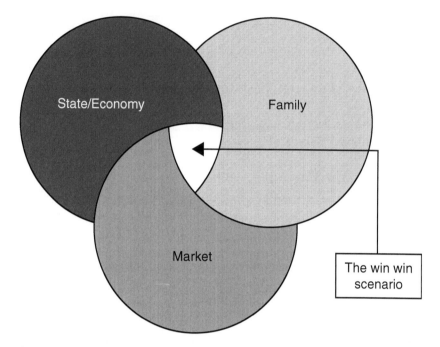

Source: Modified from CIPD (2005).

Figure 12.1   Flexibility – the economic and social agendas

identity of interests is assumed between the economic objectives of the
market, and the economic and social objectives of the state and the family,
yet in reality this ideal scenario is realised only occasionally. I begin by identifying aspects of this dual agenda before exploring some of the varied
forms of flexible working in the UK and their differentiated social impact.
Part of the argument is theoretical and part is substantiated by reference to
the growing body of quantitative and qualitative research on flexible
working, including some illustrations from a number of research projects
in which I have been involved.[2]

ECONOMIC AND SOCIAL FLEXIBILITY

With respect to other older member states of the European Union, the UK
appears as something of an aberration with its endorsement of deregulation
and flexibility as a means of expanding employment, raising competitiveness and productivity; collectively considered to be the pre-conditions for a

knowledge-based economy. Gordon Brown, the UK Chancellor of the Exchequer, captured this philosophy in his 2003 budget speech: 'the modern route – indeed, I believe, the only route – to full employment for all regions and nations is to combine flexibility with fairness' (Brown 2003, para 281). Indeed he maintains that Britain leads in job creation and suggests that the British strategy 'could help Europe's 15 million unemployed'. While he concedes that Britain has learned from Europe by introducing new maternity rights and paternity pay, he emphasises that 'in striking the balance between dynamism and social standards, our position is that no change to European regulations, like the working time directive, should risk British job creation' (Brown 2003, para 277). In this regard the government is seeking to retain the UK's opt-out of the Working Time Directive and has opposed the introduction of a Directive in relation to Temporary Agency Workers. Otherwise the UK has always implemented the EU Directives, albeit at a minimum level of compliance.[3]

Employment policies in the UK are designed to suit the Third Way politics of rights and responsibilities, encapsulated by the slogan 'work for those who can, security for those who cannot' (Hyde et al. 1999). To ensure that all those who *can, do* work, labour market activation policies were introduced in addition to tax credit policies designed to 'make work pay', discussed further in the final section. Thus one of the prime objectives of government policy has been to expand employment. In this respect it conforms to the revised Lisbon agenda (European Commission 2005a) and the European Employment Strategy (EES) guideline to 'attract more people to enter and remain in the labour market' and to create more jobs (European Commission 2005b). More specifically the UK meets two of the overarching and interrelated objectives of the EES guidelines – full employment and strengthening social cohesion (European Commission 2005b). However the way this has been done – through the development of highly flexible and non-standard working arrangements together with the working/child tax credits system (which sustains low pay) – perhaps conflicts with two other key objectives of the EES; namely, creating better jobs and 'improving quality and productivity at work', and 'strengthening social cohesion' (European Commission 2005b, p. 24). It could also conflict with the government's economic objective of moving towards a knowledge-based society with high levels of productivity. The UK government however presents flexibility, more specifically flexible labour markets, in a positive way as a means of both enhancing competitiveness and productivity on the one hand and job creation on the other. Indeed the government emphasises the UK's unique position, which enables it to exceed the US in job creation while maintaining the fairness enshrined in EU labour regulation and the EES guidelines.

These more social objectives are also emphasised in rather different debates where flexibility is advocated as a means of facilitating work life balance (Department of Trade and Industry 2003a, 2003b), though here too a win–win situation is presented between economic and social concerns. The private sector is encouraged to recognise the business case for flexibility. In principle flexibility facilitates savings on overtime, recruitment and retention costs and generates productivity gains by widening diversity and the skill base, in part by drawing on women's currently underutilised skills. Some very positive illustrations are given in the survey of 585 Human Resources professionals from a range of public and private sector organisations carried out by the Chartered Institute of Personnel Development in 2005 (Chartered Institute of Personnel Development 2005). One company for example reported reductions in overtime costs (two thirds), recruitment costs (four fifths), staff turnover (half) and secured a more diverse workforce (Chartered Institute of Personnel Development 2005). Flexibility has also been endorsed by a law, passed in 2003, which gives parents of children under the age of six (under 18 if the child is disabled) a right to request to work flexibly. The majority of such requests have been granted (Palmer 2004) and many firms have extended this right to all employees (Chartered Institute of Personnel Development 2005). As the scheme remains discretionary, however, the decisions firms make are likely to vary with the state of the labour market.[4]

Interestingly, the Equal Opportunities Commission (EOC 2005a, p. 5) in a rather different argument based on a range of research (Darton and Hurrell 2005; Grant et al. 2005) also endorse this win–win scenario. They advocate extending flexibility to a fuller range of jobs in order to unblock 'the hidden brain drain' of 5.6 million part-timers (that is one in five of the working population) working below their potential, as a consequence of choosing jobs to suit their working patterns rather than to match their skills. While calling for more flexibility however, the EOC (2005a) share many of the reservations about the current practices and limitations discussed in this chapter.

The UK government has expanded support for childcare considerably since 1998 in terms of finance and through the establishment of child centres, but coverage is not comprehensive and neither is it intended to be. Informal care combined with flexible working figure prominently in this strategy. Indeed the UK is unique in the sense of having a high female employment rate, limited childcare facilities and long working hours for men and especially fathers. As Susan Himmelweit and Maria Sigala (2004, p. 455) neatly state, this 'circle is squared' through mothers working short part-time hours fitted around their children's care. Indeed the majority of the requests for flexible working under the 2003 legislation came from

Table 12.1 Employment rates of mothers and fathers with children of different ages (%)

Employment rate	Age of youngest child			All with dependent children
	0–4	5–10	11–15	
Married/cohabiting mothers	59	77	80	71
Married /cohabiting fathers	91	91	91	91
Lone parents	34	57	65	54
Full-time employment rate				
Married cohabiting mothers	21	27	38	28
Married cohabiting fathers	87	88	87	87
Lone parents	13	24	39	28

Source: Adapted from Walling (2005).

mothers (Palmer 2004). Thus while the proportion of mothers working in the labour market has increased significantly in the late 1990s and early 2000s the presence of children continues to act as a constraint in terms of both overall labour market participation and the form of that participation.[5] Fathers by contrast are more likely to be in employment than men overall. Table 12.1 illustrates the differential employment rates of mothers and fathers with children of different ages. Both lone and partnered working parents are vastly overrepresented among those working part time and 'flexibly' (La Valle et al. 2002; Harkness 2005; Walling 2005).

FORMS OF FLEXIBILITY, AND THEIR IMPLICATIONS

The term 'flexible employment' is itself flexible and its inherently ambiguous meaning is drawn on to paint a consistently positive picture based on the connotations of adaptability, variety and adjustment. While these characteristics are correct for some people in some situations, they can be misleading and misrepresent the whole picture. Understanding the different forms of flexibility is therefore necessary in order to assess whether the economic objectives for a flexible and adjustable workforce are compatible with the social objectives of work life balance and reducing child poverty. First some of the specific forms of flexibility and their implications are considered at a general level before focusing more specifically on the link between flexibility and control over working hours and finally the impact of raising the employment rate on child poverty.[6]

Work can be flexible by task, time, contract and place. This chapter considers the latter three.[7] In terms of working times, work can be flexible in terms of the number of hours worked and by their distribution across the day, week and year. Thus full-time workers – those working over 30, usually 37–40, hours a week averaged over the year – can still be working flexibly if their hours are concentrated on particular days of the week, over certain months of the year or at atypical times. Flexibility also applies to people working less than full-time hours, which likewise may take a variety of forms ranging from permanent workers with regular hours to those with varied and unpredictable patterns. People may also be working flexibly by contract and again there are different patterns, including temporary/ temporary agency workers, and people on fixed-term contracts. All of these different forms of flexibility intersect in different ways but people with flexible contracts are also likely to be working flexible hours and are more likely, though not invariably, to be working at varied times. Finally, flexibility can also relate to the place of work, thus people working from home all or part of the time are also called flexible. Tables 12.2–12.3 provide some indication of the forms and scale of flexible working in the UK and the gender differentiated composition.

Compared to three other EU countries – France, Denmark and Sweden – the UK has by far the greatest range and dispersion of working hours (see Table 12.2 and Bishop 2004). While the modal pattern of working hours (36–40 per week) is similar between these countries, in the UK the percentage whose usual hours fall within the mode is a comparatively small 29 per cent, compared to 64 per cent in Sweden. The proportion typically working these hours in the UK is even lower: 11 per cent compared to 52 per cent in Sweden. The differences between countries can largely be attributed to prevailing legislation and traditions in relation to collective bargaining. In the UK working hours are unstandardised and increasingly negotiated on an individual level, in contrast to France, Spain or Finland where the state plays a much greater role, or in Germany, Sweden or Denmark where collective bargaining is more significant (Cousins and Tang 2005; Soskice 2005). This varied distribution in the UK also reflects the long hours worked by full-time workers, 44 on average compared with 40 for the EU overall, but also the gender-differentiated working time patterns. Men, and especially fathers, on average work longer hours than elsewhere in the EU, with 40 per cent working over 48 hours a week and one eighth over 60 hours a week (O'Brien and Shemilt 2003; Cousins and Tang 2005). Men also work longer than women, who on average have some of the shortest hours in the EU. Short hours are concentrated among mothers with dependent

Table 12.2   The varied pattern of working hours in the UK

	Usual hours		Typical hours	
	Mode (hours per week)	Per cent within the mode	Mode (hours per week)	Per cent within the mode
UK	36–40	29	40	11
France	36–40	38	39	24
Sweden	36–40	64	40	52
Denmark	36–40	54	37	45

Source: Data taken from Bishop (2004), source data Eurostat.

Table 12.3   Flexible working by time (employees' percentages) (2004)

	Men	Women	All
Full-time employees	10.2	16.1	11.6
Flexible working hours	4.9	5.1	5.0
Annualised working hours	1.4	5.1	1.5
Four and a half day week	1.4	0.9	1.2
Term-time working	1.2	5.8	2.9
Nine-day fortnight	0.3	0.3	0.3
Any flexible working pattern	18.2	28.5	22.1
Part-time employees			
Flexible working hours	6.8	9.3	8.9
Annualised working hours	3.0	4.1	3.9
Term-time working	4.2	10.9	9.6
Job sharing	0.8	2.2	1.9
Any flexible working pattern	15.8	27.3	25.0

Source: Social Trends (2006).

children. The flexible UK labour market facilitates both long and short hours, which in practice are gender differentiated, thus reinforcing gender inequality. Furthermore, class inequalities are likely to be reinforced as more regularly employed higher qualified and better paid women (likely to be partnered by men with similar attributes) are also more likely to qualify for leave entitlements and to be able to afford childcare and so retain full-time labour market attachment (Elias and Purcell 2005; Rubery et al. 2005).

Table 12.3 provides the gender composition of all forms of flexible working by time and indicates the extent of women's overrepresentation. The data show that it is women rather than men who are more likely to be working in all the different forms of flexible work. In terms of work scheduling, weekend, Sunday and night working, in 2002 approximately one third of men and a quarter of women usually worked during the evenings. Night work is considerably more prevalent among men and marginally more frequent among parents, with almost one fifth of fathers usually working at night but only one in ten mothers. In 40 per cent of families at least one parent regularly works during the evening. This is especially the case for mothers who are married or cohabiting (Harkness 2005; La Valle et al. 2002). They schedule their working hours such that one parent goes to work as the other comes home and by so doing avoid the need for childcare. Ten per cent of families with a child under five, and 7 per cent of families with a child under 12 follow this pattern, with men usually working in the day and women in the evening or night. While some professional jobs are available at this time, for example in nursing, this scheduling of work is often associated with downward occupational mobility for women as they take jobs because of their working hours rather than on the basis of their labour market skills. Supermarkets and call centres, where a wide range of working hours are offered, are particularly important and expanding sources of employment in this respect and some illustrations from work in the former are drawn on later in the chapter (Equal Opportunities Commission 2005a; Perrons 2000).[8] While mothers worked these hours to reconcile paid work with family life, the majority of men worked atypical hours out of financial necessity or because of job insecurity (La Valle et al. 2002). Professional parents worked atypical hours for both career and family reasons. People in lower socio-economic groups had less choice over working times. They were unable to negotiate a more preferable arrangement within the existing job or to find a job with better hours (La Valle et al. 2002). This differentiation reflects the way that flexibility is linked more to labour market adaptability than work life balance at the lower end of the labour market.

Serial childcare or 'shift parenting' can be extremely complicated to manage and may result in family members having little time to spend together. The following illustration comes from the UK component of a comparative study of flexible working in the retail sector in the European Union (Perrons 2000).[9] It refers to a dual-parent household where both partners work flexibly and their respective parents are also in work, not an entirely unusual scenario in the flexible UK. 'Family life' – in the sense of time spent together – most frequently took place in the car. The mother with her children would collect the father from his daytime job at a supermarket, drop them all at home before proceeding to her evening shift at a restaurant. If both parents were scheduled for weekend work then one of the grandmothers would step in, but this too had to be planned as the grandparents too worked flexibly. The father commented 'I can't remember the last full day we spent together', the interview took place in July, so when probed 'well since Christmas?', he immediately pointed out that they had not spent Christmas together, as his wife (employed in catering) was working (Perrons 2000). Another common practice for working parents in a variety of sectors is taking separate holidays to cover childcare during the school vacations: 'My husband and I . . . take most of our holidays separately so that [while I am working] he can have the children. The last couple of years we haven't actually been away on holiday, *so the arrangement has worked very well* [emphasis added].[10]

Overall an association remains between the presence of young children and lower labour market activity. The extent to which this represents a free or constrained choice is more contested, as well as the degree to which choices are shaped by internal or external constraints and whether they are durable or open to policy influence (Himmelweit and Sigala 2004). The comment above in relation to holidays reflects the way that constraints have been internalised and naturalised and indirectly raises questions about the veracity of interpretation of large-scale attitudinal data which imply that preferences are innate.[11]

The difficulty of spending time together as a family is not unusual and has been reflected in other qualitative studies (Crompton 2002) and in a nationally representative survey (La Valle et al. 2002). The precise effects of serial childcare on children have not to my knowledge been investigated, though an association between women working at night and an increased probability of couple/marital separation has been identified in the USA (Presser 2006) and similar findings in relation to family tensions are found in the UK (La Valle et al. 2002). This latter study additionally reported that 32 per cent of mothers working atypical hours had difficulty finding time to play with their children, read to them or help them with their homework, compared to 12 per cent of mothers with more standard hours. The comparable figures for men are higher, 48 per cent and 16 per cent respectively. Likewise a smaller proportion, 50 per cent compared to 75 per cent of those working standard hours, found time to have a daily meal together. On a more positive note these patterns may provide an opportunity for fathers to develop more individual relationships with their children as they have sole responsibility for longer periods. Indeed, fathers are now responsible for one third of total parental time spent with children, partly as a consequence of the increasing likelihood that their partner will be in paid employment (O'Brien and Shemilt 2003).

Employers recognise the gap in childcare provision and to some extent tailor their contracts to these constraints and the ensuing time preferences of employees, but this mainly occurs at the lower paid end of the employment hierarchy. Even where flexible employment patterns exist, however, the extent of flexibility enjoyed by any particular worker is by no means guaranteed. Implementation can depend on line managers who have to demonstrate fairness in reconciling competing staff demands, manage the work flow and satisfy company policies in relation to client expectations within the constraints arising from higher level managerial policies in relation to staffing levels (Perrons 1999; Crompton 2002; Charted Institute of Personnel Development 2005). In practice many requests for flexibility are dealt with informally on a 'give and take' basis but this clearly raises issues of transparency, monitoring and equity. For the companies surveyed by the Charted Institute of Personnel Development (2005), with the exception of part-time work less than half of the companies provided other forms of flexibility (such as job shares or annual hours) and when these were provided, fewer than half of the staff were eligible to apply. These findings are supported by an earlier survey (Institute of Employment Research/IFF Research 2001), which found that the most prevalent forms of flexibility were extended working hours at atypical times, suggesting that working times are adjusted to the rather inflexible demands of work rather than to accommodate caring responsibilities.

Thus while flexible working patterns can facilitate combining paid work with childcare and so may be said to contribute to work life balance, this interpretation rests on a very narrow conceptualisation of 'life'. For example little consideration is given to providing for leisure time and even with regard to an economically balanced life, flexible work entails both short and longer term hazards especially with respect to financial security and pensions (Warren 2004). Part-time work attracts a large pay penalty, even working less than full time for one year can have a negative effect on future earnings (Manning and Petrongolo 2004; Francesconi and Gosling 2005).

Flexible work by contract is especially hazardous in this respect and is found in the professions as well as lower paid work. It is especially prevalent in the cultural sector, thought by some to be essential for the knowledge economy (Florida 2002). Short-term contract work also has knock-on effects on childcare arrangements as the following case illustrates.[12] Jacqui (the respondent) and her partner Phil are a professional couple and illustrate the difficulties even high earners face when their working contracts are insecure. Jacqui has held a series of short-term contracts, and Phil has a rolling annual contract that was once renewed only two days before expiry. Their two children are now of school age, but the insecurity, varied hours and uncertain income had affected and continues to affect their childcare arrangements. They could not afford to pay a nanny when they were not working, the opening hours of nurseries did not match their long days and there was a limit to the extent to which they could depend on their wider family. They had been lucky to find older childminders prepared to work flexibly and match their varied needs; their current childminder had adapted her working hours to the children's after-school activity patterns. She also 'rests' when Jacqui is between jobs, though on occasions had been paid during these periods. Clearly this arrangement is highly individualised and depends on the existence of people prepared to work these patterns.

Flexibility and Control Over Working Times

The majority of people working short hours in the UK express a preference for so doing and employees comment favourably on employers who offer flexible working patterns. Sometimes these are genuine free choices – people have other things they want to do – but these patterns are also welcomed because of constraints elsewhere in their lives, for example the lack of affordable and accessible childcare. Flexible employment may enable those with caring responsibilities, generally women, to combine paid work with family life and so meet their practical gendered requirements, but these workers generally pay a high price for the flexibility in terms of pay and career development (Manning and Petrongolo 2004; Equal Opportunities Commission 2005b). Supermarkets and call centres feature as particularly important suppliers of these forms of flexibility. Typically, however, these jobs have short career ladders and so offer relatively flat employment hierarchies limiting the scope for advance within the organisation, which further reinforces occupational segregation and the pay gap experienced by part-time workers (Darton and Hurrell 2005; Crompton 2002; Perrons 1999).

However, in the UK supermarket employees are increasingly able to negotiate individual contracts, though having been negotiated these can be more difficult to change, as employers aim to retain control over the parameters of working patterns having built them into their scheduling which in turn reflects the daily, weekly, and seasonal fluctuations in sales. Thus while freely entered into by employees seeking to match their working times with childcare commitments, the ensuing patterns can work to the employees' disadvantage as the following illustrations show.[13]

Cara is a single parent of three children, living in central London. She has been out of paid employment for most of her life, is wary about paid care but is also concerned about having constantly to take time off owing to unpredictable child illnesses and school closures, revealing a combination of internal and external constraints. Now her children are all at school, she has taken a job at a local supermarket, having made clear to her employer her caring preferences and priorities, and established a working pattern to suit. The basic contract is for 16 hours a week but with a built-in commitment to work 20 if asked to do so. In practice however the number of working hours has been extremely varied, from 16 to 40 a week, yet as she points out: 'you get holiday pay after three months. My Christmas holiday will be paid. But only for 16 hours. Even if I've done 40 hours for the past three months, it doesn't make any difference. So that's where they get you as well' (Cara, supermarket worker). While she makes this critical point, Cara in general values her employers and the fact that her flexible working times enable her to be in employment. Similar remarks are made by other workers working flexibly by time and by contract. The next case refers to someone working for a temporary employment agency.

A growing proportion of people in the UK are employed through employment agencies[14] and this too can be by 'choice'. The DTI (2005) state that 52 per cent of agency temps state that they do not want a permanent job, while 25 per cent are temping because they could not get a permanent job.[15] Employees find this work attractive because in principle it allows them greater control over their working times and indeed to exceed what may be allowed within regular employment. The case of Beverley, taken from a comparative study of living and working in London and Manchester, illustrates this point. Beverley is a professional social worker and a single parent with four dependent children. She effectively works for the public sector, but via an agency, and has one full-time and one part-time job, making a working week of about 60 hours in total: 'I try to do the nights during weekends, so that's Friday, Saturday, Sunday. And then Monday to Friday during the days. Occasional midweek nights, one maybe. I have cut back a lot I must admit. I have only got one body' (Beverley, agency professional social worker).

Despite her long working hours Beverley considers that she is 'not ready for permanence' as she prioritises her children and wants to be able to manage her own time. Working for an agency, however, means that all her working time is effectively commoditised and that there is no porosity in her working day (see Rubery et al. 2005).[16] Beverley's situation contrasts markedly with another mother from the same study, Frances, with three children and similar working hours but working on a permanent contract, and who works for a news organisation. Frances however has negotiated a certain amount of flexibility within her permanent job and is trusted to manage her own time, as she comments:

> It's completely up to me, so, you know, if I want to leave at 4.30 to take a child to the dentist, or if I want to go in late because I want to see a teacher, or take an afternoon off to see a nativity play and I let my boss know, but it doesn't get monitored. (Frances, information analyst)

She is however regarded as part time even though she works between 55 and 60 hours a week. These contrasting illustrations indicate some of the complexities of flexibility in the UK and the way they are differentiated 'flexibly' between occupations, social classes and individuals.

FLEXIBILITY, THE EMPLOYMENT RATE AND CHILD POVERTY

By widening temporal and spatial horizons, flexible working has facilitated the expansion of employment in the UK. According to the government's interpretation, this contributes to the competitiveness agenda, facilitates work life balance and reduces poverty, in particular child poverty. Since 1998, the UK has adopted a policy of welfare-to-work to create 'employment opportunity for all' – 'work for those who can security for those who can't' (see Department of Social Security 1998; Hyde et al. 1999; Sefton and Sutherland 2005; Department of Work and Pensions 2004). To implement this strategy, labour market activation policies such as the New Deal were developed to encourage people to seek employment.

New Deal policies were originally introduced for young people and then extended to lone parents, but now have been generalised to a wider population including the over 25s, the over 50s, the partners of unemployed people, refugees, people affected by drug addiction, and so on.[17] These schemes provide assistance and encouragement for people to get (back) into paid employment or training. For example lone parents with children over five years of age are interviewed, advised about existing employment opportunities in their areas, the benefits they would receive if they were in employment and the availability of local childcare. These strategies have been effective such that by 2004, over half (55.8 per cent) of lone parents (92 per cent of whom are women) are in paid employment, which is almost 11 per cent higher than prior to the introduction of these policies (Department of Work and Pensions 2004 and 2005). The overall rate of worklessness among lone parent households has correspondingly fallen.[18]

The government has been particularly concerned about the comparatively high proportion of children growing up in poverty in the UK, the majority of whom are in lone parent and workless households. Child poverty has increased rapidly since the late 1960s, when one in ten children lived in poverty (McKnight 2002). By 1997, the proportion of children living in poverty, defined as households with incomes below 60 per cent of the median, was just over 25 per cent, the highest figure for all EU countries. By 2001 this figure had fallen to around 23 per cent and the UK is now fifth from bottom, with Italy, Ireland, Spain and Portugal having higher figures (Stewart 2005).

Raising the employment rate of lone parents therefore has been a central element of the strategy to reduce child poverty and, as the figures above indicate, the policy has succeeded in getting more lone parents into employment and in reducing child poverty. Overall the proportion of children living in workless households fell from 18.5 per cent to 15.9 per cent between 1997 and 2004[19] and this is one of the main reasons for the reduction in the child poverty rate.

To make these labour market activation policies effective, tax and benefit changes have also been made in order 'to make work pay' – that is, to make it economically rational to be in paid employment rather than in receipt of unemployment benefits or income support. This policy explicitly meets the Specific Guideline 19 of the European Employment Strategy: 'Enhance inclusive labour markets, enhance work attractiveness, and make work pay for job seekers, including disadvantaged people, and the inactive' (European Commission 2005b, p. 3).

People with children have benefited from the tax credit policies, initially through the working families tax credit. This measure has subsequently been divided into two payments, the child tax credit, payable to the primary carer of children on an income-related basis, and the working tax credit, payable to all people over 25 years of age working more than 30 hours a week who are in receipt of low earnings, or younger than this and working at least 16 hours a week if they have children. People with children who are in receipt of the working tax credit are also eligible to claim some financial support towards childcare costs.[20]

These policies are generally effective, except in London, where despite higher average earnings, the employment rate is below and the unemployment rate above the national average, especially for women. The high costs of housing, transport and childcare make it necessary to earn well above the minimum wage to gain financially from paid work rather than benefits, even allowing for the new tax credits (Bivand et al. 2003). For example, a lone parent with two children and childcare costs is better off returning to work at the minimum wage outside London, but needs to earn £7.76 an hour in London (that is, almost 1.75 times the minimum wage) in order to benefit financially. In recognition of the high costs of living and working in London new in-work credits are to be introduced in 2005 but for a limited period (Department of Work and Pensions 2005). These additional credits and payments are also to be made available in particularly deprived areas elsewhere in the country, which also meets the recommendations made to the UK by the Commission (European Commission 2004, p. 24).[21]

The orientation of the 'make work pay' strategies has been towards eradicating poverty, especially child poverty, raising employment and the tax base. Clearly children are likely to benefit from higher incomes, though the actual gains from the marginal increases in income for low-paid workers when offset against possible time losses and more stressed parents is less clear. There may also be gains arising from formal childcare. From the perspective of gender equality, however, the impact of these policies has been varied. While the scale of in-work benefits boosts entry into paid employment, this form of support is means-tested on the basis of family income – thus couples are assessed jointly and the current system means that the financial return from having a second earner is now lower on average than it was in 1997 when the government first came into power. Consequently there is a disincentive for the lower earner in any household, generally the female partner, to enter the labour market, even though in the longer term labour market inactivity will have a negative impact on their lifetime incomes (Brewer and Shephard 2004). Thus from the perspective of gender equality, the implementation of these policies raises some concerns, not only because of the perverse impact on the participation rate of the second earner but also because of the emphasis on subsidising rather than eradicating low-paid jobs. These are predominantly, but not exclusively, performed by women, owing to the continuing segregation in the labour market and the low pay in jobs where women are overrepresented. Thus these labour market activation and tax benefit policies have not addressed the question of the 'working poor', whose numbers have also been expanding. A further concern is that while the policies have been relatively successful in terms of getting lone parents into paid employment, the question of gender inequality in terms of time and the continuing caring deficit have not yet been adequately addressed.

While in some ways well intentioned, especially in respect of the concern to reduce child poverty, and clearly successful in raising the employment rate, the introduction of tax credit policies means that in effect the government is subsidising low pay as it is the government rather than employers that ensures people in employment are in receipt of a living wage. Some of these supplements are child related and some relate only to people who are citizens, that is, not all employees are eligible for the additional payments, which results in a segmented labour market even among comparatively low-paid employees.

Labour market activation policies, in addition to the general macroeconomic policies and policies to encourage labour market flexibility, may account for the positive annual employment growth figures since 1996 and declining unemployment. Indeed the UK has exceeded all the EU employment rate targets including those for women and older workers. However, people working flexibly often find they pay a high price for so doing, having to accept lower pay and lower status jobs; the part-time pay gap is 40 per cent. Part-time workers are also less likely to be offered training. Although the UK now has a minimum wage, this, compared to other countries in the EU is set at a low level (only 30 per cent of average wages). Only Spain has a lower figure, at 28 per cent (Stewart 2005). Low pay, defined as two thirds of the median for all employees, affected 5.4 million people or 23 per cent of UK employees in 2000/1. Thus about a quarter of all employees have hourly earnings that are insufficient to keep them out of poverty, unless they work very long hours each week (Millar and Gardiner 2004). Questions as to the quality of employment are not addressed in the same degree of depth, despite the commitment to creating a knowledge society. Neither are the time demands placed on working parents and especially lone parents.

The labour market activation policies and the expansion of non-standard forms of work may therefore also have contributed to the comparatively high numbers of working poor in the UK. Indeed, 28 per cent of UK households with a lone working parent are poor, the third highest rate in the EU (13)[22] (Stewart 2005). The generally low wage climate also sets a very low floor, the position of those workers whose legality is in question or who are subject to onerous payments to their employers for housing or transport is almost untenable (Anderson and Rogaly 2005). The circumstances in which labour can be obtained at low cost are not conducive to modernisation or training and are in conflict with the economic objective of promoting the knowledge economy.

CONCLUSION

Flexibility therefore has a multiple agenda comprising economic and social concerns. On the economic side it is designed to expand the employment rate and retain women's skills, which are considered crucial for a competitive knowledge economy. On the social side, it is believed to promote work life balance. Furthermore, by opening up employment opportunities to people with caring responsibilities, especially lone parents, flexible employment is expected to reduce child poverty. These economic and social objectives are often conflated in discussions of flexible working, which in addition refers to a wide range of working practices with quite different implications for achieving either or both of the economic or social objectives. While there is evidence of comparatively high levels of job creation there is little evidence that flexibility has contributed to productivity, and whether it has contributed to enhancing work life balance is likewise more debatable and varies according to individual circumstances. For some families combining paid work with caring results in extremely busy lives, with little time for shared leisure activities or even being together as a family unit (see also Brannen 2005; Jarvis 2005).

In relation to the economic objectives and the quest for a knowledge-based society, it is clear that what is being reproduced is a society that has experienced continuous growth for the last twelve and a half years with very high levels of employment. However productivity levels remain low, with a wide gap between the UK and other G7 countries.[23] At the lower margin flexibility seems to create and sustain a low-wage, low-skilled workforce characterised by low productivity, rather than fostering the innovation and skills that would be required in a knowledge-based society. Flexible forms of employment are sustained in many cases by the growing use of often over-skilled women and migrants who in practice have few choices. Low-paid work is also sustained by the tax credit policies which, while boosting the incomes of low-wage workers, do little to stimulate innovation or training. Furthermore the tax credits are not available to everyone, so the overall effect can be to create a low-paid and segmented labour market. Indeed in the case of migrant workers, flexibility has been shown to promote conditions more reminiscent of nineteenth century bonded labour than of a knowledge economy (Anderson and Rogaly 2005). The mechanisms for moving forward from this low-wage equilibrium sustained by tax credits are unclear. It would appear then that here, as in other areas, government policies are characterised by a high aspiration-to-evidence ratio.[24]

Further, while the feminisation of employment has increased, which generally has a positive impact on women's lives in terms of self-esteem if not necessarily empowerment or balance, gender inequalities remain. In particular paid employment remains highly segregated by gender with women overrepresented in the lower paying jobs, and in some forms of flexible employment, especially part-time work, where they experience a significant pay penalty (Manning and Petrongolo 2004).

In the case of part-time workers, children may gain from their parents' attention, though people working atypical hours report less time available to spend with their children or time spent together as a family unit. Problems also remain as a consequence of the low pay of current forms of flexible work. One possibility for improvement in these respects could arise from the commitment in the latest (2005) budget to provide wrap-around cover (between 8 am and 6 pm) for children between the ages of 3 and 14, together with a widespread provision of children's centres. The exact impact needs to be researched and will depend on the quality and cost in relation to wages. However, it is at precisely these times, an hour either side of a more usual working day, which provides the necessary margin for taking and fetching children, that people seem to want childcare. In principle this extended cover could expand the range of employment choices for working parents. It will be interesting to see whether people who have currently chosen their jobs on the basis of working times, part-time, evening or weekend work will continue to do so, or whether the extended cover will enable them to work in jobs that more closely match their skills, that at present are only available to people working more traditional patterns. Clearly the impact of extended childcare cover on working practices has yet to be investigated and both this and the impact of current practices of flexible working on children are a comparatively under-researched area.[25]

Currently flexibility is associated with varied working hours, including excessive hours for some and short hours for others, employment segregation and low pay. It is also linked with gender-differentiated lifetime earnings and contributes to explaining the 2.2 million women who have deficient or non-existent pension rights. Even in higher tier occupations the take-up of flexible working arrangements has been found to have a negative impact on career advance and interestingly, perhaps reflecting gender stereotypes, the negative effect can be greater for men than women (Almer et al. 2004).

The considerable volume of research on flexible working in recent years indicates that it is associated with both positive and negative experiences, which is to be expected given the wide variety of forms of flexibility and how these in turn mesh with people's individual attributes and circumstances. Definitive conclusions are correspondingly difficult. There are some indications from the qualitative evidence reported here, supported by quantitative survey data (Darton and Hurrell 2005) that suggest that the extent and form of flexibility varies by social class, with middle- and upper-class employees better able to shape the flexibility to meet their own agendas. Lower down the social hierarchy, however, flexibility has enabled employees to establish some control over their working hours, but in the process to work in jobs below their capabilities and with less advantageous working practices in terms of holiday and sick pay. Overall it is possible to conclude that flexible working has contributed positively to women's practical gender interests by facilitating their entry into paid employment and so enhancing their own and their children's immediate financial well-being. As this entry is only partial, however, it fails to challenge the currently unequal gender order or to meet women's strategic gender interests. The findings reported in this chapter may provide some caution to those unquestioningly advocating the high employment, highly flexible UK model elsewhere in the European Union.

NOTES

I thank the European Union for financing the project 'Flexible working and the reconciliation of paid work and family life' and my co-researcher in the UK, Jennifer Hurstfield, Linda McDowell, Colette Fagan, Kath Ray and Kevin Ward for allowing me to include references to our combined research on 'Living and labouring in London and Manchester' and the ESRC (grant number R000239470) for funding this project as well as all of the participants in both of the studies who recounted the complexity of their work life arrangements. I also thank Jane Lewis for her insightful comments on an earlier draft of this chapter.

1. Recent reports for the EU for example (Sapir 2005, Kok 2004) and the European Employment Strategy guidelines (European Commission 2005b) suggest that the EU is now looking towards greater flexibility as a means of securing the Lisbon targets of higher growth and greater employment. Thus the exceptionalism of the UK may no longer hold (see Barnard et al. 2003).

2. Two separate pieces of research are drawn on in which the author was involved: the UK component of a comparative six-country study of flexible working in the retail sector carried out with Jennifer Hurstfield (European Commission 2000; Perrons 1999, 2000) and a comparative analysis of 'Living and labouring in London and Manchester' carried out jointly with Linda McDowell, Colette Fagan, Kath Ray and Kevin Ward.

3. For example the initial transposition of the EU Directive on Parental Leave into UK legislation restricted the application to children born only after the legislation came into effect rather than all of the children meeting the age criterion. It was revised, but only after it had been successfully challenged in the European Court of Human Justice (see International Reform Monitor 2005).

4. The results of the first employee survey of the impact of the April 2003 legislation (Palmer 2004) indicate however that only just over half of all employees are aware that they have this right (55 per cent women and 49 per cent men, but slightly higher in cases where people had children). Almost one quarter of employees with children under six years old and one fifth of those with children less than 16 years old had asked to exercise this right and 83 per cent of requests were granted.

5. The proportion of couples with dependent children where both parents work increased by 8 per cent between 1994 and 2004 and the comparable figure for lone parents by 12 per cent to 54 per cent. Fathers' employment rate is 90 per cent compared to 74 per cent for men as a whole (Walling 2005 using Labour Force Survey data).

6. The more economic objectives are not specifically addressed in this chapter, for a discussion of flexibility and equal opportunities see Perrons (1999).

7. Flexible working by task or functional flexibility is important for employers but less central to the work life balance debates.

8. Estimates vary because of varying definitions but there are estimated to be around 850 000 call centre workers and numbers are continuing to grow despite offshoring, and the 1.25 million supermarket workers are another expanding sector.

9. This illustration came from a comparative study of the retail sector in six European countries.

10. This comment comes from a factory worker from the London and Manchester study, but similar remarks were made in the UK supermarket study (see Perrons 2000).

11. See Warren (2004) for a detailed critique of these limitations and Himmelweit and Sigala (2004) for a discussion of the dynamic nature of attitudes as they change with experience.

12. These illustrations come from an ESRC research project jointly carried out with L. McDowell, C. Fagan, K. Ray and K. Ward (see McDowell et al. 2005).

13. These illustrations come from the ESRC research project jointly carried out with L. McDowell, C. Fagan, K. Ray and K. Ward, and the EU study of 'Flexible work and the reconciliation of paid work and family life' (EC 2000; Perrons 2000).

14. The DTI (2002) estimates that there are 600 000 temporary agency workers in the UK or 2 per cent of the labour force. This figure was based on a specially commissioned survey during 1999 and contrasts both with the figure of 275 000 produced by the Labour Force Survey (in 2002) on the basis of self-assessment, and with that of 1.3 million produced by the Recruitment Employment Confederation (REC), an organisation of the employment agencies. The UK is believed to have the largest temporary staffing industry in Europe.

15. The DTI (2005) refer to REC (Recruitment and Employment Confederation) (which may be over-optimistic) for the data on those who say they do not want a permanent job but to the more reliable LFS data for those who say they could not get a permanent job.

16. To reduce porosity, warehouses supplying supermarkets have introduced wearable electronic devices that direct and monitor workers' movements to increase their efficiency and accountability.
17. For information on the New Deal policies see the Department of Work and Pensions website http://www.dwp.gov.uk/asd/asd1/new_deal/NDYP_ND25plus_Background_Information.pdf.
18. On slightly different figures from the Department of Work and Pensions, the Office of National Statistics estimate that the extent of worklessness was 40.8 per cent in 2004, which represents a large (7 percentage points) decrease from five years earlier (Office for National Statistics 2004).
19. In terms of absolute numbers, in autumn 2004 the number of children under 16 living in workless lone parent households was 1.2 million (Office for National Statistics 2004).
20. For the precise details of these benefits see http://www.taxcredits.inlandrevenue.gov.uk/Qualify/WhatAreTaxCredits.aspx. This is the Inland Revenue site and it provides background information, details of current schemes and an interactive service through which people can calculate whether or not they are eligible to receive these benefits. In 2005 the Childcare element in the working tax credit, available to parents working more than 16 hours a week, covered 80 per cent of costs up to £175 for one child and £300 for two children. This figure is similar to the average costs of childcare but there are regional variations, with childcare costs being higher in London (Daycare Trust 2005).
21. To 'attract more people to the labour market and making work a real option for all' it states that particular attention should be given to lone parents and people living in deprived areas. A new measure the Pathways to Work for Lone Parents will be piloted in five areas and is designed to 'give more choice and more help than ever before to lone parents to enable them to move off welfare and into work'. More specifically it intends to 'bring together extra support and childcare help with added financial incentives to look for and move into work. The new measures will ensure a clear gain from work for lone parents, as well as guarantees about childcare support and ongoing help of professional job advisers, in return for a commitment to search for and take up the offer of work.' (Department of Work and Pensions 2005).
22. No data for Ireland or Belgium.
23. UK output per worker in 2003 was similar to that of Germany, and above that of Japan but still below that of France and the USA, yet on comparative measures of flexibility the UK scores highly. On the Blanchard Wolfers (2000) (flexibility) Index for a range of OECD countries the UK is second to the USA as providing the most flexible environment when interpreted as deregulation rather than labour time or functional flexibility.
24. Robert Wade (2002) makes a similar comment in relation to the ICT for development debates.
25. See McKee et al. (2003) for a study of Scotland; and Galinski (1999) on the USA. These studies highlight the negative impact of long working hours, but also the significance of the distribution of working hours and the extent to which they allow either parent to spend quality time with their children.

BIBLIOGRAPHY

Almer, E.D., J.R. Cohen and L.E. Single (2004), 'Is it the kids or the schedule?: The incremental effect of families and flexible scheduling on perceived career success', *Journal of Business Ethics*, **54**(1), 51–65.
Anderson, B. and B. Rogaly (2005), 'Forced labour and free migration to the UK', study prepared by Compass in collaboration with the TUC, accessed at www.tuc.org.uk/international/tuc-9317-f0.cfm.

Barnard, C., S. Deakin and R. Hobbs (2003), '"Fog in the Channel, continent isolated": Britain as a model for EU social and economic policy?', *Industrial Relations Journal*, **34**(5), 461–76.

Bishop, K. (2004), 'Working time patterns in the UK, France, Denmark and Sweden. Analysis of usual hours reported in four European countries with different institutional arrangements', *Labour Market Trends*, **112**(3), 113–22.

Bivand, P., B. Gordon and D. Simmonds (2003), *Making Work Pay in London*, London: Centre for Economic and Social Inclusion.

Blanchard, O. and J. Wolfers (2000), 'The role of shocks and institutions in the rise of European unemployment: the aggregate evidence', *Economic Journal*, **110**(462), 1–33.

Brannen, J. (2005), 'Time and the study of women's work–family lives: autonomy or illusion?', *Time and Society*, **14**(1), 113–33.

Brewer, M. and A. Shephard (2004), 'Has Labour made work pay', accessed at www.jrf.org.uk/bookshop/eBooks/1859352626.pdf.

Brown, G. (2003), Hansard column 277, accessed 9 April at www.publications. parliament.uk/pa/cm200203/cmhansrd/vo030409/debtext/30409-04.htm#30409-04_spmin1.

Chartered Institute of Personnel Development (CIPD) (2005), 'Flexible working: the implementation challenge', (written by Rebecca Clarke), London: Chartered Institute of Personnel Development, www.cipd.co.uk/NR/rdonlyres/EBAA2100-EF46-43EE-9C6D-16577DCBC6DE/0/flexwork1005.pdf.

Cousins, C. and N. Tang (2005), 'Working time, gender and family: an East–West European comparison', *Gender Work and Organization*, **12**(6), 527–50.

Coyle, A (2003), 'Women and flexible working in the NHS', Equal Opportunities Commission working paper series, no 9, Manchester.

Crompton, R. (2002), 'Employment, flexible working, and the family', *British Journal of Sociology*, **53**, 537–58.

Darton, D. and K. Hurrell (2005), 'People working part-time below their potential', Equal Opportunities Commission, Manchester, accessed at www.eoc.org.uk/PDF/people_working_pt_below_potential.pdf.

Daycare Trust (2005), 'Parents pay the inflation-busting costs of childcare: results of the 2005 childcare costs survey', accessed at www.daycaretrust.org.uk/article.php?sid=245.

Department of Social Security (1998), 'New ambitions for our country: a new contract for welfare', Cm 3805, London: Stationery Office.

Department of Trade and Industry (2002), 'Proposal for a directive of the European Parliament and of the Council on working conditions for temporary agency workers, regulatory impact assessment', accessed at www.dti.gov.uk/er/agency/ria3.pdf.

Department of Trade and Industry (2003a), 'Flexible working. The business case 50 success stories, Department of Trade and Industry', accessed at http://164.36.164.20/work-lifebalance/publications.html.

Department of Trade and Industry (2003b), Worklife Balance website – information about publications, conferences and case studies, accessed at www.dti.gov.uk/work-lifebalance/.

Department of Trade and Industry (2005), 'How have employees fared? Recent UK trends', Employment Relations series no 56, London, accessed May 2006 at www.dti.gov.uk/files/file27472.pdf.

Department of Work and Pensions (2004), 'Opportunity for all sixth annual report', Cm 6239, Department of Work and Pensions, London: Stationery Office, accessed at www.dwp.gov.uk/ofa/reports/2004/summary/05.asp.

Department of Work and Pensions (2005), 'Pathways to work boost for lone parents', accessed at www.dwp.gov.uk/mediacentre/pressreleases/2005/feb/emp2510-ndlp. asp.

Dex, S. and C. Smith (2002), *The Nature and Pattern of Family-friendly Employment Policies in Britain*, Joseph Rowntree Foundation Family and Work Series, Bristol: Policy Press.

Elias, P. and K. Purcell (2005), 'Evidence on equality – reviewing the trends', paper presented at the Celebrating the 25th Anniversary of the Women and Employment Survey: Changes in Women's Employment 1980–2005 Conference.

Equal Opportunities Commission (2005a), 'Britain's hidden brain drain. The Equal Opportunities Commission's investigation into flexible and part-time working. Final report', Manchester: Equal Opportunities Commission, accessed at www.eoc.org.uk/PDF/brain_drain_final_report.pdf.

Equal Opportunities Commission (2005b), 'Part-time work is no crime so why the pay penalty? The Equal Opportunities Commission's investigation into flexible and part-time working. Interim report', Manchester: Equal Opportunities Commission, accessed at www.eoc.org.uk/PDF/flexible_working_interim_ report.pdf.

European Commission (2000), *Gender Use of Time: Three European Studies*, Brussels: Office for Official Publications of the European Communities, pp. 1–50.

European Commission (2004), 'Strengthening the implementation of the European Employment Strategy COM (2004) Final', accessed at http://europa.eu.int/ comm/employment_social/employment_strategy/prop_2004/com_2004_0239_ en. pdf.

European Commission (2005a), 'Community action for growth and employment', Community Lisbon Programme com (2005) 330 final, accessed at http:// europa.eu.int/growthandjobs/pdf/COM2005_330_en.pdf.

European Commission (2005b), 'European employment strategy guidelines for the employment policies of member states 2005/600/EC', *Official Journal of the European Commission*, l(205), 21–7, accessed at http://europa.eu.int/eur-lex/lex/ LexUriServ/site/en/oj/2005/l_205/l_20520050806en00210027.pdf.

Ferri, E. and K. Smith (1996), *Parenting in the 1990s*, London: Family Policy Studies Centre in association with the Joseph Rowntree Foundation.

Florida, R. (2002), *The Rise of the Creative Class: And How It's Transforming Work, Leisure, Community and Everyday Life*, New York: Basic Books.

Francesconi, M. and A. Gosling (2005), 'Career paths of part-time workers', Equal Opportunities Commission working paper series no 19, Manchester: Equal Opportunities Commission.

Galinski, E. (1999), *Ask the Children: What America's Children Really Think about Working Parents*, New York: William Morrow and Company.

Grant, L., S. Yeandle and S. Buckner (2005), 'Working below potential: women and part-time work', Equal Opportunities Commission working paper series, No. 40, Manchester.

Harkness, S. (2005), *Employment, Work Patterns and Unpaid Work: An Analysis of Trends Since the 1970s, Final Report*, Swindon: Economic and Social Research Council.

Himmelweit, S. and M. Sigala (2004), 'Choice and the relationship between identities and behaviours for mothers with pre-school children: some implications from a UK study', *Journal of Social Policy*, **33**(3), 455–78.

Houston, D. and J. Waumsley (2003), *Attitudes to Flexible Working and Family Life*, Joseph Rowntree Foundation, Bristol: The Policy Press.

Hyde, M., J. Dixon and M. Joyner (1999), 'Work for those who can, security for those who cannot: the new social security reform agenda for the United Kingdom', *International Social Security Review*, **52**(4), 69–86.

Institute of Employment Research/IFF Research (IER/IFF) (2001), *Work–Life Balance 2000: Baseline Study of Work–Life Balance in Great Britain*, Warwick: Institute of Employment Research.

International Reform Monitor (2005), 'Adaptation of UK labour market regulation to European Union directives', accessed at www.reformmonitor.org/httpd-cache/doc_reports_2-2650.html.

Jarvis, H. (2005), 'Moving to London time: household co-ordination and the infrastructure of everyday life', *Time and Society* **14**(1), 133–54.

Kok, W. (2004), 'Facing the challenge. The Lisbon strategy for growth and employment', report from the High Level Group chaired by Wim Kok, accessed at http://europa.eu.int/comm/lisbon_strategy/pdf/2004-1866-EN-complet.pdf.

La Valle, I., S. Arthur, C. Millward and J. Scott with M. Clayden (2002), *Happy Families? atypical Work and Its Influence on Family Life*, Joseph Rowntree Foundation, Bristol: The Policy Press.

McDowell, L., D. Perrons, C. Fagan, K. Ray and K. Ward (2005), 'The contradictions and intersections of class and gender in a global city: placing working women's lives on the research agenda', *Environment and Planning A*, **37**(3), 441–61.

McKee, L., N. Mauthner and J. Galilee (2003), 'Children's perceptions on middle class work family arrangements', in A.M. Jensen and L. McKee (eds), *Children and the Changing Family: Between Transformation and Negotiation*, London: Routledge.

McKnight, A. (2002), 'Low-paid work: drip feeding the poor', in J. Hills, J. Le Grand and D. Piachaud (eds), *Understanding Social Exclusion*, Oxford: Oxford University Press.

Manning, A. and B. Petrongolo (2004), *The Part-time Pay Penalty*, London: Department of Trade and Industry, Women and Employment Unit.

Millar, J. and K. Gardiner (2004), 'Low pay, household resources and poverty', Joseph Rowntree Foundation, accessed at www.jrf.org.uk/knowledge/findings/socialpolicy/n64.asp.

O'Brien, M. and I. Shemilt (2003), 'Working fathers: earning and caring', Equal Opportunities Commission discussion series, Manchester, accessed at www.eoc.org.uk/PDF/ueareport.pdf.

Office for National Statistics (2004), 'Workless lone parent households', ONS National Statistics website data, accessed at www.statistics.gov.uk/cci/nugget.asp?id=409.

Palmer, T. (2004), 'Results of the first flexible working employee survey', Department of Trade and Industry *Employment Relations occasional papers*, London, accessed at www.dti.gov.uk/er/emar/flex_survey_results.pdf.

Perrons, D. (1999), 'Flexible working patterns and equal opportunities in the European Union. Conflict or compatibility?', *European Journal of Women's Studies*, **6**(4), 391–418.

Perrons, D. (2000), 'Flexible working and Equal Opportunities in the UK: a case study from retail', *Environment and Planning A*, **32**(10), 1719–34.

Pocock, B. and J. Clarke (2005), 'Time, money and job spillover: how parents' jobs affect young people', *Journal of Industrial Relations*, **47**(1), 62–76.

Presser, H. (2006), 'Employment in a 24/7 economy: challenges for the family', in D. Perrons, C. Fagan, L. McDowell, K. Ray and K. Ward (eds), *Gender Divisions and Working Time in the New Economy: Changing Patterns of Work, Care and Public Policy in Europe and North America*, Cheltenham, UK and Northampton, MA, USA: Edward Elgar.

Reynolds, T., C. Callender and R. Edwards (2003), *Caring and Counting: The Impact of Mothers' Employment on Family Relationships*, Joseph Rowntree Foundation, Bristol: The Policy Press.

Rubery, J., K. Ward, D. Grimshaw and H. Beynon (2005), 'Working time, industrial relations and the employment relationship', *Time & Society*, **14**(1), 89–111.

Sapir, A. (2005), 'An agenda for a growing Europe: The Sapir Report', *Regional Studies*, **39**(7), 958–65.

Social Trends (2006), 'Social Trends no 36', 2006 edn, London: National Statistics.

Sefton, T. and H. Sutherland (2005), 'Inequality and poverty under New Labour', in J. Hills and K. Steward (eds), *A More Equal Society?*, Bristol: Policy Press.

Soskice, D. (2005), 'Varieties of capitalism and cross-national gender differences', *Social Politics*, **12**(2), 170–9.

Statham, J. and A. Mooney (2003), *Around the Clock: Childcare Services at Atypical Times*, Joseph Rowntree Foundation, Bristol: The Policy Press.

Stevens, J., J. Brown and C. Lee (2004), 'The second work life balance study. Results from the employees survey', Department of Trade and Industry working paper series 27, London, accessed at www.dti.gov.uk/er/emar/errs 27.pdf.

Stewart, K. (2005), 'Changes in poverty and inequality in the UK in international context', in J. Hills and K. Stewart (eds), *A More Equal Society?*, Bristol: Policy Press.

Wade, R. (2002), 'Bridging the digital divide: route to development or new form of dependency?', *Global Governance*, **8**(4), 443–66.

Wallace, C. (2003), 'Work flexibility in eight European countries. A cross national comparison', Vienna: Reihe Soziologie/Sociological Series 60, accessed at www.ihs.ac.at/publications/soc/rs 60.pdf.

Walling, A. (2005), 'Families and work', *Labour Market Trends*, **112**(6), 275–84.

Warren, T. (2004), 'Working part-time: achieving a successful "work–life" balance?', *British Journal of Sociology*, **55**(1), 99–122.

13. Men and women's agency and capabilities to create a worklife balance in diverse and changing institutional contexts

Barbara Hobson, Ann-Zofie Duvander and Karin Halldén

INTRODUCTION

The male breadwinner model, characterised by a traditional division of unpaid and paid work, is no longer the norm in European societies. The European Union through laws, codes of good practice and discourse has played a key role in facilitating a dual-earner family model, including statutory policies that give rights to women and men for parental leave, targets for childcare places, as well as laws removing barriers against equal treatment of women workers (Lewis and Guillari 2005; Hervey and O'Keefe 1996). These policies and their accompanying discourses on reconciling parenting with employment reflect social goals in the EU that seek to create conditions for a worklife balance, a phrase that recognises the value of caring and earning as part of a full and balanced life. Yet the promotion of worklife balance often sits uncomfortably with competing goals for productivity and competitiveness (EC 2002, 2003). These discourses convey the bifurcation in European policymaking communities between social aims and their market goals,[1] and mirror the disjuncture between two worklife scenarios: the embodied worker expected to develop strategies to reconcile having and caring for children with employment, and the disembodied worker assumed to be unencumbered by care responsibilities who is expected to devote all his or her energies to the workplace. The latter has been strengthened by neo-liberal ideologies and globalised labour markets (Hochschild 1997).

These are and have been highly gendered scenarios, mothers are the ones who are assumed to do the reconciling of employment with having children, but fathers have not been expected to adjust work hours or work schedules to family responsibilities. However, currently, the scripts appear more fluid, both because of increasing expectations for gender equality in families (McDonald 2000), alongside a growing sense of insecurity and uncertainty in male jobs and declining male wages (Walker et al. 2000).

How do parents' attitudes and practices reflect the disjunctures between changes in norms and ideologies promoting worklife balance for women and men, and the possibilities for achieving them? In an era of insecure employment and unstable marriages, what kinds of strategies around caring and earning do men and women opt for after deciding to have a family?

Our purpose in this chapter is to locate men's and women's choices around employment and care within different institutional contexts, underscoring the importance of considering parents' decision making in a complex and changing universe of work, welfare and shifting cultural norms around parenting and fatherhood. Most studies have tended to focus on women's ability to reconcile employment and motherhood (Crompton 1999; Gornick et al. 1997; Pfau-Effinger 2005). Others emphasise differences in household approaches to employment and care, concentrating on women's preferences only (Hakim 2003). Although we look at differences across Europe for both women and men in respect of the compatibility of employment with caring for children, we angle our lens more in the direction of men's possibilities and rights to care, as there is less comparative research and this is an undertheorised research area. We also concentrate on proactive policies that encourage men to increase their carework, with a specific focus on parental leave in Sweden, a society that has mandated two months for fathers' leave.

The literature on contemporary fatherhood and masculinities suggests that there is a growing number of men who would like to have a more balanced worklife to enable them to be fathers more engaged with the care of their children (Kimmel 2000; Haas et al. 2002; Hobson and Morgan 2002; Knijn and Stelten 2002). Moreover, men face increased pressures from their partners and friends to take time off from employment for care after the birth of a child. The British Prime Minister, Tony Blair, felt bound to exercise his rights for parental leave after his wife publicly announced that he would. In doing so, he was seen as setting a good example for British fathers. The assumption underlying days and months reserved for fathers is that early contact will result in bonding and closeness between fathers and children as well as lead to more equality in the family (Hobson and Morgan 2002). Governments have launched media campaigns to persuade fathers to engage in more carework, most notably in the Netherlands, Norway and Sweden (Duvendak and Stavenuiter 2004; Rostgaard 2002; Bergman and Hobson 2002). In Sweden and Norway, men who do not take time off to care for young children are the exception rather than the norm.

In emphasising the discursive shift and ideological reconstructions of fatherhood from cash to care (Hobson and Morgan 2002), we are not suggesting that men are no longer the main earners in families across Europe or that the dual earner family has been accomplished across all European countries. Rather, we see this period as one of transition in which there is declining salience of the male breadwinner norm.[2] The meaning of fatherhood has moved more toward fathering, in the sense of involvement with caretaking (Hobson and Morgan 2002). This is especially true in Northern European countries (Smith 2004). In countries with proactive policies for men to take up carework, we can begin to ask the question: what possibilities do men have to be earners and carers?

In the first section of the chapter, we focus on the European context and describe the variations across selected European countries between attitudes toward a worklife balance and practices. Using selected countries from the most recent wave of the European Social Survey of 2004, we compare the attitudes between men and women on a range of worklife balance issues with the actual working times and caretaking responsibilities. In the following section, we concentrate on proactive polices toward fathering in Nordic countries, analysing data on the Swedish case, in which there has been a survey of 4000 individuals on how they divide parental leave. We include a range of variables: income, working times, education in relation to stated reasons why they opted for their choices, what parents perceive as constraints and what they would have preferred. In the conclusion, we discuss the implications of our results and suggest research strategies for future research on men's 'capabilities' to create a worklife balance and thus to be more active and involved fathers.

Capabilities

Before turning to our analysis of worklife balance attitudes and practices in European societies, we want to clarify why and how we use a capabilities and agency approach. Taking inspiration from Amaryta's Sen's formulation of agency and capabilities, we explore men's capabilities to reconcile employment with carework for children. For Sen (1992, 2003), individual freedom to choose is bound both by means (what he or she is or does, which Sen calls functionings) and social and environmental factors, that is, the institutional context and social worlds that individuals inhabit. In our study of worklife balance, real choice (or agency freedom) involves not just the existence of specific laws and policies for reconciling employment with care, but the capabilities to exercise rights. More and more research on gender and worklife balance has turned to structural features of workplaces, expected working times and organisational cultures (Crompton 1999; den Duik 2001; Haas et al. 2002; Van der Lippe et al. forthcoming). This is a crucial dimension for understanding men's and women's agency to realise a worklife balance. Alongside the economic and social constraints that inhibit the individual's exercise of his rights are the interlocking societal norms and personal perceptions of rights and entitlements to make a claim that prioritises care for one's children over job demands. This sense of entitlement is crucial for understanding men's care claims, given the fact that the father breadwinner norm has deeper roots in most European societies than that of the father carer. An essential feature of the capabilities framework is that it situates individual agency within a multi-layered personal, social and structural environment: the individual (perceptions of his or her possibilities and entitlements), the needs and claims of other family members; the claims and tolerance of employers and workmates; and the laws and policies that undergird claims and perceptions. Therefore, it implicitly recognises that institutions, rules, and informal norms held by others (collectively) not only affect access to resources, but also subjective states of efficacy (England 2000; Takahashi 2003).[3] Agency freedom in this context is revealed in the sense of entitlement to make a claim for parenting.

A major critique of the capabilities approach is that it is a highly individualised model that does not allow us to look at the dynamics with the couple. Men's agency freedom not to take responsibility for care has limited mothers' freedom to reconcile having a family with having employment (Lewis and Guillari 2005). This is the strength of the household strategies approach (Wallace 2003), which also recognises that the family is a dynamic institution rather than the passive outcome of policies – that there are different cultures of work and care (Pfau-Effinger 2003). However, even a cultural-embedded approach to family strategies around work and care, which takes us further than models that assume static preferences (Becker 1991; Hakim 2003), does not allow for analysis of the diverse settings and situations that shape agency for worklife balance claims (Haas 2003).

A capabilities approach acknowledges that the diverse individual capabilities of men and women across education, age, ethnic and racial backgrounds in particular settings affect their sense of agency to make claims for a worklife balance (Hobson and Oláh 2006; Bygren and Duvander 2006). In employing a capabilities approach, we consider parents' agency to reconcile caring for children with employment demands considering different social environments and contexts – the couple, the workplace, and national and supra-national policy levels – and how they shape individual attitudes and practices.

THE EUROPEAN POLICY CONTEXT

There is variation across European societies with regard to the rights and protection for parents to reconcile employment with care for children (Plantenga and Remery 2005; Moss and Deven 1999). There are different policy formulas and mixes of public and private care/work solutions across European societies, including the growing tendency to rely on firms to develop reconciliation policies (Plantenga and Remery 2005). Despite the variations in the extent and type of care formulas, there is commitment at the European level to the reconciliation of employment and care, expressed in recommendations, guidelines and formal Directives, which have engendered new legislation and policy agendas at the member state level (Deven and Moss 2002).

Although the EU has prioritised reconciliation of work and employment and advocated greater sharing of care and household responsibilities (EC 2003; Hantrais 2000; Deven and Moss 2002), generally the strategies have been geared toward increasing women's labour force participation, rather than increasing men's carework. Two specific Directives – on parental leave and part-time work – have the potential to affect men's ability to spend more time caring for their children.

By making parental leave gender-neutral, the 1996 EU Directive (96/34) gave men in several countries their first opportunity to use their parental rights to take time off from their employment for fathering. Still, in most countries this does not constitute a social right to care. Whereas maternity benefit levels range between 60 to 100 per cent of previous income in most countries (based on Gauthier and Bortnik's 2001 estimates of the proportion of pay replacement for a woman industrial worker),[4] parental leave in most EU countries is a low, flat-rate benefit, in some countries it is a means-tested benefit, and it is an unpaid benefit in a few others. The exceptions are some of the Scandinavian countries with parental leave benefits between 80 and 100 per cent of previous wage. Ferrarini (2003), using estimates based on the proportion of leave benefits with the net earnings of an average industrial worker's wage in 2000, shows that for nearly all European men that amounts to about 20 per cent of their income; again the exceptions are Finland, Norway and Sweden. Of course, some fathers gain benefits through specific collective bargaining agreements or special policies in firms. Still, undeniably, the majority of European men are limited in their ability to exercise their rights to parental leave, given the minimal levels of replacement for men's income and the negative effect it would have on the household economy.

The other EU Directive on Part Time Work (97/81)[5] does not establish the right to request reduced hours, though it 'recommends' that employers facilitate part-time work at all levels and that member states adapt their social security systems to accommodate part-time work. Among EU policy makers, flexibility in working time is viewed as a strategy to promote work-life balance for parents, but it is also a strategy that offers employers the opportunity to adjust workers' hours to productivity. There are marked differences across EU countries in the extent and form of the rights of employees to reduce hours.[6] Moreover there are few measures that specifically encourage men to take up this option. The rights to reduce hours have been most pertinent for mothers' reconciliation of employment and family, and many studies note the double-edged nature of part-time work, which allows many women to have jobs who otherwise would not have been able to combine employment with raising children. Yet this option affects women's earnings, and lifetime earnings (O'Reilly and Fagan 1998; Rubery et al. 1999).

Many countries have legislation allowing all employees to reduce hours. The discourses on flexible work times and the reconciliation of work and family life have led to recent national legislation (for example in the UK, Germany and the Netherlands) aimed at men as well as women, and designed to create a worklife balance through entitlements to flexible working times. Alongside the codes of practice and enabling laws to reduce hours, there are other types of incentives to create a worklife balance through working time accounts, in which parents work more hours in some periods that can then be 'traded' when they need time off from employment for carework; Belgium, Germany and Norway are examples of countries that have introduced these initiatives to promote more broad-based flexible working times, which have the potential to increase men's ability to take on more care responsibilities.

It is perhaps too early to evaluate the effect of these options on working times. Nevertheless recent European studies suggest that there is a significant implementation gap between the formal policies that permit workers to reduce hours or create more flexible work environments, and actual practices in workplaces (Guerreiro et al. 2004, p. 26). The Netherlands is a case in point. According to Collette Fagan et al. (2006), the flexible work-time schemes in the Netherlands are the most comprehensive (see also Plantenga et al. 1999). Since 2001, all employees (not just parents) have the right to move between full-time and part-time working hours and employers have very little leeway to deny requests. So far the data suggest that this option has not been taken up by many couples. Knijn and Wel (2001), for example, show that only 9 per cent of parents with children have taken advantage of the equal sharing option.[7] The majority, over 60 per cent, follow the one and a half earner family model, with fathers continuing to work full time.

Specific policy incentives do not necessarily have an effect on practices. First, they cannot be isolated from the broader policy matrices involving childcare, school scheduling, and tax and pension schemes (Gornick and Meyers 2003). Second, the agency and capabilities of parents to achieve a worklife balance involve not only regulation of working times, but also organisational cultures, involving expected working hours as well as availability to work on weekends and overtime (Fagan 2004; Guerreiro et al. 2004).[8] And these norms are understood in gendered terms with more latitude for mothers to make claims for care and less for fathers: male employees' perceptions of their capabilities to exercise their rights to care are shaped by what other men are doing in the workplace (Bygren and Duvander 2006; Haas et al. 2002). Furthermore some studies suggest that there are working time practices in countries (working times regimes that appear as general norms in a society) and that these differ for women and men (Rubery et al. 2001; Plantenga et al. 1999). Finally, policy initiatives, even proactive polices to increase men's care, confront deeply rooted cultural norms concerning women's and men's responsibilities for care.

In the following section, we provide an overview of worklife balance norms, attitudes and practices across European societies, using the most recent wave of the European Social Survey in 2004.[9] We have selected 11 European countries from those completing the survey, representing the three welfare regime types, and the post-Socialist transition countries:[10] Belgium, the Czech Republic, Denmark, Finland, Germany, Norway, Poland, Portugal, Spain, Sweden and the UK.

Attitudes and Norms Surrounding Worklife Balance[11]

As can be seen from Table 13.1, there are variations across European societies in attitudes around male breadwinner norms and gender roles, specifically in two questions asking whether men should have priority for jobs when they are scarce and whether women should reduce hours for the sake of the family. In Portugal, the Czech Republic and Poland, we can see that a significant proportion of women and men agree[12] with the statement that women should be prepared to cut down their work for the sake of the family (over 60 per cent in Portugal, 50 per cent of women and 57 per cent of men in the Czech Republic, and about the same proportions in Poland). These countries appear to be the most traditional in their attitudes to gender roles; they also score higher than the other countries in our sample when asked if men should have more rights to a job if jobs are scarce (see Table 13.1). In contrast few Scandinavian men or women agree with either of these statements. The weakness of the male breadwinner norm is reflected in these attitudes, especially in Sweden, Denmark and Finland, with less than 6 per cent

Table 13.1   The share of men and women (per cent) between 20 and 45 years of age agreeing with or perceiving the following statements as important

		Czech Republic	Poland	Germany	Spain	Belgium	Portugal	United Kingdom	Norway	Finland	Sweden	Denmark
A woman should be prepared to cut down on her paid work for the sake of the family?	Men	57.4	56.0	44.4	43.3	31.2	60.5	34.6	23.9	18.1	14.7	11.5
	Women	50.2	51.0	46.2	48.9	34.2	63.9	43.2	26.0	18.6	13.0	16.3
When jobs are scarce men should have more right to a job than women?	Men	36.0	36.8	17.5	19.7	20.0	30.8	11.5	8.1	5.8	4.3	5.4
	Women	25.3	31.9	13.2	22.2	20.9	31.2	13.6	4.3	4.4	2.3	4.0
Men should take as much responsibility as women for the home and children?	Men	71.9	86.2	77.5	82.7	87.2	79.5	91.2	90.3	88.2	94.1	89.2
	Women	82.0	94.7	87.6	89.8	87.9	85.7	88.5	92.2	90.7	96.4	92.0
A person's family should be his or her main priority in life?	Men	82.7	95.2	85.7	78.9	82.8	81.0	90.7	78.0	84.4	83.4	67.2
	Women	85.5	93.2	81.0	71.7	78.1	80.2	87.8	73.5	82.6	79.4	66.0
How important is high income when choosing a job?	Men	90.5	98.8	82.7	93.3	83.3	96.6	76.0	91.8	69.6	78.8	61.3
	Women	85.7	96.1	69.2	92.2	65.6	94.7	58.8	85.0	65.8	69.5	43.6
How important is a job that allows you to combine work and family responsibilities when choosing a job?	Men	91.2	88.7	86.6	85.1	92.8	93.3	87.3	88.5	74.0	95.0	85.7
	Women	90.2	91.6	94.4	96.2	96.0	96.3	95.9	95.4	78.9	97.3	92.9

Source: European Social Survey 2004 (first version), selected countries. The data have been weighted to correct for differences in sample selection across countries. The number of cases is 9455 respondents in total for the first four attitudinal questions (includes all women and men aged 20–45) and 3423 cases for the latter two (includes only couples with children under 12, between ages of 20 and 45).

of men and women believing that men have precedence over women when there is a shortage of jobs. Still, the fact that over two thirds of men in most of our countries did not agree that men should have the right to a job suggests that the salience of a single male breadwinner earner is on the wane.

The belief that men and women should have *equal* responsibility for home and family has gained widespread acceptance; around 80–90 per cent of both men and women take this position, though women on average are slightly more positive (see Table 13.1). This has become an accepted norm in European societies. Most people in our sample felt that family should be the main priority in one's life, but actually slightly more men than women in nearly all our countries felt this way (see Table 13.1). However, when considering attitudes toward caretaking responsibilities, we can see that significant proportions of men and women still agree with the statement that women should reduce their hours for the sake of children; even more women take this view.

When considering priorities in choosing jobs, we limited our sample to families with children under 12 because the question is more relevant to their situation: they were asked whether they would consider combining employment and family to be important when choosing a job (Table 13.1). The responses of this group reveal how hegemonic the norms surrounding worklife balance have become. The vast majority of men and women agreed that combining work and responsibility is a priority when it comes to choosing a job. This is more so among women, but also most men give priority to being able to find jobs that allow them to combine employment with family responsibilities.

At the same time the overwhelming majority of men in all our countries also value having a high income when choosing a job – this being true for most men in our countries, but also for women in Spain, Portugal, the Czech Republic and Poland. These are countries with fairly high unemployment (except for the Czech Republic), more informal work and less secure jobs, as well as minimal care services. Those who seem to be least concerned about having a high income are Danish men and women. Still, in all the Scandinavian societies, which are dual earner societies where families are less dependent on one income, fathers and mothers attach much higher importance to reconciliation possibilities than to having a high income when choosing a job. Interestingly, this was also true for the UK.

Worklife Balance Practices

In looking at worklife balance practices, we also limit our sample to couples with children under 12. The ESS survey asks how many hours a week men and women normally work. In the Czech Republic and Poland men have extremely long weekly working hours including overtime. A majority of the men, 54 per cent in the Czech Republic and 53 per cent in Poland, work more than 45 hours per week (Table 13.2). Over a third of Polish women with children under 12 are also working more than 45 hours. For the other countries the most common pattern for both men and women is a 35–45 hour week, especially in the Scandinavian countries. A significant proportion of women work part time in the UK, Belgium, and Germany (more than 50 per cent are working 34 hours or less) compared to other countries. In Scandinavia, over a third of women are working long part-time hours. Finland with its long history of women in full-time work does not fit the pattern. Nor does part-time work seem to be an option for many women in Spain, Portugal and post-Socialist transition countries.

The average preferred working hours per week question is in fact a capabilities question since it asks how many hours a week, if any, would you choose to work, bearing in mind that your earnings would go up or down according to how many hours you work (Figure 13.1). Therefore it is not surprising that the responses are quite close to actual weekly hours. For men, in all countries but one (Poland where the averages were above 45 hours a week), the average preferred hours were slightly less than actual working hours. We might assume that when Polish and Czech men say their preferred working hours reach as high as 47 and 55.4 hours per week, they are revealing more about the economic constraints in their lives than what they might actually prefer, especially in light of the their professed strong interest in finding jobs that allow them to combine work and responsibilities (around 90 per cent). The average preferred time for most men is 40 hours per week in our other countries. Comparing men and women's preferred hours (Figure 13.1), we show that in general women claim that they would work fewer hours than men. Here the exceptions are Portuguese and Polish women who say that they would prefer to work slightly more hours, even though their average work week is near or above 40 hours per week. The gender gap in preferences is highest in the UK, Belgium and Germany (Figure 13.1). There is no gender difference in preferred work hours in Portugal (around 42 hours a week). In the Scandinavian countries we also see that most men prefer a near full-time working week, whereas most women want a shorter working week by about five or six hours.[13]

CARING WORK AND ITS CONSEQUENCES

The capabilities and agency to achieve a worklife balance are intimately connected with expectations about who takes time out to do the caring work for young children. Questions in the ESS about the amount of time

Table 13.2   Working hours in a normal week including paid and unpaid overtime (mean) for men and women living with a wife/husband/partner with at least one child below 12 years of age in the household (ages 20–45 years)

		1–19 hours	20–34 hours	35–45 hours	More than 45 hours a week
Czech Republic	Men	1.2	1.2	43.3	54.3
	Women	1.9	10.3	69.2	18.7
Poland	Men	2.0	4.0	40.9	53.0
	Women	6.5	8.4	49.0	36.1
Germany	Men	1.4	2.1	63.7	32.9
	Women	27.2	28.2	38.1	6.4
Spain	Men	0.8	4.2	51.3	43.7
	Women	5.7	13.3	63.8	17.1
Belgium	Men	4.2	3.3	60.0	32.5
	Women	13.5	37.8	37.8	10.8
Portugal	Men	4.1	1.0	60.2	34.7
	Women	10.1	2.2	68.8	18.8
United Kingdom	Men	2.0	10.7	50.0	37.3
	Women	28.7	28.0	33.8	9.6
Norway	Men	0.5	6.6	67.2	25.7
	Women	11.4	27.1	54.8	6.6
Finland	Men	0.6	5.3	68.4	25.7
	Women	3.2	16.1	69.7	11.0
Sweden	Men	0	4.4	74.2	21.4
	Women	4.1	30.1	58.9	6.8
Denmark	Men	1.7	1.7	74.8	21.8
	Women	2.8	25.5	61.7	9.9

Source: European Social Survey 2004 (first version), selected countries. The data have been weighted to correct for differences in sample selection across countries.

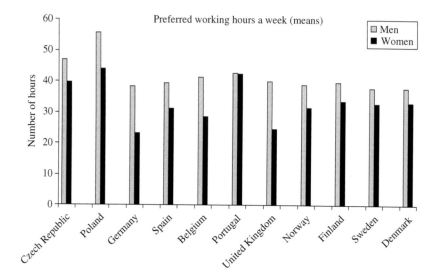

Note: Respondents living with a wife/husband/partner between the ages of 25 and 45 having at least one child below 12 years of age in the household are included in the sample. The questions posed are: '*Regardless of your basic or contracted hours, how many hours do/did you normally work a week (in your main job), including paid or unpaid overtime?*' and '*How many hours a week, if any, would you choose to work, bearing in mind that your earnings would go up and down according to how many hours you work?*'

Source: European Social Survey 2004 (first version), selected countries (3423 respondents).

Figure 13.1   What hours men and women would choose with pay rises for more hours and pay reductions for reduced hours (in selected European countries, ages 25–45)

taken in leave and about working hours were directed only to women (with at least six months labour market experience) and not to men, there being an assumption that only women take time off to care and women pay the price for interrupting employment to care. The data show that a majority of all women take one year of full-time maternity leave, except in Portugal, where only 26 per cent take any leave;[14] and in Spain, where 23 per cent of women do not use any full-time maternity leave.

A significant proportion of women in all our countries reduce their working hours when they have a family. However, this was not the case in Poland, the Czech Republic and Finland in which the vast majority of women (over 80 per cent) reported that they did not work part time after they had children. Many women in the UK (56 per cent), in Germany (50 per cent) and in Sweden (43 per cent) said that they spent more than a year working part time instead of full time because they were caring for children. The proportions are also high for Norway and Belgium (43 per cent and 41 per cent respectively).

How did these women perceive the consequences of taking leave and working part time to care for their children? Every second woman in the UK stated that maternity leave had had a negative effect on her career. The proportion was also high for Germany (44 per cent), and between 15 and 30 per cent of women in the other nine countries agreed with this statement. The same pattern of responses is shown in respect of part-time work: 55 per cent of all UK women and 45 per cent of the women in Germany think that reduced work time due to care of children had negative consequences for their careers. Both are countries with high percentages of women in short hour, part-time work; furthermore, their governments have recently passed legislation to enable parents to request a reduction in their working hours. In relation to fathers' hours, we would place both countries in the 'long hour working regimes' category (Plantenga et al. 1999), in which significant proportions of fathers – over a third – are working over 45 hours a week.

In looking across these European countries, we see a disjuncture between the value accorded to family and worklife balance that men profess as compared with the actual practices. We can surmise that there are variations in the capabilities of individual men to achieve a worklife balance allowing for the reconciliation of employment with caring for children. Considering average working times and traditional gender norms, we find the constraints are greatest in the two post-Socialist transition countries, and in Spain and Portugal. They are weakest in the Nordic countries. But actually we find the widest gap between attitudes in favour of gender-equal norms in parenting on the one hand, and the hours that men work and whether they would reduce their working hours and take lower wages on the other, in the Scandinavian countries. Our capabilities approach assumes that institutional context can increase agency. This means that the incongruity between attitudes and practices appears more pronounced given that the three Scandinavian countries, Denmark, Norway and Sweden, have initiated proactive policies to enable men to be more involved in care work for children.

PROACTIVE FATHERING POLICIES: THE SCANDINAVIAN EXPERIMENT

In the mid-1990s, Scandinavian governments (Norway, Sweden and Denmark) introduced a new policy concept – the father quota – intended to increase men's parental time with young children. We refer to this as a proactive fathering policy for several reasons. Unlike the policies on flexible working times and parental leave, the father quota was specifically aimed at men's care work: the policies enacted had incentives and penalties for parents to use the benefit. And finally, in both Norway and Sweden, the law was accompanied by orchestrated government campaigns to increase men's share of care work and caregiving, with the long-term goal of altering the gendered work/care balance.

Among the three countries, Denmark had the shortest, least flexible and most short-lived father quota. Two weeks were reserved for fathers at the end of the parental leave, which was dropped in 2001 after the change to a Liberal/Conservative government. In Norway and Sweden there was little controversy over the father quota. In both countries the impetus behind it was two-pronged: to increase men's contact and involvement with family and to equalise the care/work balance between men and women. The latter has been stressed more in the Norwegian policy, which was framed in terms of exerting pressure on fathers to assume their responsibilities as fathers; the minister of social affairs called it the 'loving force' (Rostgaard 2002).

The Swedish policy differs from the Norwegian in several respects. For example in Norway fathers have to use it as a full-time benefit compared to the highly flexible Swedish policy. The father quota or 'daddy month' was a 'use it or lose it' policy in Sweden (families lost one month if the father did not take the month off), whereas in Norway it was effectively an additional month. However despite this the Swedish public debates framed the daddy month in terms of rights rather than obligations: as an entitlement for men to have more contact with children.

In the following section we concentrate on the Swedish case and consider how and in what ways the father quota has altered work/care practices within couples after the birth of a child. The Swedish case is an ideal one to analyse capabilities for worklife balance because the dual earner model has been institutionalised for several decades; it was the first country to make parental leave an individual entitlement (in the 1970s); and the ideologies supporting gender equality have embraced both men's and women's active participation in employment and care.

The Swedish Case

The Swedish parental leave programme was introduced in 1974 and gave the right to six months of paid leave from work after the birth of a child. The entitlement period was lengthened throughout the 1970s and 1980s, reaching its peak in 1989. Employed mothers and fathers were granted an income replacement of 90 per cent of their previous earnings up to a relatively high ceiling for 12 months, with the possibility of extending the leave for three months at a low flat rate benefit, equivalent to 6 euros per day. In the 1990s the benefit level was reduced and since 1998 it has been at 80 per cent of previous earnings. Moreover, since the income ceiling for parental leave benefit has not kept pace with increases in incomes, today a large share of parents, especially fathers, are receiving less than the stipulated 80 per cent replacement, although some employers cover a larger part of the income loss. Indeed, all state employees receive 90 per cent replacement. Many private employers have similar contracts with their employees.

Another important feature of the system is that by accepting a lower benefit than 80 per cent of earnings, one can extend the duration of the leave. On average, children born in 1999 stayed at home with a parent for over 16 months before another form of childcare was selected (Berggren 2004). This option translates into a much lower benefit level for mothers who are the ones most likely to take advantage of it, an outcome that runs counter to the policy aim of tackling the gender imbalance in care work. Over a quarter of all mothers took 18 months of leave or longer.

Fathers' share of parental leave
Although the policy has been gender neutral since the mid-1970s, not until the beginning of the 1990s did men's share of parental leave reach a tenth of the days available to parents (see Figure 13.2). Today men use about 19 per cent of all parental leave days.

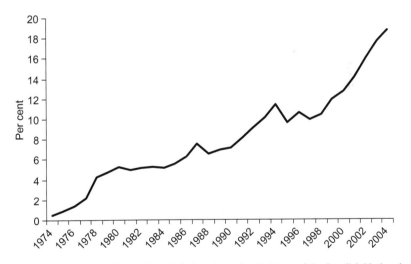

Source: Data based on Duvander calculations from the Registers of the Swedish National Social Insurance Board.

Figure 13.2 Fathers' share of all parental leave days

After the introduction of the daddy quota, the proportion of leave taken by fathers actually declined slightly, but this has been attributed to the economic crisis of the mid-1990s (Hobson and Oláh 2006). By 2000 the proportion of all parental leave days fathers take had doubled, which reflects a fall in the proportion of fathers who take no leave from one half to one fifth of all fathers (Figure 13.3). So far we have seen no such dramatic effect following the introduction of the second reserved month in 2002, but it may be too early to tell.

Most men use between one and two months of leave. The fathers who take longer leave are those with a fairly high and secure income, even though the income ceiling for the benefit discourages longer leave periods (Nyman and Pettersson 2002; Sundström and Duvander 2002). Those least likely to take the leave are fathers who have a weak attachment to the labour market: the unemployed and those with low earnings (Nyman and Pettersson 2002). In other words, fathers who would receive a low level of benefit during parental leave most often choose not to take leave. The close connection between income and family benefits is a major reason why the dual-earner family is so widespread in Sweden, but it also results in great disadvantages for the parents who are only marginally attached to the

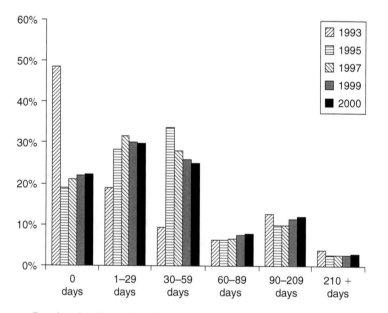

Source: Data based on Duvander calculations from the Registers of the Swedish National Social Insurance Board.

Figure 13.3   Fathers' use of parental leave up to their child's fourth birthday

labour market. As immigrants have a much worse labour market position it is reasonable to expect that immigrant parents use the leave differently from Swedish-born parents.[15] Indeed, a much smaller proportion of immigrant fathers, particularly those from African, Asian and Middle Eastern countries take up their parental leave right compared to the Swedish-born fathers and those from other Nordic countries. However, immigrant fathers who actually use the leave tend to use a larger number of days than Swedish-born fathers.

Survey of parental leave

The most recent survey of parental leave investigates factors influencing the length of leave taken by fathers and mothers in Sweden.[16] It asks parents of children born in 1993 (two years before the introduction of the daddy month), and in 1999 (four years after) about the length of their parental leave (Berggren 2004).[17] The survey includes questions on what individuals do and what they can imagine themselves doing (reflections of what Sen understood as 'means' and 'capabilities'). It reveals their strategies regarding, and reasons for taking, parental leave in relation to their partners and asks them what might lead to a balance between work and family (Table 13.3).

In Table 13.3 we show the results from separate regression analyses for men and women of the impact of various factors on their parental leave length. The better fit of the model for fathers shows that the variables chosen for these analyses explain more of the factors behind fathers' parental leave length than they do for mothers. It is obvious that one parent's longer leave reduces the length for the other parent and that fathers used more leave after the daddy quota. Age is negative for fathers' leave and positive for mothers', which suggests that different situations in employment over the life course can influence men's and women's abilities to use their rights to care. For women, a higher age at childbirth may indicate that they have a secure work position and that they can take a long parental leave period. For men, becoming fathers at a later age often means that they have positions with more responsibility, so it is difficult to make claims for a long period of parental leave. Previous studies (Sundström and Duvander 2002) and the current study show that the higher education of both the man and woman is connected with a longer leave length of the father, but not so for the mother, which may reflect gender norms as well as the tendency of women to work in gender-segregated, parent friendly workplaces.

From a capabilities perspective, the strong impact of the level of earned income before childbirth on the benefit level during parental leave (Table 13.3) reflects the powerful incentives to establish oneself in the labour market before

Table 13.3   Regression models of fathers' and mothers' parental leave use measured in weeks

	Fathers' parental leave	Mothers' parental leave
Other parent's parental leave	−0.184***	−0.731***
Child born 1993 *(referent=1999)*	−0.047	2.306**
Number of children born before this child	−0.727***	−2.402***
Age	−0.151***	0.658***
Educational level	0.343*	−0.169
Income		
Very low	−2.330**	3.545**
Middle low	1.078**	2.634**
Middle high (referent)	Ref	Ref
Very high	−0.540	−2.994
Other parent's age	0.233***	−0.184*
Other parent's educational level	0.757***	0.169
Other parent's income		
Very low	−0.935	−6.734***
Middle low	−1.020*	−1.072
Middle high (referent)	Ref	Ref
Very high	1.410	1.213
Work sector		
Municipal (referent)	Ref	Ref
Private	−2.258***	−3.526***
State	−1.768**	−4.806***
Extra benefit from employer	4.352***	4.231***
Mixed work and parental leave	4.121***	1.464
Other parent work sector		
Municipal (referent)	Ref	Ref
Private	−0.212	−0.540
State	0.279	−0.146
Other parent extra benefit from employer	1.199*	-0.455
Other parent mixed work and parental leave	0.603	1.926*
R square	0.243	0.173

Notes:
Length of parental leave is measured in weeks for both the mother and the father and is based on information from the parents. The parental leave concerns children born in either 1993 or 1999. The number of older siblings is based on siblings still living in the household at the time of interview. Age of mother and father and educational level come from register information. Educational level is presented as a continuous variable after tests showing that the effect seemed to be linear. Income is measured as income before tax in the year before childbirth (1993 or 1999). It is not possible to measure income in the same year or after childbirth as income is heavily influenced by parental leave length. Work sector is based on register data and is divided into state, municipality and private sector. We did not collapse state and municipality (into public sector) because the conditions may vary considerably, particularly regarding parental leave policies in which the state sector has been much more privileged than the municipal sector. Whether the parent has received extra benefits from the employer is based on the interviewee's answer, as no such register information exists. The same is true for the information on whether the parent mixed work and parental leave.
$*p < 0.10, **p < 0.05, ***p < 0.01$

considering becoming a parent. We know that earned income is positively related to Swedish women's entry into motherhood (Andersson 2000; Duvander and Olsson 2001; Hoem 2000). The same also holds true for men's entry into fatherhood (Duvander and Olsson 2001).

We also found that men with low income take short leave or no leave, which may be related to job insecurity or the low level of benefit that these men would receive. Both hinder the ability to exercise one's right to care. Moreover, our results show that a man's low income affects the capabilities of his partner/wife who also tends to take shorter leaves (Table 13.3) because of the need for all of her income (as opposed to the 80 per cent leave income) in a household economy with a low-paid male earner. Nevertheless, women with low paying jobs tend to take much longer leave compared to women with higher incomes, since they are able to depend on their partner/husband's economic contribution in the family, while the opposite is rarely possible for men.

Extra benefits from the employer extend the leave length for both men and women (Table 13.3). At first glance we might assume that the primary reason is that the extra income compensates for the income loss, given that we control for employment sector, but it may also signify a particular parent-friendly workplace (more often found in the public sector). In the private sector, firms that top up the benefit also display an official policy of support for parental leave.

This study supports the finding that men who work in the private sector take shorter leave and also that employees of the central state take shorter leave than men employed in municipalities. One possible explanation for longer, periods of leave in the municipalities is that this sector contains many female-dominated workplaces, which makes it easier for both men and women to take leave.

Flexibility in working life seems to have some impact on the ability of men to take a longer period of the leave. Fathers who managed to mix work and parental leave took longer parental leave; at the time of the survey, over a third of fathers had flexible working hours. True, these fathers may have been more committed to caring for children and have chosen jobs that give them flexibility. Some earlier studies make the point that employers' positive or negative attitudes is a determining factor on men's use of their parental leave (Näsman 1992), and this also may be a factor affecting flexible work schemes.

Workplace cultures and parental leave
There is some convincing evidence that workplace cultures have an effect on men's agency to take advantage of parental leave rights (Bygren and Duvander 2004, 2006).

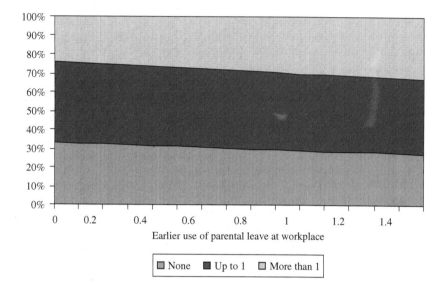

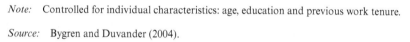

Note: Controlled for individual characteristics: age, education and previous work tenure.

Source: Bygren and Duvander (2004).

*Figure 13.4   Expected use of parental leave at father's workplace
considering the proportion of men who had taken some leave*

Looking at all men in Stockholm who had children during the years 1997 and 1999 and then linking them to their workplaces, Bygren and Duvander (2004)[18] constructed a unique database from which to capture some of the effects of workplace culture on parental leave (Figure 13.4). After controlling for age, income and education, and tenure over the past several years at the workplace, their study showed that the proportion of leave days fathers take is influenced by how many fathers before them have taken leave, a snowball effect. From the perspective of capabilities, we might assume that the more men who take leave in a firm, the less risk there is of a wage or career penalty: there is safety in numbers. Male dominated workplaces also influenced how much leave mothers took, but given the extent of vertical and horizontal gender-segregated employment in Sweden, the workplace is more important for fathers' leave length.

Reasons given for dividing the leave
Implicit in the reasons given as to why parents divide leave as they do are norms about what fathers and mothers are expected to say and do. But they

Table 13.4   Responses to what might lead to a better worklife balance

	Women (per cent)	Men (per cent)
Flexible work hours	7.7	9.7
Less work hours	48.8	61.7
Partner's flexible work hours or less work hours	12.7	5.4
Help from the other parent	6.9	1.2
Help from relatives	5.4	3.7
Better economy	18.6	18.4

Note: No response, answers of 'don't know' and 'other' are excluded from the table, together, 18 per cent of the responses.

also shed light on facets of agency and capabilities; perceptions of what is possible and the subjective states of efficacy that are needed to make a claim for oneself.

Returning to our analysis of the survey of parents' use of leave, we asked what were the reasons for the individual dividing the leave as they did. Many women responded that they wanted to be at home most of the time.[19] When parents were asked if they would have liked a different division of the leave, relatively few (particularly mothers) expressed any discontent. However, almost a fifth of all fathers would have liked to share the leave more equally, but almost no fathers claimed that they would have liked to share 50–50. Such an outcome is beyond the realm of possibility for most fathers in a society that promotes active fathering, but that also sustains highly gender-segregated work situations and gender wage differences (Hobson 2003).

Around a fifth of both men and women claim that men's work determined the division of leave. We can interpret this response as a simple function of the fact that women tend to earn less than men. However, what men and women do in relation to their partner's options and choices is conditioned by gendered norms about employment and care in the society that are mirrored in the organisation of working times and workplace organisational cultures (Bekkengen 2002). These not only limit women's agency to create a worklife balance but also men's.

When asked what might lead to a better worklife balance, a reduction in working hours appears to be the crucial component in the equation for men and women with small children (Table 13.4). Flexible work does not seem to be a solution that would enhance the capabilities of men and women to create a worklife balance. It is the time squeeze rather than the lack of flexibility that appears to weaken capabilities. A better household economy is equally important for both men and women. This might capture a range of issues involving capabilities, for example, the ability to buy services, which are quite expensive in Sweden. It might also reflect a lack of agency to reduce working hours. For men, this might involve the income pressures that force them to work in non-parent friendly workplaces, requiring them to work long hours, weekends or overtime. (In the ESS survey over 20 per cent of Swedish men work more than 45 hours per week.) In terms of the agency of one partner affecting the other, we have some indication that some women believe they would have a greater possibility of achieving a worklife balance if their partners worked less and had more flexible work. (In the ESS survey, Swedish women reported that their partners worked weekends several times a month.)

Within a capabilities framework, workplace organisational cultures and employment situations appear more and more important for both men's and women's agency in regard to the use of parental leave. Extra benefits from the employer increase the leave length for both fathers and mothers. Moreover to be able to mix work and leave also increases the length of leave for fathers. The influence of the other parent's work situation seems, however, to be negligible. Even if parents claim they give priority to the father's work situation when considering how the leave should be divided, it seems that the influence on the mother's leave length is minimal. A possible interpretation is that the flexibility in the policy that allows parents to increase the length of leave with reduced compensation leads to an outcome whereby the total leave length is less of a zero-sum game between the parents than might be expected.

CONCLUSION

Women and men who seek to create a worklife balance that allows for participation in both caregiving and employment confront issues that involve long- and short-term economic and social costs – lost income, or potential income, or less contact and bonding with their children. The rising expectations of women who desire greater attachment in the labour market after having children are often at odds with men's interests in building careers and a secure income. The rising expectations of fathers to have more time with their children sometimes clash with mothers who see themselves as more entitled to care benefits and the right to reduce working times. These normative and structural constraints affect the agency and capabilities of parents to create a worklife balance. The term 'worklife balance', a phrase that appears more and more frequently in EU working papers and funded research on European parenting, does not capture these tensions or the multidimensional framework in which parenting strategies are embedded. Moreover its essentially gender-neutral casing conceals the highly gendered norms and practices that operate in workplaces. Fathers who want to take long childcare leave or reduce working hours often meet prejudice from employers and workmates (Näsman 1992), whereas it is anticipated that mothers will be interrupting employment for mothering.[20] In fact, one Swedish study shows that individual men pay a greater care penalty in respect of future wages than women (Albrecht et al. 1999). Still, the majority of women suffer a care penalty in the statistical discrimination they experience in job recruitment and pay (Mandel and Shalev 2003). European women in our sample and in Eurobarometer studies acknowledge the negative consequences on careers and occupations that result from their taking time out to care (Sjöberg 2004).

Across our European societies, we can see that reconciling employment and family responsibilities, a mantra in EU documents and discourse, has been internalised by men and women as a norm, a goal to achieve. Between 85 and 95 per cent of fathers and mothers with children under 12 maintained that being able to combine family and employment was an important consideration when they choose a job.[21] Yet men's working hours and their ability to choose to work fewer hours reveal the gap between the norm and the practice. What we are witnessing is the demise of the male breadwinner norm, but not the assumptions that underlie it. These permeate workplaces and gendered working time regimes, and are mirrored in societal norms as to who should be responsible for care and who should have the rights to a job in tight labour markets. Alison Smith (2004) in her study of men's caring hours across European societies, argues that the further south one goes, the less care work men do. The underlying expectation is that northern countries are less traditional in their family values. In our analysis of agency and capabilities, we find a more nuanced and complex picture. The appropriate divide may only not be north and south, but also new and old EU member states. Those countries with the most conservative attitudes towards male breadwinner rights and women's responsibilities to reduce work for the family are the Czech Republic and Poland; in the Southern Rim countries, Portugal but not Spain is more in line with this group. Furthermore women as well as men in the Czech Republic and Poland are working very long hours and have the weakest capabilities to create a worklife balance. In both countries the main form of childcare is a relative.[22] With the exception of Scandinavia, most young children are being cared for by a parent at home. Turning to our Scandinavian case, we expect that fathers should be able to create a worklife balance because of laws, institutional arrangements and societal norms, all of which enhance men's ability to make claims for care in the workplace and in the family.

Still, we find that while over one-fifth of men felt that that they would have preferred to take more parental leave, almost none would have wanted an equal split. In fact the daddy months may in themselves be norm-constraining for many men who might otherwise consider making claims to take more leave.

When considering worklife balance issues, the capabilities approach allows us to understand the inconsistencies and contradictions that operate within individual agency and decision making: the pull of family and the demands and inducements of work. Expected norms are intertwined with social and economic environments – one's 'habitus', but they also limit what can be imagined, which in turn limits agency and power to make changes. This is the essence of what Sen means by agency freedom. That deeply embedded gender norms around care and breadwinning govern what we can imagine and expect is evident even in the questions within the European Social Science module on work and family, added in 2004. Only women were asked if they took time off to care or if they reduced hours after children were born. The fact that there were no questions addressing men's care work and that maternity/parental leave was operationalised as full-time leave does not acknowledge the varied tapestries that many couples are weaving around employment and family: taking days and half days of parental leave as the leave becomes more flexible in different countries; new innovative legislation in various European countries in which individuals can amass time credit accounts that they can use after children are born; and job share programmes and possibilities for organising a flexible work schedule in many firms. These innovative strategies reflect a change in the ability of families to live on the earnings of a single bread-winner and the growing insecurities in jobs. They also mirror women's ambitions to be more attached to the labour market and aspirations among men to have more contact with children. New research strategies and designs need to be developed to understand men's agency to create a work-life balance in this period of institutional change.

NOTES

1. For a discussion of these competing goals see Carson (2004).
2. In addition to cross-national differences in the amount of care men do (Smith 2004), there are also differences across educational levels in the organisation of paid and unpaid work (Gershuny and Sullivan 2003).
3. This goes beyond saying that institutional settings shape preferences (Folbre 1994), to argue that institutional settings shape the ability to transform means (our resources) into what we are and what we do and what we value (Sen 1992, 2003).
4. Looking at EU countries up to 1999, Gauthier and Bortnik (2001) show that the UK was the exception with the replacement rate for a woman industrial worker being below

50 per cent. Gornick and Meyers (2003) use a leave index (in the year 2000) in which they multiply number of weeks by replacement pay. Among their European countries, only the UK had a maternity leave index below 12, although recent legislation should improve this. Hobson and Oláh (2006) have similar findings, and they include post-Socialist transition countries.

5. The 1997 Directive provides statutory protection for the equal treatment of part-time workers on a pro-rata basis with comparable full-time workers.

6. Ronnie Eklund (2001) refers to the Directive as the 'Chewing Gum Directive', and highlights its vague and elastic parameters. He makes the point that the Directive follows a tendency in the EU to leave the regulation of social policy to the social partners, assuming they will take over the initiative in collective bargaining agreements.

7. More recent studies even suggest a slight decline: see Emancipatiemonitor (2004). I am grateful to Monika Kremer for providing me with these statistics

8. In their summary of seven European country-level reports, Guerreiro et al. (2004), found that an 'ethic of care' and ethic of business existed in all organisations, but in the private sector the ethic of business dominated.

9. The European Social Survey has been conducted twice, 2002 and 2004 within several European countries (25 countries in the latter round). The aim of this joint survey is to collect information about changing attitudes, beliefs and behaviour patterns; in 2004 an additional module on employment and family was added (www.europeansocialsurvey. org; 2005-11-28). The sample is representative for all persons above 15 years of age within private households in each country. The response rate varies from 46.9 to 79.3 per cent depending on country, with an effective sample of about 1500 individuals (see ESS 2005a, 2005b).

10. We have chosen these countries from the 17 that are included in the first edition of the European Social Survey because they represent different welfare regime types: Scandinavian or dual earner (Denmark, Finland, Norway and Sweden), liberal or market-oriented (UK), conservative or family welfare regime type (Belgium, Germany, Portugal, Spain), and post-Socialist (Czech Republic and Poland), leaning more toward the liberal and market-oriented policy configuration, but which would also fit Korpi's dual earner type: see Esping-Andersen (1990); and Korpi (2000).

11. We have selected two samples in this analysis: 1) for attitudes toward gender roles, we selected all individuals between 20 and 45 years of age (a sample of 9631 respondents); 2) when analysing specific working-life balance preferences and practices the sample is reduced to married or cohabitant men and women of 20–45 years of age having at least one child below 12 years of age in the household (3546 individuals). Singles or individuals living alone are excluded as well as those without young children.

12. In these questions the response alternatives *Agree strongly* and *Agree* are collapsed into one category and *Disagree strongly* and *Disagree* into another. The same goes for *Not important at all – Not important* and *Very important – Important*.

13. Policy addressing a shorter working week has been a longstanding gendered debate in Sweden with the industrial unions (mainly composed of men) claiming longer paid holidays – now up to six weeks – and the service sector unions (comprising mostly women) pressing for a shorter working week, without success.

14. A significant proportion of women in Portugal, Spain and Poland take only up to six months of the leave: 46 per cent in Portugal; 29 per cent in Spain; 24 per cent in Belgium; and 20 per cent in Poland.

15. During the economic crisis of the 1990s, the period when the daddy month was introduced, the labour market situation of these immigrants worsened.

16. Few studies investigate the factors influencing both mothers' and fathers' leave use. The survey does this. Conducted in 2003 by the Swedish National Social Insurance Board, the survey is a random sample of biological or adoptive parents of children born in 1993 and 1999. Based on telephone interviews, the sample includes 4000 parents, with a response rate of 80 per cent. The parents' responses were linked to register data on income, parental leave and other social insurance schemes (for more details see National Social Insurance Board 2003).

17. As many parents divide the leave into parts of days, this measure of how long a leave a parent took is more useful than one using register data of benefit days taken.
18. They use a sub-sample from a database of all residents in Stockholm during the 1990s and then register data to link individuals to their workplaces.
19. The question in the survey was whether the leave was divided because the father wanted to be home most of the time, but very few men or women answered positively to this because few men take most of the leave. Thus we cannot analyse men's entitlement or advocacy for the division of leave. However, Haas et al. (2002) found this to be significant.
20. As of yet, there are no men who have taken a case to the European Court of Justice for loss of jobs after parental leave. There are two cases in which men have claimed rights as fathers. One, the oft-cited Hoffman case (C-184/83), concerned the Court's denial of the petition of a father for rights to parental leave; it was made moot after the parental leave Directive was passed. Another case involved denial of a claim by 144 male employees at the Renault company who became fathers and challenged a benefit given only to mothers after the birth of a child (C-218798: Obdoulaye and Others). The Court accepted the argument that women (even though they receive full salary) are hindered in their careers, wages, training, and so on because of maternity leave. The Court did not allow for the possibility that men might take leave for care.
21. In Finland the percentages are about 10 percentage points lower.
22. A question in the ESS asked parents of children not in school what was their main source of childcare.

REFERENCES

Albrecht, J.W., E. Per-Anders, M. Sundström and S.B. Vroman (1999), 'Career interruptions and subsequent earnings: a re-examination using Swedish data', *Journal of Human Resources*, **294**, 294–321.

Andersson, G. (2000), 'The impact of labor-force participation on childbearing behavior: pro-cyclical fertility in Sweden during the 1980s and the 1990s', *European Journal of Population*, **16**, 293–333.

Becker, G.S. (1991), *A Treatise on the Family*, Cambridge, MA: Harvard University Press.

Bekkengen, L. (2002), *Man får välja – om föräldraskap och föräldraledighet i arbetsliv och familjeliv*, Malmö: Liber.

Berggren, S. (2004), 'Flexibel föräldrapenning – hur mammor och pappor använder föräldrapenningen och hur länge de är föräldralediga', *RFV Analyserar*, 2004, 14, Stockholm, RFV, Riksförsakringsverket, National Social Insurance Board.

Bergman, H. and B. Hobson (2002), 'Compulsory fatherhood: the coding of fatherhood in Sweden', in B. Hobson (ed.), *Making Men into Fathers: Men, Masculinities and the Social Politics of Fatherhood*, Cambridge: Cambridge University Press.

Bruning, G. and J. Plantenga (1999), 'Parental leave and equal opportunities: experiences in eight European countries', *Journal of European Social Politics*, **9**(3), 195–209.

Bygren, M. and A. Duvander (2004), 'Ingen annan på jobbet har ju varit pappaledig. Papporna, deras arbetsplatser och deras pappaledighetsuttag', in M. Bygren, M. Gähler and M. Nermo (eds), *Familj och arbete. Vardagsliv i förändring*, Stockholm: SNS Förlag.

Bygren, M. and A. Duvander (2006), 'Parents' workplace situation and fathers' parental leave', *Journal of Marriage and the Family*, **10**(2), forthcoming.

Carson, M. (2004), *From Common Market to Social Europe? Paradigm Shift and Institutional Change in European Union Policy on Food, Asbestos and Chemicals, and Gender Equality*, Stockholm University Studies in Sociology, Stockholm: Alqvist & Wicksell.

Crompton, R. (1999), *Restructuring Gender Relations and Employment: The Decline of the Male Breadwinner*, Oxford: Oxford University Press.

Den Duik, L. (2001), *Work–Family Arrangements in Organisations: A Cross-national Study in the Netherlands, Italy, the UK, and Sweden*, Rotterdam: Rozenberg.

Deven, F. and P. Moss (2002), 'Leave arrangements for parents: overview and future outlook', *Community, Work and Family*, **5**(3), 237–55.

Duvander, A. and S. Olsson (2001), 'När har vi råd att skaffa barn?', *RFV analyserar*, 2001, 8, Stockholm: National Social Insurance Board.

Duvendak, J.W. and M. Stavenuiter (ed.) (2004), *Working Fathers, Caring Men*, The Hague: Verwey-Jonker Institute.

Eklund, R. (2001), 'The chewing-gum directive – part-time work in the European Community', in '*Festskrift till Hans Stark*', Stockholm: Liber Amicorum, pp. 59–78.

Emancipatiemonitor (2004), SCP fact sheet on parental job sharing.

England, P. (2000), 'Conceptualizing women's empowerment in countries of the north', in H. Presser and G. Sen (eds), *Moving Beyond Cairo*, Oxford: Oxford University Press.

Esping-Andersen, G. (1990), *The Three Worlds of Welfare Capitalism*, Cambridge: Polity Press.

European Commission (2002), '*Increasing labour force participation and promoting active ageing*', COM, 9, final, Brussels: European Commission.

European Commission (2003), *Scoreboard on Implementing the Social Policy Agenda*, COM, 57, final, Brussels: Final.

European Social Survey (2005a), 'Sampling for the European social survey – round 2: principles and requirements', accessed at www.europeansocialsurvey.org; 2005-11-28.

European Social Survey (2005b), 'Weighting European social survey data', accessed at www.europeansocialsurvey.org; 2005-11-28.

Fagan, C. (2004), 'Gender and working-time in industrialized countries: practices and preferences' in J. Messenger (ed.), *Finding the Balance: Working-time and Workers' Needs and Preferences in Industrialized countries*, London: Routledge/ Institute for Labour Studies of the International Labour Organisation.

Fagan, C., A. Hegewisch and J. Pillinger (2006), 'Out of time: why Britain needs a new approach to working time flexibility', report for the Trades Union Congress.

Ferrarini, T. (2003), '*Parental leave institutions in eighteen post-war welfare states*', Swedish Institute for Social Research dissertation series no 58, Stockholm University, Stockholm.

Folbre, N. (1994), *Who Pays for the Kids? Gender and the Structures of Constraint*, New York and London: Routledge.

Gauthier, A.H. and A. Bortnik (2001), Comparative Maternity, Parental, and Childcare Database, version 2, University of Calgary, accessed at http://soci.ucalgary.ca/fypp/family_policy_databases.htm

Gershuny, J.O. and O. Sullivan (2003), 'Time use, gender, and public policy regimes', *Social Politics*, **10**(3), 205–28.

Gornick, J.C. and M.C. Meyers (2003), *Families that Work: Policies for Reconciling Parenthood and Employment*, New York: Russell Sage Foundation.

Gornick, J.C., M.C. Meyers and K.E. Ross (1997), 'Supporting the employment of mothers: policy variation across fourteen welfare states', *Journal of European Social Policy*, **7**(1), 45–70.

Guerreiro, M.D., P. Abrantes and I. Pereira (2004), 'Transitions: case studies summary reports', CIES/SCETE, November, accessed at www.workliferesearch. org/transitions.

Haas, Barbara. (2003), 'The reconciliation of work and family obligations: a comparison between Austria, the Netherlands and Sweden', in C. Wallace (ed.), *HWF Survey Comparative Report Volume 2: Thematic Paper*, Vienna: Institute for Advanced Studies, HWF Project.

Haas, L., K. Allard and P. Hwang (2002), 'The impact of organizational culture on men's use of parental leave in Sweden', *Community, Work and Family*, **5**(3), 319–42.

Hakim, C. (2003), 'A new approach to explaining fertility patterns: preference theory', *Population and Development Review*, **29**(3), 349–74.

Hantrais, L. (ed.) (2000), *Gendered Policies in Europe: Reconciling Employment and Family Life*, Basingstoke: Macmillan.

Hervey, T. and D. O'Keefe (eds) (1996), *Sex Equality Law in the European Union*, Chichester: Wiley.

Hobson, B. (2003), 'The individualised worker, the gender participatory and the gender equality models in Sweden', *Social Policy and Society*, **3**, 75–83.

Hobson, B. and D. Morgan (2002), 'Introduction: making men into fathers', in B. Hobson (ed.), *Making Men into Fathers: Men, Masculinities and the Social Politics of Fatherhood*, Cambridge: Cambridge University Press.

Hobson, B. and L. Oláh (2006), 'Birthstrikes? Agency and capabilities in the reconciliation of employment and family', *Journal of Marriage and the Family Review*, forthcoming.

Hochschild, A.R. (1997), *The Time Bind When Work Becomes Home and Home Becomes Work*, New York: Henry Holt and Company.

Hoem, B. (2000), 'Entry into motherhood in Sweden: the influence of economic factors on the rise and fall in fertility, 1986–1997', *Demographic Research*, **2**, accessed at http://www.demographic-research.org/Volumes/Vol2/4.

Kimmel, M. (2000), *What Do Men Want?*, Cambridge, MA: Harvard Business School Press.

Knijn, T. and P. Stelten (2002), 'Transformations in fatherhood in the Netherlands', in B. Hobson (ed.), *Making Men Into Fathers*, Cambridge: Cambridge University Press.

Knijn, T. and F. Wel (2001), *Een wankel evenwicht. Arbeid en zorg in gezinnen met jonge kindern*, Amsterdam: SWP.

Korpi, W. (2000), 'Faces of inequality: gender, class, and patterns of inequalities in different types of welfare states', *Social Politics*, **7**(2), 127–91.

Lewis, J. and S. Guillari (2005), 'The adult worker model family, gender equality and care: the search for new policy principles and the possibilities and problems of a capabilities approach', *Economy and Society*, **34**(1), 76–104.

Lippe, T. van der, A. Jager and Y. Kops (forthcoming), *Work-Family Balance in European Countries*.

McDonald, P. (2000), 'Gender equity, social institutions and the future of fertility', *Journal of Population Research*, **17**, 1–16.

Mandel, H. and M. Shalev (2003), 'Class conditioning of welfare state effects on gender inequality: a preliminary comparative analysis', paper prepared for the Annual Conference of Research Committee 19, 21–24 August Toronto.

Moss, P. and F. Deven (1999), *Parental Leave: Progress or Pitfall. Research and Policy Issues in Europe*, Brussels: NIDI/CBGS Publications.

Näsman, E. (1992), '*Parental Leave in Sweden – a Workplace Issue?*', Stockholm University research reports in demography 73, Stockholm.

National Social Insurance Board (2003), *Social Insurance in Sweden 2003: Family Assets – Time and Money*, Stockholm: National Social Insurance Board.

National Social Insurance Board (2005), *Social Insurance in Sweden 2005*, Stockholm: National Social Insurance Board.

Nyman, H. and J. Pettersson (2002), 'Spelade pappamånaden någon roll? – pappornas uttag av föräldrapenning', *RFV Analyserar*, 2002, 14, Stockholm, National Social Insurance Board.

O'Reilly, J. and C. Fagan (eds) (1998), *Part-time Prospects: An International Comparison of Part-time Work in Europe, North America and the Pacific Rim*, London: Routledge.

Pfau-Effinger, B. (2005), 'Culture and welfare state policies: reflections on a complex interaction', *Social Policy*, **34**(1), 1–18.

Plantenga, J. and C. Remery (2005), 'Reconciliation of work and private life: a comparative review of thirty European countries', final report of Expert Group of Gender, Social Inclusion and Employment for the Equal Opportunities Unit of the European Commission.

Plantenga, J., J. Schippers and J. Siegers (1999), 'Towards an equal division of paid and unpaid work: the case of the Netherlands', *Journal of European Social Policy*, **9**(2), 99–110.

Rostgaard, T. (2002), 'Setting time aside for the father: father's leave in Scandinavia', *Community, Work and Family*, **5**(3), 343–64.

Rubery, J., M. Smith and C. Fagan (1999), *Women's Employment in Europe: Trends and Prospects*, London: Routledge.

Sen, A. (1992), *Inequality Re-examined*, Oxford: Oxford University Press.

Sen, A. (2003), 'Capability and well-being', in M. Nussbaum and A. Sen (eds), *The Quality of Life*, Oxford: Oxford University Press.

Sjöberg, O. (2004), 'Attitudes related to fertility and childbearing in the EU countries', report.

Smith, A.J. (2004), 'Who cares? European fathers and the time they spend looking after children', Oxford University sociology working papers.

Sundström, M. and A. Duvander (2002), 'Gender division of child care and the sharing of parental leave among new parents in Sweden', *European Sociological Review*, **18**(4), 433–47.

Takahashi, M. (2003), '*Gender dimensions in family life: a comparative study of structural constraints and power in Sweden and Japan*, Stockholm University Studies in Sociology no 15, Stockholm.

Wallace, C. (2003), 'Household strategies: their conceptual relevance and analytical scope in social research', *Sociology*, **36**(2), 275–92.

Walker, R, R. Goodwin and E. Cornwall (2000), 'Work patterns in Europe and related social security issues', in D. Pieters (ed.), *Changing Work Patterns and Social Security*, London: EISS Yearbook.

Index